Handbook of Research on IMPROVING STUDENT ACHIEVEMENT

Third Edition

Gordon Cawelti, Editor

 Educational Research Service

Because research and information make the difference.

Educational Research Service
2000 Clarendon Boulevard, Arlington, VA 22201-2908
Tel: (703) 243-2100 or (800) 791-9308
Fax: (703) 243-1985 or (800) 791-9309
Email: ers@ers.org • Web site: www.ers.org

Educational Research Service is the nonprofit foundation serving the research and information needs of the nation's K-12 education leaders and the public. Founded by seven national school management associations, ERS provides quality, objective research and information that enable education leaders to make the most effective school decisions, in terms of both day-to-day operations and long-range planning. Refer to page 257 of this publication to learn how you can benefit from the services and resources available through an annual ERS subscription. Or visit us online at www.ers.org for a more complete overview of the wealth of K-12 research and information available through ERS subscriptions and resources.

This report is intended to provide a summary of research and best practices appearing in the current research and literature. The inclusion of any specific assertion or opinion here is not intended to imply approval or endorsement by Educational Research Service or any of its founding organizations.

ERS Founding Organizations:
American Association of School Administrators
American Association of School Personnel Administrators
Association of School Business Officials International
Council of Chief State School Officers
National Association of Elementary School Principals
National Association of Secondary School Principals
National School Public Relations Association

Ordering information: Additional copies of *Handbook of Research on Improving Student Achievement, Third Edition* may be purchased at the base price of $44 each (ERS Comprehensive Subscriber price: $22; ERS Individual Subscriber price: $33). Quantity discounts available. Stock No. 0538. ISBN 1-931762-29-5.

Order from: Educational Research Service, 2000 Clarendon Boulevard, Arlington, VA 22201-2908. Telephone: (800) 791-9308. Fax: (800) 791-9309. Email: ers@ers.org. Web site: www.ers.org. Add the greater of $3.50 or 10% of total purchase price for postage and handling. Phone orders accepted with Visa, MasterCard, or American Express.

ERS Management Staff:
John M. Forsyth, Ph.D., President and Director of Research
Katherine A. Behrens, Senior Director of Marketing and Member Services
Patrick R. Murphy, Senior Director of Finance and Administration

Contents

Foreword

In the fall of 1995, Educational Research Service was pleased to publish the original edition of the *Handbook of Research on Improving Student Achievement*, a report designed to help education practitioners use accurate, comprehensive research in their instructional decisions and practices. The groundbreaking publication, edited by distinguished educator Gordon Cawelti, provided a synthesis of the knowledge base about effective practices for improving student learning in all of the major subject fields in elementary and secondary education.

Passage and enactment of the No Child Left Behind Act have made this research even more valuable to education leaders tasked with finding ways to ensure *all* children and youth in their schools and school districts succeed. The *Handbook*, now in its third edition, makes a unique contribution to the literature because it examines the research by subject fields. It is hoped that the inclusion of information from the various disciplines in one source will inspire curriculum developers and teachers to look outside their own areas of expertise and learn from and about the other discipline areas. We believe the *Handbook* provides a basic framework from which solid interdisciplinary curricula can be built, leading to higher student achievement.

School and school district leaders and teachers across the country responded enthusiastically to earlier editions of the *Handbook*. They told us they have used the *Handbook* in professional development activities, as a reference for teacher evaluation, as a guide for faculty study groups, and in many other productive ways. The overwhelmingly positive response to the first and second editions supported our decision to produce this revised edition, to ensure readers have access to the most current research.

This revised edition contains updated chapters by all of the *Handbook's* original authors. With the addition of Susan J. Paik, who assisted in updating the Effective General Practices chapter, this group of respected scholars brought to the project a wealth of research experience and objectivity. Based on a thorough review of the research since publication of the last edition in 1999, chapters have been expanded and new practices have been added to reflect the most current thinking on each subject. In addition, other experts within the education field (all colleagues of the authors) were invited to review chapters to ensure a broad, objective summary of the research and practices.

We appreciate the support of the Alliance for Curriculum Reform for the *Handbook of Research on Improving Student Achievement*. ACR's sponsorship of the original *Handbook* and the financial support of the Rockefeller Foundation for the first edition were crucial to the development of this valuable information source.

Ever since ERS was established in 1973, a primary mission of the organization has been to promote research-based decision making in local schools and school districts by providing the research and information needed by education leaders. This *Handbook of Research on Improving Student Achievement* represents a major contribution to this mission. ERS hopes education leaders, administrators, and teachers will continue to find this new edition of the *Handbook* useful and relevant.

John M. Forsyth, Ph.D.
President and Director of Research

Acknowledgments

Publication of the *Handbook of Research on Improving Student Achievement, Third Edition* is the result of the serious interest and considerable effort of many people over nearly a decade. It is appropriate to recognize here both those people who were instrumental in initiating the first and second editions of the *Handbook* in 1995 and 1999, respectively, and those whose efforts supported this revision.

The knowledge base the original *Handbook* helped to establish was made possible by the financial support of the Rockefeller Foundation and the insight of Hugh B. Price, its former vice president, who saw the need for providing such information to teachers and other instructional leaders in clear and concise language.

The Advisory Panel for the initial *Handbook* met in May 1994 and provided valuable advice on the general format and procedures to be followed, as well as suggested scholars to be invited to contribute to the *Handbook*. Panel members included Herb Walberg of the University of Illinois at Chicago, Robert Slavin of The Johns Hopkins University, Dennis Sparks of the National Staff Development Council, Thomas Romberg of the University of Wisconsin, Jay McTighe of the Maryland State Department of Education, Denise McKeon of the Alliance for Curriculum Reform, and Glen Robinson, former president of Educational Research Service.

After carefully reviewing the qualifications of many scholars who had contributed to research in the fields represented in the *Handbook,* the editor extended invitations to 10 individuals to prepare chapters in their disciplines of specialty. All of the original invitees accepted the challenge. Those authors—along with Robin Sawyer, who prepared the current chapter on Health Education, and Kristin Cebulla, who collaborated on revising the Mathematics chapter for the second edition—are all certainly due thanks for their diligence in conducting a thorough search of the literature and articulating those practices shown by research to have the most promise for improving student achievement. Each author contributed an extensive bibliography section, which readers of the *Handbook* are invited to use for further study.

The authors were supported in their work on the revised editions by information collected by three seasoned educators: Al Slawson in Tucson, Joan Brady in Denver, and Martha Bruckner in Omaha, and by Leila Beasley McLaurin, a former ERS research specialist, who contacted a sample of *Handbook* users and solicited their suggestions for changes.

Thanks are also due to the Alliance for Curriculum Reform, which sponsored the original project; to Glen Robinson, former ERS president, who was highly supportive of the project from its inception; and to John Forsyth, current ERS president, who has continued his support through each of the revisions of the *Handbook*. Deborah Perkins-Gough, former ERS editor-in-chief, spent many hours on the original manuscript, and Katherine Behrens, senior director of ERS marketing and member services, has helped enormously in developing wide distribution of this handbook. Jeanne Chircop, manager of ERS editorial services, greatly assisted in editing this third edition.

Special recognition must go to my esteemed colleague, Nancy Protheroe, director of ERS special research projects. She has been directly involved from the outset of planning and has helped a great deal to ensure the consistent format, highly readable style, and accurate information that have made the *Handbook* so popular. Without the many hours of hard work she contributed, we would never have had this valuable edition for use in these times when using research-based teaching strategies is being rightfully stressed.

Gordon Cawelti
Editor and Project Director

About the Authors

Gordon Cawelti (Editor), *High-Performing School Systems*

Among his many current projects and activities, Gordon Cawelti serves as a research consultant for Educational Research Service and a project director for the Laboratory for School Success. He was executive director of the Association for Supervision and Curriculum Development (ASCD) from 1973-1992. Prior to that, he served as superintendent of the Tulsa Public Schools, executive director of the North Central Association in Chicago, and a high school principal and teacher in Iowa. He has authored some 150 articles and books on curriculum and has carried out national studies on school innovation and restructuring. His current focus of study is the effects of school restructuring on student achievement and other outcomes. He received his Ph.D. from the University of Iowa.

Richard Colwell, *The Arts*

Richard Colwell is chair of music education at the New England Conservatory of Music in Boston and a visiting professor at the University of Michigan. He formerly taught at Boston University, University of Illinois, and Eastern Montana College. He has published extensively on research and issues in music education. He is the editor of the *Handbook of Research in Music Education* (Macmillan 1992), the *Handbook of Research on Music Teaching and Learning* (Oxford University Press 2002), and author of the chapter on arts education in ASCD's *Curriculum Handbook*. He serves as a consultant on music education to colleges and universities and has directed several U.S. Department of Education grants for music projects. He has been active with the Music Educators National Conference and is a member of that organization's hall of fame. He received his Ed.D. in music education from the University of Illinois.

Catherine D. Ennis, *Physical Education*

Catherine D. Ennis serves as professor in the Department of Kinesiology at the University of Maryland in College Park. She previously taught at the University of Wisconsin, University of Georgia, University of North Carolina at Greensboro, and Duke University. She has authored numerous articles on her research in refereed journals and is author of *The Curriculum Process in Physical Education* and editor of *Student Learning in Physical Education: Applying Research to Enhance Instruction.* Her research interests have focused on student misconceptions in science-based physical education, student engagement, and value orientations in the formation of teacher and student knowledge structures and problem-solving heuristics. She received her Ph.D. from the University of Georgia.

Dorothy Gabel, *Science*

Dorothy Gabel is professor of science education at Indiana University in Bloomington and has previously worked for the National Science Foundation, the University of Maryland, and Purdue University. She served as editor of the *Handbook of Research on Science Teaching and Learning* (Macmillan 1994) and has published 25 articles in refereed journals, including the *Journal of Research in Science Teaching.* She has published two textbooks on high school chemistry and has won several grants from the National Science Foundation. Gabel is the recipient of seven awards for outstanding research from the National Association for Research on science teaching, and the Carleton Award for outstanding leadership in science education from the National Science Teachers Association. She received her Ph.D. from Purdue University.

Douglas A. Grouws, *Mathematics*

Douglas A. Grouws is professor of mathematics education at the University of Iowa. He was editor of the *Handbook of Research on Mathematics Teaching and Learning* (Macmillan 1992) and has written a large number of other publications on research in mathematics education. He has made invited research presentations in England, Scotland, Australia, Hungary, India, Mexico, Thailand, Japan, China, and Guam. He has directed several research projects for the National Science Foundation (NSF) and other agencies in the areas of mathematical problem solving and classroom teaching practices. His current NSF work involves mathematics and technology. He received his Ph.D. from the University of Wisconsin.

Myriam Met, *Foreign Language*

Myriam Met currently serves as deputy director of the National Foreign Language Center, a think tank dedicated to language policy, planning, and infrastructure development. She was previously coordinator of foreign languages for the Montgomery County Public Schools in Rockville, Md. She has published extensively on the topics of curriculum and teacher development for foreign language, bilingual education, and ESL programs and has provided consultant services to school districts, departments of education, and postsecondary institutions in more than 40 states, Europe, Asia, South America, and Canada. She received her Ed.D. from the University of Cincinnati.

Susan J. Paik, *Effective General Practices*

Susan J. Paik is an assistant professor at the University of San Francisco in the School of Education, Department of Learning and Instruction. She has participated in education projects in Africa, Asia, Central America, Europe, and the United States, where she founded and directed a character-development program for inner-city youth. She has presented her work not only at the American Educational Research Association annually, but also at Oxford University in England, the University of Cape Town in South Africa, and the University of Bologna in Italy, as well as at professional meetings in South America, Australia, Germany, and the United States. She has received several awards, fellowships, and grants and has authored numerous publications.

Carolyn Dunkle Perry, *Oral Communication*

Carolyn Dunkle Perry has been assisting the National Communication Association with numerous K-12 communication standards projects and publications since 1995. She has had several years of teaching experience at the middle and high school levels in Florida, North Carolina, and Virginia, and is currently an English instructional supervisor in the Loudoun County Public Schools in Virginia. She has done much research on developing communication and composition skills in students and integrating communication education across the K-12 curriculum. She received her M.A. in speech communication from the University of North Carolina.

Robin G. Sawyer, *Health Education*

Robin G. Sawyer is associate professor and acting chairperson in the Department of Public and Community Health at the University of Maryland in College Park. He previously taught middle and high school health education in both the United States and his native England. His particular area of interest and expertise is the subject of adolescent sexuality; in addition to having published numerous research articles in refereed journals, he also has produced four award-winning films on sexuality and is a regular presenter at colleges and universities throughout the United States. He is a co-author of the text *Health*

Education: Creating Strategies for School and Community Health. He received his Ph.D. from the University of Maryland.

James P. Shaver, *Social Studies*

James P. Shaver is professor emeritus of secondary education at Utah State University. He edited the *Handbook of Research on Social Studies Teaching and Learning* (Macmillan 1991) and has published articles on social studies curricular issues, research findings, and epistemological and methodological research issues. Among other books, he is the author of *Teaching Public Issues in High Schools* (with Donald Oliver). He is a past-president of the National Council for the Social Studies. He received his Ed.D. from Harvard University.

Dennis Sparks, *Staff Development*

Dennis Sparks serves as executive director of the National Staff Development Council in Ann Arbor, Mich. He was a teacher, counselor, and co-director of an alternative high school before becoming the director of the Northwest Staff Development Center in Livonia, Mich. He has taught at the University of Michigan, Eastern Michigan University, and the University of Alaska. He is executive editor of *The Journal of Staff Development* and has published widely on the topic of staff development. He received his Ph.D. from the University of Michigan.

James R. Squire, *Language Arts*

The late James R. Squire taught at Harvard University Teachers College, Columbia University, UCLA, University of Illinois, and Southern Illinois University. He was the former executive secretary of the National Council of Teachers of English and senior vice president and editor-in-chief for Ginn and Company. He authored and edited 14 books and more than 100 articles, including serving as editor (with others) of the *Handbook of Research on Teaching the English Language Arts* (Macmillan 1991). He received his Ph.D. from the University of California at Berkeley.

Herbert J. Walberg, *Effective General Practices*

Herbert J. Walberg is university scholar and research professor emeritus of Education and Psychology at the University of Illinois at Chicago and formerly served as assistant professor at Harvard University. A distinguished visiting fellow at the Stanford University Hoover Institution, he has written and edited more than 50 books and contributed more than 380 articles to educational and psychological research journals on the topic of educational productivity and related subjects. He served as chairman of the Technical Committee on International Education Indicators for the Paris-based Organization for Economic Cooperation and Development and was a founding member and chairman of the Design and Analysis Committee of the National Assessment Governing Board. He received his Ph.D. from the University of Chicago.

Introduction

Gordon Cawelti

The third edition of the *Handbook of Research on Improving Student Achievement* is being released at a critical time for schools. For many schools and districts, the accountability element of the No Child Left Behind Act has led to an unprecedented press to quickly and substantially improve student achievement as measured by standardized tests. To meet the provisions of No Child Left Behind, schools must first decide how to focus their improvement efforts.

On a positive note, research provides helpful direction for this effort. In an addition to this *Handbook*, recent research on effective districts—those that have substantially improved the achievement of students who typically have not done well in school—provides a road map for districts. In this new chapter, the emphasis the successful districts placed on curriculum, instruction, and curricular alignment is identified as a key element of this road map. In addition, the successful districts recognized the importance of using the knowledge base to improve teaching.

The *Handbook* is designed to help schools and districts with the critical task of improving teaching; its underlying assumption is that efforts to improve instruction must focus on the existing knowledge base about effective teaching and learning in order to succeed. The practices included here can help teachers to expand their instructional repertoire to successfully address the wide range of interests and aptitudes of students found in most classrooms.

In addition, this third edition of the *Handbook*, like its earlier editions in 1995 and 1999, can be considered an important contribution to the field because, in one volume, it discusses

research related to all major disciplines currently taught in elementary and secondary schools. By bringing together what is known about effective instruction across disciplines, the *Handbook* is intended to encourage readers to learn about, discuss, and try promising approaches from other subject areas.

Design of the *Handbook*

Before the first edition of the *Handbook of Research on Improving Student Achievement* was written, everyone involved with the project—the advisory group, the authors, the editor, and ERS staff working on the project—discussed how it might be used most effectively. The results of that discussion provided direction for both the content and the format of the *Handbook*. To make the *Handbook* most useful to educators, it was decided that it should:

- include both research and classroom implications for each of the practices, as well as references for use by readers desiring more information;

- use a format that allowed busy teachers and other school leaders to read the information on each practice in a short period of time; and

- provide research on all of the major content areas so that teachers could learn from the research base developed in content areas other than their own.

Work on the second edition of the *Handbook* was preceded by intensive efforts to ask people who had used the first edition how they would suggest changing the format. The reaction was unanimous: use the original approach. Repeatedly we heard that the format—a description of a teaching practice followed by a brief overview of research findings and an "in the classroom" section—greatly contributed to the usefulness of the *Handbook*. This same format is used again in this third edition.

All of the scholars selected to prepare the sections of the *Handbook* have had extensive research experience in their particular fields, as their biographies indicate. As a group, they have the particular expertise needed to judge the quality of research, to conduct extensive searches of the literature, and to prepare the syntheses appearing in the *Handbook*. Perhaps most importantly, they are relatively free of bias, unlike some scholars who are strong advocates of particular approaches in their own fields.

What Is Included

After considerable discussion about what practices to include in each of the sections of the *Handbook*, the authors agreed to include not only classroom practices with a broad research base but also those practices reflected in the educational standards that have recently emerged and for which less substantive research currently exists.

Thus, in some instances a particular practice is included mainly because of the scholar's judgment that it reflects a serious attempt to accomplish "higher-order thinking skills" or the development of more personal meaning for individual students. Those who use this *Handbook* will see a mixture of emerging strategies and "tried and true" practices.

Another decision made in preparing the *Handbook* was to avoid creating separate sections for practices aimed at students who might be categorized as "at-risk"—for example, those from poor socioeconomic backgrounds, racial minorities, those with learning disabilities, and those for whom English is a second language.

The authors recognize many schools have an urgent need to develop plans directed toward significantly improving the achievement of these students. However, in a thorough analysis of programs designed specifically for at-risk children at the preschool and elementary level and for special education students, Slavin, Karweit, and Madden (1989) stress the qualities of effective teachers for disadvantaged students in these programs tended to be similar to the qualities of effective teachers for all students. And the most intensive classroom observational study of effective teaching practices relating to at-risk children conducted in recent years, titled *Academic Challenge for the Children of Poverty* and financed by the U.S. Department of Education, found:

> The results present clear evidence that alternative [teaching] practices work at least as well for low-performing as high-performing students. In all three subject areas [mathematics, reading, and writing], instruction aimed at meaning and understanding appeared to work as well for students at the low end as those at the high end of the achievement distribution (Knapp, Shields, and Turnbull 1992, 27).

However, this does not mean the research supports "one size fits all" instruction. Grant characterizes "ceaseless diversity of America's student population, which public schools must accept and accommodate," as an irresistible force and state standards as an immovable object (2003, 48). Teacher attention to the strengths, background knowledge, and needs of individual students supports high levels of achievement for all students within the context of assessment-based accountability. For example, teachers need to be knowledgeable about cultural differences that may affect learning and be able to respond to them in meeting the child's instructional needs.

The definition of achievement used in the *Handbook* is clearly a very critical issue. While much of the scholarly research over the years has relied on standardized test results in cognitive areas of knowledge and skills, this is not the only outcome expected of schools. If a particular classroom practice in science, for example, results in students liking science better and taking more classes, this is also an important achievement, as is an approach enabling students to understand and value diversity in people. A goal of a school district might be to raise minority students' academic performance, but an equally important type of achievement would be to increase minority students' access to social networks and institutions of higher education.

In short, the authors were encouraged to use a broad definition of achievement as they identified research-based practices that lead to improved achievement in concepts, values, or skills. Even so, the preponderance of studies reported here rely on more traditional kinds of testing of knowledge and skills. This is not to say that other kinds of achievement are not important, but rather that less research has been done in associating classroom practices with the highly important kinds of nontraditional achievement measures just described.

A final issue during the preparation of the *Handbook* involved the decision to present these effective practices by subject area. This may appear to disregard the trend toward greater integration of the separate subjects in the curriculum. Interdisciplinary approaches to organizing the curriculum can help students make connections between ideas and knowledge in different subject fields. In addition, it has become increasingly apparent that the newly emerging voluntary curriculum standards stand little chance of being implemented through a separate-subjects curriculum, because of the large body of knowledge they represent and the limited time available in a given school day.

The key elements of the current educational system, such as teacher training, schedules, textbooks, and assessment, tend to be discipline based. Despite this, teachers themselves have increasingly come to recognize that students need to be helped to see the relationships among important concepts, and have forged ahead in developing more interdisciplinary approaches, or what has come to be called an integrated curriculum. Elementary teachers have a natural setting for such instruction in their self-contained classrooms. At the secondary level, the organization and schedule changes required for such curriculum

integration have made the practice less prevalent, yet significant numbers of high schools are changing to block schedules, teaming arrangements, and interdisciplinary teaching (Cawelti 1994).

While there is much advocacy for curriculum integration, however, its very nature has tended to limit reliable research on its efficacy, and the vast body of research on effective instructional practices has typically been reported by broad subject fields. According to Goodlad and Zhizin, "almost all the literature on curriculum organization is conceptual or prescriptive and rarely experimental" (1992, 339). Carefully conceived longitudinal research on the effects of curriculum integration is needed, and no doubt will be forthcoming.

The research available on integrated approaches within the disciplines is included in this *Handbook* when judged to be appropriate. Although these chapters are arranged by broad subject fields, readers will note many commonalities between the research-based practices identified by the scholars in different subject fields.

Preparing the Third Edition of the Handbook

When the *Handbook of Research on Improving Student Achievement* was originally published in 1995, it was recognized that this publication would need to be updated periodically to include the most current research and thinking on best practices in the various subject areas.

For both the second and third editions of the *Handbook*, the original authors were invited to update their chapters. In some cases, chapters were not changed at all because the research on teaching in the content area still supported inclusion of the practices originally used. Some authors included their original practices, but substantially revised the list of references provided in support of each practice. Finally, some authors added practices.

Using This *Handbook*

The *Handbook of Research on Improving Student Achievement* provides a synthesis of the knowledge base that exists about effective practices for improving teaching and learning. It is intended for use by teachers, principals, other instructional leaders, and policy makers who are undertaking the quest to attain world-class standards while meeting the needs of an increasingly diverse student body.

The research findings presented in the *Handbook* should be viewed as reliable information to be used as a starting point in developing comprehensive school improvement plans, rather than as a prescription equally applicable to all classrooms. In her chapter on foreign language, Myriam Met makes this point clearly:

> Research cannot and does not identify the right or best way to teach, nor does it suggest certain instructional practices should always or should never be used. But research *can* illuminate which instructional practices are most likely to achieve desired results, with which kinds of learners, and under what conditions.

James Shaver, author of the chapter on social studies instruction, elaborates on the importance of meshing both the research base and the expertise of experienced educators when making instructional decisions. In Shaver's view, there are:

> . . . reasons that the prescription of classroom practice from research findings should be avoided. Research findings must be applied in specific classroom and school settings. In particular, sound instructional decisions must be based on the educational values of the teacher, the school, the school district, and the community, as well as on district and state guidelines and requirements. Skilled, thoughtful, and motivated teachers must adapt and implement techniques or approaches suggested by research findings to achieve desired student outcomes.

> Research findings can be of assistance in instructional decision making by stimulating thought and suggesting alternatives, and as a source of information on options as teachers consider how to teach. However, the experiences and practical knowledge of the individual teacher and his or her colleagues are crucial in deciding upon applications. In addition, each teacher knows his or her students' interests and motivations, their prior experiences, and their expectations, as these will influence each student's reactions to instructional techniques and approaches. Each teacher is also aware of the extent to which his or her students find social studies interesting and challenging, and of the extent to which meaningful learning is occurring.

This acknowledgement that both the research and professional experience are important is consistent with an oft-repeated, NCLB-related phrase—evidence-based education. Grover Whitehurst, assistant secretary for Educational Research and Improvement of the U.S. Department of Education, describes evidence-based education as the "integration of professional wisdom with the best available empirical evidence in making decisions about how to deliver instruction" (2002, online). This *Handbook* is designed to provide educators with a thoughtful, comprehensive, and user-friendly overview of the empirical evidence.

The Context for Using the Handbook

In the chapter on the research about high-achieving districts, the importance of context in efforts to improve schools is highlighted. Over and over again, researchers visiting these districts heard that the need to improve quickly generated systemic responses that were powerful in their impact. The importance of focusing on curriculum and instruction was paramount. Teachers were more likely to be provided with time to collaborate. They were encouraged to observe and learn from other teachers whose "best practices" had been identified as having significant positive effects on student learning. The importance of using the knowledge base about effective practices was recognized. Finally, improvement came from implementation of several initiatives carefully planned to reinforce, not compete with, each other. Such an organizational context is ideally suited for broad-based and effective use of the *Handbook* to improve teaching.

Collaboration among Educators—Putting the knowledge base on improving student achievement to work in classrooms is a complex business. Dennis Sparks, in his chapter on staff development in the *Handbook's* first edition, clearly articulated the responsibility of schools and school districts to establish a culture in which teachers can exercise their professional competence, explore promising practices, and share information among themselves, while keeping the focus on the ultimate goal of staff development—the improvement of student learning.

Within such a culture, much of the best staff development occurs on a daily basis. Teachers report observing their peers' classrooms and participating in discussion groups with other teachers provide powerful learning experiences and generate excitement for expanding their own repertoires to include new practices.

Teachers and school leaders inevitably will need time for further study of, discussion of, and exposure to what a particular practice entails before deciding to include it in their school's plans. Time, and particularly the lack of it for reflection on practice, has been identified repeatedly as a barrier to school improvement efforts. Although many teachers report how helpful it is to them to be able to see a particular practice applied in the classroom, limited time for sharing and professional conversation often leaves them unaware that another teacher in the building is already using the practice. This fellow-teacher resource is important as a person who can both demonstrate the practice and provide support until the teacher newly using the practice gains facility and confidence.

While much staff development based on the *Handbook* typically will occur in content area-based settings, teachers also should be encouraged to talk about what their experiences in their subject field or grade level bring to the profession as a whole. Through such discussions, an important goal of the *Handbook* project will be served—to ensure the adoption of effective instructional practices is not limited by barriers between content areas.

Ultimately, the value of the *Handbook* as a resource devoted to increasing student achievement depends on the willingness of schools and districts to invest the energy and time needed for reflection, for discussion, for sharing expertise, and for the inclusion of new instructional strategies in classroom practice. It is only a tool, and is best used by teachers and other educators who are collaborating to continuously improve instruction.

Multiple Changes—In considering the instructional practices discussed in the *Handbook*, readers should be aware that, in most cases, the results of research on specific teaching practices show only small or moderate gains. In education, we need to understand, carefully select, and use combinations of teaching practices that together increase the *probability* of helping students learn, knowing these practices may not work in all classrooms all the time.

The strongest probability of improving student learning will emerge where schools are able to implement multiple changes in the teaching and learning activities affecting the daily life of students. For example, if the aim is to improve the quality of student composition skills in the eighth grade, the school might plan to introduce training for teachers in: 1) tutoring; 2) instruction in writing as a process; and 3) appropriate assessment techniques. The research summarized in this *Handbook* supports the efficacy of each of these instructional practices in improving students' writing achievement.

School Restructuring—It can be anticipated that the need to restructure schools will become more and more important as schools continue the task of significantly improving student achievement by expanding the knowledge base of teachers. Experience has shown teachers need time to absorb new information, observe and discuss new practices, and participate in the training needed to become confident with new techniques.

This often requires changes in traditional schedules to give teachers regular opportunities to team with their colleagues both in acquiring new skills and in providing instruction. When employees in other work settings have been provided with such opportunities to assume direct responsibility for improving the quality of services, the results have been positive. It is hoped that expanding the knowledge base and changing the culture of schools to promote such empowerment will result in higher student achievement and schools in which students, parents, and the community have a high degree of confidence.

Suggestions for Use

Preparation for the second edition of the *Handbook* included interviews of purchasers of the book who were asked how they used it. Their responses were both interesting and informative, and so they were summarized and included as ideas for other educators in use of the *Handbook*. This information—in the broad categories of teacher staff development, curriculum development, evaluation of teachers, development of principals and other administrators, support for school improvement activities, and in higher education programs—is again included and is presented briefly below.

For teacher professional development:

- Some social studies teachers suggested reviewing one practice a month through the school year at department meetings. The practice would provide a focus for discussion, with teachers who already used the practice available as resources and mentors for other teachers interested in using the practice in their own classrooms. As one teacher re-marked, "Staff development doesn't work when teachers are *told* what they need—often, they then just go along for the ride."

  Using the *Handbook*, the teachers would select the practices that seemed to hold the most value for their needs and those of the students they taught and then use these practices to guide their own development. They also saw value in the *Handbook* as an anchor around which they might structure a professional discussion about teaching and learning. In their view, departmental meet-

ings often included too much "business" and not enough instructionally related content.

- One school reported using the *Handbook* as a resource when teachers met to discuss alternative approaches that might be used with students who were not experiencing success. It "provided ideas and was a guide to other resources."

- Curriculum specialists in one district were given copies of the *Handbook* and asked to read the Introduction, the Staff Development chapter, and the chapters relating to their disciplines. As a group, the specialists discussed practices that were common across content areas; in addition, each individual highlighted practices within his or her own discipline holding promise for adaptation and application in other content-area classrooms. Specialists then met with teachers in their own content areas to review both the contents of the subject-area chapter and the ideas shared among the specialists. Each teacher was asked to identify one research-based practice that would expand his or her personal repertoire of instructional strategies and to introduce its use during the first three months of school. Follow-up discussions were held by content-area teachers and specialists, as well as by the specialists who met as a group to share ideas generated by the teachers with whom they worked.

- One respondent identified an important use for the *Handbook*: to validate the instructional practices teachers already employ. In his words, "It is as important for teachers to know what they know as well as what they still have to learn." Another made a related comment: "We had some 'Aha!' experiences. The *Handbook* rekindled some knowledge that we already had, but perhaps had forgotten."

- Teachers in one district reviewed and dis-cussed the research findings, then received training and follow-up support in strategies in which they were interested.

- One lead teacher reported sharing one or two practices for his content area during each departmental meeting.

- Curriculum and staff development specialists in one district used the *Handbook* as a guide to planning staff development opportunities. The focus was on expanding the breadth of teaching techniques teachers felt comfortable applying in each of their classrooms.

- One principal—while expressing concern about the time teachers in her school spend at the copy machine—kept a copy of the *Handbook* by the machine. She reported teachers liked the short format allowing them to quickly read about one of the practices.

- Another suggestion made by teachers was the use of the *Handbook* to help less-experienced teachers "take the rough edges off." More experienced teachers would work collaboratively with them to help the newer teachers expand and refine their repertoire of teaching strategies.

For curriculum development and improvement:

- One administrator reported a standard practice in her district is the development of literature reviews for use by knowledge-based study teams. The *Handbook* had provided a shortcut toward developing these reference lists.

- One district used the *Handbook* to help strengthen areas of weakness identified by standardized assessments.

- Another provided it as background material for all district committees charged with reviewing, renewing, and aligning curriculum.

- Several respondents reported using the *Handbook* to provide background reading for focus/study groups.

- The *Handbook* was used in one district in content-area study committees (made up of a representative group of teachers—at least one from each school—and an assistant princi-

pal) tasked to plan content-area lessons for the district.

- The *Handbook* was used during one district's systematic curriculum review cycle as a compendium of source materials and perspectives on individual content areas.

- Another district used the *Handbook* as a resource when reviewing curriculum and teacher strategies related to a new state-required math assessment.

- One respondent commented, "It has helped support improvement efforts in the different content areas since it focuses our efforts on instructional strategies that research indicates are effective."

- Copies of the *Handbook* were made available to all members of one district's Curriculum Renewal Committee for use during an intensive, four-day planning session held during the summer.

As a resource during the teacher evaluation process:

- One principal reported: "I found it useful when observing teachers. It helped me focus on the essentials of good teaching while encouraging me to look for a variety of strategies."

- Training held for principals in teacher evaluation incorporated the *Handbook* as a reference/discussion item on quality teaching practices.

- One new principal reported feeling more comfortable when observing teachers in content areas with which he had little personal experience. He reported that reading the practices before the observation provided him with a valuable resource and a "common ground" on which he could focus during post-observation discussions with the teacher.

- The *Handbook* was provided as a resource for building administrators to be "shared, quoted, and used when providing written or oral feedback" to teachers after classroom observations.

- The *Handbook* was used in one district to alert principals to characteristics that should be observed in teachers using these "best practices."

- Principals used the *Handbook* with teachers during post-evaluation meetings as a source from which to develop professional growth plans.

In development activities and as a reference for principals and other administrators:

- Members of a district committee of principals and curriculum specialists used the *Handbook* as a focal point in their monthly meetings. The responsibility for studying and reporting on a chapter was rotated among the members, although all committee members were expected to come prepared with examples of strategy implementation in their own schools.

- One administrator responded that the *Handbook* "helped him keep abreast" of research in a variety of content areas, a task that had always been difficult.

- A principal in a small school district felt the *Handbook* was especially valuable to him because it greatly increased the "resources available" to him.

- One administrator had used content from the *Handbook* in preparing presentations for regional and state association meetings.

- Several respondents reported using the *Handbook* to facilitate communication with parents. For example, one principal noted the *Handbook* had provided some information helpful to answering a parent's question about an instructional strategy.

- Several administrators reported using the *Handbook* as a reference, both to answer questions and to explain something. They also made the *Handbook* available to others interested in research-based information about teaching.

In school improvement and planning activities:

- One building administrator reported: "We were interested in building 'learning teams' in our school. Discussing some of the content in the *Handbook* provided a good activity on which to base the rest of our efforts."

- In a district in which each content area annually develops an Academic Action Plan, teachers reviewed specific content-area practices and identified some as focus areas for additional teacher training and practice.

- An administrator in a district using the Effective Schools model reported that, because they try to approach all decisions with research as a base, the *Handbook* provided a solid base of general guidance.

- A consultant who works with several districts found the *Handbook* valuable as a resource focusing school improvement efforts on student learning. He then works with these districts to "develop policies and procedures supportive of learning and use of these best practices" by teachers.

- One district incorporated the *Handbook* as a source document for research-based ideas in its systematic curriculum review cycle.

- School staff in one district used the *Handbook* to stimulate discussion about the critical role of instructional practice in school improvement efforts.

- One district provided copies of the *Handbook* to each of its school improvement teams. It was used in training activities as a way to focus the teams on their primary goal—increasing the level of student learning.

- Instructional models—some of them commercially prepackaged—already being used by one district were reviewed to see whether they incorporated the "best practices" identified in the *Handbook*.

- Several districts reported using the *Handbook* as a reference and as supporting documentation when preparing grant requests.

- One assistant superintendent used the *Handbook* as a resource during the district's accreditation process. School officials had decided to identify "target goals" and used the *Handbook* in the "instructional practices" portion of the improvement plan.

- The *Handbook* was viewed as an excellent starting point for district improvement discussions involving teachers, building administrators, and curriculum specialists. Volunteers from within the study group collected additional material about selected practices and then led in-depth group discussions.

For higher education programs:

- One professor reported using the *Handbook* as a text for a graduate education course related to curriculum improvement and differentiation.

- Another considered it an important tool for Ph.D. candidates, recommending they use it in their work as school or district administrators.

These brief descriptions of how educators used the first edition of the *Handbook* provide only a starting point. The culture of the classrooms, schools, and districts in which the *Handbook* is used will ultimately determine whether its content has an impact on the daily classroom lives of students and teachers.

Bibliography

Cawelti, Gordon. 1994. *High School Restructuring: A National Study.* Arlington, VA: Educational Research Service.

Cawelti, Gordon, and Protheroe, Nancy. 2001. *High Student Achievement: How Six School Districts Changed into High-Performance Systems.* Arlington, VA: Educational Research Service.

Goodlad, John I., and Su Zhizin. 1992. "Organization of the Curriculum." In *Handbook of Research on Curriculum,* Philip Jackson, editor. New York: Macmillan Publishing Company.

Grant, Jim. 2003. Differentiating for Diversity. *Principal* (January/February 2003), 48-51.

Knapp, Michael, Patrick Shields, and Brenda Turnbull. 1992. *Academic Challenge for the Children of Poverty: The Summary Report.* Washington, DC: U.S. Department of Education, Office of Policy and Planning. [Reprinted from original by Educational Research Service, Arlington, VA.]

Louis, Karen Seashore, and Robert A. Dentler. 1988. "Knowledge Use and School Improvement." *Curriculum Inquiry* Vol. 18, No. 1: 34-61.

Mullis, Ina V.S. et al. 1994. *NAEP 1992 Trends in Academic Progress.* Washington: National Center for Education Statistics.

Slavin, Robert E., Nancy L. Karweit, and Nancy A. Madden. 1989. *Effective Programs for Students at Risk.* Boston: Allyn and Bacon.

Whitehurst, Grover J. 2002. *Evidenced-Based Education. U.S. Department of Education.* Retrieved from http://nclb/methods/whatworks/eb/edlite-index.html

Chapter 1. A Synthesis of Research on High-Performing School Systems

Gordon Cawelti

The primary focus of this *Handbook* is on improvement of instruction at the classroom level, but there has been renewed recognition during recent years that improving classroom by classroom, or even school by school, is too slow. While the practices in this *Handbook* can be used to help teachers expand their repertoire, and thus successfully teach more of their students, the district can provide an important context for these efforts. It is for this reason a chapter is included in this edition of the *Handbook* on the emerging "lessons learned" from recent research on high-achieving districts—those that have developed the culture and practices that move the process of improvement more quickly, sometimes radically so.

It also should be noted, however, that no matter how powerful a central-office initiative may appear, or how strongly policy "wonks" may favor a particular practice, no significant increase in student achievement will be forthcoming unless students receive higher quality and more focused instruction in their classrooms on a day-to-day basis. That is, class size reduction may be very helpful for teachers, or site-based management may be a way to increase accountability, but it is entirely conceivable that neither would result in a better quality instructional life for students or improved test scores.

It is for this reason that educating teachers about instructional practices research—such as the best practices presented in this book— has been shown to make a difference in student achievement and is so important.

Some History of Related Research

A substantial number of studies over almost three decades have been carried out to identify factors describing individual schools that have defied the odds by accomplishing high levels of achievement while serving significant numbers of children from low-income or minority families. But, until recently, there has been little research focused on school *districts* as the locus for improvement efforts.

For information about efforts to improve larger systems, educators often turned to research done in the corporate world. Perhaps the most famous of these studies was done by Peters and Waterman (1982), who studied 62 companies ranking high on six measures of long-term financial health. The study contributed to a revolution in many American businesses that responded to the findings describing several characteristics of the successful companies in the study. The following are some of the key findings of Peters and Waterman's study of high-performing corporations:

- They were "close to their customers," and they listened to what their customers or clients said about their products and services.

- They had a "bias for action"—for trying new ways of doing things and then trying something else if this did not work.

- They shifted responsibility for improving quality to the workers themselves—those dealing directly with clients and customers. (Hiring more supervisors and middle managers was not the way to get better motorcycles or hotel services!) This practice is reflected in high-performing schools and districts where teacher teams are given responsibility for making use of data about student performance in efforts to improve instruction and diagnose the need of some students for additional instruction.

A more recent and also popular study by Jim Collins (2001) took another look at companies operating successfully in a very competitive, global economy. In his view, a key element of their success was developing a culture encouraging people to try new ideas, test them, and then try something else if the first new approaches don't pay off.

The School District Studies

The research studies on school districts seem to have their genesis in several common themes. First, there was increasing understanding that while not all the lessons learned from corporate studies might be directly applicable to education, there was one key element: The corporate research focused on high-performing *systems*, complex organizations with many interrelated parts. School districts, in particular large districts, could certainly be viewed as systems facing challenges similar to corporations. And, if very large corporations could improve significantly through a systemwide initiative, logic said school districts could as well.

Second, the pressure of state standards-based reform and accountability required, in some cases, substantial improvement by hundreds of schools statewide. Some of the state accountability systems also brought with them a new resource. For example, the Texas assessment system reported results disaggregated by major racial/ethnic groups and for poor students. Trend data were also available so that progress—or lack of it—could be tracked year to year. These data both jump-started improvement efforts and provided a way to identify schools and districts achieving rapid and substantial improvement.

Finally, it was quickly recognized—by both school districts and researchers—that more radical and intense efforts were needed than the typical school-by-school improvement. Some school districts began to take a much more aggressive role in school improvement efforts. And, as the state accountability programs began

to identify districts in which improvement was evident across many schools, researchers began to ask if key factors could be identified in these high-performing *systems*. If the factors could be reliably identified and replicated, the process of improving student achievement on a broad scale could be accelerated.

This chapter represents an effort to synthesize the findings of studies focusing on school districts as the locus for school improvement efforts. For their data, the researchers looked to districts serving high percentages of children who typically do less well than White, middle- or upper-class students and who were *improving*. Thus, these studies do not present a picture of school systems that had been high-performing on a long-term basis. Typically, these systems tend to be in suburban America, monitored closely by their middle-class parents and school boards, better supported financially, focused on the college-prep mission, and serving a far less diverse student body than many large districts. While there are definitely lessons to be learned from these districts, this chapter will highlight what low-performing districts did to improve.

Improvements in Student Achievement

This summary of the district-focused research is too brief to provide detailed student achievement data from all the districts studied, but some highlights provide a picture of the often dramatic improvement experienced by some districts:

- In the San Benito district, for example, the percentage of White students passing the math portion of the Texas assessment increased from 67.2 percent in 1994 to 90.9 percent in 1999, from 50.3 percent to 86.7 percent for Hispanic students, and from 47.1 percent to 85.5 percent for economically disadvantaged students (Dana Center study).

- In Wichita Falls ISD in Texas, the pass rates for mathematics increased from 68.5 percent (1994) to 93.1 percent (1999) for White students; corresponding pass rates for Hispanic students were 40.7 percent and 87.2

In the following sections of this report, findings from the four studies of school district improvement are summarized. The reports discussed include:

- *Equity-Driven Achievement-Focused School Districts*, a report summarizing results from a study conducted by the Charles A. Dana Center at the University of Texas at Austin (2000).

- *High Student Achievement: How Six School Districts Changed into High-Performance Systems*, a report summarizing a study conducted by Educational Research Service with support from the Laboratory of School Success, a regional laboratory of the U.S. Department of Education located in Philadelphia. Six districts serving significant numbers of low SES children were studied (2001).

- *Foundations for Success: Case Studies of How Urban School Systems Improve Student Achievement*, a report summarizing results from a study conducted by the Council of the Great City Schools. Three urban districts, with part of another, were studied along with comparison districts doing less well in their efforts to improve student achievement (2002).

- *Beyond Islands of Excellence: What Districts Can Do to Improve Instruction and Achievement in All Schools*, a report summarizing findings from a study conducted by the Learning First Alliance. Five high-poverty districts were studied (2003).

percent, and for economically disadvantaged students, 43.0 percent and 84.3 percent (Dana Center study).

- Figure 1 demonstrates the dramatic progress made in the Brazosport, Tex., school district in eliminating gaps in reading achievement between subgroups of students. This elimination of the gaps in reading achievement was replicated in mathematics and writing. At least 95 percent of the students, or more in each of the subgroups, received a passing score on the state tests by 2000 (ERS/LSS study).

- In the Twin Falls School District in Idaho, scores on the Iowa Tests of Basic Skills at the fifth-grade level in mathematics rose from the 55th percentile in 1995 to the 89th percentile in 1999, and a similar pattern was seen at the other grade levels (ERS/LSS study).

- In Ysleta ISD in Texas, all 49 schools were in the two lowest-performing categories in 1993, but by 2000, 43 of these schools had moved to either the "recognized" or "exemplary" category (ERS/LSS study).

- In the Barbour County, W.Va., school district, student scores at the third-grade level on the SAT-9 tests in all subjects rose during the 1997-2000 years from the 47th percentile to the 65th percentile (ERS/LSS study).

- In the Houston Independent School District, SAT-9 reading achievement at the fifth-grade level improved substantially from 1998 to 2001. In 1998, 46.7 percent of students overall scored in the lowest quartile; by 2001, this had been reduced to 31.7 percent. Almost half (48.7 percent) of African American students were in the lowest quartile in 1998; this had dropped to 32.6 percent in 2001. Results for Hispanic students showed a 17.8 percent reduction in the number scoring in the lowest quartile. Finally, there was a 10-12 point reduction in the gaps between White and minority achievement (CGCS study).

- Between 1998 and 2000, Sacramento fifth-grade reading scores falling in the lowest quartile fell from 46.2 percent (in 1998) to 41.6 percent (in 2000), with a reduction in the gap between the scores of African

American and Hispanic students, compared with White students (CGCS study).

- Between 1995 and 2001, the percentage of African American students in the Charlotte Mecklenburg (N.C.) School District scoring in the two lowest categories on the grade 5 math test fell from 58 percent to 27 percent, while for White students it fell from 18 percent to 5 percent, a significant improvement for both groups as well as a reduction in the gap between them (CGCS study).

- In Aldine, the percentage of African American students who passed the math portion of the Texas assessment increased from 65 percent in 1994 to 94 percent in 2002, with corresponding pass rates for White students at 84 percent and 96 percent. This also

resulted in a significant reduction in the gap between the two groups (LFA study).

- Kent County increased the proportion of students scoring "satisfactory" on Maryland assessments and was the highest-scoring district in the state in 1999 and 2000 (LFA study).

- Between 1999 and 2002, the percentage of second-grade Hispanic students in the Chula Vista Elementary School District scoring at or above the 50th percentile on the Stanford-9 increased from 37 percent to 55 percent (LFA study).

The Charles A. Dana Center Studies

Skrla, Scheurich, and Johnson (2000) identified four school districts with 1997 enrollments

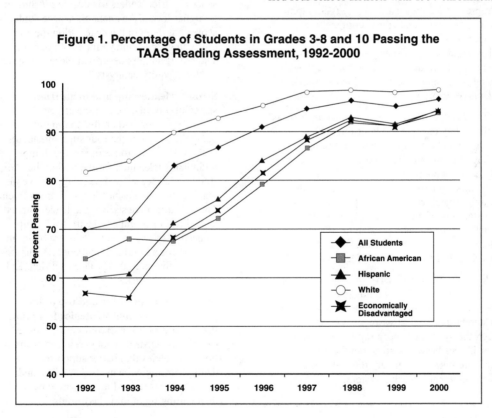

Figure 1. Percentage of Students in Grades 3-8 and 10 Passing the TAAS Reading Assessment, 1992-2000

of 5,000 or more students that showed substantial progress in moving their schools from the "low-performing" category up to the "recognized" or even "exemplary" category, where 90 percent of the students needed to have passed the state tests in reading, writing, and mathematics. A third or more of each district's low-SES schools had moved up to the two highest state categories based on test scores. The districts selected also needed to have at least two middle or high schools among these high-performing schools. In addition, districts with exemption rates for testing special education or LEP students above the state average, excessive dropout rates, or excessive ninth-grade retention rates were eliminated.

Of the 11 districts identified, four districts were chosen—Aldine, Brazosport, San Benito, and Wichita Falls Independent School Districts—to "represent the greatest diversity (geographic, district size, and racial/ethnic composition) possible" (Skrla, Scheurich, and Johnson 2000, 3). Each had accomplished gains in student achievement among all student subgroups while serving substantial numbers of low-SES and/or students of color.

The research team visited these four districts in 1999. They interviewed board members, superintendents, central-office leaders, principals, teachers, parents and other community leaders, and also gathered large amounts of data and documents from the districts. The goal of the research project was to "develop an in-depth understanding of the ways in which the study districts organized and operated to educate all children to high levels of success" (Skrla, Scheurich, and Johnson 2000, 5).

It is important to observe that this report out of the University of Texas tends to admire the state system for evaluating schools through use of a standards-based assessment system. Although the system has been replicated in other states, it does have its critics, but there are only minor references here to any flaws that are perhaps inherent in such a system.

The factors these researchers believe contributed most to the successes of the four districts center around five areas:

1. **Motivation by virtue of the state's accountability plan.** The research team found the state's new plan for improving results among all students was a highly motivating factor in the changes that had been made. Use of criterion-referenced tests, requiring a sorting out of test results by student subgroups (disaggregation), and public access to such data all tended to highlight for teachers and principals where they most needed to improve.

2. **Pressure placed on leaders by community members.** Public access to results from low-achieving schools resulted in pressure from parents and other community groups on school district leaders to educate *all* students to higher levels. Any schools whose students' scores put them in the state's "low-performing" category became a focus of attention. The report authors described these pressures as "local equity catalysts."

3. **Stronger leadership and focus from superintendents.** Seeing the effects this public reporting had on the community compelled each of the four superintendents, in their own way, to become a much more articulate spokesman for the notion that "all students can learn" and more aggressive in making the changes needed for improvement. The researchers described the leadership as an "ethical or moral one" with leadership consisting of two aspects: "sincere belief in learning for all children and concrete actions based on that belief" (Skrla, Scheurich, and Johnson 2000, 16).

4. **More serious quest for and use of improved instructional strategies to support the pursuit of educational equity and excellence.** District leaders realized instructional strategies that better supported students' learning were needed and directed district efforts toward identifying these and then getting them into classrooms. Teachers

were helped to maintain better focus to their teaching, to align the curriculum with the tests, and to grow professionally as they acquired new strategies for getting the job done. They began to see how they could assist students who had not mastered the state objectives in basic skills and so began to believe that low-SES students and students of color could achieve at high levels. Schools were organized into teams that examined this new state data as they planned how to do better. The expression "proactive redundancy" began to be used to acknowledge that several changes or approaches were needed to ensure higher levels of achievement.

5. **Everyday equity.** The Texas accountability system had made it unacceptable to accept low performance from some groups of students. Although the ethical challenge of educating all students to high levels was accepted, the focus at the beginning of the change efforts was on getting schools off the low-performing list. However, "in the study districts, under the new system, the assumptions about children of color and poor children began to change. As educators experienced new success with these children, the educators began to see that they could accomplish even higher success" (Skrla, Scheurich, and Johnson 2000, 37-38).

The net effect of all these changes was to carve out new roles for superintendents, principals, teachers, and board members that facilitated the changes required to transform the districts from sluggish, low-performing systems to districts that achieved high pass rates on state assessments and much smaller student achievement gaps. All of these required a great deal of time in meetings and staff development for all staff as they were helped to acquire the new skills they needed.

Aldine Superintendent Sonny Donaldson put it "The main thing is to keep the main thing (student learning) the main thing."

The Educational Research Service and Laboratory for School Success Study

One of the first national studies of high-performing districts was conducted by Cawelti and Protheroe of Educational Research Service with support from the Mid-Atlantic Regional Educational Laboratory for Student Success in Philadelphia. The primary focus of the study was on obtaining a clear picture of systemwide changes that had a positive effect on the daily instructional life and performance of students in the districts' schools.

The process to select study districts took several months as the investigators sought to identify school districts that had been successful in raising student achievement while serving large numbers of low-SES and/or minority children. Recommendations were sought from the regional educational laboratories, chief state school officers and state agency assessment directors, and other organizations. State department of education Web sites comprised a very useful tool for corroborating reports of student achievement.

Some interesting problems were encountered in this search: some of the suggested districts had only one school; standards were much higher in some states than others; and in some states (i.e., Virginia, which is a state identified as having relatively high standards reflected in the assessments), no districts met the criteria. Some chief state school officers readily admitted there were no such districts in their state, or that while achievement gains may have been made in one area such as mathematics, reading results were flat or had declined. One district meeting the criteria was located, but its school officials felt they already had been "studied to death" and didn't need further interruptions.

Six districts that had experienced major gains on either state assessments or national, norm-referenced tests during the preceding five to six years were selected for study. Four of these districts met the original criterion of at least 25 percent growth in achievement during this time. Two urban districts not meeting this criterion were added because they came the closest to having accomplished this degree of improvement. The six districts were Barbour County School District in West Virginia; Twin Falls School District in Idaho; Brazosport, Ysleta, and Houston Independent School Districts in Texas; and Sacramento City Unified School District in California.

Each district had its own story to tell, and, although there were similarities among their improvement efforts, each identified one or two changes as central to its success. The Barbour County School District in rural Appalachia had focused much of its early efforts on aligning the local curriculum with the state's curriculum framework. The Twin Falls School District in southern Idaho had also done this and, in addition, had made extensive use of a practice program ensuring pupil retention of skills taught earlier in the year.

Superintendent Jim Sweeney and his Sacramento staff worked hard to reach, define, and then stay focused on seven "Vital Signs of Student Performance," such as readiness for kindergarten, graduation rates, and proficiency in math and reading. Sacramento also gave perhaps the most attention of the six districts studied to how various parts of the total *system* did (or did not) contribute to better achievement.

Houston leaders placed responsibility for improvement squarely at the school and teacher levels, but gave principals and teachers strong support—for example, by providing extensive staff development focused on the newly developed common math and reading curriculum. Brazosport identified a few teachers who were already successful in their efforts to have high percentages of their students pass the state tests, observed them to gather information about their practices, and then trained other teachers in their daily classroom instructional strategies. In Ysleta, district leaders began by repeatedly stressing "all students can learn," but followed up with a strong focus on teaching the objectives of the state curriculum and encouraging teachers to demonstrate *"cariño"*—a caring feeling toward students in this heavily Hispanic district.

But while each district had particular approaches that were working for them, it was also apparent it was a *combination of changes* that resulted in major progress toward raising student

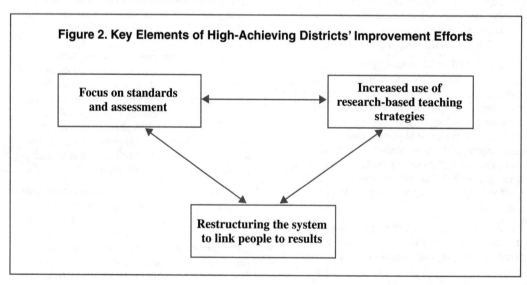

Figure 2. Key Elements of High-Achieving Districts' Improvement Efforts

Focus on standards and assessment

Increased use of research-based teaching strategies

Restructuring the system to link people to results

achievement while reducing achievement gaps. These changes centered around three key elements (see figure 2) present in all of the districts studied, although there was obviously variation in the *degree* to which each element was present.

1. **Superintendents and other leaders developed and focused on shared beliefs.** Each district reveals an interesting story of how leaders began to back the rhetoric about learning with a focus on results, an understanding that every staff member was personally accountable, and a "no excuses" attitude. In no instance was a passive, laissez-faire style observed. In most cases, the superintendent moved well beyond articulating this focus by developing staff skills through staff development and hands-on activities, such as analysis of achievement data.

"If any one idea about leadership has inspired organizations for thousands of years, it's the capacity to hold a shared vision of the future we seek to create" (Senge 1990, 9).

---

2. **Restructuring the organization linking people to results.** Restructuring in this instance refers to shifting the direct responsibility for improvement downward to principals and their staffs, encouraging or requiring teacher teams be established to work together on planning improvement, increasing school-level responsibility for making best use of resources, and fostering development of a more optimistic culture about student learning with no excuses. The roles of central-office staff changed from supervisors, controllers, regulators, or resource allocators to support people who helped schools perfect the processes and instructional strategies used at the school level to improve achievement. For example, a common practice was to help teacher teams analyze disaggregated student achievement data to plan instructional improvement.

3. **Aligning local curriculum with state standards and making increased use of benchmarking testing throughout the year to assess mastery.** It was clear that teachers in these districts were both more directly focused on teaching the skills and knowledge prescribed by the state and seeking ways to measure how well their students were performing on a daily basis. Some states provided a good deal of information to schools about how particular students did with each test item, while other states sent back more general results that were of more limited diagnostic value. Good feedback of test results also helped with alignment activities. For example, if a significant number of students answered incorrectly on test items related to a particular objective, it helped the school to see it needed to focus more (or better) on teaching that skill. Tests used in these districts included the Texas Assessment of Academic Skills (TAAS), the Standard Achievement Test 9, and the Iowa Tests of Basic Skills.

4. **Training was provided for teachers on research-based teaching strategies to expand their use in the classroom.** Leaders in each of the districts knew that just to restructure the organization, or to do more testing, was not going to result in higher levels of achievement. Extensive staff development was provided to support specific instructional goals, for example, improving early-grades reading achievement or student writing abilities. The Brazosport district trained all of its teachers in its 8-Step Teaching Cycle process incorporating use of state assessment data and benchmark testing data to continuously adjust/improve instruction. The data also are used to identify students needing additional support or enrichment as determined by a student's nonmastery or mastery of particular objectives. Perhaps most impressive was the earnestness with which teachers and principals were seeking strategies that worked in helping students to achieve better. At the

heart of these strategies was use of direct instructional techniques plus considerable (some say too much) time spent directly preparing students for the tests.

5. **Focusing on the state standards of learning and the state assessment instrument.** It is apparent the recent standards-based movement in America has provided an increased focus on basic skills, with a corresponding reduction in time spent on content not tested. Whether or not teachers support state assessment programs, the stakes have become too great in most communities for them to ignore state standards and assessment. On the contrary, it seems clear that, in these districts, it has been necessary to "teach to the test" to some degree—although this is justifiably viewed by these teachers as teaching to the standards. Since both the establishment of standards and use of state assessment necessarily involve sampling of all that could be taught and all that could be tested, the curriculum has necessarily narrowed.

As with other studies described here, all six districts realized they must move ahead with needed changes in several areas—restructuring and refocusing the organization, hard work on standards and assessment issues, and helping teachers expand their use of research-based strategies. For example, simply introducing a new teaching strategy will not substantially improve student achievement through the system known as the district.

Cawelti and Protheroe also noted a number of less desirable side effects also alluded to in the other reports reviewed here. These included:

- An obvious decrease in the amount of time spent on other subjects, such as science, health, art, and social studies, particularly at the elementary level. That these subjects, were not even tested in most states was of great concern for teachers of these subjects, with the problem more severe at the high school level.

- Apprehension on the part of teachers and principals that their continued employment would come to be based on improved achievement. This was not a major concern, but rather one that surfaced from time to time.

- A very heavy load created for teachers by a constant influx of new approaches being urged on them to raise student achievement.

- A feeling that too much time was spent preparing students to take tests. This was a dominant concern in some schools.

These concerns, however, were offset by a feeling of pride and sense of accomplishment—often expressed in celebrations at the time new test scores were released.

The Council of Great City Schools Report

The CGCS is a coalition of the major urban districts in the country that works to advance its interests through legislative advocacy and other traditional association activities that serve to improve the quality of schooling for children in the cities.

In addition to studying urban districts making positive progress in raising student achievement and reducing the racial gap in achievement, the CGCS research study compared the experiences of these districts to other districts making little progress. The focus of the study was on the "potential role of the school district as an initiator and sustainer of academic improvement." This report contributes to a better understanding of what strategies are needed in large, complex systems if major gains in achievement are to be accomplished.

Three school districts and a part of a fourth were selected for study because they were making greater gains than other cities in mathematics and reading achievement, and in reducing the achievement gaps between White and minority students. The three districts chosen for intensive study were the Houston Independent School District, Sacramento City Unified School District, and the Charlotte-Mecklenburg (N.C.) Schools. A partial study was also made of a fourth district in the New

York City school system, where the chancellor had selected some schools that were given particular attention in dealing with the achievement issue.

The reform in Houston began after a state audit documented gross mismanagement and the voters voted down a much needed bond election. School board members elevated one of their own, Rod Paige, to the superintendency, and he presented an extensive plan that included assigning more accountability for results to schools, more parental involvement and greater choice in choosing schools, and replacement of principal tenure with rewards for progress. The plan also called for a centralized curriculum in math and reading in order to provide greater focus on the state's curriculum and massive staff development to improve teacher skill in these basic instructional areas. Schools identified as "low performing" were given technical assistance in preparing a plan to get better results.

In Sacramento, the mayor played a key role in getting a new school board who then hired an "in house" staff member, Jim Sweeney, who promptly began a series of reforms substantially altering how this large bureaucracy had been used to functioning. He pushed the community to reach agreement on seven vital signs to be used in judging progress, and these included defined levels of proficiency in math and reading, 95 percent attendance in each school, 90 percent graduation rates, and helping ensure a higher level of proficiency among entering kindergarten students. Sweeney also kept the focus on nine so-called "puzzle pieces" needing attention if the system was to ensure progress on the achievement issue. These included things such as high standards, quality instruction, a uniform curriculum (Open Court in reading and Saxon math), accountability for results, staff development, and decentralized decision making.

The citizens in Charlotte had also expressed their disappointment in the school system by defeating a bond issue just before Eric Smith arrived as superintendent in 1996. He moved quickly to lay out a plan similar in many ways to Houston's and Sacramento's. These included a more uniform curriculum in reading and math, plus extensive training for teachers in these areas. Schools were provided with data on student achievement for each school, teacher and student, and teacher teams were trained on how to plan together for needed improvements. Interim tests were developed and used on a quarterly basis to monitor student progress in basic skills. Pre-school instruction was developed, focusing on the skills students would need to succeed in kindergarten, and better counseling and teaching moved larger numbers of high school students into advanced placement courses.

Summary Findings

1. **There was an intense focus on improving student achievement.** From the leader on down it was clear scores on state or national assessments were to be the focus and results were expected. The case-study districts typically focused on student achievement and specific achievement goals, on a set schedule with defined consequences; aligned curricula with state standards; and helped translate these standards into instructional practice. The goal-setting process was considered an important exercise in consensus building, and the achievement goals—with timelines— were used as road maps for the reform efforts.

2. **Clear systems of accountability were put in place.** To be sure, this change was brought about by the state's emphasis on standards-based reform, but these district leaders tended to go beyond the requirements of that system to tie results to people.

3. **A districtwide curriculum was adopted for the system in math and reading.** The combined factors of high mobility among low-SES children and misalignment of curriculum to state standards in many schools made it clear the latitude once afforded schools on curriculum could not be continued. Latitude was given, however, on particular strategies to be used in improving achievement. The extra time given to reading

and math often took away from time normally given to other subjects such as science and social studies. The districts supported these districtwide instructional strategies at the central office through professional development and support for "faithful" implementation throughout the district, even in the face of some teacher resistance to "prescribed" strategies.

4. **Special help was given to low-performing schools.** Because of the many challenges facing these schools it was not sufficient to adopt the "shape up or ship out" philosophy. The districts provided support and assistance to those schools whose students were in the low-performing category.

5. **Roles for central-office staff were changed to focus on improving instruction.** Many urban systems have reduced the number of central-office people they have, but all of the districts studied also have substantially altered the kind of roles these people play. They now focus on the *processes* used to improve instruction at the building level, such as working in teams, using data to analyze performance, or finding best practices in the system.

The CGCS study found, although the comparison districts described their efforts as similar to those of the improving districts, they were different in certain key ways that hampered their improvement efforts. Specifically, they had not developed the "preconditions for success" the study identified as important; specifically:

• They lacked a clear consensus among key stakeholders about district priorities or an overall strategy for reform.

• They lacked specific, clear standards, achievement goals, timelines, and consequences.

• The district's central office took little or no responsibility for improving instruction or creating a cohesive instructional strategy throughout the district.

• The policies and practices of the central office were not strongly connected to intended changes in teaching and learning in the classrooms.

• The districts gave schools multiple and conflicting curricula and instructional expectations, which they were left to decipher on their own (Snipes, Doolittle, and Herlihy 2002a, xviii).

Finally, the difference between case study and comparison districts in the use of data to support improvement efforts was considered striking. The case-study districts were "far more sophisticated in using data to better understand the challenges they faced, to monitor progress toward their goals, and to refine their approaches to reaching them" (Snipes, Doolittle, and Herlihy 2002b, 55).

The Learning First Alliance Study

This relatively new alliance consists of organizations representing state education agencies, parents, students, principals, superintendents, school board members, and other kinds of professionals in education. For this reason, this study tended to be interested in the nature of the roles played by various segments of the educational enterprise that have not always functioned collaboratively in the past.

The Learning First Alliance study focused, as did the other three, on high-poverty districts that had made substantial progress in improving student achievement. The intent of the study was to identify characteristics of district-level initiatives that supported school improvement. Specifically, researchers were "interested in learning more about how districts promoted good instruction across their systems" (Togneri and Anderson 2003, 1).

Five school districts were selected that served diverse populations of students and had shown at least three years of improvement in mathematics and reading achievement among all the subgroups of students. These districts were: Aldine Independent School District (Tex.), Chula Vista Elementary School District (Calif.), Kent County Public Schools (Md.), Minneapolis

Public Schools (Minn.), and Providence Public Schools (R.I.). The districts ranged from an enrollment of 3,000 in Kent County to over 50,000 in Minneapolis and Aldine. All have seen a recent growth in the numbers of low-SES students and minority students. As in the other studies of school districts, there had been very positive growth in student achievement in mathematics and reading, but there remained a number of students in some districts who still had not been reached by the instructional changes that had been made. However, overall *trends* were very positive.

As with the other studies, the research team identified certain characteristics found to some extent in all the districts, although with varying degrees of emphasis. Perhaps a central finding was that a sense of trust among board members, teachers, administrators, and the community had enabled them to make many changes that were needed. There tended to be more stability in the superintendency than is often the case, thus enabling new initiatives to be given a fair chance before being abandoned.

1. The districts had the **courage to acknowledge poor performance and the will to seek solutions**. Key leaders were willing to accept ownership of difficult challenges and seek solutions without placing blame.

2. The districts studied by LFA made instruction the centerpiece of their improvement efforts. To support staff in their efforts to improve student achievement, the districts **put in place a systemwide approach to improving instruction** and built the necessary infrastructure to support instructional improvement. This step represented a sharp break from past practice.

3. The districts **instilled visions focusing on student learning and guiding instructional improvement**. Each district's one-line vision connected to the goal of improving student achievement, and stakeholders had internalized the vision and spoke about it in their own words. In addition to the one-line vision

statements, each of the five districts had a more detailed set of goals and strategies comprising the strategic plan.

4. The five districts **made decisions based on data, not instinct**. Specifically, they systematically gathered data on multiple issues, developed multimeasure accountability systems to gauge student and school progress, and encouraged teachers and administrators to use data to guide decision making.

5. Study districts **adopted new approaches to professional development** to support instructional improvement efforts characterized as "remarkable shifts" from previous practice. The districts used research-based principles of professional development— such as connecting development to district goals—to guide their work. They developed networks of instructional experts, such as instructionally proficient principals and teacher leaders (e.g., content specialists, mentor teachers), to support teachers. They provided extensive support systems for new teachers, and they were strategic in their allocation of financial resources for development efforts.

6. Districts included in the LFA study **redefined and extended leadership roles** beyond the superintendent and principals because district leaders quickly determined "no single stakeholder could tackle instructional improvement alone."

7. Finally, the study districts were **committed to sustaining reform over the long haul**.

This study is perhaps the most sensitive of the four to the issue of teacher stress and overload. Teachers who have seen administrators come and go, and have faced the impact of new regulations and laws tend to reach a point where they feel they cannot respond to conflicting demands on their time.

In Summary

When one examines the findings from these four studies, it is apparent there are some factors common to all the districts studied as well as some differences (see figure 3, which summarizes the findings from the four studies). The standards-based reform movement has compelled teachers in the districts to narrow the focus of their teaching to the objectives of the state's curriculum framework and the assessments being used in conjunction with these requirements. Much more attention is being given to accountability for student performance within these districts by making it clear principals and their teachers were to be held responsible for improvement. A new part of the jargon of the profession appears in the often-cited expression "data-driven," and clearly, these teachers and principals had moved to make use of this practice as a part of their professional life.

Very little was said in these reports about the tradeoffs being made in exchange for higher test scores. There can be but little doubt that the curriculum has been narrowed for many students by reducing the time spent on their general education in subjects such as science, health, art, and social studies, or on more general goals such as developing a sense of civic responsibility in students. For now, this may mean students will learn significantly less about content areas other than those emphasizing tested skills. However, some states and districts have expressed plans to "raise the bar" in terms of the content tested—and so taught.

Clearly, some students are essentially unchallenged by state assessments and so are bored by the instruction they receive as other students are being "prepared for the tests." This too will likely change in the years ahead as such students and their parents demand a more challenging curriculum be provided to students as they prepare for either college or the work world.

While one can see similarities from these findings in the public sector compared with the corporate studies of high-performing systems, even the improving school systems discussed in these reports face some continuing problems of sluggishness. For example, while these districts tended to have restructured by decentralizing responsibility for improving achievement down to the principals and their staffs, some of these building leaders were clearly more aggressive than others in their work to improve student achievement.

Put another way, the incentives or motivation for principals to engage teachers in activities that would result in tangible gains on state-level assessments for students from low-income families continue to be lacking in many systems. The tendency of public education traditions, union policies, and a concern for personal needs exists to a greater extent in schools than in some corporate environments. Thus while Jack Welch, recent CEO of General Electric, was famous (some say infamous) for "ranking and tanking" his top managers, there is little evidence of such a harsh policy in school districts. At the same time, several decades of failing to deal with the incentive issue has resulted in perhaps too high a tolerance for those principals and teachers who evidence too little concern for making the changes needed to ensure all students attain higher standards.

Finally, what use is to be made of the lessons from these studies of high-performing school districts? The Task Force on School District Leadership suggests it is important for everyone involved with the planning for districtwide improvement to understand:

> There are no easy solutions and that the process may become messy and ridden with dilemmas…. Since experts in systems change say it usually takes five years for change to occur at all levels of an organization, the restructuring plan should include a multi-year timeline, a realistic number of changes to be implemented, resources to support the process, and the commitment of district leaders and stakeholders to see the process through without rushing it (2001, 17).

The success stories presented here make it clear this "messy" process is one that needs strong district-level support. It is also obvious that districts

Figure 3. Summary of Characteristics of Reform Initiatives in High-Performing Districts Identified by the Four Studies

Dana Center Study of Four School Districts in Texas	ERS/LSS National Study of Six School Districts	Council of Great City Schools Case Studies of Urban Districts	Learning First Alliance Study of Five School Districts
Motivation provided by Texas accountability plan	Superintendents and other leaders focused on shared beliefs	An intense focus on improving student achievement	Districts had the courage to acknowledge poor performance and the will to seek solutions
Pressure by local community groups for improvement	Restructuring the organization to link people with results and encourage teamwork	Clear systems of accountability put in place	Systemwide approach to improving instruction put in place along with the necessary infrastructure
Strong leadership and focus provided by superintendents	Extensive curriculum work, including alignment and use of benchmark testing to assess student mastery	Districtwide curriculum adopted in mathematics and reading	Instilled visions focusing on student learning and guided instructional improvement
Serious quest for and use of instructional strategies supporting high levels of student learning	Training for teachers to expand use of research-based strategies in classrooms	Special supports provided to low-performing schools	Made decisions based on data, not instinct
Appearance of "everyday equity" driving people's beliefs	Focus on teaching standards and use of assessment data for instructional improvement	Roles for central-office staff changed to focus on instruction at the building level	Redefined and extended leadership roles beyond the superintendent and principals
	Process established to ensure students needing additional help received it		Adopted new approaches to professional development to support instructional improvement efforts
			Committed to sustaining reform over the long haul

differ in the extent to which they are currently capable of supporting school improvement. As the mandates of NCLB require districts and states to provide assistance to low-performing schools and districts, these "lessons learned" can provide a valuable road map for improvement efforts.

Ultimately, these studies mark a major transition in public education as its institutions struggle to replace the rhetoric of "all children can learn" with the reality of becoming high-performing systems. And facing reality is clearly the first step.

Bibliography

Cawelti, G., & Protheroe, N. 2001. *High student achievement: How six school districts changed into high-performance systems.* Arlington, VA: Educational Research Service.

Collins, J. 2001. *Good to Great: Why Some Companies Make the Leap . . . and Others Don't.* New York: Harper Collins.

Evaluation Section, Division of Accountability Services, North Carolina Department of Public Instruction. 2000. *Improving student performance: The role of district-level staff.*

Peters, T., & Waterman, R. 1982. *In Search of Excellence: Lessons from America's Best-Run Companies.* New York: Warner Books.

Senge, P. 1990. *The Fifth Discipline.* New York: Currency Doubleday.

Skrla, L., Scheurich, J., & Johnson, J., Jr. 2000. *Equity-driven achievement-focused school districts: A report of systemic school success in four Texas school districts serving diverse student populations.* Austin, TX: The Charles A. Dana Center, The University of Texas at Austin. Retrieved from http://www.utdanacenter.org/research/reports/equitydistricts.pdf

Snipes, J., Doolittle, F., & Herlihy, C. 2002a. *Foundations for success: Case studies of how urban school systems improve student achievement—An Abstract.* Washington, DC: Council of the Great City Schools.

Snipes, J., Doolittle, F., & Herlihy, C. 2002b. *Foundations for success: Case studies of how urban school systems improve student achievement.* Washington, DC: Council of the Great City Schools.

Task Force on School District Leadership. 2001. *Leadership for student learning: Restructuring school district leadership.* Washington, DC: Institute for Educational Leadership.

Togneri, W., & Anderson, S.E. 2003. *Beyond islands of excellence: What districts can do to improve instruction and achievement in all schools.* Alexandria, VA: Learning First Alliance.

Chapter 2. Effective General Practices

Herbert J. Walberg and Susan J. Paik

The practices in this section are general in that they can be applied widely to the academic subject matter of kindergarten through 12th grade. They show powerful and consistent effects for students in widely varying circumstances. As with all educational practices, of course, they can be effectively or ineffectively planned and conducted, and the results will vary accordingly.

The research on these practices has accumulated over a half-century. The references include several by our colleagues and us that were funded by grants from the U.S. Department of Education and the National Science Foundation. These studies compiled the results of research summaries and synthesized several hundred investigations of educational practices by many scholars. The practices were further investigated by analyzing large national achievement surveys of U.S. elementary and secondary students. Information from European countries and Japan was also analyzed to shed light on why students in these countries often do better than American students on achievement tests.

Most of the research employed standardized achievement test scores as learning criteria, rather than measures of "higher-order processes" such as critical thinking as revealed on essay examinations. Research usually shows students must know the essential facts and principles of the subject as prerequisites to the deepest understanding, which may only be possible through years of study. It would be astonishing, for example, to find a student who could explain the causes of wars in American history but who had little knowledge of basic facts such as presidents or important dates. Nor can students play musical instruments well without knowing the scales and elementary musical theory. Nor is it easy to learn mathematical division before addition and subtraction, or calculus before algebra.

Some authorities, nonetheless, believe conventional tests do not measure all that is valuable to learn in their fields, including attitudes, values, and special skills. Many science specialists, for example, believe scientific insights, skeptical attitudes, and strong interests are supported by laboratory experiences, even though it is difficult to observe or measure such effects. Similarly, many teachers of writing believe essays, rather than standardized tests, are the best measures of writing mastery. And knowing the musical scales and music theory hardly guarantees musical artistry.

Experiences fostering positive attitudes, values, and higher-order learning are valuable in their own right even if their effects cannot be clearly shown. The teamwork seen in science laboratory work and the excitement of discovery may be considered self-justifying. Humming a classical tune on the way home after learning it in a music class may be justification enough. Surely, writing ability is a valuable skill in many aspects of life, although it is difficult to measure quantitatively. Thus, assessments of these types of student achievement are a valid part of classroom teaching even though research on them is less than definitive.

The other chapters of this *Handbook* recommend more specific practices that appear particularly useful in achieving the special goals of each subject. Although the practices in this chapter can be generally recommended, they should be considered companions rather than substitutes for the particular practices of the other sections.

As mentioned above, the practices in this section are generally powerful and consistent in promoting learning. Some other practices can be cited that are nearly as good. For further reading on the practices in this section and others, the following works may be consulted: Husén and Postlethwaite 1994; Lipsey and Wilson 1993; Walberg 1984; Wang, Haertel, and Walberg 1993; Waxman and Walberg 1991, 1999; and Wang and Haertel, 1997.

We thank the following people for their review of previous versions of this chapter: Lorin Anderson, professor of education, College of Education, University of South Carolina, Columbia; Jere Brophy, professor of education, College of Education, Michigan State University, East Lansing; Margaret Wang, professor of education, Center for Research on Human Development and Education, Temple University, Philadelphia; and 14 advanced doctoral students. Any shortcomings of this chapter, however, are attributable to the authors.

2.1. Parental Involvement: Learning is enhanced when schools encourage parents to stimulate their children's intellectual development.

Research findings:

Dozens of studies in the United States, Australia, Canada, England, and elsewhere show the home environment powerfully influences what children and youth learn within and outside school. This environment is considerably more powerful than the parents' income and education in influencing what children learn in the first six years of life and during the 12 years of primary and secondary education. One major reason parental influence is so strong is children, from infancy through age 18, spend approximately 92 percent of their time outside school under the influence of their parents.

Cooperative efforts by parents and educators to modify these alterable academic conditions in the home have strong, beneficial effects on learning. In 29 controlled studies, 91 percent of the comparisons favored children in such programs over non-participant control groups.

In the classroom:

Sometimes called "the curriculum of the home," the home environment refers to informed parent-child conversations about school and everyday events; encouragement and discussion of leisure reading; monitoring and critical review of television viewing and peer activities; deferral of immediate gratification to accomplish long-term goals; expressions of affection and interest in the child's academic and other progress as a person; and perhaps, among such unremitting efforts, laughter, caprice, and serendipity. In the years before school, reading to and with the child and animated discussion of everyday events prepare children for academic activities in school.

A home-school connection explaining the benefits of these approaches and providing support for parents who wish to develop a strong academic environment for their children exerts a positive influence on student learning.

Sources:

Epstein 1995; Graue, Weinstein, and Walberg 1983; Iverson and Walberg 1982; Paik 2001; Peng and Wright 1994; Redding 2000; Stevenson, Lee, and Stigler 1986; Walberg 1984; Walberg and Paik 1997.

2.2. Graded Homework: Students learn more when they complete homework that is graded, commented upon, and discussed by their teachers.

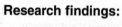 **Research findings:**

A synthesis of more than a dozen studies of the effects of homework in various subjects showed the assignment and completion of homework yield positive effects on academic achievement. The effects are almost tripled when teachers take time to grade the work, make corrections and specific comments on improvements that can be made, and discuss problems and remedies with individual students or the whole class. Homework also seems particularly effective in high school.

 In the classroom:

Among advanced countries, the United States has the least number of school days because of the long summer vacation. U.S. students also spend less time, on average, doing homework. Extending homework time is a proven way to lengthen study time and increase achievement, although the quality of the assignments and completed work are also important.

Like a three-legged stool, homework requires a teacher to assign it and provide feedback, a parent to monitor it, and a student to do it. If one leg is weak, the stool may fall down. The role of the teacher in providing feedback—in reinforcing what has been done correctly and in reteaching what has not—is key to maximizing the positive impact of homework.

Districts and schools that have well-known homework policies for daily minutes of required work are likely to reap benefits. Homework "hotlines" in which students may call in for help have proven useful. To relieve some of the workload of grading, teachers can employ procedures in which students grade their own and other students' work. In this way, they can learn cooperative social skills and how to evaluate their own and others' efforts.

The quality of homework is as important as the amount. Effective homework is relevant to the lessons to be learned and in keeping with students' abilities.

 Sources:

Paik 2001; Paik, Wang, and Walberg 2002; Paschal, Weinstein, and Walberg 1984; Stevenson, Lee, and Stigler 1986; Walberg 1984, 1994; Walberg and Haertel 1997.

2.3. **Aligned Time on Task:** Students who are actively focused on educational goals do best in mastering the subject matter.

Research findings:

More than 130 studies support the obvious idea that the more students study, other things being equal, the more they learn. It is one of the most consistent findings in educational research, if not all psychological and social research. Time alone, however, does not suffice. Learning activities should reflect educational goals. This alignment or coordination of means with goals can be called "curricular focus." A similar reform term is "systemic reform," which means the three components of the curriculum—1) goals; 2) textbooks, materials, and learning activities; and 3) tests and other outcome assessments—are well matched in content and emphasis.

In the classroom:

The amount learned reflects both study time and curricular focus. Curricular focus represents efforts to decide what should be learned by a given age or grade level and then concentrating attention, time, and energy on these elements. Consequently, students at a given grade level should have greater degrees of shared knowledge and skills as prerequisites for further learning; teachers can avoid excessive review; and progress can be better assessed.

Teachers have the most direct role in ensuring this emphasis is carried into the classroom. The teacher's skillful classroom management, by taking into account what is to be learned and identifying the most efficient ways to present it, increases effective study time. Students who are actively engaged in activities focused on specific instructional goals make more progress toward these goals.

Sources:

Anderson and Walberg 1994; Fredrick 1980; Fredrick and Walberg 1980; Paik 2001; Paik, Wang, and Walberg 2002; Stigler, Lee, and Stevenson 1987; Walberg and Fredrick 1992; Walberg and Haertel 1997; Walberg and Paik 1997; Waxman and Walberg 1999.

2.4. Direct Teaching: Direct teaching is most effective when it exhibits key features and follows systematic steps.

Research findings:

Many studies show direct teaching can be effective in promoting student learning. The process emphasizes systematic sequencing of lessons, a presentation of new content and skills, guided student practice, the use of feedback, and independent practice by students. The traits of teachers employing effective direct instruction include clarity, task orientation, enthusiasm, and flexibility. Effective direct teachers also clearly organize their presentations and occasionally use student ideas.

In the classroom:

The use of direct teaching can be traced to the turn of the 20th century; it is what many citizens and parents expect to see in classrooms. Done well, it can yield consistent and substantial, although perhaps not the very best, results. Whole-class teaching of diverse groups may mean lessons are too advanced for slower students and too repetitive for the quick. In the last decade or two, moreover, theorists have tried to transfer more control of lesson planning and completion to students themselves so that they "learn to learn," as several subsequent practices exemplify.

Six phased functions of direct teaching work well:

1. Daily review, homework check, and, if necessary, reteaching.

2. Presentation of new content and skills in small steps.

3. Guided student practice with close teacher monitoring.

4. Corrective feedback and instructional reinforcement.

5. Independent practice in seatwork and homework with a high (more than 90 percent) success rate.

6. Weekly and monthly reviews.

Sources:

Brophy 1999; Brophy and Good 1986; Gage and Needles 1989; Walberg and Haertel 1997; Wang, Haertel, and Walberg 1993a, 1993b; Waxman and Walberg 1999.

2.5. Advance Organizers: Showing students the relationships between past learning and present learning increases its depth and breadth.

Research findings:

More than a dozen studies show when teachers explain how new ideas in the current lesson relate to ideas in previous lessons and other prior learning, students can connect the old with the new, which helps them to better remember and understand. Similarly, alerting them to key points to be learned allows them to concentrate their attention on the most crucial parts of the lessons.

In the classroom:

Advance organizers help students focus on key ideas by enabling them to anticipate which points are important to learn. Understanding the sequence or continuity of subject matter development, moreover, can be motivating. If students simply learn one isolated idea after another, the subject matter may appear arbitrary. Given a "mental road map" of what they have accomplished, where they are presently, and where they are going can avoid unpleasant surprises and help them to set realistic goals. Similar effects can be accomplished by goal setting, overviewing, pretests before lessons that sensitize students to points to learn, and pre-questions stated in textbooks and by teachers.

It also may be useful to show how what is being learned solves problems that exist in the world outside of school and that students are likely to encounter in later life. For example, human biology that features nutrition and exercise applications is likely to be more interesting than abstract biology.

Teachers and textbooks can sometimes make effective use of graphic advance organizers. Maps, timetables, flow charts depicting the sequence of activities, and other such devices may be worth many hundreds of words. They also may be easier to remember.

Sources:

Ausubel 1968; Brophy 1999; Walberg and Haertel 1997; Walker 1987; Weinert 1989.

2.6. Teaching of Learning Strategies: Delegating some control to students for the learning goals and the monitoring of personal progress in achieving them yields learning gains.

Research findings:

In the 1980s, cognitive research on teaching sought ways to encourage self-monitoring, self-teaching, or "metacognition" to foster achievement and independence. Skills are important, but the learner's monitoring and management of his or her own learning has primacy. This approach transfers part of the direct teaching functions of planning, allocating time, and review (see Practice 2.4) to learners. Being aware of what goes on in one's mind during learning is a critical first step to effective independent learning.

Some students have been found to lack this self-awareness and must be taught the skills necessary to monitor and regulate their own learning. Many studies have demonstrated this can be done and positive effects can accrue.

In the classroom:

Students with a repertoire of learning strategies can measure their own progress toward explicit goals. When students use these strategies to strengthen their opportunities for learning, they simultaneously increase their skills of self-awareness, personal control, and positive self-evaluation.

Three possible phases of teaching about learning strategies include:

1. Modeling, in which the teacher exhibits the desired behavior.

2. Guided practice, in which students perform with help from the teacher.

3. Application, in which students act independently of the teacher.

As an example, a successful program of "reciprocal teaching" fosters reading comprehension by having students take turns in leading dialogues on pertinent features of texts. By assuming the roles of planning and monitoring ordinarily exercised by teachers, students learn self-management. Perhaps that is why tutors learn from tutoring, and why it is said, "To learn something well, teach it."

Sources:

Brophy 1999; Haller, Child, and Walberg 1988; Palincsar and Brown 1984; Pearson 1985; Walberg and Haertel 1997.

2.7. Tutoring: Teaching one student or a small number with the same abilities and instructional needs can be remarkably effective.

Research findings:

Tutoring, because it gears instruction to needs, has yielded large learning effects in several dozen studies. It yields particularly large effects in mathematics—perhaps because of the subject's well-defined sequence and organization. If students fall behind in a fast-paced mathematics class, they may never catch up unless their particular problems are identified and remedied. This individualized assessment and follow-up process is the virtue of tutoring and other means of adaptive instruction.

In the classroom:

Peer tutoring (tutoring of slower or younger students by more advanced students) appears to work nearly as well as teacher tutoring; with sustained student practice it might be equal to teacher tutoring in some cases. Significantly, peer tutoring promotes effective learning in tutors as well as tutees. The need to organize one's thoughts to impart them intelligibly to others, to become conscious of the value of time, and to learn managerial and social skills are probably the main reasons for benefits to the tutor.

Even slower-learning students and those with disabilities can be in the position of teaching to others if they are given the extra time and practice that may be required to master a skill. This can give them a positive experience and increase their feelings of self-esteem. The success of two other practices in this section— the teaching of learning strategies and cooperative learning—is attributable to instructional features similar to those of tutoring.

Sources:

Cohen, Kulik, and Kulik 1982; Ehly 1980; Medway 1991; Topping 2000; Walberg and Haertel 1997.

2.8. **Mastery Learning:** In subject matter to be learned in a sequence, thorough mastery of each step is optimal.

Research findings:

More than 50 studies show careful sequencing, monitoring, and control of the learning process raises the learning rate. Pretesting helps determine what should be studied; this allows the teacher to avoid assigning material that has already been mastered or for which the student does not yet have the requisite skills. Ensuring students achieve mastery of initial steps in the sequence helps to ensure they will make satisfactory progress in subsequent, more advanced steps. Frequent assessment of progress informs teachers and students when additional time and corrective remedies are needed. Mastery learning appears to work best when the subject matter is well organized.

learners' time. It allows more time and remediation for students who need it. It also enables faster learners to skip material they already know. In these ways, it is superior to whole-class instruction because it suits instruction to small groups and individuals, while direct instruction gears instruction to the average class member, making it too difficult for some and too easy for others.

Mastery learning programs require special planning, materials, and procedures. Teachers must be prepared to identify the components of instruction, develop assessment strategies so that individual students are appropriately placed in the instructional continuum, and provide reinforcement and corrective feedback—while continuously engaging students in lessons.

In the classroom:

Because of its emphasis on outcomes and careful monitoring of progress, mastery learning can save

Sources:

Bloom 1988; Guskey 1990; Kulik, Kulik, and Bangert-Drowns 1990; Topping 2000; Walberg and Haertel 1997; Waxman and Walberg 1999.

2.9. Cooperative Learning: Students in small, self-instructing groups can support and increase each other's learning.

Research findings:

Learning, as shown by more than 50 studies, proceeds more effectively than usual when exchanges among teachers and learners are frequent and specifically directed toward students' problems and interests. In whole-class instruction, only one person can speak at a time, and shy or slow-learning students may be reluctant to speak at all. When students work in groups of two to four, however, each group member can participate extensively, individual problems are more likely to become clear and to be remedied (sometimes with the teacher's assistance), and learning can accelerate.

In the classroom:

With justification, cooperative learning has become widespread in American schools. Not only can it increase academic achievement, but it has other virtues. By working in small groups, students learn teamwork, how to give and receive criticism, and how to plan, monitor, and evaluate their individual and joint activities with others.

It appears that American workplaces increasingly require such partial delegation of authority, group management, and cooperative skills. Like managers, teachers may need to become more like facilitators, consultants, and evaluators than supervisors. Nonetheless, researchers do not recommend cooperative learning take up the whole school day; use of a variety of procedures, rather than cooperative learning alone, is considered to be most productive.

In addition, cooperative learning means more than merely assigning children to small groups. Teachers must also carefully design and prepare for the small-group setting. Students need instruction in the skills necessary to operate successfully in small groups. Decisions must be made about the use of individual or group accountability. Care must be taken in establishing the mix of strengths and needs represented by students in the groups. Attention to these details will increase the likelihood that the cooperative groups will produce increased learning.

Sources:

Aronson and Patnoe 1997; Hertz-Lazarowitz and Miller 1992; Johnson and Johnson 1989; Walberg and Haertel 1997; Waxman and Walberg 1999.

2.10. Adaptive Education: Employing a variety of instructional techniques to adapt lessons to individual students and small groups raises achievement.

Research findings:

Adaptive instruction is an integrated diagnostic-prescriptive process combining several preceding practices—tutoring, mastery and cooperative learning, and instruction in learning strategies—into a classroom management system to tailor instruction to individual and small-group needs. Achievement effects of adaptive programs have been demonstrated. The broader effects of adaptive instruction are probably underestimated, because it aims at diverse ends that are difficult to measure, including student autonomy, intrinsic motivation, teacher and student choice, and parental involvement.

In the classroom:

Adaptive education requires implementation steps executed by a master teacher, including planning, time allocation, task delegation to aides and students, and quality control. Unlike most other practices, it is a comprehensive program for the whole school day rather than a single method requiring simple integration into one subject or into a single teacher's repertoire. Its focus on the individual student requires that barriers to learning first be diagnosed and then a plan be developed to address those needs.

A student with special needs or experiencing academic difficulties becomes the shared respon-sibility of a team of teachers and specialists. Such an approach to education calls for teachers to develop a broad spectrum of teaching ap-proaches, along with a knowledge of when to use each of them most productively, and to coordi-nate their efforts with those of other professionals providing support to a student. Time and oppor-tunity to do this are crucial for implementation of adaptive education.

Skillful professional management is re-quired to integrate all aspects of the program. For example, curricular coordination means more than a plan for the teaching of subject matter skills and knowledge across grade levels as it applies to *all* students. Instead, it encom-passes the relationship of that curriculum to the abilities and needs of *each* student. Conse-quently, central-office staff, principals, and teachers need more than the usual training to install and maintain adaptive programs.

As goals for school become more clear and uniform, it should be increasingly possible to develop and employ systemic approaches such as adaptive education.

Sources:

Walberg and Haertel 1997; Wang 1992; Wang, Haertel, and Walberg, 1998; Wang, Oates, and Whiteshew 1995; Wang and Zollers 1990; Waxman and Walberg 1999.

Bibliography

Anderson, L.W., and H.J. Walberg. 1994. *Time Piece: Extending and Enhancing Learning Time.* Reston, VA: National Association of Secondary School Principals.

Aronson, E., and S. Patnoe. 1997. *The Jigsaw Classroom: Building Cooperation in the Classroom.* (2nd edition). New York: Addison Wesley Longman.

Ausubel, D.P. 1968. *Educational Psychology: A Cognitive View.* New York: Holt, Rinehart, and Winston.

Bloom, B.S. 1988. "Helping All Children Learn Well in Elementary School—and Beyond." *Principal* Vol. 67, No. 4: 12-17.

Brophy, J. 1999. *Teaching.* UNESCO Publications.

Brophy, J., and T. Good. 1986. "Teacher-Effects Results." In *Handbook of Research on Teaching,* M.C. Wittrock, editor. New York: Macmillan.

Cohen, P.A., J.A. Kulik, and C.L. Kulik. 1982. "Educational Outcomes of Tutoring: A Meta-Analysis of Findings." *American Educational Research Journal* Vol. 19, No. 2: 237-248.

Ehly, S.W. 1980. *Peer Tutoring for Individualized Instruction.* Boston: Allyn and Bacon.

Epstein, J.L. 1995. "School-Family-Community Partnerships: Caring for the Children We Share." *Phi Delta Kappan,* 76, 701-712.

Fredrick, W.C. 1980. "Instructional Time." *Evaluation in Education* Vol. 4: 148-158.

Fredrick, W.C., and H.J. Walberg. 1980. "Learning as a Function of Time." *Journal of Educational Research* Vol. 73: 183-194.

Gage, N.L., and M.C. Needles. 1989. "Process-Product Research on Teaching." *Elementary School Journal* Vol. 89: 253-300.

Graue, M.E., T. Weinstein, and H.J. Walberg. 1983. "School-Based Home Reinforcement Programs: A Quantitative Synthesis." *Journal of Educational Research* Vol. 76: 351-360.

Guskey, T.R. 1990. "Cooperative Mastery Learning Strategies." *Elementary School Journal* Vol. 91, No. 1: 33-42.

Haller, E., D. Child, and H.J. Walberg. December 1988. "Can Comprehension Be Taught: A Quantitative Synthesis." *Educational Researcher* Vol. 17, No. 9: 5-8.

Hertz-Lazarowitz, R., and N. Miller (editors). 1992. *Interaction in Cooperative Groups.* New York: Cambridge University Press.

Husén, T., and T.N. Postlethwaite. 1994. *International Encyclopedia of Education (Second Edition).* Oxford, England: Elsevier Science.

Iverson, B.K., and H.J. Walberg. 1982. "Home Environment and Learning: A Quantitative Synthesis." *Journal of Experimental Education* Vol. 50: 144-151.

Johnson, D.W., and R. Johnson. 1989. *Cooperation and Competition: Theory and Research.* Edina, MN: Interaction Book Co.

Kulik, J.A., C.L. Kulik, and R.L. Bangert-Drowns. 1990. "Effectiveness of Mastery Learning Programs: A Meta-Analysis." *Review of Educational Research* Vol. 60, No. 2: 265-299.

Lipsey, M.W., and D.B. Wilson. December 1993. "The Efficacy of Psychological, Educational, and Behavioral Treatment: Confirmation from Meta-Analysis." *American Psychologist* Vol. 49: 1181-1209.

Medway, F.J. 1991. "A Social Psychological Analysis of Peer Tutoring." *Journal of Developmental Education* Vol. 15, No. 1: 20-26.

Paik, S.J. 2001. "Educational Productivity in South Korea and the United States." *International Journal of Educational Research* 35, 535-607. Pergamon Press Elsevier Science Ltd.

Paik, S.J., D. Wang, and H.J. Walberg. 2002. "Timely Improvements to Learning." *Educational Horizons* (Winter 2002), pp. 69-71.

Palincsar, A.M., and A. Brown. 1984. "Reciprocal Teaching of Comprehension Fostering and Comprehension Monitoring Activities." *Cognition and Instruction* Vol. 1: 117-176.

Paschal, R., T. Weinstein, and H.J. Walberg. 1984. "Effects of Homework: A Quantitative Synthesis." *Journal of Educational Research* Vol. 78: 97-104.

Pearson, D. 1985. "Reading Comprehension Instruction: Six Necessary Steps." *Reading Teacher* Vol. 38: 724-738.

Peng, S., and D. Wright. 1994. "Explanation of Academic Achievement of Asian American Students." *Journal of Educational Research* Vol. 87, No. 6: 718.

Redding, S. 2000. *Parents and Learning.* UNESCO Publications.

Stevenson, H.W., S.Y. Lee, and J.W. Stigler. 1986. "Mathematics Achievement of Chinese, Japanese, and American Children." *Child Development* Vol. 56: 718-734.

Stigler, J., S. Lee, and H. Stevenson. 1987. "Mathematics Classrooms in Japan, Taiwan, and the United States." *Child Development* Vol. 58: 1272-1285.

Topping, Keith. 2000. *Tutoring.* UNESCO Publications.

Walberg, H.J. 1984. "Improving the Productivity of America's Schools." *Educational Leadership* Vol. 41, No. 8: 19-27.

Walberg, H.J. 1986. "Synthesis of Research on Teaching." In *Handbook of Research on Teaching,* M.C. Wittrock, editor. New York: Macmillan.

Walberg, H.J. 1994. "Homework." In *International Encyclopedia of Education (Second Edition),*

T. Husén and T.N. Postlethwaite, editors. Oxford, England: Pergamon.

Walberg, H.J., and W.C. Fredrick. 1992. *Extending Learning Time*. Washington, DC: U.S. Department of Education, Office of Educational Research and Improvement.

Walberg H.J., and G.D. Haertel (editors). 1997. *Psychology and Educational Practice*. Berkeley, CA: McCutchan Publishing.

Walberg, H.J., and S.J. Paik. 1997. "Home Environments for Learning." In Herbert J. Walberg and Geneva D. Haertel, (editors). *Psychology and Educational Practice*. Berkeley, CA: McCutchan Publishing.

Walker, C.H. 1987. "Relative Importance of Domain Knowledge." *Cognition and Instruction* Vol. 4, No. 1: 25-42.

Wang, M.C. 1992. *Adaptive Education Strategies: Building on Diversity*. Baltimore: Paul H. Brookes Publishing.

Wang, M.C., G.D. Haertel, and H.J. Walberg. 1993a. "Toward a Knowledge Base for School Learning." *Review of Educational Research* Vol. 63: 249-294.

Wang, M.C., G.D. Haertel, and H.J. Walberg. 1993b. "What Helps Students Learn?" *Educational Leadership* Vol. 51, No. 4: 74-79.

Wang, M.C., G.D. Haertel, and H.J. Walberg. 1998. "Models of Reform: A Comparative Guide." *Educational Leadership* Vol. 55, No. 7: 66-71.

Wang, M.C., J. Oates, and N. Whiteshew. 1995. " Effective School Responses to Student Diversity in Inner-City Schools: A Coordinated Approach." *Education and Urban Society* Vol. 27, No. 4: 32-43.

Wang, M.C., and N.J. Zollers. 1990. "Adaptive Education: An Alternative Service Delivery Approach." *Remedial and Special Education* Vol. 11, No. 1: 7-21.

Waxman, H.C., and H.J. Walberg. 1991. *Effective Teaching: Current Research*. Berkeley, CA: McCutchan Publishers.

Waxman, H.C., and H.J. Walberg. 1999. *New Directions for Teaching Practice and Research*. Berkeley, CA: McCutchan Publishers.

Weinert, F. 1989. "The Relation Between Education and Development." *International Journal of Educational Research* Vol. 13, No. 8: 827-948.

Wittrock, M.C. 1986. *Handbook of Research on Teaching*. New York: Macmillan.

Chapter 3. The Arts

Richard Colwell

The arts are the most flexible subjects in the school curriculum. This capacity leads to the perception by many educational leaders that the arts are not essential in and of themselves, although they may have a role to play in gifted and special education, in attaining goals in personal development, in focusing school esprit, in enhancing "academic" subjects, and in contributing to a variety of cognitive and affective domains. The arts are often considered a luxury, to be put aside when pressure to cover the "essentials" and to pass mandated tests is too strong.

Deficiencies in school-based arts education programs are compensated for by interested parents through private lessons and involvement in community arts experiences, and the success of most after-school programs results from the inclusion of elective arts offerings that exert a powerful role in student motivation. Such evidence of the importance of the arts to parents and students has, in the past, not been taken as seriously by educational leaders as it would have been had it occurred in other subjects. If a large proportion of parents felt it necessary to hire math tutors for their children, for example, there would be serious questions about the adequacy of school mathematics offerings.

Even a definition of arts education is problematic, thus confusing any data on the extent of student involvement with systematic arts instruction. The National Art Education Association, however, reports more than half (52.7 percent) of the students graduating from high school in 1998 obtained at least one credit in visual arts education (Roey et al. 2001).

Music, visual arts, theater, creative drama, dance, architecture, media, and literature constitute a common list, but it is not unusual to find state educational agencies including foreign language and the applied arts under the arts umbrella. To some, arts education means a sequential curriculum extending over several years and taught by a state certified teacher. To others, arts education means concert and museum attendance, artists in the schools, and many informal arts experiences. There also is a vast difference between arts education in elementary and secondary schools, presumably caused by differences in required and elective experiences. A further movement in arts education is to stress the arts as a cognitive activity—a way of knowing—an emphasis that has resulted in some arts programs becoming humanities offerings. The adaptability, in addition to the lack of an "approved" definition, broadens the scope of arts research and especially arts evaluation. School leaders are often less rigorous in evaluating their arts program than they are with other core subjects. Mediocre performances and processes slip by. Those who care most about quality are usually those who have themselves experienced a quality program with recognized standards.

The voluntary national standards in the arts have addressed both the place of the arts in the curriculum and the definition of what is to be included. Under the standards, music, visual arts, dance, and theater are to be required for all students, a requirement that moves the arts into the area of liberal arts as opposed to the fine arts, a major shift in thinking within the educational community. The idea that elementary school students should attain competency in at least four arts is revolutionary, renaissance-like in intention, and clearly implies study of the arts adds meaning, understanding, and value to all aspects of a civilized society. This stance derives from the belief that the schools work within a cultural context and that inclusion of the arts is necessary to define our contemporary American culture.

Lacking a firm position in the education scheme, the arts also have lacked educational research. This lack exists in reverse proportion to the prevalence of the art form in the school; there is more research in music and visual arts than there is in theater and dance. Much of the research that does exist is in need of replication. Recent practice has focused on the use of art objects and/or artist performers to enrich instruction, as opposed to the solving of lingering instructional questions. For instance, dance research journals contain delightful reports on dances, dancers, and descriptions of performance conditions, but almost nothing on the effects of differing instructional practices.

The paucity of systematic research studies, however, does not mean there is little knowledge about teaching toward the national standards and other objectives in arts education. Musicians, artists, actors, and dancers have been successfully taught for generations, and audiences for these artists have learned how to understand and appreciate the best the various cultures have to offer. The arts also have been used as therapy, accomplishing major objectives for special populations. What may be different if schools respond to the challenge of the new standards, especially the performance standards speaking to excellence, is that instructional programs may need to be modified so they can be used with a wider population and with students of differing ages.

A recent up-tick in research activity has been prompted by arts advocates and arts advocacy organizations in an effort to document the many observed, important non-arts outcomes of experiences in the arts. These and other studies reporting non-arts outcomes were subjected to a meta-analysis by Ellen Winner, Lois Hetland, and their colleagues at Project Zero, which was reported in articles in Volume 34 (2000) of the *Journal of Aesthetic Education*. Seven electronic databases

were searched from their inception until 1998. In addition, the researchers searched 41 journals, with issues published beginning in 1950, plus analyzed personal contacts with more than 200 arts education researchers. Altogether, the information resulted in 1,135 research "records."

The researchers found causation difficult to document because students enrolled in arts courses, regardless of SES level, typically have parents who are interested in education and the arts, and also attend better schools that have strong arts programs and that employ enthusiastic arts teachers; further, the students were usually self-selected. Correlations identified are significant, however, with the most positive school outcomes ranging from academic achievement to character building and school retention; causation is most apparent in drama/theater education. The strong and positive relationship with academic outcomes, with critical thinking, self-confidence, perseverance, motivation, discipline, bonding, and more are not to be ignored. These non-arts outcomes are characteristic of students who actively participate in the arts and are a defining feature. With increased student participation in the arts, researchers will have increased opportunities to study the possibility of causality.

The practices reported in this section are specific and are applicable to all grade levels. The research emphasis is on interventions that begin in the lower grades, as the arts have many uses and many applications even for very young children. Students move, sing, paint, and act out events as early as preschool. Arts education in early childhood education has produced important learning in each of the art forms, and the voluntary national standards cannot be attained without consistent, long-term instruction.

Focused instruction in each of the arts is advocated here; the arts have, however, as many commonalities with other school subjects as they do with one another, and integration is not unusual. Visual arts education has been successful when integrated, on occasion, with other subjects, largely because of the interest it brings to academics and also the stimulus it provides to the teacher who must now be better prepared. The fact that dance is usually accompanied by music and theatrical practices does not mean the instructional objectives of dance, theater, and music are identical. Cognitive integration is desirable, but it must be based on reasonably strong student competence in at least one of the arts. There are major differences affecting the difficulty of tasks that should be recognized and that have implications for emphasis and sequence. The teaching practices presented here often apply to several or all of the arts. In the presentation of the practices, a specific art may be cited with generalizations where appropriate; references are listed in the several arts.

Most of the practices in arts education can be conducted by the generalist classroom teacher, if that teacher is interested in the arts and believes in their importance for the children in his or her class. The Interstate New Teacher Assessment and Support Consortium (INTASC) teacher certification requirements, if implemented, will facilitate subject matter integration because the classroom teacher will be better informed about the arts, and most integrated instructional activities will not require the assistance of the arts specialist. This seriousness of purpose is itself the essential practice, as indicated by considerable research and experience. Treating the arts seriously in teaching and learning is necessary for the acquisition of knowledge and skill; in addition, it leads to expanded imagination and creativity in the art form itself, to the application of understanding from the arts to other subjects, and to a way of living. Much of the valid research substantiates the importance of focus and reflection in both the performing and the visual arts. The arts are also marked by attention to detail; subtleties in looking, seeing, and hearing are of supreme importance, and symbols and metaphors must be understood.

There is something incomplete about an education that does not include minimal competence in the ability to perform and discriminate in at least one art form. Although arts educators do not always intentionally teach for transfer,

intense, quality experiences in the arts have often resulted in multiple outcomes. Thus, the arts teach not only directly but also through metaphors and stories, providing students with answers to questions about the human condition that have not, as yet, been asked. Educators could find clues to many educational issues from a study of arts education, because arts education involves private as well as very large group instruction, heterogeneous (at risk, mainstreamed, varied SES, and gifted students in a single class) and homogeneous instruction, multiple age- and grade-level classes, partnered instruction with the community, cooperative and rigorous competitive instructional strategies, sequenced and rote instruction, and much more.

The arts are not an isolated quantity; students must be competent in other subjects in order for the arts to be meaningful. Knowledge of Greek and Roman myths and the Bible is useful, if not necessary, to understand much of Western theater, music, and visual arts; a sense of European history and culture is important for study in music. The arts continue to be prevalent in society, more so than in the school curriculum. Students listen to music and view images in their free time; these experiences are influenced by the media, their peers, and current trends.

One of the attractions of the arts is that so much is accomplished by doing. One learns to draw by drawing; one learns to dance not only by viewing *The Nutcracker* on TV at Christmastime, but also by moving and dancing by oneself and with others. Students enjoy developing these skills. The arts continue their importance as an avocation and as a necessity. Many large medical centers have superb musical ensembles composed of health providers. Similar powerful avocational activities exist in visual arts, dance, and theater. The opportunity to "do" in the arts implies sufficient time to practice. The arts do not lend themselves to six weeks of exploration in middle school. Although there are many subjects in the applied arts—driver training, for example—where much can be accomplished in a six-week or nine-week period, the standards in the fine arts do not accommodate to such an instructional pattern.

Arts education can thrive with block or regular scheduling with the following caveat: Students must be given the opportunity to learn; the most important element is access to instruction by a qualified, enthusiastic teacher on a frequent basis, with "frequent" defined as two to three times a week or more in the elementary school—a schedule comparable to that of the high school. Alternating instruction among the arts has never resulted in substantive school-based arts learning. Learning in the arts can occur, and does occur, with no more difficulty than learning in the other basic subjects of language arts, mathematics, and the social sciences. Talent and interest are important factors, as they are in all subjects. The teacher shares responsibility with the community for improving student interest, but the teacher assumes primary responsibility for emphasizing the importance of attaining knowledge, skill, and experience in at least one art form.

The author wishes to thank the following people for their valuable assistance in reviewing this section: Jerry Housman, formerly director of curriculum and instruction for Urban Gateways; Susan Stinson, chair, Department of Design, University of North Carolina at Greenville; Karen Bradley, chair of dance, University of Maryland; Lois Hetland, Project Zero, Harvard University; Thomas Brewer, coordinator of art education, University of Central Florida; Keith Swanwick, academic dean, University of London; Lin Wright, chair, Department of Drama, Arizona State University; Ann Podlozny, University of California, Los Angeles, and consultant to the film industry; Folkert Haanstra, Institute for Educational Research, University of Amsterdam; Read Diket, chair of art, William Carey College; Jean Morrow, New England Conservatory of Music; and Marionette Cano, University of Michigan.

3.1. Direct Instruction: Direct instruction, including modeling, leads to not only greater production/performance skill but also to improvement in understanding the art form.

Research findings:

Both practice and research in all four art fields—music, visual arts, dance, and theater—indicate direct instruction, including modeling, is most effective in attaining the standards related to performance/production. Extensive research findings of the Aesthetic Education Project at the Central Midwestern Regional Educational Laboratory (CEMREL) on non-performance objectives revealed the more focused the instruction, the more dramatic the results.

Most research in visual arts was done in the first half of the 20th century; most drawing research since that time has focused on racial, gender, and socioeconomic differences. Brewer (1998) found when instruction is minimal, age and gender are more persuasive than instruction. Wilson and Wilson's (1977) seminal research, Brewer and Colbert's (1992) study of seventh-grade students, and Neperud's (1966) study of fifth-grade students all found direct instruction led to a higher level of drawing skill. Sang (1987) discovered the teacher's ability to model and the frequency of that modeling positively affected student performance level. Delzell (1989) found modeling to be important in developing musical discrimination skills, as did Francisco (1994) in his research with secondary school ensembles. Musical improvisation is taught successfully almost entirely by teacher-centered modeling (Bitz 1998). Unrau (1999) enhanced learning in dance using Merce Cunningham's techniques as models.

Instruction for young children in the arts is typically both direct and developmentally appropriate. For example, Colprit (2000) as well as Duke (1999) report that with the eminently successful Suzuki method of violin instruction, 66 percent of instruction is teacher-centered and 34 percent student performance, with almost no off-task talk or behavior. Modeling by peers is effective both with and without peer critique.

Research shows students who were taught performance were no better at analyzing parts of artworks, but they did excel in deriving meaning, because the holistic evaluation incorporated more of the historical and contextual aspects of the work of art.

In the classroom:

Students learning to create works of art benefit from direct teacher intervention and teacher modeling as distinguished from a discussion-based or lecture-based curriculum. With production objectives, teacher-centered instruction is more successful regardless of the student's learning style. Instruction in visual arts continues to be 65 percent production; performance instruction is even higher in music, dance, and theater.

The essence of performance in the arts is the development of a wide range of skills—perceptual, aural, visual, and psychomotor—that facilitate dancing, acting, drawing, painting, working in media, and making music. Artistry can be more easily taught by demonstration than by words. Skills education is related to mastery education, as indicated by the extensive research of Rosenshine (1997) in all subjects. Enhancement of skills is possible once the basic mastery level is attained. The Guildhall School of Music and Drama found an inspiring role model—physical, artistic, and mental—is crucial for the projection of intentions and the conveying of meaning in the performing arts.

Instruction by demonstration, coaching, close and direct observation, and modeling is most effective for a "trial and error" model of instruction. Correct initial skills learning is crucial; awkward and inefficient techniques obstruct and inhibit progress in performance. The need to avoid mastery of negative skill performance (bad habits) reinforces the importance of direct instruction. Direct instruction in developing skill competency is also the primary factor in enhanced self-esteem through the arts.

Use of the knowledge of self-theories explicated by Dweck (1999) and confirmed in music by Smith (2002) are critical in teaching, especially through direct instruction, as about half of the students believe talent is fixed and half believe improvement is possible. Students who believe talent in the arts is a stable entity thrive on easy, low-level successes and undeserved reinforcement, while these students (often the males) believe they could attain the goals if they tried. Austin and Vispoel (1998) report an even larger percentage of adolescents who think of ability as

stable, which may account for students' rationalizing failures in the arts as a "lack of talent" and not a lack of instruction, effort, or practice. The setting and modeling of appropriate goals create the difference in the classroom.

 Sources:

Austin and Vispoel 1998; Bitz 1998; Brewer 1998; Brewer and Colbert 1992; Chen 1996; Colprit 2000; Cox 1992; Delacruz 1997; Delzell 1989; Duke 1999; Dweck 1999; Francisco 1994; Green 1987; Grey 1983; Kototski, Davidson, and Coimbra 2001; Lagne 1970; Langan 1995; Lansing 1981; Makin, White, and Owen 1996; Neperud 1966; O'Neill 1997; Rosenshine 1997; Rosenthal 1984; Sang 1987; Smith 2002; Thompson 1991; Unrau 1999; Wilson and Wilson 1977.

3.2. **Immediate Feedback:** Providing immediate feedback to individuals, whether performing alone or in a group, is superior to delayed, group, or no feedback in promoting skill development in all areas of the arts.

Research findings:

Extensive research on skill development has yielded a consistent finding, whether in the initial trials or during refinement: Immediate reinforcement, whether positive or negative, facilitates learning. Practicing mistakes (the beta hypothesis) to sensitize performers is not effective. Immediate correction is better for both short-term and long-term learning.

Makin, White, and Owen (1996) found feedback is effective when it is immediate and provides specific information addressing a student's own objectives. Fewer than 25 percent of the questions of art teachers in their study were evaluative; teachers asked "display" questions rather than genuine questions. Visual arts teachers, to avoid any interference in the process of self-expression, provided only 1 percent negative comments in their feedback to students, and 79 percent of the positive comments lacked any specific information on why the work of art was praised; this kind of feedback led to a drop in students' intrinsic motivation. Kassing and Mortensen (1981-82) in dance found immediate feedback by peers greatly reduced the instructional time needed, while Burton (2001) found feedback from classroom posting of artwork was the second-most important instructional variable. Sheridan and Byrne (2002) found, with immediate feedback, experiences become autotelic and any worry of failure in performance disappears, resulting in a balance between challenge and skill.

In the classroom:

On-the-spot corrections may take any format—a positive or negative comment, a demonstration of the error, the correct rendition, or both in a comparison mode. It is the timing and the individualization of the correction that are critical in performance improvement. The immediate interruption of an individual or a group performance emphasizes the importance of correcting the error(s); corrections made at the end of the performance have less impact, less specificity, and less power to focus attention. Bad performance habits form quickly and tend to have permanence.

Improvement is most dramatic in music, theater, and dance, but the importance of immediate individual corrections is also evident in the teaching of performance practices in visual arts and media arts. Practical experience indicates, as an intervention, immediate individual correction is most difficult in music because of multiple performers on a single part and the fact that aural discrimination in these situations requires more training than does visual. Dance and theater teachers use both the visual and aural (spoken/sung) senses, while visual arts teachers often rely on an unchanging visual stimulus. The coaching nature of instruction in visual arts, theater, and dance is effective because of the manner and immediacy of feedback; this is also part of private instruction in music.

The need to reflect on the work as a whole to improve interpretive abilities in music, dance, theater, and the visual arts—the product of focused instruction—is a different, though equally important, instructional practice. Delays in feedback are occasioned in the arts when excessive use is made of the portfolio approach. This delayed feedback and self-criticism develops audience, not performance, competencies.

Sources:

Baxter and Stauffer 1988; Bloom 1985; Brunelle and de Carufel 1982; Burton 2001; Fitterling and Ayllon 1983; Fortin 1986; Gates and Bradshaw 1994; Kassing and Mortensen 1981-82; Makin, White, and Owen 1996; Sevigny 1977; Sheridan and Byrne 2002; Siegesmund, Diket, and McCulloch 2001; Stokrocki 1988.

3.3. Interdisciplinary Learning: Teaching visual/spatial skills together with historical/technical information enables students to comprehend and respond to visual art as well as comparable tasks in music, dance, theater, and media.

Research findings:

Widespread experience with the power of arts programs to enhance schooling prompted support for a comprehensive meta-analysis of research. The meta-analysis covered the research completed in the past 50 years in the four primary arts, in order to verify causality. Some of the research findings reported here reference these meta-analysis studies, as reported in the *Journal of Aesthetic Education*, rather than individual studies because the effect sizes are more informative.

Research studies indicate the studio approach alone is not very successful in educating students to the aesthetic properties of a work of art. Two meta-analyses were conducted by the Dutch researcher Folkert Haanstra, who searched three computer bases—Dissertation Abstracts International, ERIC, and PSYCHinfo—as well as the Index of British Studies, Art and Design Education, Dutch Bibliography of Research in Arts Education, Studies in Art Education, and Visual Arts Research. He found 108 relevant titles; studies not meeting the criteria for treatment or outcome measures, or not providing sufficient statistical information, were excluded. The relevant studies, including 30 on visual-spatial ability and 39 investigating aesthetic perception, indicated studio education that is solely performance based has no effect on visual-spatial ability and only a modest effect on aesthetic perception (Haanstra 1994). Warner (1975) and Hoffer and Anderson (1970, 1971) found a comprehensive musicianship approach combining music history and theory in the rehearsal improved performance. Other researchers have found no loss of skill with interdisciplinary teaching. Discipline-based art education, the project of the Getty Institute, champions incorporating history, analysis, and aesthetics with production. Getty has 15 years of research-based results indicated in the bibliography, although production remains the primary teaching objective.

Eccles and Barber (1999), Marsh and Kleitman (2002), Catterall, Chapleau, and Iwanaga (1999), and College Board Studies, among others, indicate students in the arts are academically more successful, more typically remain in school, and develop better habits than students who do not participate. Quest (1999) and Blutzlaff (2000) each reported reading gains among music students; both Rose (2003) and Gilbert (1994) found similar gains with dance classes; and Fast (2000) claimed gains in visual arts. Podlozny (2000) found major improvement in these indicators as a result of theater education. Modest support for music improving mathematics is reported in the meta-analysis of Vaughan (2000) and spatial-temporal gains in the meta-analysis of Hetland (2000). Creativity and dance are related, based on the research of Minton (2000) and the meta-analysis of Moga, Burger, Hetland, and Winner (2000).

College Board studies provide research data on thousands of students over time, and those data show that whereas the verbal SAT mean is 400 for non-arts students, it ranges from 433 for dance students to 465 for actors. The mean math SAT score is 464, but it's 504 for music students, and dance students report the lowest of the scores of all arts students with 477, still well above the mean.

In the classroom:

Choosing, reflecting, and evaluating are important goals in the music and visual arts education standards. Effective in developing abilities contributing to these goals is a structured curriculum stressing the ability to categorize art objects by concepts such as style, historical period, subject, and medium, and to make evaluations based on aesthetic properties rather than less relevant characteristics. Primary-age students can improve the perceptual skills that go beyond simple description. For example, mental transformations that move, expand, fold, and rotate shapes contribute to seeing and retaining a visual form within a two-dimensional plane, and thus are necessary in making aesthetic judgments of two-dimensional artworks. The arts are not known for their adherence to a curriculum; however, the Getty materials provide classroom teachers with a structure and a knowledge base representing both research and practice. Research reinforces the importance of planning for specific instructional objectives when selecting among the rich arts experiences available.

These findings from visual arts have implications for the other arts: The development of aesthetic perceptual abilities in the arts does not automatically result from performance experiences; the teachable aspects in such development are knowledge-intensive and dependent on direct, focused learning experi-ence, and so they are also more powerful with older students than with younger ones. Such focused instruction is equally important in music, dance, theater, and media education as well as the traditional visual arts.

Finally, the multicultural role of the arts is evident but has not been documented, other than its ability to add interest to classes such as social studies. Teachers must be sensitive to the cultural beliefs of students, as themes related to sex, drugs, and alcohol are sometimes found in contemporary art forms such as music, theater, and the visual arts.

Sources:

Allison 1986; Baker 1996; Butzlaff 2000; College Board 1988-1998; Eccles and Barber 1999; Efland 1990; Fast 2000; Gilbert 1994; Haanstra 1994, 1996; Harris 2002; Hetland 2000; Hoffer and Anderson 1970, 1971; Kannegeiter 1971; Koroscik 1982; Lindblade 1995; Mark 1996; Marsh and Kleitman 2002; Minton 2000; Moga, Burger, Hetland, and Winner 2000; Podlozny 2000; Quest 1999; Rose 2003; Salome 1965; Turner 2000; Vaughan 2000; Warner 1975; Wilson 1997; Winner and Cooper 2000.

3.4. Questioning Techniques: Specific questioning techniques lead to an understanding of art products and the process of creating them.

Research findings:

Most research on questioning techniques and their sequence has been completed in visual arts education, although dance and theater also have employed this genre of research study. Research has found formulating questions that "set a direction, discover, analyze, classify, personalize, hypothesize, reorder, synthesize, evaluate" (in approximately that order) leads to understanding in the act of criticizing. Short-term studies in music, theater, and visual arts consistently find that through use of questioning strategies, the teacher can get beyond superficialities and subject matter to the content of the art object. Questioning techniques, however, do not aid in attaining immediate results in improved arts production.

In the classroom:

Teaching students to think reflectively and objectively about the arts is an important goal. The sequence of questions identified by the research ("set a direction, discover, analyze, classify, personalize, hypothesize, reorder, synthesize, evaluate") is also effective in teaching production or creation. Variations of this sequence of questions have also been successful.

Questioning techniques are a teaching tool of good teachers in the arts. To be effective, questioning techniques must use the precise language of the discipline and focus on the construct.

Giving approval to students who have only "a general idea" of the artwork does not lead to understanding or transfer of learning. One powerful component of the arts is that individuals must be able to talk about art using the vocabulary of context and expression.

Questioning techniques are especially useful with abstract art or with art that is potentially offensive because of its content. Questioning techniques can objectify the content and place the emphasis on the formal, technical, sensuous, and expressive dimensions of the work. Extensive experience with "artists in the schools" programs has revealed pre- and post-materials (that is, preparation and evaluation) are ineffective unless they make use of insightful questions that follow a set sequence and use vocabulary related to the art being experienced. The most successful model has been a trip to an art gallery, play, or concert, preceded by careful preparation in the classroom, and making use of a docent/assistant working with small groups of students (six to eight) during the art experience. The questions asked before, during, and after the field trip and their sequence are the crucial elements.

Sources:

Armstrong 1986, 1993; Barrett and Rab 1990; Brewer and Colbert 1992; Cooper 1983; Diket 1991; Feldman 1983; Hamblen 1984; Saldaña 1989; Taunton 1983.

3.5. Reflecting on Learning/Non-Learning: Writing and/or reflecting about one's own (and others') performance/production experiences heightens discrimination and improves future performance.

Research findings:

Private arts teachers have long emphasized reflecting on one's own performance as a method of self-evaluation. Extensive research projects in error identification in group settings were spurred by the visual arts and music research in the Arts PROPEL program, the Pittsburgh schools' classroom application of a cognitive approach to arts education developed by Harvard Project Zero. Widely researched in recent years, error identification is found to be especially helpful in dance and theater, two art forms that have not had the advantages of tape recordings and visual products.

Visual arts researchers have found writing important as a method of reflective criticism; music, dance, and theater research indicates writing is an effective means for teaching students to identify seminal events in an artwork. Writing can also help students recognize performance inadequacies. Cummings (1995) analyzed student critical interpretations of works of art. Ryan (2001) found untutored students were unable to make any more than descriptive comments, indicating art criticism is not a natural ability. Similar findings were present in studies of music. Williams (1997) identified difficulties in listening critically while performing, and Kerchner (1996) found unique responses to music in students' verbal, visual, and kinesthetic representations of a listening experience.

Ericsson (1998) has applied research findings from other fields to practicing in music, identifying strategies that lead to expertise in performance. McPherson, working with Zimmerman (2002), has taken the ideas of self-regulation and applied them to music students of all ages. This use of metacognition that develops concentration, planning, and monitoring of practice is supported by considerable research in music (McPherson and McCormick, Renwick and McPherson, Hallam, Chaffin and Imreh, Cecconi-Roberts, Hewitt, Lehmann and Davidson, and Jorgensen) and the use of Laban Movement Analysis as a framework, as well as by Unrau's (1999) research in dance.

In the classroom:

Although writing about dance, theater, music, and visual arts is not in itself an arts experience (except for script writing in theater), it is a valuable teaching technique that makes learning a more active process when combined with performing, creating, or viewing/listening. Writing about what one has just done requires the use of artistic memory to focus not only on the events and their sequence but also on the quality, relationships, and meaning of these events. The writing does not replace, however, teacher evaluation and teacher feedback based on what should be.

Writing need not entail a critique; even a task requiring minimal writing can be a powerful means of focusing on expressive devices and moments. "Call charts"—which pinpoint specific spots in the musical recording or score for which students are to give written answers to specific questions—may be used as a means to make listening active rather than passive. Theater and dance employ both memory and reproduction through videos to direct thought and attention to artistic events, and these can be used to elicit written responses, either general or specific. The writing is only a supplement to the important performance experience, and should always be subordinate to the performance itself.

Research has found that criticism often lacks precision. If the objective is the teaching of criticism, then systematic instruction with examples is needed. Without focus, writing becomes just an exercise to be completed, and attention is on the superficial. In contrast, theater students rehearse their lines, dance students count and memorize, both aided by classroom videotaping that provides not only immediate feedback but also an opportunity to reflect and focus on specific details. A re-analysis of the 1997 NAEP by Diket (2001) in visual arts found holistic scoring to be ineffective and scoring of parts necessary for student improvement.

Sources:

Alter 1995; Bridges 1996; Carpenter 1996; Cecconi-Roberts 2001; Chaffin and Imreh 2001; Cummings 1995; Diket 2001; Erickson 1998; Hallam 2001; Hewitt 2000; Jorgensen 2001; Jorgensen and Lehmann 1997; Kerchner 1996; Lavender and Oliver 1993; Lehmann and Davidson 2002; McPherson and McCormick 2000; McPherson and Zimmerman 2002; McSorley 1996; Renwick and McPherson 2002; Ryan 2001; Stavropoulos 1992; Swinton 1989; Unrau 1999; Williams 1997; Wilson 1986.

3.6. Individual Performance: Individual participatory experiences in the arts lead to better understanding and higher-level skills than does group experience.

Research findings:

The established practice in music is the private lesson; visual arts, dance, and theater also emphasize individual production, although often conducted in a group setting. Students who are taught individually not only advance at their own pace, but also receive direct and immediate feedback on their strengths and weaknesses. The research has investigated only young students; however, the problem of masking errors when performing in a group has been demonstrated at all ages. The successful Suzuki instructional program, which began in strings education, is based on individual performance. Although confounded by the effects of self- and parental selection, research in each of the arts indicates the importance of individual instruction and/or individual performance. Odam (2000) found 53 percent of the students in a music composition class also composed out of school, and more than 80 percent of the students in AP visual arts draw outside of school. Davis and Pulman (2001) found individual public performance is necessary to trigger independent learning. Performing opportunities in the innovative D'Amboise dance program were effective in improving the skills of at-risk students, according to Seham (1997). Because expertise takes time, Jorgensen (2001) found not only individual attention was necessary but also lessons should begin as early as possible.

In the classroom:

Performance is a crucial goal for each of the arts. Teaching practices that avoid putting students in situations where they sing, play, or otherwise perform alone contribute to lower levels of competence

and to the perception that individual performance is more difficult and potentially embarrassing.

Tradition might promote the idea that learning to sing or otherwise perform in music is best conducted in a group situation, where the individual receives reinforcement and clues from peers. Research and practice, however, indicate not only do individuals learn how to sing by singing alone, but the quality of the vocal performance of young children is better when a student sings by himself or herself rather than in a group. Learning to sing accurately is actually easier when done alone. The voices of others mask one's own efforts and interfere with one's ability to judge pitch, rhythm, and tonal quality as well as to think about what is desired before producing the sound.

Group performance goals in music, dance, and theater stress different competencies and should come later in the learning sequence. Practice indicates the superiority of private lessons or instruction in small groups where students receive feedback from other class members as well as the teacher. Although Suzuki violin students are known for performing in large groups, they receive individual instruction, as do college music majors. The successful apprentice model of skill learning is based on individual performance even when the eventual goal is to work as a member of a team. Individual performance requires individual instruction and practice.

In dance, theater, and the visual arts, the individual is more prominent, less obscured by the group activity, and hence, more readily habituated to individual exposure. The principle obtains equally in all of the arts; it is simply more difficult to apply in music. Burton (2001) documented the importance of immediate display of individual work. The classroom teacher must provide opportunities for individuals to not only perform for the entire class but also to have paired students or students in small groups perform for each other; critiquing leads to not only interest but better outcomes in skill, disposition, and understanding.

Sources:

Blaker 1995; Burton 2001; Carsillo 1996; Davis and Pulman 2001; De Spain 1997; Goetze 1985; Jorgensen 2001; Kellet 2000; Kozan 1995; Odam 2000; Seham 1997; Seipp 1976; Szekely 1995.

3.7. **Use of Creative Drama and Theater:** Creating a story to be acted out by themselves and others can improve students' language arts skills, self-concept, peer relationships, and creativity.

Research findings:

Research in theater has focused on creative drama, an area with its own distinct objectives. Students may be given a situation to portray—or even as few as two randomly selected words—and asked to improvise a few meaningful sentences or actions that are part of a story or the entire story. Research results vary in impact and power, but more than 70 percent of studies in this area show student learning can be improved significantly through creative drama, as students assume roles and interact in improvisation or in role playing.

Research with at-risk youth indicates older students who become involved in acting scenes and events gain a greater understanding of language and literature, in addition to finding relationships in the literature to their own lives, resulting in improved attitudes toward the class and also toward school attendance.

Research with younger students has been in creative drama, not children's theater. This improvisatory activity is most effective when guided by trained and imaginative leaders. Teachers with as few as two to four hours of professional development can help students accomplish objectives related to creativity in the arts. Research also shows the action part of creative drama is important; the same results have not been observed with creative writing or oral interpretation.

In the classroom:

Teachers who relate creative drama to other subjects have found students make increased cognitive gains and find more personal meaning in whatever subject is involved. The skills required to create and to involve other students in one's creation include listening skills, fluency, flexibility, and originality of language. Students learn to concentrate, control vivid images, make themselves believable, give structure to the plot, and make effective use of whatever space and props are available.

These findings also apply to the goal of the other art forms in promoting creativity. For example, the student may be asked to create a sculpture or painting from a few clues, compose or improvise music based on a short melody or motif, create a dance based on a word or term, or carry out similar projects in photography, architecture, and media.

Theater is often cross-disciplinary—theater as government is one example. The study of and participation in serious theater enable participants to experience feelings of humanness: love, greed, loneliness, disease, and masculinity and femininity. Seidel (1996) found leadership was a consistent outcome in addition to artistic competencies.

Podlozny (2000) reports there have been 200 experimental studies assessing the relationship of theater education to outcomes in reading, oral language, and writing. Kardash and Wright's (1987) meta-analysis of 16 studies supported the causality of drama education in several cognitive outcomes and suggested instruction at earlier ages is strongest.

Conard's (1992) meta-analysis found support for improvement of reading readiness, reading achievement, story understanding, oral language development, and writing, which inspired Podlozny (2000) to analyze drama instruction in terms of enactment, plot, and leader. Beginning with 265 possible research studies, 80 were identified as being of substantive quality. Important findings were that the length of instruction was not as important as frequency of instruction, that drama helps students understand and recall, and that enacting one text makes a new text more comprehensible. The leader as instructor (teacher-centered, direct instruction) was more effective than was teacher as facilitator. Drama experiences were even more effective in improving reading ability with low SES populations. Podlozny's findings were powerful and causal, documenting the value of the arts in directly involving the student in learning and further involving the student as an individual rather than as a class member. Students not only understood and derived meaning from the literature, but their ability to write improved significantly.

Sources:

Barufaldi 1992; Bennett 1982; Burke 1980; Burton, Horowitz, and Abeles 2000; Conard 1992; Dallett 1996; Dupont 1989; Heathcote and Bolton 1995; Kardash and Wright 1987; Podlozny 2000; Rosenberg 1989; Saab 1988; Seidel 1996; Sharples 1992; Shiavi 1998; Vitz 1983; Wagner 1998.

3.8. Visual and Aural Thinking: The use of visual and aural thinking improves performance, creation, and discrimination in arts education.

Research findings:

"Audiation" is a word coined by researcher Edwin Gordon (1997, 1998) to better describe "tonal thinking" or the ability to think sounds before attempting to sing or play. Other investigators have pointed out the need for wide experience in hearing sounds before attempting to read musical notation. Ability to connect the sound, real or imagined, with the notation enables the learner to grasp the meaning of the symbols and thus gain musical literacy. In order to produce the correct pitch with the correct duration, a performer thinks about the characteristics of the note before producing it. As the habit of "prior thinking" becomes stronger, the time between thinking and producing is reduced. Dancers, actors, and visual artists describe or use gestures (mentally or physically) before moving, acting, or drawing.

Extensive research and practice indicate mental and mental/physical practice without an instrument or going through the actions of dance or theater improves performance. Edwin Gordon's more than 10 years of research on mental thinking of sounds prior to production has helped focus the research results of others that confirm the importance of mental imagery of physical tasks. Woody (1999, 2002) found mental expectation influenced the expressiveness of production; Krasnow, Chatfield, Barr, Jensen, and Defek (1977) identified the importance of imagery in dance, as did Hanrahan (1994) and Overby (2000).

In the classroom:

Teachers need to provide opportunities for students to learn and practice aural and visual thinking. Imagining what the music will sound like, imagining what one will draw, paint or sculpt, and visualizing in one's mind dance movements and theatrical gestures before one begins to sing, play, dance, act, create, view, or listen set up the expectations against which actual performance is judged. The understanding of art requires the cognitive act of going beyond what is seen or heard.

Tonal thinking is important in creating music, improvising, and adding harmony to familiar melodies. Tonal thinking creates listening expectations used in comprehending a musical work. Accomplished musicians and dancers practice mentally without producing a sound; Mozart's ability to hear an entire symphony prior to writing it is well established, and many architects and choreographers visualize their work in detail before setting it on paper.

Visual and aural thinking are fundamental to the many uses of imagination that are valued outcomes of arts instruction. The ability to have a vivid imagination is important not only for mental health but as a first step in creativity. A major benefit of any arts instruction is release from the ordinary, the experience of magic worlds, people, and events. Classroom and everyday events can dull the imagination. The arts place responsibility on teachers to encourage visual and aural thinking, which are the foundation of innovation and creativity. Theater stresses the use of vivid imaginations in portraying characters in published and student-constructed plays.

Maxine Greene, with 20 years of research at Lincoln Center, has long advocated the primacy of the imagination in all learning; learning that is most clear in the arts occurs when one projects himself or herself into a world of "becoming." The entire focus of *Contact Quarterly* is on the teaching of improvisation for theater and dance, two art forms where communicating one's thinking to fellow performers is necessary for both adequacy and quality of the performance.

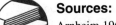

Sources:

Arnheim 1969; Bennett 1994; Bradford 1995; Coffman 1987; Denis 1995; Fiske 1993; Gordon 1997, 1998; Hanrahan 1994; Hoffman 2002; Kassing and Mortensen 1981-82; Kellman 1998; Koopman 2002; Krasnow, Chatfield, Barr, Jensen, and Defek 1977; McCurry 1998; Miceli 1998; Overby 2000; Pinciotti 1982; Rideout 1992; Rosenberg with Pinciotti et al. 1987; Roush 1995; Weaver 1996; Wells 1995; Woody 1999, 2002.

3.9. Sequencing for Understanding: Systematically following a sequence of activities relative to an artwork enables students to learn the process of arts criticism.

Research findings:

The development of competencies in the affective domain (appreciation, attitude, values, and preferences) requires systematic and long-term instruction.

For example, Feldman (1983), whose research in visual arts criticism is among the most extensive, used a sequence of description, formal analysis, interpretation, and evaluation. Several of Feldman's doctoral students have successfully taught criticism to students of all ages. Feldman's system has been shown to help disadvantaged first-graders in learning the basic concepts of art, and the system has been successfully researched in music as well. The research of discipline-based education requires analysis, comparison, and criticism.

The emphasis on understanding the material and seeking instructional efficiency has resulted in Nielsen's (1999) sequence of independent learning strategies in music and Kindler's (2000) findings in art, which support a teaching and learning sequence based on age. The same concept underlies Welch, Fitt, and Thompson's (1994) finding that one must teach from the fundamentals forward and not begin with the product and then dissect the learning process (in dance), and also Geahigan's (1998) research findings on the importance of sequence for critical inquiry outcomes.

In dance, Lord (2001) found direct instruction requires centering: setting up the situation, presenting the task orally and through demonstration, providing a transition to the execution, and then feedback, guiding the task's execution, and revisiting the situation, often necessitating imagery through the use of metaphors common to all arts instruction.

In the classroom:

The goal of the individual creating a work of art is to affect the lives of the viewer/listener. Early interpretation, out of sequence, leads to intellectual passivity, as the viewer focuses only on the subjective/responsive aspects of the experience rather than on the intellectually knowable aspects. The use of precise language in the sequence is necessary. In visual arts, for example, students are first given training in perception that includes techniques to identify shape, location, size, texture, and other critical elements. Details of a work of art are named and described, a method that is both heuristic and phenomenological. Next, form is analyzed, and relationships of size, quality, singularity, and recurrence, etc., are systematically sought by the viewer. Only then is the focus turned to interpreting and evaluating. Research in music indicates music of the classical period is easier to hear with respect to form and the elements comprising form—moving from obvious to subtle and from simple to complex.

The arts involve acting and responding, making and using, offering and accepting—dictating that precision of language and sequence is of importance. Listeners to music and viewers of theater and dance must use their memory to make sequential mental comparisons in the process of describing, analyzing, interpreting, and evaluating. This process is aided by examining smaller segments in sequence. For example, museums arrange visual arts products to facilitate comparison and contrast, using historical sequences or lines of social change to highlight elements of style, period, genre, and so forth. Both the student and the teacher must first understand the work of art and its dimensions before they can engage in criticism and become discriminating. The visual artist seeks to understand where the performing arts benefit from authentic performances.

To be effective, advance organizers that provide the framework should be at a more obvious level in the beginning stages of instruction: in music, students listen for dynamics, tessitura, or who is performing; viewers of dance identify forms and styles of choreography and roles and performers. On successive listenings/viewings and in successive years, the framework may direct attention to more subtle components, such as counter melodies in music, supporting background in visual arts, or gestures in theater or dance. The sequence of experiences in the arts separates entertainment from education; fortunately, education in the arts can also be entertaining.

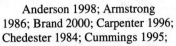

Sources:

Anderson 1998; Armstrong 1986; Brand 2000; Carpenter 1996; Chedester 1984; Cummings 1995; Feldman 1983; Fisher 1989; Geahigan 1998; Kindler 2000; Lang and Ryba 1976; Lord 2001; McSorley 1996; Millsap 1999; Nielsen 1999; Ragans 1971; Richardson 1988; Short 1998; Stephens 1996; Twiggs 1970; Vallance 1995; Welch, Fitt, and Thompson 1994; Williams 1997; Wilson 1997.

3.10. Use of Psychomotor Principles: Performance skill is enhanced through systematic instruction based on principles derived from the motor and psychomotor domain.

Research findings:

Physical tension is inhibiting to all activities involving bodily movement; hence, it is not surprising that research studies indicate physical disposition has a major impact on musical performance. Regular rhythmic movement in one or more parts of the body reduces physical tension. Primary-age students often cannot move to a regular pulsation; those who can tend to be higher achievers in the arts and in other subjects than those who cannot. (Not all large-body muscles develop before small muscles; students can often clap with a steadier pulse than they can move their bodies or walk).

Research findings differ by age and by extent of impairment due to tension. However, exercise, good posture, mental thinking, and improved skill each contribute to lessening of tension. Almost all studies found improvement when the principles of movement were taught. Music, theater, and dance employ findings from the Dalcroze, Weikert, and Alexander techniques to improve performance. Psychomotor principles can reduce stage fright. Research based on Weikert also suggests preschool children who are taught movement do better in most school subjects.

Kimmarle's (2001) research in dance illustrates the need for the teacher to understand the physical domain as well as the mental in a developmentally appropriate way. Kimmarle found that when dance movements are taught from only one side and when the student is asked to execute the same movement using the other side of the body, the skill has not transferred. Mental tension often has a physical basis and the principles of Alexander, Pilates, and Laban have been found to be especially effective in minimizing stress on muscles required for performance, ranging from Wiest's (1997) research on minimizing stress on the vocal cords to Stinson's (1997) stress reduction through large, dance movements.

In the classroom:

The formation of correct bodily habits requires time and instruction; teachers must not only provide daily reminders and systematic feedback to students who exhibit bodily tension in performance, but also use instructional devices such as videos, demonstrations, modeling, and specific (nonmusical) exercises designed to reduce body tension. For example, exercises requiring students to pick up heavier objects result in reduced tension in holding musical instruments, violin bows, etc. With all physical movements, "follow through" such as that practiced by golfers is important to avoid jerky and quick changes of motion. Musicians should be able to move all body parts—not only those required for performance—while performing, and such movements are a gauge of the degree of bodily tension present.

For acting, dancing, or musical performance to be relaxed and natural, instruction must include work toward making body motions relaxed and natural. Biofeedback and other mental exercises have a direct impact on the physical actions basic to the best artistic production. For example, stage fright is a recognized condition that can be attenuated by deep breathing and other relaxation exercises.

Interventions as short as two weeks' duration lead to observable improvements in performance. Teachers may need little more guidance than that provided by the Paul Rolland videos on violin instruction, which show how to apply a few selected principles of relaxation in appendages. Teachers cannot expect that students will develop tension-free performance without instruction.

Sources:

Chappell 1999; Croom 1998; Dennis 1984; Holm 1997; Kalliopuska 1989; Kimmarle 2001; McCullough 1996; Rideout 1992; Rohwer 1997; Rolland, Mutschler, and Colwell 1971; Rose 1995; Stinson 1997; Vanmiddlesworth 1996; Wade 1990; Waite 1977; Weikert 1982; Wiest 1997; Yang 1994; Yontz 2001.

3.11. Correct Body Use: Correct use of the body is necessary for achievement of acceptable standards in the performance arts.

Research findings:

Correct body use depends, of course, on employing appropriate psychomotor principles, but research findings also indicate the importance of nutrition as well as the teaching and practicing of exercises that develop stamina, enlarged lung capacity, and the ability to use one's body to project communication and convey nonverbal meaning. The well-crafted research of Bonbright (1989) in dance relates nutrition to the success of 15- to 18-year-old ballet dancers. Research with arts students in performance has also documented the negative effects of smoking, alcohol, and poor diet with large-scale surveys such as that of Eccles and Barber (1999), indicating students who participate in music ensembles, theater, and dance clubs avoid health risks such as alcohol usage more than the average high school student.

Incorrect posture, identified in extensive and well-executed research through photographs, video, x-rays, and fluoroscopes, is the most frequently identified factor in preventing students from attaining performance standards in music, dance, and theater. Breathing is affected, as are other muscles. Improper breath support affects tone production in vocal and instrumental performance, projection in theater, and the ability to move properly in dance. Research supports practical experience in concluding that posture makes a major difference.

In the classroom:

Artists must be as concerned as athletes about their bodies. Objectives in the arts that require the use of muscles depend on the correct use of these muscles. Warm-up exercises that help students in the correct use of the body and its muscles are critical in acting, singing, and dancing, and very important in playing a musical instrument. Painters and other art producers find proper position and relaxation exercises important in executing proper technique.

The proper use of the body can be guided by specific exercises. For example, one of the goals of elementary school music is to establish the "head tone" physically and in the student's ear. This can be done by singing from second-space A to third-space C, a range that is higher than the student's speaking voice. Chest singing is harmful; young singers should not force the muscles to match vocal styles such as gospel and rock. Preventive "medicine" is now a responsibility of the classroom teacher. For example, poor posture must be corrected in dance and theater before planned instruction can be effective. Standing helps facilitate proper breathing and reduces tension. Students can learn to sing incorrectly as well as correctly; correct singing may require the student to unlearn habits of poor posture and voice placement.

Dance requires similar instruction in posture, use of the muscles, warm-ups, and cool-downs. Alignment, centering, gravity, balance, breathing, and use of tension and relaxation are necessary concepts to learn and apply in practice. The basic posture for music, dance, and theater can be simply described: head, chest, and pelvis are supported and in alignment, shoulders are down and back but relaxed, body weight is well distributed. Posture must be erect, balanced, and relaxed, whether sitting, standing, or moving. Theater is being aided by the digital camera that graphically displays incorrect weight and balance. Movement is now a key component in early childhood education for "readiness" in several subjects.

The teaching of correct posture is an intervention both to improve performance and to prevent bad habits that are difficult to identify and correct.

The desirable habits are the same ones that contribute to good health in general—good health being one of the standards in dance education.

 Sources:

Adar 1995; Batson 1989; Bonbright 1989; Bosh and Hinch 1999; Cardinal and Hilsendager 1995; De Spain 1997; Dunkin 1998; Eccles and Barber 1999; Education Committee of the International Association for Dance Medicine and Science 2001; Fitt, Sturman, and McClain-Smith 1993; Gackle 1987; Holm 1997; McCullough 1996; Miller 1986; Minton 1981, 1989; Montgomery 1997; Phillips 1992; Richmond 1994; Riley, 1987; Rohwer 1997; Rose 1995; Sehmann 2000; Turon 2000; Vanmiddlesworth 1996; VonRossberg-Gempton 1998.

3.12. Improving Memory: "Chunking," or grouping by units to form pitch and rhythm patterns, leads to improved musical memory.

Research findings:

Musical memory is essential for listening, performing, creating, and understanding. Petzold's (1966) seminal six-year study in music with children ages one to six established the importance of patterns to musical memory. Walters' (1992) research on sequencing for declarative and procedural memory and Bamberger's (1991) lifetime of well-known research on developmental patterns in young students demonstrate pattern or gestalt learning. According to Starkes, Caicco, Boutilier, and Sevsek (1990), performance improves one's memory for dance and theater, with experience indicating the same is true for music. Chan, Ho, and Cheung (1998) found that music training improves verbal memory; further research shows improving musical memory greatly improves one's memory in learning a different language, with considerably more positive results for education experiences before the age of 12. Gonzalez (1996) found having the ability to make decisions about one's performance enhances memory. Madsen and Madsen (2002) documented the out-of-school experiences that enhance memory—homework is overwhelmingly a positive experience. Memory leads to learning and understanding in the arts as well as to improved performance. Research is limited, however, because of the existence of successful practices in remembering plays, dances, and music.

In the classroom:

The memory of students, even those with minimal talent, can be improved by "chunking" pitches into commonly used patterns. Patterns may be as short as two notes or as long as a complete melody. Chords and scales provide beginning structures for chunking pitches. Duration can be grouped by the meter of the piece into measures, by notes in a beat, or by patterns representing styles of music; the rhythm of dances from the 17th century to the present provides an example of rhythmic chunking.

These patterns are further chunked into phrases, sequences, melodies, and counter-melodies that are the building blocks of musical form. Performers and listeners must remember those building blocks in order to follow and make sense out of the musical composition. Other aids to musical memory, such as repetition and contrast, texture, voicing, and style, all depend upon chunking.

Because perception is constantly used by musicians, chunking provides a sufficient framework so educated musicians are not affected by inexact page turning or temporary loss of the musical score. Musical memory is influenced by the ability to improvise and play by ear, which are related to chunking.

This practice also applies to other performance arts. For example, dancers learn the choreography by using music as an aid in chunking by phrases and more, as well as by visualizing their own movements in units; actors use chunking to learn the script of a play. Memory is also important for audiences at museums and performances. Chunking of form, style, genre, theme, and motif can improve an audience's understanding. The de-emphasis of memory in other subjects makes it more important in the arts. There is a relationship between artistic memory and visual and aural thinking.

Sources:

Amuah 1994; Bamberger 1991; Chan, Ho, and Cheung 1998; Cziko 1988; Feinstein 1984; Gaynor 1995; Gonzalez 1996; Levitin 1996; Madsen and Madsen 2002; Petzold 1966; Price, Blanton, and Parrish 1998; Starkes, Caicco, Boutilier, and Sevsek 1990; Starr 1996; Vaughan 2002; Walters 1992.

3.13. Instruction in the Role of Symbols: The ability to read, interpret, and understand an art discipline's symbol system enables students to perform more fully and more independently in that art.

Research findings:

Performance of notated dance and music can be learned independently only if one can read the notation. Similarly, theater attainment requires the ability to accurately interpret the symbols of language beyond the reading of words. However, each of the performing arts requires the ability to perform beyond the written page, because the symbols, as critical as they are, provide only the basic structure. The motif, a musical symbol made famous by Richard Wagner, requires one to follow motives in making sense of the music. Motif writing in dance was found by Venable (1998) to enhance not only the production but also the improvisation and vocabulary of the art form. Metaphor as a verbal symbol is used in all of the arts, as it provides the necessary flexibility in the search for meaning. Asking students to construct their own notation systems is an important teaching/learning tool. Research studies in Great Britain and the United States that have been extensive and conforming to high standards indicate achievement of performance goals in dance is facilitated by a knowledge of dance notation—usually Laban, although Benesh and Stepanov have proven to be effective. Children as young as age three have been taught Laban notation.

The research on the relationship of spatial ability in visual arts and temporal-spatial ability in music is based on a symbol system. Spatial ability is not related directly to the ability to draw, nor is temporal-spatial ability related directly to musicality.

In the classroom:

The ability to read and understand what the composer, choreog-rapher, or author intended is crucial for independent growth in performance. The better reader of words—the one who understands sentence structure and possesses a wide vocabulary—is more likely to appropriately interpret a play script; understanding notation in music and dance is similarly helpful. There exists a continuum in precision and meaning of symbol systems from words in literature and poetry to metaphors in visual arts. These symbol systems have levels of difficulty and require instruction and practice.

Slavish adherence to notation/gestures may result in nonexpressive, sterile performance, but without symbols, performance would often become imitative rather than original and creative. For example, videos and CDs are important teaching tools, but they have a major drawback in that they limit artistic thinking and imagination when the student's goal is only to imitate the performance as seen or heard. Symbols are the trigger for improvisation in music and dance, with chord symbols often being the only notation in jazz and improvisational music; dancers have even less specific instructions in the choreographer's score. Use of Laban Movement Analysis, Bartenieff Fundamentals, Gandlin Focusing, and Stanislawski's Actor Training encourages personal risk taking and encourages performers to express deeply felt life experiencess. They provide embellishing and creative experiences in visual arts and theater. A symbol or metaphor, a new meaning to a word or a deeper meaning, is the actor's cue. The richness of the human experience is derived from learned parameters of symbols. Arnheim (1969) speaks of visual thinking in visual art, although this is the most concrete art form because of its lack of a recognized symbol system. Differences in symbolic meaning mark cultural differences.

The purpose of arts education is to offer a key that will unlock the meaning of the metaphors and symbols of which art is made. However, the written symbols that make it possible to remember and reproduce an artistic creation will be learned more easily and more meaningfully if introduced after students have had vivid and successful experiences with the art form.

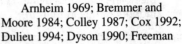

Sources:

Arnheim 1969; Bremmer and Moore 1984; Colley 1987; Cox 1992; Dulieu 1994; Dyson 1990; Freeman 1980; Gaynor 1995; Golomb 1992; Guest 1995; Hodges 1992; Kindler and Darras 1998; Klemish 1970; Kurath 1986; Langan 1995; Lavender and Predock-Linnell 1996; Lee-Chao 1997; Lin-Meng 1999; Marion 1997; Moirs 1996; Moses 1992; Orde 1996; Venable 1998; Willats 1997; Wilson and Wilson 1977.

3.14. Nonverbal Aids to Reading: The use of syllables and nonverbal gestures leads to the ability to read musical notation.

Research findings:

Notation systems of all cultures have marked similarities, and children create notational systems that are recognizable. Literally hundreds of research studies have investigated music reading systems: pitch, rhythm, fixed or moveable "do." The evidence shows syllables and moveable "do" improve one's ability to read music. The teaching of music composition has spawned research on children's invented notation. Researchers believe invented notation is a highway to understanding children's musical thinking. In dance, the Laban notation is helpful in teaching and standardizing a dance. Dance educator Alter (1995) indicates Laban notation has the same result as the use of syllables in music—it gives exact words to indefinite places in space and directions for sequences. For example, Indian dance depends on the use of syllables and rhythms.

Gesture is used in addition to the verbal and nonverbal symbols on the written page to communicate idea and feeling among performers. These gestures convey desired artistic tension that leaders and performers convey to one another and to any audience. Proper use of psychomotor principles provides a unique type of important motor recall in both dancers and musicians and, to a lesser degree, in actors. The importance of interpreting what is written to derive meaning and understanding has led to considerable research and also to a sharing of gestures and symbol systems among the performing arts.

In the classroom:

Reading the symbol system in music and dance is a two-step process: one first learns the meaning of the symbols and then learns how to use the symbols to read with understanding. In music, the first step might be the use of Curwin hand signs, signs that represent the sol-fa syllables. The Kodaly instructional program uses the Curwin hand symbols in a program that emphasizes the importance of music reading, and instruction in Kodaly has recently been related to higher academic scores. For the teacher, student competency in mastering nonverbal aids has no known negative impact on learning. Research and practice indicate the importance of using syllables to read the notation and produce music independently. Becoming facile with notation, whether music or dance, is of course the reason for learning to translate the symbols.

Research and practice indicate performing music with the words or a neutral syllable does not lead to the ability to read music; learning remains at the rote level. The use of syllables is preferred to numbers, note names, and other techniques, because the sounds produced are more musical and the syllable system provides for pitch alterations, such as sharps and flats. Mastering a discipline's notation system facilitates the transfer of learning as well as making one independent of teachers and peers to engage in performance for personal satisfaction. The present attraction to making music and students' organization of "garage bands" are strong motivation to become competent in reading music.

Sources:

Alter 1995; Appelman 1967; Benge 1996; Billingham 2001; Burnard 2002; Choksy 1988; Christy 1974; Colley 1987; Dunn 1995; Finnas 2001; Frego 1999; Fuelberth 2001; Gaynor 1995; Goetze 1985; Hongsermeier 1995; Marion 1997; McLean 1999; Phillips 1992; Starkes, Caicco, Boutilier, and Sevsek 1990; Walker 1990; Yang 1994.

3.15. Focus on the Arts as Separate Disciplines: Focused study of a particular art discipline provides greater achievement in that art than when it is integrated into the study of non-art subjects or when the arts are related to each other. However, other academic subjects can benefit from arts integration.

Research findings:

Research by arts advocates has seldom documented what students are learning in the art form—their emphasis being learning in non-arts objectives. Substantive learning in the arts universally occurs when the art form, itself, is studied and practiced. The performance arts are successful when students have a disposition toward learning, have excellent instruction, and practice both at home and at school. Diket (2001), in reanalyzing the scores of 3,000 students from the 1997 NAEP, found home learning (practice) accounted for 23 percent of the variance and classroom practice, 7 percent. Brewer (2002) found 70 percent of students in his high quartile drew at home, but 50 percent of the low quartile also drew at home. Brown (2001) found students needed high levels of accomplishment in skills before they were able to function artistically and before any learning transfer could occur. This meta-cognition based on accomplishment applied to all of the performing arts. Stinespring (2001) found without good craftsmanship, students suffered a loss of standards of judgment, a loss of attention to effective design, and a replacement of masterworks with merely a visual expression when visual arts were incorporated with social studies.

Thompson (1991) attempted to relate visual arts and science. She found that when art was taught separately, enthusiasm for the course was greater, scores on the Torrance Test of Creativity were higher, and students outperformed the combined class on thinking skills, fantasy projects, and also on basic visual arts skills. Walters (1992) has compiled extensive research upholding this finding in music as well.

Research and practice, however, suggest the arts can reinforce learning in other subjects. For example, LEAP (Learning through an Expanded Art Program) has been used in the classroom for 20 years. Results from this program show art-centered learning experiences can promote reading, writing, and mathematics skills even as students react to and perform art. Other positive by-products are: improved motivation, problem-solving skills, and understanding of subject matter. A related program is RITA (Reading Improvement Through Art), which integrates reading in art classes and art concepts in reading classes. Creative drama improves reading skills, communication skills, and person-perception skills. Other outcomes include improved self-confidence, self-concept, leadership, self-esteem, moral reasoning skills, and assorted other personal characteristics. The potential of the arts means that arts instruction aids learning in most other subjects. A few of the many "connections" are provided in the bibliography.

In the classroom:

The objectives and standards of the arts themselves are not well-served by integrated or interdisciplinary approaches. The arts must be taught and learned as separate disciplines with their own sequence. Arts objectives are unique; transfer of learning is never easy; and many of the national standards in the arts are learned by doing and studying the arts themselves. Students' enthusiasm for the curriculum in a particular art is also increased when the objectives for the course are carefully focused. Educational journals have popularized arts instruction for its contribution to cognitive development as editors have become aware of the importance of the arts in education.

The arts are most valuable, however, for their unique contribution to the human experience. In the classroom, this spurt of research findings indicates primarily there is little danger of overemphasizing the arts in the curriculum.

Teachers in other disciplines should be aware, moreover, that the use of arts examples and even learning about art processes can make non-art curricular subjects not only more interesting but also more real. The arts have always been a major part of life and culture; language arts, science, history, and other subjects cannot be thoroughly taught without using examples from the arts.

Sources:

Bachstrom 1988; Baker 1996; Benes-Lafferty 1995; Boston 1996; Brewer 2002; Brown, K. 2001; Chen 1996; Conn 1993; Crosswhite 1996; Dean and Gross 1992; Diket 2001; Duvall 1995; Ginsburg 1996; Gordon 1998; Hamblen 1992; Kardash and Wright 1987; Lindblade 1995; Lowe 1995; Miller 1995; Rauscher et al. 1997; Schramm 1997; Stephens 1996; Stinespring 2001; Thompson 1991; Trent 1996; Wagner 1988; Walters 1992; Wright 2002.

3.16. Arts and Special Needs Students: Among special education students, production experience in the arts, such as singing, playing, drawing and painting, acting, and dancing, enhances motivation and self-concept and improves attitude toward school.

Research findings:

Longitudinal research indicates the arts are essential in the education of special needs students. Dance, art, theater, and music therapy are separate disciplines created originally to provide services in hospitals and institutions catering to special populations. Use of selected principles from these arts therapy disciplines can help in modifying inappropriate social behaviors, improving attention span, reducing distractibility, improving attitude toward school and learning, and acting as a stimulant and/or sedative depending on the procedure selected. For special education students, these production experiences contribute to improved self-perception and self-confidence that transfer to other school subjects and other experiences. In addition to arts therapy, hospital arts, performing arts medicine, and the arts and neuroscience have important research findings in stress reduction, prevention of muscular problems, and the arts relationship to synapse firings within the brain. Codding (2000) found movement experiences with music aided visually impaired students in moving in a sighted society; Boswell and Mentzer (1995) found movement poetry aided the creative efforts of students with behavioral disorders. Bond's (1992) work in dance resulted in increased ability of students with hearing impairment and dual vision to express themselves.

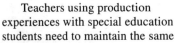

In the classroom:

Teachers using production experiences with special education students need to maintain the same standards but allow for more practice and slower progress; they need to minimize teacher talk and allow students to experiment and discover. Music notation in Braille is available

from the Library of Congress; the National Theatre of the Deaf provides a model for meaningful experiences; and there is a wide choice of activities in visual arts to satisfy students of varied talent and background. Evelyn Glennie, the famous percussion soloist, has convinced the most reluctant teachers of the potential of music for the deaf.

Arts instruction for special learners is equally successful at all age levels and works well in mixed-age and mixed-grade grouping. Students with like interests and like abilities work well together. Success or failure is often related to the specific etiology. Down Syndrome children matched for mental age with non-disabled children can be successful, especially in visual-motor tasks. Golomb (1996) has a lifetime of research on the drawing development and artistry of people with mental disabilities, supported by the research of Ellen Winner (1979). For more than three decades, the National Theatre of the Deaf has stood as testimony to the power of drama for the special needs student. Further, its signature style of visual language and American Sign Language has proved the ability of artistic symbols to communicate deep and profound meanings of the human experience. Podlozny's (2000) meta-analyses of research in theater education documents a heightened understanding and readiness for reading with learning disabled students.

In the area of music, rhythmic tasks must be introduced in their simplest form, with few distracters, until the basic rhythmic tasks are mastered. There is less research in melodic responses with this population, but it appears students grouped for mental age do equally well. Music and dance for the deaf has become a discipline, and deaf students can successfully master the elements.

Students with mental and physical disabilities require the same instructional patterns, with more attention to behavioral management needed for students with mental disabilities. Positive role models, use of pictures, graphs, physical gestures, modeling, and similar aids may need to be exaggerated. Behavior issues are often due to overstimulation and overenthusiasm, and so motivation must be used with care.

Sources:

Allen 1989; Bond 1992, 1994; Boswell and Mentzer 1995; Codding 2000; Crain etal. 1983; Exiner and Kelynack 1994; Fedorenko 1996; Golomb 1996; Goodwin 1985; Kuebhausen 1996; Moon 1994; Nocera 1981; Podlozny 2000; Puretz 1992; Rosene 1976; Standley 1992; Tooker 1995; Vogel 1975; Wilkinson 1993; Winner 1979.

3.17. Understanding of Culture in and through the Arts: The arts are markers of cultures providing the appropriate entrée for understanding one's own culture and cultures of other times and places.

Research findings:

Sculptures, paintings, architecture, literature, dance, and music are the dominant characteristics of Western civilization through which we interpret the essence of earlier civilizations. Greek plays and Greek architecture are the tangible evidence of Greek culture. Chinese opera, the Great Wall, Japanese crafts, paintings, legends, and Indian shrines and music historically studied provide the key to understanding these peoples, their beliefs, and what they prized. With several thousand years of history and multiple cultures, researchers in the arts have demonstrated how the use of theater, dance, visual arts, and music can facilitate instruction and understanding in any subject and in any culture.

Both Congdon (1989) and Anderson (1998) demonstrated the use of multicultural approaches to arts criticism; Hamblen (1990) did the same in aesthetics. Aubuchon (1995) experimented with the affective response of secondary band students to nonwestern music, while Campbell's (1991) research has improved our understanding of young children. Dunkin (1998) applied multicultural dance to play. Floyd (1997) used multicultural art to improve the self-concept of African American students, while Silveira (1995) had similar success with Hispanic American students.

Lowe (1995, 2002) found connections are made through knowledge of fables, art forms, styles, and melodies, while Radford (2001) identified objectives related to understanding the mystery and meaning of human life to require knowledge of religion and aesthetics. To improve an understanding of culture, Erickson (1998) experimented with improving students' ability to interpret artwork contextually. First, students were required to demonstrate some knowledge of what happened when an artwork was produced, and then the students were challenged to interpret a work of a different culture at the same or different time and then respond, "It would help if I knew…." Explicit comparisons were found to be an important transfer strategy in the arts. Pinker's (2002) extensive research indicates the stability of memes acquired from one's culture facilitate that which is to be learned; this finding argues for increased attention to the valued aspects of one's culture.

In the classroom:

Inadequate education in the arts of so many classroom teachers creates a void in their teaching and an inability to discuss and understand the cultures of the world, including the native cultures of some of the students in their classes. Arts teachers have temporarily set aside their own sequential instruction to demonstrate the importance of cross-cultural knowledge throughout the curriculum. The study of unfamiliar cultures and customs adds interest to the classroom and is also a useful motivation. International language experts suggest knowing the language of a culture is important to understanding that culture. Inspecting a painting, listening to music, or observing a dance are only introductory, and may produce only superficial or erroneous learning.

The classroom teacher may not have sufficient time for an intensive approach, but it may be possible to study aspects of one's own culture—music, art, dance, and theater—and relate these to other academic subjects. A second culture cannot be understood without a firm understanding of one's own culture, including its history and development. With this accomplished, it is then possible to add an additional culture and study it sufficiently for understanding to occur and relationships among cultures to be perceived. Students prefer familiarity in all subjects, including the arts, and a sampling of many cultures is usually unprofitable. Student preference is anchored in their own culture and the culture of the dominant peer group; these are more persuasive than the culture of their parents.

Sources:

Alvarez 1995; Anderson 1998; Aubuchon 1995; Bramwell 1990; Bridges 1996; Campbell 1991, 1998; Chalmers 1992, 1996; Congdon 1989; Davis 1994; Dunkin 1998; Erickson 1998; Floyd 1997; Fung 1996; Ginsburg 1996; Gleason 1995; Hamblen 1990; Lowe 1995, 2002; Makin, White, and Owen 1996; Pinker 2002; Planchat 1994; Radford 2001; Silveira 1995; Stuhr, Petrovich-Mwaniki, and Wasson 1992; Wagner 1998.

Bibliography

Adar, I. 1995. *Differences Among Measurements of Vital Lung Capacity and Forced Expiration Volume in Performers of Western Classical Wind Instruments.* Unpublished doctoral dissertation. University of Missouri, Columbia.

Allen, B.J. 1989. *The Effect of Dance/Movement on the Self-Concept of Developmentally Handicapped Fourth and Fifth Grade Students.* Unpublished doctoral dissertation. Ohio State University, Columbus.

Allison, B. 1986. *Index of British Studies in Art and Design Education.* Aldershot: Gower Publishing Group.

Alter, J. 1995. Personal correspondence based on results of pilot testing of National Assessment measures.

Alvarez, A. 1995. *Effects of an Augmented Art Curriculum on the Attitudes of High School Art Students Toward Diversity in Art.* Unpublished doctoral dissertation. Florida International University, Miami.

Amuah, I. 1994. *Memory for Music and Its Relationships to Aspects of Musical Behavior and Environmental and Personal Factors.* Unpublished doctoral dissertation. Northwestern University, Evanston.

Anderson, T. 1998. "Toward a Cross Cultural Approach to Arts Criticism." *Studies in Art Education* Vol. 36, No. 4: 198-209.

Appelman, R.D. 1967. *The Science of Vocal Pedagogy: Theory and Application.* Bloomington, IN: Indiana University Press.

Armstrong, C. 1986. "Stages of Inquiry in Art: Model, Rationale, and Application to a Teacher Questioning Strategy." *Studies in Art Education* Vol. 28, No. 1: 37-48.

Armstrong, C. 1993. "Effect of Training in an Art Production Questioning Method on Teacher Questioning and Student Responses." *Studies in Art Education* Vol. 34, No. 4: 209-221.

Arnheim, R. 1969. *Visual Thinking.* Berkeley, CA: University of California Press.

Aubuchon, S. 1995. *Information Dependent Affective Response of Secondary Instrumental Music Students to Excerpts of Unfamiliar Music from Nonwestern Cultures.* Unpublished doctoral dissertation, University of Montana, Missoula.

Austin, J., and W. Vispoel. 1998. "How American Adolescents Interpret Success and Failure in Classroom Music: Relationships Among Attributional Beliefs, Self Concept and Achievement." *Psychology of Music* Vol. 26: 26-45.

Bachstrom, E. 1988. *The Effects of Creative Dramatics on Student Behaviors and Attitudes in Literature and Language Arts.* Unpublished doctoral dissertation. University of California, Los Angeles.

Baik, Y. 1999. *Art Activities for Developing the Preadolescent's, Understanding for Self and Others through Art-making and Reflection.* Unpublished doctoral dissertation. New York University, New York.

Baker, T. 1996. *Integritas: Modern Relationship between Music and Architecture.* Unpublished doctoral dissertation. University of Washington, Seattle.

Bamberger, J. 1991. *The Mind Behind the Musical Ear.* Cambridge, MA: Harvard University Press.

Barrett, T., and S. Rab. 1990. "Twelve High School Students, a Teacher, a Professor, and Robert Mapplethorpe's Photographs: Exploring Cultural Difference through Controversial Art." *Journal of Multicultural and Cross-Cultural Research in Art Education* Vol. 8, No. 1: 4-17.

Barufaldi, J. 1992. *Creative Drama and the Enhancement of Elementary School Students' Understanding of Science Concepts.* Unpublished doctoral dissertation. University of Texas, Austin.

Batson, G. 1989. "Stretching Technique: A Somatic Learning Model." *Impulse* Vol. 1, No. 2: 126-140.

Baxter, S., and S. Stauffer. 1988. "Music Teaching: A Review of Common Practice." In *The Crane Symposium: Toward an Understanding of the Teaching and Learning of Music Performance*, C. Fowler, editor. Potsdam, NY: State University of New York.

Benes-Lafferty, K. 1995. *An Analysis of Using Musical Activities in a Second Grade Mathematics Class.* Unpublished doctoral dissertation. Indiana University of Pennsylvania, Indiana.

Benge, T. 1996. *Movements Utilizing Conductors in the Stimulation of Expression and Musicianship.* Unpublished doctoral dissertation. University of Southern California, Los Angeles.

Bennett, O. 1982. *An Investigation into the Effects of a Creative Experience in Drama on the Creativity, Self Concept and Achievement of Fifth and Sixth Grade Students.* Unpublished doctoral dissertation. Georgia State University, Atlanta.

Bennett, S. 1994. *Can Simple Vocalization Help Improve the Intonation of Wind Players?* Unpublished doctoral dissertation. Arizona State University, Tempe.

Beston, L. 1995. *Integration of the Expressive Arts and Academic Curricula: Creating a Climate for Student Success.* Unpublished doctoral dissertation. The Union Institute, New York City.

Billingham, L. 2001. *The Development of Gestural Vocabulary for Choral Conductors Based on the Movement Theory of Rudolf Laban.* Unpublished doctoral dissertation. University of Arizona, Tucson.

Bitz, M. 1998. *A Description and Investigation of Strategies for Teaching Classroom Music Improvisation.*

Unpublished doctoral dissertation. Teachers College of Columbia University, New York.

Blaker, S. 1995. *A Survey of Suzuki Violin Programs in Community Music Schools in the United States.* Unpublished doctoral dissertation. Ohio State University, Columbus.

Bloom, B. 1985. *Developing Talent in Young People.* New York: Ballantine.

Bonbright, J. 1989. "The Nutritional Status of Female Ballet Dancers 15-18 Years of Age." *Dance Research Journal* Vol. 21, No. 2: 9-14.

Bond, K. 1992. *Dance for Children with Dual Sensory Impairments.* Unpublished doctoral dissertation. LaTrobe University, Australia.

Bond, K. 1994. "Personal Style as a Mediator of Engagement in Dance: Watching Terpsichore Rise." *Dance Research Journal* Vol. 26, No. 1: 15-26.

Bonifeti, L. 1997. *The Impact of the Home Environment on Scores in Instrumental Music.* Unpublished doctoral dissertation. Teachers College, New York City.

Bosh, A., and J. Hinch. 1999. "The Application of the Alexander Technique to Flute Teaching: Two Case Studies." *British Journal of Music Education* Vol. 16, No. 3: 245-251.

Boston, B. 1996. *Connections: The Arts and the Integration of the High School Curriculum.* New York: College Board.

Boswell, B., and M. Mentzer. 1995. "Effects of a Movement Poetry Program on Creativity of Children with Behavioral Disorders." *Impulse* Vol. 3: 183-190.

Bradford, P. 1995. *The Aural/Oral Difficulty Levels of Selected Rhythm Patterns Among Kindergarten Children.* Unpublished doctoral dissertation. University of Oklahoma, Norman.

Bramwell, R. 1990. *The Effect of Drama Education on Children's Attitudes to the Elderly and to Aging.* Unpublished doctoral dissertation. University of British Columbia, Vancouver.

Brand, M. 2000. "Music Teachers' Role in Preparing Students for Live Symphonic Experiences." *Research Studies in Music Education* Vol. 15: 24-30.

Bremmer, J., and S. Moore. 1984. "Prior Visual Inspection and Object Naming: Two Factors that Enhance Hidden Feature Inclusion in Young Children's Drawings." *British Journal of Developmental Psychology* Vol. 2: 371-376.

Brewer, T. 1998. "The Relationship of Art Instruction, Grade Level, and Gender on 3rd and 7th Grade Student Drawings." *Studies in Art Education* Vol. 39, No. 2: 132-146.

Brewer, T. 2002. An Examination of Intrinsic and Instrumental Instruction in Art Education." *Studies in Art Education* Vol. 43, No. 4: 354-372.

Brewer, T.M., and C.B. Colbert. 1992. "The Effect of Contrasting Instructional Strategies on Seventh-Grade Students' Ceramic Vessels." *Studies in Art Education* Vol. 34, No. 12: 18-27.

Bridges, B. 1996. *Eighth Grade Students' Reflections on the Relationship between Art, Culture, and Self.* Unpublished doctoral dissertation. University of Minnesota, Minneapolis.

Brown, K. 2001. *Effects of Fixed and Moveable Sight-Singing Systems on Undergraduate Music Student's Ability to Perform Diatonic, Modulatory, Chromatic, and Atonal Melodic Passages.* Unpublished doctoral dissertation. University of Oregon, Eugene.

Brown, N. 2001. "The Meaning of Transfer in the Practices of Arts Education." *Studies in Art Education* Vol. 43, No. 1: 83-102.

Brunelle, J., and F. de Carufel. 1982. "Analyse des Feedback Emis par des Mitres de l'Enseignement de la Danse Moderne." *Revue Quebecois de l'Activite Physique* Vol. 2, No. 1: 3-9.

Burke, J. 1980. *The Effect of Creative Dramatics on the Attitudes and Reading Ability of Seventh Grade Students.* Unpublished doctoral dissertation. University of Michigan, Ann Arbor.

Burnard, P. 2002. "Investigating Children's Meaning-making and the Emergence of Musical Interaction in Group Improvisation." *British Journal of Music Education* Vol. 19, No. 2: 157-172.

Burton, D. 2001. "A Quartile Analysis of the 1997 NAEP Visual Arts Report Card." *Studies in Art Education* Vol. 43, No. 1: 35-44.

Burton, J., R. Horowitz, and H. Abeles. 2000. "Learning in and thru the Arts: The Question of Transfer." *Studies in Art Education* Vol. 41, No. 3: 228-257.

Butler, J. 1995. *A Process for Effective Graphic Design Curriculum Development.* Unpublished doctoral dissertation. University of Wisconsin, Madison.

Butzlaff, R. 2000. "Can Music be Used to Teach Reading?" *Journal of Aesthetic Education* Vol. 34, No. 3-4: 164-178.

Cahan, S., and Z. Kocur, (Eds.) 1996. *Contemporary Art and Multicultural Education.* New York: The New Museum of Contemporary Art.

Campbell, P. 1991. *Lessons from the World: A Cross Cultural Guide to Music Teaching and Learning.* New York: Schirmer Books.

Campbell, P. 1998. *Songs in Their Heads: Music and its Meaning in Children's Lives.* New York: Oxford University Press.

Cardinal, M., and S. Hilsendager. 1995. "Incorporating Dance Wellness Related Components into Higher Education Programs." *Impulse* Vol. 3, No. 4: 238-248.

Carpenter, B. 1996. *A Meta-critical Analysis of Ceramics Criticism for Art Education: Towards an Interpretive Methodology.* Unpublished doctoral dissertation. Pennsylvania State University, College Park.

Carsillo, P. 1996. *A Study of Learning Style Grouping in an Art Studio Classroom: Observation, Implications, and Suggestions.* Unpublished doctoral dissertation. University of Georgia, Athens.

Catterall, J., R. Chapleau, and J. Iwanaga. 1999. "Involvement in the Arts and Human Development: General Involvement and Intensive Involvement in Music and Theater Arts." In *Champions of Change: The Impact of the Arts on Learning*, E. Fiske, editor. Washington: Arts Education Partnership and the President's Committee on the Arts and Humanities.

Cecconi-Roberts, L. 2001. *Effect of Practice Strategies on Improvements of Performance of Intermediate Woodwind Students*. Unpublished doctoral dissertation. University of Missouri, Columbia.

Chaffin, R., and G. Imreh. 2001. "A Comparison of Practice and Self Report as Sources of Information About the Goals of Expert Practice." *Psychology of Music* Vol. 29: 39-69.

Chalmers, F. G. 1992. "DBAE as Multicultural Education." *Art Education* Vol. 45, No. 3: 16-24.

Chalmers, F.G. 1996. *Celebrating Pluralism: Art, Education, and Cultural Diversity*. Occasional Paper 5. Los Angeles: The Getty Education Institute for the Arts.

Chan, A.S., Y.C. Ho, and M.C. Cheung. 1998. "Music Training Improves Verbal Memory." *Nature* Vol. 396: 128.

Chappell, S. 1999. "Developing the Complete Pianist: A Study of the Importance of Whole Brain Approach to Piano Teaching." *British Journal of Music Education* Vol. 16, No. 3: 253-262.

Chedester, G. 1984. *An Art Critical Strategy toward the Enhancement of Reading Comprehension among Selected High School Students*. Unpublished doctoral dissertation. University of Georgia, Athens.

Chen, C. 1996. *Conceptions of Art of Young Children and Adolescents: A Developmental Study*. Unpublished doctoral dissertation. University of Illinois, Urbana.

Chetelat, F. 1981. "Visual Arts Education for the Gifted Elementary Level Art Student." *Gifted Child Quarterly* Vol. 225, No. 4: 154-158.

Choksy, L. 1988. *The Kodaly Method. Second Edition*. Englewood Cliffs, NJ: Prentice Hall.

Christy, V.A. 1974. *Foundations in Singing*. Dubuque, IA: William C. Brown.

Clark, G., and E. Zimmerman. 1984. *Educating Artistically Talented Students*. Syracuse, NY: Syracuse University Press.

Codding, R. 2000. Music Therapy Literature and Clinical Application for Blind and Severely Visually Impaired Persons: 1940-2000. In *Effectiveness of Music Therapy Procedures: Documentation of Research and Clinical Practice* (third edition), C.E. Furman, editor. Silver Spring, MD: American Music Therapy Association, Inc.

Coffman, D.D. 1987. *The Effects of Mental Practice, Physical Practice, and Aural Knowledge of Results on Improving Piano Performance*. Unpublished doctoral dissertation. University of Kansas, Lawrence.

College Board, The. 1988-1998. College Bound Seniors Profile of SAT and Achievement Test Takers. New York: The College Board.

Colley, B. 1987. "A Comparison of Syllabic Methods for Improving Rhythm Literacy." *Journal of Research in Music Education* Vol. 35, No. 4: 221-235.

Colprit, E. 2000. "Observation and Analysis of Suzuki String Teaching." *Journal of Research in Music Education* Vol. 48, No. 3: 206-221.

Conard, F. 1992. *The Arts in Education and a Meta-Analysis (Creative Dramatics)*. Unpublished doctoral dissertation. Purdue University, Purdue.

Conard, F., and J.W. Asher. 2000. "Self Concept and Self-esteem through Drama: A Meta-Analysis." *Youth Theate Journal* Vol. 14: 78-83.

Congdon, K.G. 1989. "Multicultural Approaches to Art Criticism." *Studies in Art Education* Vol. 30, No. 3: 176-184.

Conn, A. 1993. *Arts Integration and Curricular Change: A Case Study of Five First and Second Grades*. Unpublished doctoral dissertation. University of Missouri, Columbia.

Connor, L. 1974. *An Investigation of the Effects of Selected Educational Dramatics Techniques on General Cognitive Abilities*. Unpublished doctoral dissertation. Southern Illinois University, Carbondale.

Cooper, J.L. 1983. *A Study of the Effects of Pre-Performance Materials on the Child's Ability to Respond to Theatrical Performance*. Unpublished doctoral dissertation. University of Georgia, Athens.

Cox, M.V. 1992. *Children's Drawings*. London: Penguin Books.

Crain, C. et al. 1983. "The Social and Physical Effects of a Ten Week Drama Program on Educable Mentally Retarded Adolescents." In *Education and Training of the Mentally Retarded*. Pp. 301-312. Washington, DC: American Association for Health, Physical Education, and Recreation.

Croom, P. 1998. *Effects of Locomotor Rhythm Training Activities on the Ability of Kindergarten Students to Synchronize Nonlocomotor Movements to Music*. Unpublished doctoral dissertation. Temple University, Philadelphia.

Crosswhite, J. 1996. *Effect of Music Instruction on Language Development of Preschool Children*. Unpublished doctoral dissertation. University of North Carolina, Greensboro.

Cummings, J. 1995. *An Analysis of Secondary Students' Untutored Art Critical Interpretations*. Unpublished doctoral dissertation. University of Georgia, Athens.

Cziko, G. 1988. "Implicit and Explicit Learning: Implications for and Applications to Music Teaching." In *The Crane Symposium: Toward an Understanding of the Teaching and Learning of Music Performance*, C. Fowler, editor (Chapter 7). Potsdam, NY: State University of New York.

Dallett, A. 1996. *Theater as Government*. Unpublished doctoral dissertation. Harvard University, Cambridge.

Davis, M.H. 1994. *Five Wind Band Works of Hale Smith and Their Implications for A Multicultural Curriculum*. Unpublished doctoral dissertation. Washington University, St Louis.

Davis R., and M. Pulman. 2001. "Raising Standards in Performance." *British Journal of Music Education* Vol. 18, No. 3: 251-259

Dean J., and I. Gross. 1992. "Teaching Basic Skills through Art and Music." *Phi Kelta Kappan* Vol. 73, No. 8: 613-616.

Deasy, R. (Ed.) 2002. *Critical Links: Learning in the Arts and Studen Academic and Social Development.* Washington: Arts Education Partnership.

Delacruz, E. 1997. *Instruction: Design for Inquiry.* Reston, VA: National Art Education Association.

Delzell, J. 1989. "The Effects of Musical Discrimination Training in Beginning Instrumental Music Classes." *Journal of Research in Music Education* Vol. 37, No. 1: 21-31.

Demmond, J. 1997. *The Use of Role Playing Improvisation and Performance in the Teaching of Literature.* Unpublished doctoral dissertation. Georgia State University, Atlanta.

Denis, F. 1995. *Aesthetic Perception Metacognition and Transfer: Thinking in the Visual Arts.* Unpublished doctoral dissertation. University of California, Los Angeles.

Dennis, A. 1984. "The Effect of Three Methods of Supporting the Double Bass on Muscle Tension." *Journal of Research in Music Education* Vol. 32, No. 1: 95-103.

De Spain, K. 1997. *Solo Movement Improvisation: Constructing Understanding through Lived Somatic Experience.* Unpublished doctoral dissertation. Temple University, Philadelphia.

Diket, R.M. 1991. *Art Criticisms: Relationships to Critical Thinking, Appreciation, and Creativity among the Gifted.* Unpublished doctoral dissertation. University of Georgia, Athens.

Diket, R.M. 2001. "A Factor Analytic Model of 8th Grade Learning: Secondary Analysis of NAEP Arts Data." *Studies in Art Education* Vol. 43, No. 1: 5-17.

Duke, R. 1999. "Teacher and Student Behavior in Suzuki String Lessons: Results from the International Symposium on Talent Education." *Journal of Research in Music Education* Vol. 47, No. 4: 293-307.

Dulieu, J. 1994. *Language of Dance for All.* London: The Language of Dance Centre.

Dunkin, A. 1998. *Making Time and Space Together: An Interpretation of Young People's Dancing as Cultural Play.* Unpublished doctoral dissertation. University of California, Riverside.

Dunn, D. 1995. *The Effect of Structured Task Presentations and Reinforcement on Attention, Achievement, and Attitude of Selected High School Choirs.* Unpublished doctoral dissertation. Louisiana State University, Baton Rouge.

Dupont, S. 1989. *The Effectiveness of Creative Drama as an Instructional Strategy to Enhance the Reading Comprehension Skills of Fifth Grade Remedial Readers.* Unpublished doctoral dissertation. Pennsylvania State University, College Park.

Duvall, S. 1995. *The Effects of a Related Studio Art Activity upon Art History, Learning and Retention in Secondary Schools.* Unpublished doctoral dissertation. University of Mississippi, University.

Dweck, C. 1999. *Self-Theories: Their Role in Motivation, Personality, and Development.* Philadelphia: Taylor and Francis.

Dyson, A.H. 1990. "Research in Review: Symbol Makers, Symbol Weavers: How Children Link Play, Pictures, and Print." *Young Children* Vol. 45, No. 2: 50-57.

Eccles, J., and B. Barber. 1999. "Student Council, Volunteering, Basketball, or Marching Band: What Kind of Extracurricular Involvement Matters?" *Journal of Adolescent Research* Vol. 14, No. 1: 10-43.

Education Committee of the International Association for Dance Medicine and Science. 2001. "The Challenge of the Adolescent Dancer." *Journal of Dance Education* Vol. 1, No. 2: 74-76.

Efland, A. 1990. "An Approach to the Assessment of Art Learning." *Arts and Learning Research* (The Journal of the Arts and Learning Special Interest Group, AERA) Vol. 8, No. 1: 50-65.

Erickson, M. 1998. "Effects of Art History Instruction on Fourth and Eighth Grade Students' Abilities to Interpret Artworks Contextually." *Studies in Art Education* Vol. 39, No. 4: 309-320.

Evans, T. 1988. "In Art Education, More DBAE Equals Less Art." *Design for Arts in Education*, Vol. 89: 35-42.

Exiner, J., and D. Kelynack. 1994. *Dance Therapy Redefined: A Body Approach to Therapeutic Dance.* Springfield, IL: C.C. Thomas.

Fast, L. 2000. "Investigating the Use of Children's Art Work as an Observation Tool in Early Reading Programs." *Visual Arts Research* Vol. 51: 1-12.

Fedorenko, J. 1996. *Integrating Arts in the Special Education Curriculum through University and Community School Collaboration: Implications for Teacher Preparation.* Unpublished doctoral dissertation. Ohio State University, Columbus.

Feinstein, H. 1984. "The Metaphoric Interpretation of Paintings: Effects of the Clustering Strategy and Relaxed Attention Exercises." *Studies in Art Education* Vol. 25, No. 2: 77-83.

Feldman, E.B. 1983. "Objectives and Images, Museums and Schools: Using Them to Teach." *Journal of Aesthetic Education* Vol. 17, No. 3 (Fall 1983): 39-52.

Finnas, L. 2001. "Presenting Music Live, Audio-visually, or Aurally: Does It Affect Listeners' Experiences Differently?" *British Journal of Music Education* Vol. 18, No. 1: 55-78.

Fisher, C. 1989. *Effects of a Developmental Drama-Inquiry Process on Creative and Critical Thinking Skills in Early Adolescent Students.* Unpublished doctoral dissertation. Kansas State University, Manhattan.

Fiske, H. 1993. *Music Cognition and Aesthetic Attitudes.* Lewiston, NY: Edwin Mellen Press.

Fitt, S., J. Sturman, and S. McClain-Smith. 1993. "Effects of Pilates-based Conditioning on Strength, Alignment, and Range of Motion in University Ballet and Modern Dance Majors." *Kinesiology and Medicine for Dance* Vol. 16, No. 1: 36-51.

Fitterling, J., and T. Ayllon. 1983. "Behavioral Coaching in Classical Ballet: Enhancing Skill Development." *Behavior Modification* Vol. 7, No. 3: 345-368.

Floyd, M. 1997. *The Enhancement of Self Concept in African American Students Through Discipline Based Multicultural Art Curricula.* Unpublished doctoral dissertation. Florida State University, Tallahassee.

Fortin, S. 1986. *Characteristics of Efficient and Inefficient Feedback as Perceived by Experienced Students and Teachers in Modern Dance.* Heidelberg: AISEP World Convention Abstracts.

Fraleigh, S., and P. Hanstein. (Eds.) 1999. *Researching Dance.* London: Dance Books.

Francisco, J. 1994. *Conductor Communication in the Ensemble Rehearsal: The Relative Effects of Verbal Communication, Visual Communication, and Modeling on Performance Improvement of High School Bands.* Unpublished doctoral dissertation. Indiana University, Bloomington.

Freeman, N.L. 1980. *Strategies of Representation in Young Children.* London: Academic Press.

Frego, R.J. 1999. "Effects of Aural and Visual Conditions on Response to Perceived Artistic Tension in Music and Dance." *Journal of Research in Music Education* Vol. 47, No. 1: 165-176.

Fuelberth, R. 2001. *The Effect of Conductor Gesture on Inappropriate Vocal Tension in Individual Singers.* Unpublished doctoral dissertation. University of Missouri at Kansas City.

Fung, V.C. 1996. "Musicians' and Nonmusicians' Preference for World Musics: Relation to Musical Characteristics and Familiarity." *Journal of Research in Music Education* Vol. 44, No. 1: 60-83.

Gackle, M.L. 1987. *The Effect of Selected Vocal Techniques for Breath Management, Resonation, and Vowel Unification Tone Production in the Junior High School Female Voice.* Unpublished doctoral dissertation. University of Miami, Coral Gables.

Gallagher, K. 2000. "Interrupting 'Truths,' Engaging Perspectives, and Enlarging the Concept of 'Human' in Classroom Drama." *Youth Theater Journal* Vol. 14: 13-25.

Gates, A., and J.L. Bradshaw. 1994. "Effects of Auditory Feedback to a Musical Performing Task." *Perception and PsychoPhysics* Vol. 16: 105-109.

Gaynor, J. 1995. *Music Reading Comprehension: The Effect of Aid on Chunking and Melodic Prediction on Sight Reading Performance Achievement of Secondary School Instrumental Music Students.* Unpublished doctoral dissertation. University of San Francisco, San Francisco.

Geahigan, G. 1998. "From Procedures to Principles and Beyond: Implementing Critical Inquiry in the Classroom." *Studies in Art Education* Vol. 39, No. 4: 293-308.

Gilbert, A.G. 1994. "Teaching the Three R's Through Dance. *Think! The Magazine on Critical and Creative Thinking* (December 1994): 33-38.

Ginsburg, A. 1996. *Envisioning Dance as a Humanity: An Analysis of Undergraduate Courses Focused on Dance as a Cultural and Aesthetic Phenomenon for the Liberal Arts College Student.* Unpublished doctoral dissertation. Temple University, Philadelphia.

Gleason, B. 1995. *The Effects of Beginning Band Instruction Using a Comprehensive, Multicultural, Interdisciplinary Method on the Knowledge, Skills, Attitudes, and Retention of Sixth-grade Students.* Unpublished doctoral dissertation. University of Iowa, Iowa City.

Goetze, M. 1985. *Factors Affecting Accuracy in Children's Singing.* Unpublished doctoral dissertation. University of Colorado, Boulder.

Golomb, C. 1992. *The Child's Creation of a Pictorial World.* Berkeley, CA: University of California Press.

Golomb, C. 1996. "Drawing Development and Artistry in Mentally Handicapped Persons." *Visual Arts Research* Vol. 22, No. 2: 90-95.

Gonzalez, R. 1996. *The Internal Processes in Memorizing, Making Expressive Decisions, and Beginning a Performance at the Piano.* Unpublished doctoral dissertation. University of Texas, Austin.

Goodwin, D.A. 1985. "An Investigation of the Efficacy of Creative Drama as a Method for Teaching Social Skills to Mentally Retarded Youth and Adults." *Youth Theater Journal* Vol. 34, No. 2: 23-26.

Gordon, E.E. 1997. *Learning Sequences in Music.* Chicago: GIA.

Gordon, E.E. 1998. *Introduction to Research and the Psychology of Music.* Chicago: GIA.

Green. G.A. 1987. *The Effect of Vocal Modeling on Pitch Matching Accuracy of Children in Grades One through Six.* Unpublished doctoral dissertation. Louisiana State University, Baton Rouge.

Grey, J. 1983. "The Science of Teaching the Art of Dance: A Description of a Computer-aided System for Recording and Analyzing Dance Instructional Behaviors." *Journal of Education for Teaching* Vol. 9, No. 3: 264-279.

Guest, A. 1995. *Your Move: A New Approach to the Study of Movement and Dance.* New York: Gordon and Brach.

Haanstra, F. 1994. *Effects of Art Education on Visual-spatial Ability and Aesthetic Perception: Two Meta Analyses.* Amsterdam, The Netherlands: Thesis Publishers.

Haanstra, F. 1996. "Effects of Art Education on Visual-Spatial Ability and Aesthetic Perception: A Quantitative Review." *Studies in Art Education* Vol. 37, No. 4: 197-209.

Hallam, S. 2001. "The Development of Metacognition in Musicians: Implications for Education." *British Journal of Music Education* Vol. 18, No. 1: 27-39.

Hamblen, K.A. 1984. "An Art Criticism Questioning Strategy Within the Framework of Bloom's Taxonomy." *Studies in Art Education* Vol. 26, No. 1: 41-50.

Hamblen, K.A. 1990. "Beyond the Aesthetic of Cash-CulturalLiteracy." *Studies in Art Education* Vol. 31, No. 4: 216-223.

Hamblen, K.A. 1992. "Performing and Visual Arts Programs that Promote Literacy: Visual Arts." Washington, DC: U.S. Department of Education. Unpublished manuscript, Chapter 5.

Hanrahan, C. 1994. "Creating Dance Images: Basic Principles for Teachers." *Journal of Physical Education, Recreation and Dance* Vol. 62, No. 2: 36-39, 48.

Hargreaves, D., and A. North. (Eds.) 1997. *The Social Psychology of Music*. New York: Oxford University Press.

Harris, D. 2002. "A Report on the Situation Regarding Teaching Music to Muslims in an Inner-City School." *British Journal of Music Education* Vol. 19, No. 1: 49-60.

Heathcote, D., and G. Bolton. 1995. *Drama for Learning*. Portsmouth, NH: Heinemann.

Henley, P. 2001. "Effects of Modeling and Tempo Patterns as Practice Techniques on the Performance of High School Instrumentalists." *Journal of Research in Music Education* Vol. 49, No. 1: 21-32.

Hetland, L. 2000. "Learning to Make Music Enhances Spatial Reasoning." *Journal of Aesthetic Education* Vol. 34, No. 3-4: 179-238.

Hewitt, M. 2000. The Effects of Self Evaluation, Self Listening, and Modeling on Junior High School Instrumental Music Performance and Practice Attitude. *Journal of Research in Music Education* Vol. 49, No. 3: 307-322.

Hodges, D. 1992. "The Acquisition of Music Reading Skills." In *The Handbook of Research on Music Teaching and Learning*, R.J. Colwell, editor (Chapter 30). New York: Schirmer Books.

Hoffer, C., and D.K. Anderson. 1970, 1971. *Performing Music with Understanding*. Belmont, CA: Wadsworth Publishing Co.

Hoffman, D. 2002. *Auditory Imagery of Conductors: An Examination of the Electroencephalographic Correlates of Score Reading Before and After Score Study*. Unpublished doctoral dissertation. University of Minnesota, Minneapolis.

Holm, C. 1997. *Correction to Breathing Hindrances in Flute Performance with Emphasis on the Alexander Technique*. Unpublished doctoral dissertation. Southern Baptist Seminary, Louisville.

Hongsermeier, J. 1995. *Kodaly-inspired Musicianship Training and the Beginning Piano Student: Integrating Musical and Technical Skill Development*. Unpub-

lished doctoral dissertation. Catholic University of America, Washington.

Hurwitz, A. 1983. *The Gifted and Talented in Art: A Guide to Program Planning*. Worcester, MA: Davis Publications.

Jackson, J. 1993. *The Effects of Creative Dramatics Participation on the Reading Achievement and Attitudes in Elementary Level Children with Behavioral Disorders*. Unpublished doctoral dissertation. Southern Illinois University, Carbondale.

Jorgensen, H. 2001. "Instrumental Learning: Is an Early Start a Key to Success?" *British Journal of Music Education* Vol. 18, No. 3: 227-239.

Jorgensen, H., and A. Lehmann. (Eds.) 1997. *Does Practice Make Perfect? Current Theory and Research on Instrumental Music Practice*. Oslo: Norges Musikkhogskole.

Kalliopuska, M. 1989. "Empathy, Self Esteem, and Creativity Among Junior Ballet Dancers." *Perceptual and Motor Skills* Vol. 69: 1227-1234.

Kannegeiter, R.B. 1971. "The Effects of a Learning Program in Activity upon the Visual Perception of Shape." *Studies in Art Education* Vol. 12, No. 2: 18-27.

Kardash, C.A., and L. Wright. 1987. "Does Creative Drama Benefit Elementary School Students? A Meta Analysis." *Youth Theater Journal* Vol. 1, No. 3: 11-18.

Kassing, G., and L. Mortensen. 1981-82. "Critiquing Student Performance in Dance." *Dance Research Journal*. Vol. 14, No. 1-2: 36-43.

Kellett, M. 2000. "Raising Musical Esteem in the Elementary Classroom: An Exploratory Study of Young Children's Listening Skills." *British Journal of Music Education* Vol. 17, No. 2: 157-181.

Kellman, J. 1998. "Ice Age Art, Autism, and Vision: How We See/How We Draw." *Studies in Art Education* Vol. 39, No. 2: 117-131.

Kendall, J. 1966. *Talent Education and Suzuki*. Reston, VA: Music Educators National Conference.

Kerchner, J. 1996. *Perceptual and Affective Components of the Music Listening Experience as Manifested by Children's Verbal, Visual, and Kinesthetic Representations*. Unpublished doctoral dissertation. Northwestern University, Evanston.

Kimmarle, M. 2001. "Lateral Bias in Dance Teaching." *The Journal of Physical Education, Recreation, and Dance* Vol. 72, No. 5: 34-47.

Kindler, A. 1998. "Artistic Development and Art Education, Translations from Theory to Practice." *Studies in Art Education* Vol. 7, No. 2.

Kindler, A. 2000. "From the U Curve to Dragons: Culture and Understanding of Artistic Development." *Visual Arts Research* Vol. 52: 15-28.

Kindler, A., and B. Darras. 1998. "Culture and Development of Pictorial Repertoires." *Studies in Art Education* Vol. 39, No. 2: 147-167.

Klemish, J.J. 1970. "A Comparative Study of Two Methods of Teaching Music Reading to First Grade

Children." *Journal of Research in Music Education* Vol. 18: 355-364.

Koopman, C. 2002. Broadly Based Piano Education for Children Aged 5-7." *British Journal of Music Education* Vol. 19, No. 3: 269-284.

Koroscik. J.S. 1982. "The Effects of Prior Knowledge, Presentation Time, and Task Demands on Visual Art Processing." *Studies in Art Education* Vol. 23, No. 3: 13-22.

Kototski, D., J. Davidson, and D. Coimbra. 2001. "Investigating the Assessment of Singers in a Music College Setting: The Student's Perspective." *Research Studies in Music Education* Vol. 16: 15-32.

Kowalchuk, E. 1996. "Translations from Theory to Practice." *Studies in Art Education* Vol. 6, No. 1.

Kozan, A. 1995. *Perceptual Judgments of the Effects of Vocal Warm-up on the Singing Voice*. Unpublished doctoral dissertation. University of Minnesota, Minneapolis.

Krasnow, D., S. Chatfield, S. Barr, J. Jensen, and J. Defek. 1977. "Imagery and Conditioning Practices for Dancers." *Dance Research Journal* Vol. 29, No. 1: 43-63.

Kuebhausen, D. 1996. *Art Made Accessible: Redefining Accessibility and Cross Cultural Communication for the Deaf and Hard of Hearing in the American Theater Institution*. Unpublished doctoral dissertation. University of Minnesota, Minneapolis.

Kurath, G.P. 1986. *Half a Century of Dance Research*. Flagstaff, AZ: Cross Cultural Dance Research.

Lagne, W.V. 1970. *The Effects of Curricular Dramatics on Children's Acting Skill*. Unpublished doctoral dissertation. Northwestern University, Evanston.

Lang, R.J., and K. Ryba. 1976. "The Identification of Some Creative Thinking Parameters Common to the Artistic and Musical Personality." *British Journal of Educational Psychology* Vol. 46: 267-279.

Langan, J. 1995. *The Influence of Visual Models and Instructional Methods on the Development of Students' Graphic Representations*. Unpublished doctoral dissertation. University of Illinois, Urbana.

Lansing, K. 1981. "The Effect of Drawing on the Development of Mental Representation." *Studies in Art Education* Vol. 22, No. 3: 15-23.

Lavender, L., and W. Oliver, 1993. "Learning to 'See' Dance: The Role of Critical Writing in Developing Students' Aesthetic Awareness." *Impulse* Vol. 1, No. 1: 10-20.

Lavender, L., and J. Predock-Linnell. 1996. "Standing Aside and Making Space: Mentoring Student Choreographers." *Impulse* Vol. 4, No. 3: 235-252.

Lazaroff, E. 2001. "Performance and Motivation in Dance Education." *Arts Education Policy Review* Vol. 103, No. 2: 23-29.

Lee-Chao, E. 1997. *A Study of the Relationship between Children's Artistic Ability and Spatial Proficiency*. Unpublished doctoral dissertation. University of Pittsburgh, Pittsburgh.

Lehmann, A., and J. Davidson. 2002. "Taking an Acquired Skills Perspective on Music Performance." In *The New Handbook of Research in Music Teaching and Learning*, R. Colwell and C. Richardson, editors. New York: Oxford University Press.

Levitin, D. 1996. *Mechanisms of Memory for Musical Attributes*. Unpublished doctoral dissertation. University of Oregon, Eugene.

Lin-Meng, Y. 1999. *The Effect of Teaching Representational Notation Versus Conventional Notation on Music Reading Skills of Third Grade Students in Taiwan*. Unpublished doctoral dissertation. University of Illinois, Urbana.

Lindblade, T. 1995. *Tactical Measures: The Interactions of Drama with Music*. Unpublished doctoral dissertation. Stanford University, Palo Alto.

Lineburgh, N. 1994. *The Effects of Exposure to Musical Prototypes on the Stylistic Discrimination Ability of Kindergarten and Second-grade Children*. Unpublished doctoral dissertation. Kent State University, Kent.

Lord, M. 2001. "Fostering the Growth of Beginner's Improvisational Skills: A Study of Dance Teaching Practices in the High School Setting." *Research in Dance Education* Vol. 2, No. 1: 19-40.

Lowe, A. 1995. *The Effect of the Incorporation of Music Learning into the Second Language Classroom on the Mutual Reinforcement of Music and Language*. Unpublished doctoral dissertation. University of Illinois, Urbana.

Lowe, A. 2002. "Toward Integrating Music and Other Art Forms into the Language Curriculum." *Research Studies in Music Education* Vol. 18: 12-23.

McCullough, C. 1996. *The Alexander Technique and the Pedagogy of Paul Rolland*. Unpublished doctoral dissertation. Arizona State University, Tempe.

McCurry, M. 1998. *Handchime Performance as a Means of Meeting Selected Standards in the National Standards of Music Education*. Unpublished doctoral dissertation. University of Georgia, Athens.

McKean, B., and P. Sudol. 2002. "Drama and Language Arts: Will Drama Improve Student Writing?" *Youth Theater Journal* Vol. 16: 28-37.

McLean, C. 1999. "Elementary Directed Listening to Music: A Singing Approach Versus a Nonsinging Approach." *Journal of Research in Music Education* Vol. 47, No. 3: 239-250.

McPherson, G., and J. McCormick. 2000. "The Contribution of Motivational Factors to Instrumental Performance in Music Examinations." *Research Studies in Music Education* Vol. 15: 31-39.

McPherson, G., and B. Zimmerman. 2002. "Self-Regulation of Musical Learning: A Social Cognitive Perspective." In *The New Handbook of Research on Music*

Teaching and Learning, Colwell, R. and C. Richardson, editors. New York: Oxford University Press.

McSorley, J. 1996. " Primary Schoolteachers' Conception of Teaching Art Criticism." *Studies in Art Education* Vol. 37, No. 3: 160-169.

Madsen, C., and K. Madsen. 2002. "Perception and Cognition in Music: Musically Trained and Untrained Adults Compared to 6th and 8th Grade Children." *Journal of Research in Music Education* Vol. 50, No. 2: 111-130.

Makin, L., M. White, and M. Owen. 1996. "Creation or Constraint: Anglo-Australian and Asian-Australian Teacher Response to Children's Art Making." *Studies in Art Education* Vol. 37, No. 4: 226-224.

Mang, E. 2001. "A Cross Language Comparison of Preschool Children's Vocal Fundamental Frequency in Speech and Language Production." *Research Studies in Music Education* Vol. 16: 4-14.

Marion, S. 1997. *Notation System and Dance Style: Three Systems Recording and Reflecting 100 Years of Western Theatrical Dance*. Unpublished doctoral dissertation. New York University, New York.

Mark, M. 1996. *Comprehensive Musicianship in Contemporary Music Education, 3rd edition*. New York: Schirmer Books.

Marsh, H., and S. Kleitman. 2002. "Extracurricular School Activities: The Good, the Bad, and the Nonlinear." *Harvard Education Review* Vol. 72, No. 4: 464-513.

Miceli, J. 1998. *An Investigation of an Audiation-Based High School General Music Curriculum and its Relationship to Music Aptitude, Music Achievement, and Student Perception of Learning*. Unpublished doctoral dissertation. University of Rochester, Rochester.

Miller, B. 1995. *Integrating Elementary Music Instruction with a Whole Language First Grade Classroom*. Unpublished doctoral dissertation. University of Illinois, Urbana.

Miller, R. 1986. *The Structure of Singing: System and Art in Vocal Technique*. New York: Schirmer Books.

Millsap, T. 1999. *The Daily Implementation of Sequential Sustained Tone Exercises as a Means of Improving the Ensemble Intonation and Tone Quality of Second Year Middle School Bands*. Unpublished doctoral dissertation. University of Georgia, Athens.

Milne, W. 2000. *Reflective Art Making: Implications for Art Education*. Unpublished doctoral dissertation. University of Pittsburgh, Pittsburgh.

Minton, S. 2000. *Assessment of High School Students' Creative Thinking Skills*. Unpublished manuscript. Greeley, CO: Author.

Minton, S. 2001. "Assessment of High School Dance Students' Self-esteem." *Journal of Dance Education* Vol.1, No. 2: 63-73.

Minton, S.C. 1981. *The Effects of Several Types of Teaching Cues on Postural Alignment of Beginning Modern Dancers: A Cinematographic Analysis*. Unpublished doctoral dissertation. Texas Women's University, Denton.

Minton, S.C. 1989. *Body and Self: Partners in Movement*. Champaign, IL: Human Kinetics Books.

Minton, S., and K. McGill. 1988. "A Study of the Relationships between Teacher Behaviors and Student Performance on a Spatial Kinesthetic Test." *Dance Research Journal* Vol. 30, No. 2: 39-52.

Moga, E., K. Burger, L. Hetland, and E. Winner. 2000. "Does Studying the Arts Engender Creative Thinking: Evidence for Near but Not Far Transfer." *Journal of Aesthetic Education* Vol. 34, No. 3-4: 91-104.

Moirs, K. 1996. *Exploring the Relationship between Spatial Ability and Artistic Production: An Evaluation of Arts Education Methods*. Unpublished doctoral dissertation. University of Iowa, Iowa City.

Montgomery, A. 1997. *The Influence of Movement Activities on Achievement in Melodic Pitch Discrimination and Language Arts Reading Readiness Skills of Selected Kindergarten Music Classes*. Unpublished doctoral dissertation. University of Southern Mississippi, Hattiesburg.

Moody, B.J. 1983. *Visual Arts in Gifted Programs: Thirty-one Current Programs Described*. Greeley, CO: Creative Arts Center.

Moon, B. 1994. *Introduction to Art Therapy: Faith in the Product*. Springfield, IL: Charles Thomas.

Moses, N. 1992. "The Effects of Movement Notation on the Performance, Cognition, and Attitudes of Beginning Ballet Students at the College Level." In *Dance: Current Selected Research Volume II*, L. Overby and J. Humphrey, editors. New York: AMS Press.

Neperud, R.W. 1966. "An Experimental Study of Visual Elements, Selected Art Instruction Methods, and Drawing Development at the Fifth Grade Level." *Studies in Art Education* Vol. 7, No. 2: 3-13.

Nielsen, S. 1999. "Learning Strategies in Instrumental Music Practice." *British Journal of Music Education* Vol. 16, No. 3: 275-291.

Nocera, S.D. 1981. *A Descriptive Analysis of the Attainment of Selective Musical Learnings by Normal Children and by Educable Mentally Retarded Children Mainstreamed in Music Classes at the Second and Fifth Grade Levels*. Unpublished doctoral dissertation. University of Wisconsin, Madison.

Norris, J. 2000. "Drama as Research: Realizing the Potential of Drama in Education as a Research Methodology." *Youth Theater Journal* Vol. 14: 40-51.

O'Neill, S. 1997. "The Role of Practice in Children's Early Musical Performance Achievement." In *Does Practice Make Perfect? Current Theory and Research on Instrumental Music Practice*, H. Jorgensen and A.C. Lehmann, editors. Oslo, Norway: NMH-publikasjoner.

Odam, G. 2000. "Teaching Composing in Secondary Schools: The Creative Dream." *British Journal of Music Education* Vol. 17, No. 2: 109-127.

Oliver, A. 1997. *A Study of Selected Treatments of Performance Anxiety with a Survey of Performance Anxiety Among Participants of the 1994 International Horn Symposium.* Unpublished doctoral dissertation. University of Iowa, Iowa City.

Orde, B. 1996. *A Correlational Study of Drawing Ability and Spatial Ability.* Unpublished doctoral dissertation. University of Wyoming, Laramie.

Overby, L. 2000. "The Body Image: A Review of Literature." In *Dance: Current Selected Research* 4, L.Y. Overby and J.H. Humphrey, editors. New York: AMS Press.

Petzold, R.G. 1966. *Auditory Perception of Musical Sounds by Children in the First Six Grades.* Madison, WI: Cooperative Research Project, U.S. Office of Education.

Phillips, K.H. 1992. "Research on the Teaching of Singing." In *Handbook of Research on Music Teaching and Learning*, R.J. Colwell, editor (Chapter 39). New York: Schirmer Books.

Pinciotti, P.A. 1982. *A Comparative Study of Two Creative Drama Approaches on Imagery, Ability, and Dramatic Improvisation.* Unpublished doctoral dissertation. Rutgers, The State University of New Jersey, New Brunswick.

Pinker, S. 2002. *The Blank Slate: The Modern Denial of Human Nature.* New York: Penguin Group.

Planchat, J. 1994. *The Usefulness of Educational Drama as a Means of Improving the Communicative Competence of Early French Immersion Students.* Unpublished master's thesis. Memorial University of Newfoundland, St. Johns.

Podlozny, A. 2000. "Strengthening Verbal Skills through the Use of Classroom Drama: A Clear Link." *Journal of Aesthetic Education* Vol. 34, No. 3 & 4: 239-276.

Price, H., F. Blanton, and R. Parrish. 1998. "Effects of Two Instructional Methods on High School Band Students' Sight Reading Proficiency, Music Performance, and Attitude." *Applications of Research in Music Education* Vol. 17, No. 1: 14-20.

Puretz, S.C. 1992. "Dance Movement Therapy: A Review and Analysis of the Literature." In *Current Selected Dance Research Vol. II*, L. Overby and J. Humphrey, editors (Chapter 10). New York: AMS Press.

Quest, U. 1999. "The Effect of Music on Acquiring Vocabulary with Technically Gifted Students." *Gifted Education International* Vol. 14, No. 1: 12-21.

Radford, M. 2001. "Aesthetics and Religious Awareness Among Pupils: Similarities and Differences." *British Journal of Music Education* Vol. 18, No. 2: 151-159.

Ragans, R.D. 1971. *The Effects of Instruction in a Technique of Art Criticism Upon the Responses of Elementary Students to Art Objects.* Unpublished doctoral dissertation. University of Georgia, Athens.

Rauscher, F.H., G.L. Shaw, L.S. Levine, W.R. Dennis, and R.L. Newcomb. 1997. "Music Training Causes Long-Term Enhancement of Pre-School Children's Spatial-Temporal Reasoning." *Neuorological Research* Vol. 19, No. 1: 1-8.

Reith, E. 1990. "Development of Representational Awareness and Competence in Drawing Production." *Archives de Psychologies* Vol. 58: 369-379.

Renwick, J., and G. McPherson. 2002. "Interest and Choice: Student Selected Repertoire and its Effect on Practicing Behaviours." *British Journal of Music Education* Vol. 19, No. 2: 173-188.

Richardson, C.P. 1988. *Musical Thinking as Exemplified in Musical Criticism.* Unpublished doctoral dissertation. University of Illinois, Urbana.

Richmond, P. 1994. "The Alexander Technique and Dance Training." *Impulse* Vol. 2, No. 1: 24-38.

Rideout, R.R. 1992. "The Role of Mental Presets in Skill Acquisition." In *Handbook of Research on Music Teaching and Learning.* R.J. Colwell, editor (Chapter 31). New York: Schirmer Books.

Riley, A. 1987. "Is Creative Dance Responsive to Research?" *Design for Arts in Education* Vol. 88: 36-40.

Roey, S., N. Caldwell, K. Rust, E. Blumstein, T. Krenzke, S. Legum, J. Kuhn, M. Waksberg, and J. Haynes. 2001. *The 1998 High School Transcript Study Tabulations: Comparative Data on Credits Earned and Demographics for 1998, 1994, 1990, 1987, and 1982 High School Graduates.* Washington, DC: National Center for Education Statistics, U.S. Department of Education.

Rohwer, D. 1997. *The Effect of Movement Instruction on Sixth Grade Beginning Instrumental Music Students' Perception, Synchronization, and Performance with a Steady Beat.* Unpublished doctoral dissertation. Ohio State University, Columbus.

Rolland, P., M. Mutschler, and R. Colwell. 1971. *Development and Trial of a Two Year Program of String Education.* Washington, DC: U.S. Office of Education, Project 5-1182.

Rose, D. 2003. "The Impact of Whirlwind's Basic Reading thru Dance Program on First-grade Students' Basic Reading Skills-Study II." *Journal of Evaluation Reviews.* In press.

Rose, S. 1995. *The Effects of Dalcroze Eurhythmics on Beat Competency Performance Skills of Kindergarten, First, and Second Grade Children.* Unpublished doctoral dissertation. University of North Carolina, Greensboro.

Rosenberg, H. 1989. "Transformations Described: How 23 Young People Think About and Experience Creative Drama." *Youth Theater Journal* Vol. 4, No. 1: 21-27.

Rosenberg, H. with P. Pinciotti et al. 1987. *Mental Imagery with Theater, Creative Drama, and Imagination: Transforming Ideas into Action.* New York: Holt Rinehart.

Rosene, P.E. 1976. *A Field Study of Wind Instrument Training for Educable Mentally Handicapped*

Children. Unpublished doctoral dissertation. University of Illinois, Urbana.

Rosenshine, B. 1997. "Advances in Research in Instruction." In *Educating Students with Disabilities*, J. Lloyd, E. Kameanui, and D. Chard, editors. Mahwah, NJ: Erlbaum Publications.

Rosenshine, B.,H. Froehlich, and I. Fakhouri. 2002. "Systematic Instruction." In *The New Handbook of Research in Music Teaching and Learning*, R. Colwell and C. Richardson, editors. New York: Oxford University Press.

Rosenthal, R.K. 1984. "The Relative Effects of Guided Model, Model Only, Guide Only, and Practice Only Treatments on the Accuracy of Advanced Instrumentalists' Musical Performance." *Journal of Research in Music Education* Vol. 32: 265-273.

Ross, P. 2000. "Young Children's Opera: Having a Multiple Literacy Experience from the Inside-out." *Youth Theater Journal* Vol. 14: 26-39.

Roush, C. 1995. *The Effects of Imagined and Anatomical Imagined Approaches to Resonance Training and Choral Experiences on High School Students Vocal Tone Quality*. Unpublished doctoral dissertation. University of Nebraska, Lincoln.

Rowe, P.A. 1967. "Research in Dance in Colleges and Universities in the U.S.: 1901-1967." *Dance Research Annual I*, Richard Bull, editor (pp. 3-13). New York: Congress of Research on Dance.

Ryan, D. 2001. "Self Assessment in Performance." *British Journal of Music Education* Vol. 18, No. 3: 215-226.

Saab, J.F. 1988. *Creative Dramatics Experience and its Relations to Creativity and Self-Concept of Elementary School Children*. Unpublished doctoral dissertation. University of West Virginia, Morgantown.

Saldaña, J. 1989. "A Quantitative Analysis of Children's Responses to Theater from Probing Questions: A Pilot Study." *Youth Theater Journal* Vol. 3, No. 4: 7-17.

Saldaña, J. 1995. "Is Theater Necessary? Final Exit Interviews with Sixth Grade Participants from the ASU Longitudinal Study." *Youth Theater Journal* Vol. 9: 14-30.

Salome, R.A. 1965. "The Effects of Perceptual Training Upon the Two Dimensional Drawings of Children." *Studies in Art Education* Vol. 7, No. 1: 18-33.

Sang, R.C. 1987. "A Study of the Relationship Between Instrumental Music Teachers' Modeling Skills and Pupil Performance Behaviors." *Bulletin of the Council for Research in Music Education* Vol. 91: 155-159.

Sawyer, R. 1995. *The Performance of Pretend Play: Enacting Peer Culture in Conversation*. Unpublished doctoral dissertation. University of Chicago.

Schramm, S. 1997. *The Quest for a Balanced Curriculum: The Perceptions of Secondary Students and Teachers who Experienced an Integrated Art and Science Curriculum*. Unpublished doctoral dissertation. University of Miami.

Seham, J. 1997. *The Effects on At-risk Children of an In-school Dance Program*. Unpublished doctoral dissertation. Adelphi University, Garden City.

Sehmann, K. 2000. "The Effects of Breath Management Instruction on the Performance of Elementary Brass Players." *Journal of Research in Music Education* Vol. 48, No. 2: 136-150.

Seidel, K. 1996. *Leader's Theater: A Case Study of How High School Students Develop Leadership Skills through Participation in Theater*. Unpublished doctoral dissertation. University of Cincinnati, Cincinnati.

Seipp, N.F. 1976. *A Comparison of Class and Private Music Instruction*. Unpublished doctoral dissertation. University of West Virginia, Morgantown.

Sevigny, M. 1977. *A Descriptive Study of Instructional Interaction and Performance Appraisal in a University Studio Art Setting: A Multiple Perspective*. Unpublished doctoral dissertation. Ohio State University, Columbus.

Sharples, G. 1992. *Intrinsic Motivation and Social Constraint: A Meta Analysis of Experimental Research Utilizing Creative Activities*. Unpublished doctoral dissertation. University of Oregon, Eugene.

Sheridan, M., and C. Byrne. 2002. "Ebb and Flow of Assessment in Music." *British Journal of Music Education* Vol. 19, No. 2: 135-143.

Shiavi, M. 1998. *Staging Effeminacy in America*. Unpublished doctoral dissertation. New York University, New York.

Short, G. 1998. "A High School Studio Curriculum and Art Understandings: An Examination Study in Art Education." *Studies in Art Education* Vol. 40, No. 1: 46-65.

Sidwell, D. 2001. "Harpooning the Hippo Cake: Drama as Ritual Architecture in Classroom Communities." *Youth Theater Journal* Vol. 15: 70-80.

Siegesmund, R., R. Diket, and S. McCulloch. 2001. "Revisioning NAEP: Amending a Performance Assessment for Middle School Art Students." *Studies in Art Education* Vol. 43, No. 1: 45-56.

Silveira, C. 1995. *An Exemplary Multicultural Unit of Art Instruction for Use in Elementary Education Designed to Help Mexican American Students Develop More Positive Attitudes Toward Different Racial, Ethnic, Cultural, and Religious Groups*. Unpublished doctoral dissertation. Texas Tech University, Lubbock.

Sink, P. 2002. "Behavioral Research on Direct Music Instruction." *In The New Handbook of Research in Music Teaching and Learning*, R. Colwell and C. Richardson, editors. New York: Oxford University Press.

Siskar, J. 2000. *Promoting Understanding in the Art Classroom: Connecting Theories of Understanding to Art Education Practice*. Unpublished doctoral dissertation. State University of New York at Buffalo, Buffalo.

Smith, B. 2002. *The Role of Selected Motivational Beliefs in the Process of Collegiate Instrumental Practice*.

Unpublished doctoral dissertation. University of Michigan, Ann Arbor.

Smith, L. 1999. *Effects of DBAE and Interdisciplinary Art Education on Artistic Development and Production, Higher Level Thinking, and Attitudes toward Science and Social Studies.* Unpublished doctoral dissertation. University of Memphis, Memphis.

Standley, J. 1992. "Meta Analysis of Research in Music and Medical Treatment: Effect Size as a Basis for Comparison Across Multiple Dependent and Independent Variables." In *Music Medicine*, R. Spintge and R. Droh, editors (pp. 364-378). St Louis, MO: MMB Music.

Starkes, J., M. Caicco, C. Boutilier, and B. Sevsek. 1990. "Motor Recall of Experts for Structured and Unstructured Sequence in Creative Modern Dance." *Journal of Sport and Exercise Physiology* Vol. 12: 317-321.

Starr, G. 1996. *Auditory Short Term Memory for Timbre and Pitch: Interference Effects from Grouping and Same-Dimension Similarity.* Unpublished doctoral dissertation. Ohio State University, Columbus.

Stavropoulos, C. 1992. *A Diagnostic Profile of Art Understandings Based on Verbal Responses to Works of Art.* Unpublished doctoral dissertation. Ohio State University, Columbus.

Stephens, P. 1996. *Discipline Based Art Education as the Structural Support of a Language Arts Intervention Program: Documentation of Cognitive Changes in Certain Elementary Age Students.* Unpublished doctoral dissertation. University of North Texas, Denton.

Stewart, E. 1999. *The Relationship between Drawing Ability and General Critical Thinking.* Unpublished doctoral dissertation. University of Missouri, Columbia.

Stinespring, J. 2001. "Preventing Art Education from Becoming a Handmaiden to the Social Studies." *Arts Education Policy Review* Vol. 102, No. 4.

Stinson, S. 1997. "A Question of Fun: Adolescent Engagement in Dance Education." *Dance Research Journal* Vol. 29, No. 2: 49-69.

Stokrocki, M. 1988. "Teaching Preadolescents During a Nine-Week Sequence: The Negotiator's Approach." *Studies in Art Education* Vol. 30, No. 1: 39-46.

Stuhr, P.L., L. Petrovich-Mwaniki, and R.F. Wasson. 1992. "Curriculum Guidelines for the Multicultural Art Classroom." *Art Education* Vol. 45, No. 1: 16-24.

Swinton, S. 1989. "Assessment of Production, Perception, and Reflection in Beginning Music Portfolios." *The Newsletter of Arts Propel.* Princeton, NJ: Educational Testing Service.

Szekely, G. 1995. "Art at Home: Learning from a Suzuki Education." In *The Visual Arts and Early Childhood Education*, C. Thompson, editor (pp. 15-22). Reston, VA: National Art Education Association.

Tambling, P. 1999. "Opera, Education, and the Role of Arts Organizations." *British Journal of Music Education* Vol. 16, No. 2: 139-156.

Taunton, M. 1983. "Questioning Strategies to Encourage Young Children to Talk about Art." *Art Education* Vol. 36, No. 4: 40-43.

Thompson, K. 1991. *Assessing the Creative Effectiveness of Two Approaches to Teaching Art at the Middle School Level.* Unpublished doctoral dissertation. University of Georgia, Athens.

Tooker, P. 1995. *A Case Study of a High School Special Education Beginning Band Class.* Unpublished doctoral dissertation. Teachers College, New York.

Trent, D. 1996. *The Impact of Instrumental Music Education on Academic Achievement.* Unpublished doctoral dissertation. East Texas State University, Commerce.

Turner, D. 2000. *The Developmental Experiences of Students in a Dance Program at a Rural Middle School.* Unpublished doctoral dissertation. Santa Barbara: The Fielding Institute.

Turon, C. 2000. *Education Prerequisites for Piano Teachers Assisting in the Prevention, Detection, and Management of Performance-related Health Disorders.* Unpublished doctoral dissertation. University of Oklahoma, Norman.

Twiggs, L. F. 1970. *The Effects of Teaching a Method of Art Criticism on the Aesthetic Responses of Culturally Disadvantaged Junior High School Students.* Unpublished doctoral dissertation. University of Georgia, Athens.

Unrau, S. 1999. *Children's Dance: An Exploration through the Techniques of Merce Cunningham.* Millennium Conference Proceedings 213-233.

Vallance, E. 1995. "The Public Curriculum of Orderly Images." *Educational Researcher* Vol. 24, No. 2: 4-13.

Van Weelden, K. 2002. "Relationships between Perceptions of Conducting Effectiveness and Ensemble Performance." *Journal of Research in Music Education* Vol. 50, No. 2: 165-176.

Vanmiddlesworth, J. 1996. *The Effects of Physiology-based Breath Management Instruction on Performance Achievement of Sixth Grade Clarinetists.* Unpublished doctoral dissertation. University of North Carolina, Greensboro.

Vaughan, K. 2000. "Music and Mathematics: Modest Support for the Oft-claimed Relationship." *Journal of Aesthetic Education* Vol. 34, No. 3-4: 149-166.

Vaughan, V. 2002. "Music Analysis in the Practice Room." *British Journal of Music Education* Vol. 19, No. 3: 255-268.

Venable, L. 1998. "Demystifying Motif Writing." *Journal of Physical Education, Recreation, and Dance* Vol. 69, No. 6: 32-36.

Vitz, K. 1983. "A Review of Empirical Research in Drama and Language." *The Children's Theater Review* Vol. 32, No. 4: 17-25.

Vogel, M.R. 1975. *The Effect of a Program of Creative Dramatics on Young Children with Specific Learning*

Disabilities. Unpublished doctoral dissertation. Fordham University, New York.

VonRossberg-Gempton, I. 1998. *Creative Dance Potentiality for Enhancing Psychomotor, Cognitive, and Social Affective Functioning in Seniors and Young Children*. Unpublished doctoral dissertation. Simon Fraser University, Burnaby.

Wade, M. 1990. "Motor Skills and the Making of Music." In *Music and Child Development: Proceedings of the 1987 Denver Conference*, F. Wilson and F. Roehmann, editors (pp. 157-178). St. Louis, MO: MMB Music.

Wagner, B. 1998. *Educational Drama and Language Arts: What Research Shows*. Portsmouth, NH: Heinemann.

Wagner, B.J. 1988. "Research Currents: Does Classroom Drama Affect the Art of Language?" *Language Arts* Vol. 65, No. 1: 46-55.

Waite, J.R. 1977. *Reducing Music Performance Anxiety: A Review of the Literature and a Self Help Manual*. Unpublished doctoral dissertation. University of Oregon, Eugene.

Walker, R. 1990. *Musical Beliefs: Psychoacoustic, Mythical, and Educational Perspectives*. New York: Teachers College Press.

Walters, D. 1992. "Sequencing for Efficient Learning." In *Handbook of Research on Music Teaching and Learning*, R.J. Colwell, editor (Chapter 36). New York: Schirmer Books.

Warner, R. 1975. *A Design for Comprehensive Musicianship in the Senior High School Band Program*. Unpublished doctoral dissertation. Washington University, St Louis.

Weaver, M. 1996. *An Investigation of the Relationships Between Performance-based Aural Musicianship, Music Achievement, and Socialization of First-year Music Majors*. Unpublished doctoral dissertation. University of Michigan, Ann Arbor.

Weikert, P. 1982. *Teaching Movement and Dance: A Sequential Approach to Rhythm in Movement*. Ypsilanti, MI: The High/Scope Press.

Welch, T., S. Fitt, and W. Thompson. 1994. "A Comparison of Forward and Backward Chaining Strategies for Teaching Dance Movement Sequences." *Impulse* Vol. 2, No. 4: 262-274.

Wells, S. 1995. *The Effect of Music on Abstract, Visual Reasoning Performance in High School Music and Nonmusic Students*. Unpublished doctoral dissertation. East Texas State University, Commerce.

Wiest, L. 1997. "Techniques for Vocal Health." *Teaching Music* Vol. 4, No. 4: 36-37, 62.

Wilkinson, J., (Ed.). 1993. *Guided Symbolic Dramatic Play as the Missing Link to the Symbolic Dramatic Play Literacy Connections, Whole Brain, Whole Body, Holistic Learning*. Needham Heights, MA: Ginn.

Willats, J. 1997. *Art and Representation*. Princeton, NJ: Princeton University Press.

Williams, D. 1997. *Listening While Performing: Music Listening Processes as Revealed Through Verbal Reports of Wind Instrumentalists During Rehearsal*. Unpublished doctoral dissertation. Northwestern University, Evanston.

Willis, S. 1999. *A Descriptive Analysis of Aesthetic Procedures Used in the AP Studio Art Program and the International Baccalaureate Art and Design Programme*. Unpublished doctoral dissertation. Florida State University, Tallahassee.

Wilson, B. 1986. "Art Criticism as Writing as Well as Talking." In *Research Readings for Discipline Based Art Education: A Journey Beyond Creating*. M. Dobbs, editor. Reston, VA: National Art Education Association.

Wilson, B. 1997. *The Quiet Evolution: Changing the Face of Arts Education*. Los Angeles: The Getty Education Institute for the Arts.

Wilson, B., and M. Wilson. 1977. "An Iconoclastic View of the Imagery Sources in the Drawings of Young Children." *Art Education* Vol. 30, No. 1: 5-11.

Winner, E. 1979. "New Names for Old Things: The Emergence of Metaphoric Language." *Journal of Child Language* Vol. 6, No. 3: 469-491.

Winner, E., and M. Cooper. 2000. "Mute Those Claims: No Evidence (Yet) for a Causal Link between Arts Study and Academic Achievement." *Journal of Aesthetic Education* Vol. 34, No. 3-4: 11-75.

Winner, E., and L. Hetland. 2000. "The Arts and Academic Achievement: What the Evidence Shows." *The Journal of Aesthetic Education* Vol. 34, No. 3-4.

Woody, R. 1999. "The Relationship between Explicit Planning and Expressive Performance of Dynamic Variations in an Aural Modeling Task." *Journal of Research in Music Education* Vol. 47, No. 4: 331-342.

Woody, R. 2002. "The Relationship between Musicians' Expectations and their Perception of Expressive Features in an Aural Model." *Research Studies in Music Education* Vol. 18: 53-61.

Wright, R. 2002. "Music for All? Pupil's Perceptions of the BCSE Music Examinations in one South Wales Secondary School." *British Journal of Music Education* Vol. 19, No. 3: 227-241.

Yang, Y. 1994. *The Effects of Solmization and Rhythmic Movement Training on the Achievement of Beginning Group Piano Students at the Elementary School Level*. Unpublished doctoral dissertation. University of Michigan, Ann Arbor.

Yontz, T. 2001. *The Effectiveness of Laban-based Principles of Movement and Previous Musical Training on Undergraduate Beginning Conductor's Ability to Convey Intended Musical Context*. Unpublished doctoral dissertation. University of Nebraska, Lincoln.

Zimmerman, E. 1985. "Towards a Theory of Labeling Artistically Talented Students." *Studies in Art Education* Vol. 17, No. 1: 31-42.

Chapter 4. Foreign Language

Myriam Met

Foreign language teachers make important instructional decisions every day as they plan and implement lessons. Research can make a significant contribution in informing these decisions, so that daily instruction reflects the best of what is known about foreign language teaching and learning. Research cannot and does not identify the right or best way to teach, nor does it suggest certain instructional practices should always or should never be used. But research *can* illuminate which instructional practices are most likely to achieve desired results, with which kinds of learners, and under which conditions.

Foreign language professionals know more today than ever about how learners acquire new languages and about the conditions under which language acquisition is likely to occur. The prevailing view among foreign language educators today is that the goal of instruction is to prepare students to function effectively in the real-life situations they are likely to encounter. This view, most frequently associated with the terms "proficiency-oriented instruction" or "communicative language teaching," has had a substantial impact on foreign language teaching practices in the last decade. National Standards for Foreign Language Learning continue the movement toward communication as a primary goal of the foreign language profession. The five goals that comprise the Standards (Communication, Cultures, Connections, Comparisons, Communities) emphasize language as a tool for interaction with others and with texts, as a tool for learning, for personal enrichment, and for use in the broader community.

The research base for communicative language instructional practices is both direct and indirect. Some evidence directly supports prac-
tices associated with communicative approaches; other practices may be inferred from the research on cognition, information processing, and sociocultural theory. While some of the evidence to support emerging approaches may be indirect or limited, it should also be noted there is a scant body of research to support past approaches to foreign language teaching, particularly grammar-based approaches.

Current constructivist and social constructivist theories of learning are consistent with the communicative approach to foreign language teaching and learning. As a result, foreign language educators share many beliefs about good instruction with those in other disciplines:

- Learners must be actively engaged in constructing their own understandings and knowledge.

- New knowledge builds on previous knowledge, and the learners' background knowledge plays a significant role in their construction of meaning.

- Social interaction is important in the construction of knowledge and the integration of knowledge into increasingly improved performance.

- Classroom tasks should closely parallel the real-life tasks to which students may expect to apply their knowledge and skills.

- Real-life tasks are meaningful, purposeful, and rooted in context.

- Approaches to assessment should reflect the complexity of integrating knowledge and skills into performance.

Some cautions about interpreting the research reported in this chapter and its implications for classrooms are in order. The research base in foreign language education, particularly in secondary schools, is not extensive. Educators and pedagogical theoreticians, therefore, frequently rely on studies drawn from English as a Second Language (ESL) settings, on research conducted primarily with postsecondary learners, or on research based on short-term studies. In addition, implications for foreign language instruction are occasionally extrapolated from research in first language development, particularly in the area of reading and writing skills development.

Beyond these cautions in interpreting the research, it appears learners benefit from:

- extensive exposure to meaningful, understandable language in use;

- opportunities to use the target language to interact with others, to understand others, and to make oneself understood;

- opportunities to use the target language in tasks reflecting real-life purposes and requiring the exchange of meaning;

- culture instruction linking cultural information, skills in observation and analysis, and ways to make meaning in a socioculturally appropriate manner;

- explicit instruction in strategies facilitating language awareness, learner autonomy, and making meaning when reading or listening to the foreign language; and

- the use of certain technological resources to assist in language learning and practice.

There are a number of areas of interest to foreign language educators where research is equivocal or minimal. Research is equivocal on the role of explicit grammar instruction and on the benefits of error correction. Further research evidence is needed that elucidates:

- the variables that affect the ways in which technology can enhance language learning, particularly in the area of distance learning;

- effective ways to teach culture, teach cross-cultural communication, and reduce ethnocentrism;

- the relationship between length and frequency of class meetings (i.e., spaced practice) and language attrition/loss, a question of particular interest to those considering block scheduling; and

- the development of reading and writing skills in secondary foreign language learners.

While research may provide direction in many areas, it provides few clear-cut answers in most. Teachers continue to be faced daily with critical decisions about how best to achieve the instructional goals embedded in professional or voluntary state or national standards. A combination of research-suggested instructional practices and professional judgment and experience is most likely to produce students who can fill the need for a language-competent America.

The author wishes to thank the following colleagues who reviewed the 2003 edition of this chapter: Dr. Richard Donato, University of Pittsburgh; Dr. Judith Liskin-Gasparro, University of Iowa; and Dr. Robert Terry, University of Richmond. Previous editions were reviewed by Dr. Terry Ballman, California State University, Channel Islands; Dr. Craig Chaudron, University of Hawaii; Dr. Joan Kelly Hall, University of Georgia; ; Dr. Judith Liskin-Gasparro, University of Iowa; and Dr. Leo Van Lier, Monterey Institute of International Studies.

4.1. Begin Instruction Early: There are significant benefits to beginning language learning early and continuing through an articulated sequence of study.

Research findings:

Research on brain development suggests the young brain is predisposed to learning language(s). While it is possible to learn additional languages when older, languages are not learned in the same ways nor, perhaps, to similar levels of attainment, particularly in the area of oral proficiency.

Programs of early foreign language instruction flourished in the 1950s and 1960s, declined in popularity, and have proliferated once again in the last decade. The most widely researched of early language programs is immersion, in which at least half the school curriculum is taught through the medium of a foreign language. Numerous studies have shown immersion students acquire high levels of proficiency in the foreign language at no detriment to their native language or achievement in school subjects, even when the latter are not taught in English. Two-way (also called dual-language) immersion uses the immersion model to instruct two linguistically mixed groups of learners: half come to school speaking English as a native language; the others speak the target language (e.g., Spanish). These programs are demonstrating positive results for both groups of students in terms of academic achievement and development of bilingual proficiencies.

Another popular model in the United States is Foreign Language in the Elementary School (FLES). Studies have shown taking time out of the school day for foreign language instruction has no detrimental effects on achievement in other subjects. In addition, a number of studies have shown a positive relationship between foreign language study in the elementary grades and academic achievement in the areas of reading, language arts, and mathematics. Both recent and older studies have found students in elementary school foreign language programs also demonstrate cognitive benefits when compared with non-language learners in the areas of metalinguistic awareness, creative thinking, and nonverbal reasoning. Research also suggests the higher the level of foreign language proficiency attained, the more pronounced the relationship with higher cognitive functioning.

In the classroom:

To attain the levels of proficiency indicated in national and many state standards, it is important for students to begin foreign language learning in the early grades and continue for as long as possible. It is unlikely that students who begin language learning in high school will have sufficient time to achieve a useful level of foreign language proficiency.

Time and intensity may be important factors in considering the program model used in the early grades. Students who have brief and/or infrequent contact with the foreign language (e.g., fewer than 75 minutes per week in fewer than three class sessions per week) may not achieve the desired levels of proficiency. Studies demonstrating a relationship between early language learning and cognitive/academic performance have been conducted on students who participate in programs where students have more than brief or infrequent encounters with the foreign language. Intensity of experience is related to motivation: students who experience a need to use language to communicate meanings that are interesting and important to them are more likely to be engaged and to persist in tasks. Engagement and persistence are needed for learning to occur. As a result, many practitioners favor using the content of the elementary school curriculum as a source for identifying appropriate curriculum, tasks, and activities for young foreign language learners. In addition, instructional practices must be developmentally appropriate to the needs, interests, and abilities of younger learners.

Assessment of student progress in early language programs remains a challenge. There are only a few instruments currently available that provide standardized, reliable information regarding student learning. New standards and accompanying assessments under development will soon be available to help measure student progress and program effectiveness.

Sources:

Armstrong and Rogers 1997; Christian, Montone, Lindholm, and Carranza 1997; Curtain and Pesola 1994; Day and Shapson 1996; Donato, Tucker, Wudthayagorn, and Igarashi 2000; Education Commission of The States 1996; Genesee 1987, 1994; Haas 1998; Harley 1986, 1998; Krashen, Scarcella, and Long 1982; Lee 1996; Ottawa Board of Education 1996; Pinker 1994; Robinson 1998; Swain and Lapkin 1991; Thomas, Collier, and Abbott 1993.

4.2.1. Language Acquisition: Extensive access to comprehensible input, as well as opportunities for meaningful, engaging interaction, are required for acquisition of the target language.

Research findings:

Most researchers and classroom practitioners today acknowledge the critical role comprehension plays in language acquisition. Comprehensible input is a term coined by Krashen (1982) to describe language (oral or written) that is understandable. For language growth to occur, Krashen posits that input must not only be understandable, but must also contain language that is just beyond the learner's current capacity. Research suggests comprehensible input is not simply a matter of quantity of exposure, but of quality as well.

Comprehension of written texts can be a significant source of vocabulary. Reading can be a form of comprehensible input that provides multiple exposures to new words, providing learners with varying examples of the varied contexts and collocations (words that tend to be used with other words) of target language vocabulary.

Language development requires that features in the input must be "noticed" by the learner in order for syntactic processing and "intake" to occur. That is, merely understanding the message may be insufficient; learners must also take note of the way the message is conveyed. Intake requires student attention, engagement, and processing. Student intake is not necessarily identical to the input they receive, but depends on how each individual attends to and processes features in the input.

Language development proceeds, then, from understanding what is heard (comprehensible input); noticing salient features in the input (intake), particularly those that are not yet part of the learner's repertoire; and internalizing language features that eventually become part of the learner's production.

In the classroom:

The learners' need for comprehensible input suggests teachers should use the target language extensively. Over-use of English decreases opportunities for comprehensible input and intake; conversely, extensive use of the target language can provide an important source of input.

Teachers' language must be understandable to the learner, with multiple clues to meaning. These may include visuals, body language, and contextual cues to promote student understanding. Input must demonstrate the topical coherence and purposes associated with language as used in real life. Input should also be structured or enhanced so that students attend to the form in which meanings are conveyed. Structured input facilitates student intake. In addition, comprehensible input and subsequent intake can be facilitated through use of readings that are understandable to students because of students' prior knowledge, visual cues, and contextual cues within the text itself. For example, reading an advertisement in a foreign language can be facilitated by knowledge of the text type (how advertisements are structured and where information can be found), prior knowledge of the advertised service or product, visuals, or linguistic cues (recognizing word families or cognates). Listening to and following commands and listening to books on tape while reading the print versions are also effective forms of comprehensible input.

Sources:

Asher 1984; Ellis 1990, 1993; Gass 1999; Hall 1999; Krashen 1982; Larsen-Freeman and Long 1991; Lee and VanPatten 1995; Leow 1999; Lightbown 1992; Paribakht and Wesche 1999; Van Lier 1996; VanPatten 2000.

4.2.2. Opportunities for Interaction: Frequent opportunities for interaction in the language, especially with other learners, help students develop language proficiency.

Research findings:

A number of studies have examined the role of interaction in language learning. Interaction allows learners to exchange information, to use language as it exists in the real world, and as a cognitive tool for problem solving. The "comprehensible output" hypothesis holds that interaction requires learners to express their meanings in ways that are comprehensible to others, which in turn pushes them to consider the relationships between meaning and form, and thereby refine their language. Thus, while research supports the importance of comprehensible input as a necessary condition for language development, research also suggests input by itself is insufficient for the development of the ability to speak or write another language.

Interaction helps students learn how to solve problems in communication using diverse problem-solving mechanisms. Peer-peer dialogue, in which students use the target language to collaboratively solve linguistic problems, contributes to language learning. Tasks in which students need to negotiate meaning (that is, make themselves understood and work to understand others) contribute to language growth, because student-to-student interaction may require more negotiation of meaning than teacher-student interaction. Teachers all too often are able to understand student utterances regardless of how poorly formed and communicated, while classmates may be less capable of deciphering their peers' messages, increasing the need for students to work on understanding and being understood. Student interaction and negotiation of meaning are more likely to take place when students are engaged and motivated to communicate.

Tasks that depend on a meaningful exchange of information among students generate more negotiation of meaning than do those in which information exchange is not required. In addition, research has shown students working in pairs or groups do not produce more errors than in teacher-conducted instruction, students can successfully correct one another, and students are unlikely to learn one another's mistakes.

Studies have shown teacher-student interactions shape the language students learn: the ways in which teachers provide and structure communication opportunities for individual students affect how each student develops language. Students in classrooms where teachers use student contributions to maintain an ongoing classroom dialogue in which students build on one another's contributions demonstrate higher levels of achievement.

The interaction between reader and text—"interactive reading"—shares many characteristics with oral tasks in terms of input, intake, form/meaning relationships, and negotiation of meaning. Collaborative interaction in peer revision of writing also has been found to be beneficial. Thus, interaction through reading and writing also promotes language growth.

In the classroom:

The research findings suggest engaging, purposeful, collaborative tasks in which students jointly construct meaning, orally or through print, should play a dominant role in classrooms. Teachers should provide extensive opportunities for students to interact with one another.

Interactive tasks are most beneficial when they require students to negotiate meaning, solve problems, and exchange information in order to complete the task. These tasks may involve an information gap (each student in a pair may have one part of the information needed) or an opinion gap (each student needs to find out the other's views/opinions). An information-gap task may require students to negotiate purchases based on the shopping list that one of the students has and the various store advertisements the other has, in order for the pair to buy a given set of items within a fixed amount. An opinion-gap task may require students to find out their partners' preferences and then compare and contrast how these preferences are similar to and/or different from their own. Interactive peer-to-peer tasks allow learners opportunities to develop authentic communicative behaviors found beyond the classroom walls, where it is rare to find situations in which one person poses a series of questions to numerous others, and then responds.

Sources:

Brooks and Donato 1994; DeGuerrero and Villamil 1994; Devitt 1997; Donato 2000; Dörnyei 1997; Dörnyei and Kormos 1998; Doughty and Pica 1986; Gass and Varonis 1985; Hall 1999; Hall and Walsh 2002; Long and Porter 1985; Nunan 1991; Oxford 1997; Pica 1994; Platt and Brooks 1994; Swain 1985; Swain, Brooks, and Tocalli-Beller 2002; Swain and Lapkin 1998; Van Lier 1996.

4.3. Communicative Language Practice: When classroom language practice is set in a context and requires meaningful and purposeful language use, students are enabled to communicate in a foreign language.

Research findings:

Theorists have proposed that communicative competence is complex and is composed of discourse competence, linguistic competence, sociocultural competence, actional competence, and strategic competence. Extensive participation in authentic types of communicative tasks in the classroom is needed for students to develop the array of communicative competencies they will need outside it. Engagement in interactive communication is necessary for students to develop fluency and to construct an understanding of the grammatical structure of the target language.

Cognitive theory suggests language learners need to develop *automaticity* (speed, fluency, and efficiency) of language use, and be enabled to put their knowledge of the language to use in performance. Research suggests learners can achieve automatic control of knowledge through practice under real operating conditions. That is, classroom practice needs to parallel authentic communication to the fullest extent possible, and students need adequate opportunities to develop the procedural knowledge necessary for real-life communication.

In the classroom:

National standards define communication as the skills of interaction (which allow for active negotiation of meaning), interpretation of meaning (skills used in listening and reading), and presentational skills (used to effectively present information orally or in writing when the possibility for active negotiation is absent). Communicative language teaching is organized around the purposes people have for communicating and the things people do when they communicate.

Communication is a process of collaborative meaning-making. It involves interpreting the meanings conveyed by others, expressing one's own meanings, and negotiating meanings to ensure that one understands and is understood. If the goal of language learning is communication, it follows that the classroom should provide opportunities for language practice and use that include the critical features of communication: *it is always set in a context, has a purpose, and involves interpreting and/or expressing meaning.*

Foreign language educators have proposed principles for foreign language instruction derived from the research on language learning:

- Foreign language activities should be set in a meaningful context, be sufficiently engaging to motivate students to communicate, and be meaning-driven.

- Students should have opportunities to practice using language that reflect the range of contexts they are likely to encounter and the functions (tasks) they may need to carry out outside of the classroom.

- Students should be encouraged to express their own meanings.

- Students need to be stretched to the limits of their language repertoire.

- Students should communicate frequently with diverse partners in the classroom to allow for interaction among more and less expert peers as well as between teacher and student.

Sources:

Celce-Murcia, Dörnyei, and Thurrell 1995; DeKeyser 1997; Ellis 1990; Hadley 2001; Hall 1999; Savignon 1991, 1997; Shrum and Glisan 2000; Van Lier 1996; VanPatten 1998.

4.4. Instruction in Learning Strategies: Explicit instruction in learning strategies can help students learn languages more easily and increase student autonomy.

Research findings:

Learning strategies are mechanisms through which students engage in the process of learning and by which they can become more autonomous learners. A number of studies have shown teaching students the purpose, nature, and appropriate use of language-learning strategies has long-term benefits. Explicit strategy instruction has been found to contribute to learner autonomy and enhanced language acquisition. Training in metacognitive and cognitive strategies has improved students' overall writing skills.

Students who use strategies frequently and effectively are self-directed and autonomous learners who can manage their own learning with less dependence on teachers for guidance and direction. Researchers have also found instruction in communication strategies helps students cope with communication problems.

Some studies on direct instruction in language-learning strategies have shown the benefits may be influenced by learner variables. Other studies have suggested socioculturally mediated strategy training provides more powerful results than does direct instruction.

In the classroom:

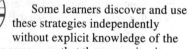

Some learners discover and use these strategies independently without explicit knowledge of the strategy or awareness that they are using it. Researchers have investigated the strategies used by successful learners with the end goal of teaching these strategies explicitly to all students. These include:

- *Metacognitive strategies*—processes such as monitoring one's comprehension and production (checking to ensure one understands the text as one is reading), self-assessment (evaluating the effectiveness of one's communication), and planning (brainstorming needed vocabulary and structures or outlining ideas prior to undertaking a writing task).

- *Cognitive strategies*—those used to organize information for learning (making a vocabulary web, or pairing synonymous or antonymous adjectives), elaborating information (explaining to oneself how one aspect of cultural behavior is like another, drawing inferences about a grammar rule from given examples, or calling on prior knowledge), or practicing, including rehearsal, experimentation, and imitation.

- *Social/affective strategies*—interactions such as asking peers or the teacher for assistance or clarification, collaborating with others, requesting feedback on one's communicative efforts, and self-talk to lower anxiety and urge oneself on.

Teachers can help students be more successful learners by teaching them what learning strategies are and when to use them. In addition, instruction can help students develop problem-solving strategies that improve their ability to communicate in another language.

Sources:

Chamot and Kupper 1989; Donato and McCormick 1994; Dörnyei 1995; O'Malley and Chamot 1990, 1993; Oxford 1990; Reichelt 2001; Rubin 1981, 1995; Wenden 1991.

4.5. Instruction in Listening and Reading for Meaning: Teaching students effective ways to listen and read results in more fluent listeners and readers.

Research findings:

Listening and reading involve the interpretation of oral language and written text. Background knowledge, topic interest, and familiarity with text type help students interpret texts. High interest in and knowledge of text topic has been shown to affect the reading comprehension of average and below-average readers more than above-average readers. Interaction among peers in discussing texts, as well as internal (private) speech aids in retention of information and comprehension of texts.

Research has identified a number of strategies used by effective listeners and effective readers. Local strategies include using cognates and contextual clues, skipping over unknown words, and using linguistic knowledge (e.g., grammatical structures and word families). Global strategies include using background knowledge or evaluating/validating one's predictions and hypotheses.

Fluent *readers* are able to predict text content and developments; they synthesize information from the text with their own background knowledge to construct an understanding of the text; and they self-monitor (check for comprehension) and self-regulate (consciously use strategies). Similarly, effective *listeners* use top-down strategies, such as predicting based on background knowledge, to construct meaning. They also monitor their own comprehension, and they set a purpose that guides what they listen for. They synthesize their background knowledge with the context and message of what they hear. The most successful listeners use a greater number and variety of strategies.

At lower levels of foreign language proficiency, students are less effective at using the comprehension strategies that underlie successful first-language reading, and they do not use all the strategies they use in their first language.

In the classroom:

Students are likely to comprehend texts better if teachers select texts consistent with students' topic interest and background knowledge (e.g., text type and structure, familiarity with topic and/or vocabulary used). Text organization and culture also influence the ability to interpret meaning. Certain text organizations facilitate recall (for example, cause-effect, compare-contrast). Because different cultures tend to organize texts differently, teachers can aid student comprehension by capitalizing on text organization where it is facilitative or by pointing out organizational differences when they may interfere with processing meaning. Both reading and listening require an extensive vocabulary and knowledge of the structure of the language. Since foreign language readers know many fewer words than do native speakers, vocabulary development is critical to reading ability in another language. This is not to suggest, however, that pre-teaching vocabulary using lists of new words is beneficial. Rather, it is more effective to present new vocabulary in the context and topic of the text (oral or written).

Teachers can improve foreign language students' ability to listen and read for meaning by providing explicit instruction in effective listening and reading strategies. Although listening and reading differ in terms of time constraints and the opportunity to go back to parts of the message that were not understood, there are, nonetheless, great similarities in what is involved in successful listening and reading.

Tasks that help students make meaning from oral or written materials generally fall into three phases:

1. *Prior to listening or reading:*

    • *Pre-reading/pre-listening activities* help students anticipate and predict based on background knowledge, use of advance organizers, and contextual cues. Teachers may need to supply cultural background information and establish a purpose for listening. Teachers can use pre- and post-reading/listening activities to link vocabulary to linguistic knowledge, such as word families, synonyms, and how context affects meaning.

2. *While listening, listening again, reading and/or re-reading:*

    *   *Skimming/scanning tasks* help students to locate specific information.

    *   *Decoding/intensive reading activities* may include guessing content or the meaning of unknown words and phrases and using connecting words to ascertain relationships within and between sentences. Decoding helps students develop rapidity by teaching them to cope with unknowns that might slow them down as they read. Intensive reading helps to identify main ideas and related supporting details.

    *   *Comprehension activities* include checks to see whether students have fulfilled the purpose for reading or listening, and having students summarize information

or compare their interpretations with supporting evidence in the text.

3. *After listening or reading:*

    *   *Transfer activities* and personal reactions allow students to apply reading/listening strategies to new tasks or contexts. Students personally respond to what they have read or listened to, and compare their own perspective with that given in the oral or written materials.

Other research-based recommendations for teaching reading comprehension skills include: 1) instructing students in specific strategies and 2) extensive reading for long, concentrated periods to help students develop automaticity, increase their vocabulary and awareness of language and text structures, and develop confidence and motivation.

 Sources:

Appel and Lantolf 1994; Bacon 1992; Barnett 1986, 1995; Carrell 1984; Carrell and Wise 1998; Chamot et al. 1987; Glisan 1988, 1995; Grabe 1991; Hall 1999; Phillips 1984; Shrum and Glisan 2000; Vandergrift 1997.

4.6. Writing Instruction: Effective approaches to the teaching of writing in the foreign language classroom should reflect student needs, abilities, and purposes for writing.

Research findings:

Most research on the teaching of writing has been done with students writing in their first language. Research on writing in a second language has been done primarily with learners of English as an additional language, not with English-speaking students learning a foreign language. Of these studies, very few have been done with students below the college level or below the intermediate level of language proficiency.

Among the findings in an extensive review of the literature on teaching writing in the student's first language (L1) were: teaching grammar in isolation does not improve writing; sentence combining can contribute to improved writing; and the use of criteria/checklists for peer editing can improve writing. However, while L1 writing research may provide some guidance for foreign language instruction, there is some question as to whether L1 writing is similar to writing in a foreign language and whether writing skills from L1 transfer.

Research on foreign language writing reflects varied views of the purposes of writing in a foreign language. As a result, research has examined varied aspects of writing: the role of extensive writing and journal writing, the effects of grammar, computer use, task types and classroom activities, and process instruction. Research has demonstrated some positive effects on student writing of metacognitive strategy instruction, process writing, extensive writing, and computer-mediated interactive writing.

Communicating through writing in a foreign language shares many characteristics with first language writing. Composing text requires planning, drafting, and editing text. As they plan to write, students can communicate more effectively when considering their audience and their purpose for writing.

In contrast, grammatical knowledge seems to be independent of the skill of composing text, and reviews of the foreign language research related to error correction have found most studies show limited, if any, benefit. The effectiveness of error correction approaches for second language writers seems to vary by student cognitive style, student attitudes toward the teacher, student proficiency level, teacher approach to error correction, and purpose. Research studies suggest that under some conditions, error correction may be beneficial, such as when teachers provide a code for composition errors that students use for self-correcting and rewriting their text, or when teachers underline errors and students then rewrite. One study found grading compositions did not affect the quantity of errors, but did result in longer compositions with more complex language.

In the classroom:

Methods used to teach writing may be determined by the proficiency level of students, the purposes for writing, the intended audience, and the needs and preferences of the students.

Students of foreign languages may benefit from learning the writing strategies used by good L1 writers: they plan, pause frequently to reread what has been written and plan what will come next, and revise. They are recursive—that is, they go back over and over again to make sure their meaning will be clear to the reader. Good writers have an awareness of their audience and bear in mind the needs of the reader.

Teachers can help students improve the quality of their writing by using techniques that promote good planning. For example, writing prompts identifying the purpose, audience, and text type can remind students to write with these factors in mind. Pre-writing activities, such as brainstorming ideas, needed vocabulary, and grammar structures—whether done individually or collaboratively—can stimulate recall, and thus availability, of language. Graphic organizers not only help students organize their thoughts, they can also help students organize the language they will use when they write. Peer editing use helps students become aware of how effectively their writing communicates their intended meanings while also promoting interactive oral language.

Although the benefits and effectiveness of error correction are questionable, some studies show students want their errors corrected. Error correction may range from teacher comments without corrections, to comments with correc-

tions embedded, to suggestions for improvement, to identification of the type of error without help, to a coding system for student self-correction, to explicit error correction. In addition, teachers may choose when to correct errors: always? only on the final product? only on early drafts? Teacher decisions may also depend on the kind of writing to be done and its purpose.

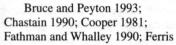

Sources:

Bruce and Peyton 1993; Chastain 1990; Cooper 1981; Fathman and Whalley 1990; Ferris 1999; Gass and Magnan 1993; Hadley 2001; Hillocks 1986; Kaplan 1966; Krapels 1990; Krashen 1984; Lalande 1982; Reichelt 2001; Rieken 1991; Scott 1995; Truscott 1996, 1999.

4.7. Explicit Grammar Instruction: Some types of explicit grammar instruction can improve students' grammatical competence.

Research findings:

The role of formal grammar instruction in language learning has occasioned great debate in the last decade, with research showing moderate, but not conclusive, value for some types of explicit grammar teaching. Studies comparing students who receive explicit grammar instruction with those who do not have shown varied results, in part because of the limitations of research designs themselves: length of the study, nature of the grammar point in light of each student's readiness to learn it, and method of assessment. Some studies have shown a positive role for form-focused instruction and input enhancement (directing student attention to targeted grammatical features). Researchers note further information about form-focused instruction is needed to determine when to focus on form, which forms to focus on, and how to do so without separating it from the primary goal of communicative language teaching and learning. Researchers also distinguish between *focus on form* (attention to grammar within the context of communicative activities) and *focus on forms* (grammar instruction as the organizing principle of curriculum and instruction).

The question of error correction is closely aligned with questions about how learners develop grammatical accuracy. Reviewers of the research on error correction in foreign language instruction have found the results are inconclusive, with contradictory evidence for the value of error correction of written work or during oral communicative activities. A series of studies focused on how learners use error correction showed some types of error correction are more likely to lead to self-correction and others are less likely to be perceived as correction at all.

In the classroom:

Despite evidence that explicit grammar instruction is useful in certain contexts for given types of structures, grammar continues to play a major role in instruction, aimed at immediate production of the form(s) taught. However, the value of grammar instruction may be to highlight the structure or morphology in the input to facilitate intake by helping students gain a heightened awareness (that is, notice features in the input they might otherwise ignore). Through form-focused instruction/input enhancement students can gain an understanding of how meanings are conveyed by forms. Teachers can promote language development by providing students with enhanced input that highlights new grammar points. Teachers may use explicit instruction combined with implicit activities to draw students' attention to significant language features. Or, tasks may require students to demonstrate their comprehension of the feature (for example, "Which word in this sentence tells whether the event took place already?"). Over time, with sufficient exposure to comprehensible input containing the language feature, students will incorporate it into their own internalized system and produce it with ever-increasing frequency and accuracy. In contrast, grammar instruction aimed at immediate production is unlikely to be successful.

If the purpose of grammar instruction is to enable students to notice features in the input (leading to intake), then grammar instruction should emanate from meaningful oral and written materials in which the feature is deliberately embedded and in which the feature is noticeably salient (for example, a story contrasting events that took place in the past vs. events yet to take place). Teachers may then draw students' attention to the feature through a series of well-designed, meaning-focused input activities (oral and/or written) that require students to attend to the new features at the sentence and discourse level. This type of interactive, guided-induction approach can help students construct their own understanding of the grammatical principles involved.

Teachers should have realistic expectations about the ability of students to accurately produce grammatical utterances, especially while students are still gaining an understanding of a new grammar concept. Practice producing grammatical utterances may lead to automaticity in the long term, but teachers should be mindful that it takes time for students to gain control over grammar.

There is a wide range of options for correcting student errors to determine which errors should be corrected, under which circumstances, and the form of correction in light of the purposes of the activity. Decisions about when and how to correct errors will depend on the purpose of the lesson, the nature of the error, and student variables. There is a range of options for correcting errors in students' oral and written production. Some researchers have noted that students often do not perceive recasts (teacher re-phrasing a student utterance in correct form) as error correction;

students are more likely to self-correct when teachers ask for clarification or elicit the correct form. Some theorists have argued only certain types of errors should be corrected. For example, since discourse-level errors (such as word order) are more likely to result in miscommunication than are sentence-level errors (such as the wrong ending on the verb), the former may be more important to correct. Others suggest assessment of each learner's language be made so that error correction can be tailored to the developmental needs of students.

 Sources:

Adair-Hauck, Donato, and Cumo 1994; Aljaafreh and Lantolf 1994; Celce-Murcia 1991; DeKeyser 1993, 1997; Doughty and Varela 1998; Doughty and Williams 1998; Ellis 1993, 1995, 2002; Fotos 1994; Gass and Magnan 1993; Heilenman 1995; Larsen-Freeman and Long 1991; Lee and VanPatten 1995; Long, Inagaki, and Ortega 1998; Long and Robinson 1998; Lyster and Ranta 1997; Mings 1993; Schmidt and Frota 1986; VanPatten 1993, 1996; White, Spada, Lightbown, and Ranta 1991.

4.8. Integration of Culture: Integrating culture in language instruction improves students' ability to communicate and function in another culture.

Research findings:

A number of theoretical models for the teaching of culture have been proposed. One useful model suggests the goal of language/culture learning is to produce an "intercultural speaker." The intercultural speaker demonstrates knowledge and skill in five domains:

- *attitudes*—the ability to be open to other cultures;

- *knowledge*—the knowledge of one's own culture and of the target culture;

- *skill in interpreting and relating*—the skill of interpreting texts, documents, and interactions in light of existing knowledge and attitudes;

- *skill in discovery and interaction*—the skill of learning new behaviors, beliefs, and values, and the ability to use knowledge and skills in successful interactions; and

- *critical awareness/political education*—the ability to consciously use explicit criteria to evaluate other cultures and one's own.

Research and reviews of research on cross-cultural communication have shown cultures vary in the ways in which individual factors such as gender, age, and the relationship between interlocutors play a role in determining how one may speak to whom, and in the ways variables inherent in the social relationships and context of communication influence how messages determine choice of lexicon or grammatical forms. The rules governing the expression of apologies, complaints, requests, and compliments also vary across languages.

A review of the research on the teaching of culture reported four factors important in preparing students for success. Teachers need to understand: 1) the roles of student attitudes toward language learning in general and their willingness to learn about and understand another culture; 2) the process of acculturation: learning to see the world through the perspectives of others is a process that teachers must facilitate and support, as this process can be emotionally provocative for students; 3) readiness for culture learning: because culture learning goes beyond facts to an understanding of the beliefs, behaviors, and values of a culture, students must be prepared to deal with the process of culture learning, and to cope with frustration and ambiguity; and 4) the role of self-awareness: students must understand how they are bound to their own cultural beliefs, behaviors, and values. Research also has shown student attitudes toward other cultures are enhanced when students have information and direct contact with other cultures.

In the classroom:

The goals of culture learning are to help students gain an understanding and knowledge of other cultures, deepen their insight into their own culture, and be enabled to communicate effectively by understanding the cultural rules of communication. Ultimately, language educators hope to develop positive student attitudes toward the people whose language and culture they are learning.

To gain an understanding and knowledge of other cultures, students need to understand the interaction among cultural perspectives (attitudes, values, beliefs), cultural practices (what people do, how people behave, how they carry out the daily lives and institutions of a culture), and cultural products (aesthetic products such as art, music, and literature; artifacts of daily life, such as household items, vehicles of transportation, wedding attire).

Culture instruction takes several forms: developing skill in cross-cultural communication, informational knowledge about the civilization and daily life patterns of the target culture, and students' ability to observe and analyze another culture. Culture instruction cannot and should not be separated from language instruction, because culture is the playing field on which language use takes place. Culture gives meaning to words, and cultures may have differing associations with words (e.g., family, home, bread, and work). Communicating accurately is more than using grammar and vocabulary correctly; it is ensuring one can convey and interpret meanings accurately within the cultural context of communication. Learners may not be able to parallel native speaker usage, but research on cross-cultural communication can help to make students aware of potential differences in how meanings are conveyed and sensitize them to the possibilities of miscommunication.

Many theorists suggest the purpose of culture instruction is not to teach facts, but rather to enable students to interpret the facts they encounter in order to organize facts into patterns of understanding. This problem-solving (as opposed to a facts-based) approach is desirable because facts are always changing; teaching facts may reinforce stereotypes rather than dispel them; and teaching facts alone will not prepare students for successful encounters with the culture outside of the classroom. Students need to recognize how their own culture pervades their attitudes and beliefs, and the dangers of projecting these onto another culture.

Sources:

Byram 1997; Byram and Esarte-Sarries 1991; Fantini 1999; Hadley 2001; Klee 1998; Lange 1999; Mantle-Bromley 1992; Olshtain 1993; Robinson 1981; Seelye 1993.

4.9. Appropriate Assessment of Student Progress: The design and methods of student assessment should be appropriate to measure the kinds of information desired about student progress.

Research findings:

Authentic assessment measures what students can do with what they know and is consistent with how they are taught. In foreign language, this has meant integrating knowledge about language into using knowledge to engage in real-life tasks. Assessment tools, then, must be authentic to the communicative goals and activities of the language classroom. Assessments tailored to objectives help link curriculum, instruction, and assessment into a coherent whole.

Beginning in the early 1980s, researchers have focused on assessing students' ability to use their knowledge to communicate in real or simulated situations. To find out whether students could explain how to get from one place in town to another, researchers had students role-play giving directions. To find out whether students could listen with comprehension to gain information, researchers asked students to listen to a weather report to determine which types of activities and clothing would be appropriate on a given day. These tasks look at student performance—the ability to use knowledge and integrate skills—rather than at knowledge or skills in isolation. Such assessment provides different information from traditional testing methods.

Researchers have found the means by which students are assessed affects the information the assessments provide about student ability to use knowledge. For example, the extent and type of language that students produce in an oral task vary according to whether students are face-to-face with their interlocutor or speaking to a recording device. Oral production may also vary according to other testing conditions: whether the test requires spontaneous or prepared speech;

whether the student speaks to the teacher, to other students, or into a recording device; and whether the task requires responses to specific questions, picture description, or is conversational in nature. Performance on reading comprehension tasks varies both by the nature of the task and the language of response—students perform differently on tasks requiring constructed responses (such as open-ended questions) than on those requiring recognition and/or selection (e.g., multiple choice). Portfolios have been shown to correlate positively with students' ability to engage in self-assessment and their investment in learning language.

In the classroom:

Teachers assess students for diagnostic purposes as well as to ascertain how much students have learned. Teachers may find written tests of knowledge one of many useful sources of information. But these tests should be part of a broader assessment approach that looks at the student's ability to integrate knowledge in use. That is, performance with language (interacting, interpreting, or presenting) is the goal of instruction, and assessment should measure progress toward that goal.

Complementary assessments that provide multiple sources of evidence of student learning, including tests, should be used to measure and evaluate student progress. Oral performances, whether spontaneous or rehearsed, are important if the goal of language learning is to use language to communicate. Similarly, the ability to communicate in writing needs to be assessed through communicative writing tasks. Among the many possible sources of information about student progress are: dialogue journals, teacher-student interviews, teacher observations, student reports, exhibits, and demonstrations, student self-assessment, and portfolios of student work.

Finding out what students know and can do in their new language requires multiple sources of information and varying types of assessments. If the goal of instruction is to enable students to use the language to communicate, then tests should examine whether, indeed, students can communicate. It is helpful for teachers to link curriculum, instruction, and

assessment by clearly stating desired outcomes and identifying what would constitute evidence of student attainment of those objectives.

Sources:

Donato 1998; Donato and McCormick 1994; Genesee and Upshur 1996; Hall 1999; Huebener and Jensen 1992; Padilla, Aninao, and Sung 1996; Phillips 1995; Shohamy 1984, 1991, 1994; Underhill 1987; Wiggins 1998; Wolf 1993.

4.10. Use of Technology: Use of various forms of technology can result in improved skills in comprehending and producing a second language.

Research findings:

Because the use of technology in foreign language instruction is relatively new, the research base relating technology to language learning is recent but growing rapidly.

Computer-mediated communication has been shown to benefit language development and intercultural learning. Real-time online interactions provide opportunities for input, output, and negation of meaning; they allow students time to process input, monitor their output, and increase opportunities for individual students to use the target language in meaningful interactions with others. As noted in sections 4.2.1 and 4.2.2, these variables have been shown to contribute to language development. Research studies have found students use more language, demonstrate greater accuracy, and initiate more interactions communicating through email interactions. International electronic projects, such as online discussions of literary texts among students of different countries, have been shown to foster communication and intercultural learning.

Studies have shown the use of word processors for composing in a foreign language improved student attitudes toward writing, increased accuracy in spelling and grammar, increased complexity of expression, and improved student writing. Writing with computers facilitates drafting and editing, two important phases of the writing process. Other studies have reported students who used networked computers demonstrated increased sophistication and complexity in their written language. Some researchers suggest online writing in real-time (synchronous writing) may have qualitatively different benefits from asynchronous writing.

Other forms of technology have also been researched. The Internet has been shown to be an effective tool for students to learn about the target culture and to use their foreign language skills to acquire new information, including "virtual study abroad." In Web-based projects between students in the United States and abroad, students analyze and compare materials from each other's cultures. Participating in discussion forums and listservs of the target culture can give foreign language learners opportunities to gain specific knowledge and information, as well as to learn the cultural norms and conventions for online communication.

Video-supported instruction, including use of captioned video and multimedia, have been shown to improve listening comprehension. Video that allows students to call on prior knowledge and experience, and that provides visual cues to the meaning of what students hear, results in greater student learning. Captioning, whether in English or the target language, enhances student comprehension, with English captions showing greater impact on comprehension. Video has been shown to be superior to print-only texts in student ability to learn and remember information. Similarly, multimedia and hypermedia also can contribute to improved reading skills.

A study of distance learning found individual learner characteristics, such as strategy use, learning style, motivation, and gender, significantly affected its effectiveness. Despite the proliferation of distance learning opportunities, little research is available to document its effectiveness. Many foreign language educators believe that while distance learning can contribute to language learning, by itself it probably cannot meet the objectives of most language curricula or standards, particularly those related to spoken language. Since the ability to communicate orally depends on opportunities to negotiate meaning through purposeful interaction, the efficacy of distance learning may rest, in part, on the quality and quantity of provision made for student interaction.

In the classroom:

Technology is increasingly used in all subjects as part of the teaching/learning process: video provides a rich source of visual information that can be used to promote skills in analyzing and observing other cultures as well as in using visual cues as links to meaning. There are a number of pilot projects involving Web-based foreign language teaching and testing. An area offering great promise, with a growing research base, involves computer communication. Computer communication, particularly the online chat mode, has many of the features of oral discourse. They involve spontaneous, unrehearsed, informal language use focusing on meaning rather than on form. Communication networks have a number of positive features contributing to language development, including increased student participation and the lowered anxiety levels made possible by the psychological distance imposed by computer-mediated communication. Furthermore, while online communication is extemporaneous, as is speech, it provides additional time to process input and to formulate output.

The Internet and World Wide Web can provide access to resources that are richer and far more extensive than those available in most school or community libraries. Because these provide immediate access to authentic language and cultural resources, they can have significant impact on the ways in which language is practiced and can enrich opportunities for meaningful contact with the target language without physically leaving the classroom. One Web site that is a popular source for teachers—and with innumerable links to other useful sites—is www.cortland.edu/www/flteach/flteach.html.

Sources:

Beauvois 1997; Bruce and Peyton 1993; Furstenberg, Levet, English, and Maillet 2001; Garza 1991; Gonzalez-Bueno 1998; Hanna and de Nooy 2003; Herron 1994; Joiner 1997; Kern 1995; Kinginger 1998; Lafford and Lafford 1997; Lee 1997, 2002; Markham, Peter, and McCarthy 2001; Martinez-Lage 1997; Müller-Hartmann 2000; Oxford et al. 1993; Pertusa-Seva and Stewart 2000; Pusack and Otto 1995; Rubin 1990; Secules, Herron, and Tomasello 1992; Swaffar and Vlatten 1997; Warschauer 1997.

Bibliography

Adair-Hauck, B., R. Donato, and P. Cumo. 1994. "Using a Whole Language Approach to Teach Grammar." In *Teacher's Handbook: Contextualized Language Instruction,* J. Shrum and E. Glisan, editors (pp. 90-111). Boston: Heinle & Heinle Publishers.

Aljaafreh, A., and J.P. Lantolf. 1994. "Negative Feedback as Regulation and Second Language Learning in the Zone of Proximal Development." *Modern Language Journal* Vol. 78, No. 4: 465- 483.

Appel, G., and J.P. Lantolf. 1994. "Speaking as Mediation: A Study of L1 and L2 Text Recall Tasks." *Modern Language Journal* Vol. 78, No. 4: 437-452.

Armstrong, P., and J. Rogers. 1997. "Basic Skills Revisited: The Effect of Foreign Language on Reading, Math, and Language Arts." *Learning Languages* Vol. 2, No. 30: 20-31.

Asher, J. 1984. *Learning Another Language Through Actions: The Complete Teacher's Guidebook.* Los Gatos, CA: Sky Oaks Publications.

Bacon, S. 1992. "Phases of Listening to Authentic Input in Spanish: A Descriptive Study." *Foreign Language Annals* Vol. 25: 317-324.

Barnett, M. 1986. "Syntactic and Lexical/Semantic Skill in Foreign Language Reading: Importance and Interaction." *Modern Language Journal* Vol. 70: 343-349.

Barnett, M. 1995. "Reading." In *Research Within Reach II,* C. Herron and V. Galloway, editors (pp. 85-95). Valdosta, GA: Southern Conference on Language Teaching.

Beauvois, M.H. 1997. "Computer-Mediated Communication: Technology for Improving Speaking and Writing." In *Technology-Enhanced Language Learning,* M. Bush and R. Terry, editors (pp. 165-184). Lincolnwood, IL: National Textbook Co.

Brooks, F.B., and R. Donato. 1994. "Vygotskyan Approaches to Understanding Foreign Language Learner Discourse During Communicative Tasks." *Hispania* Vol. 77, No. 2: 262-274.

Bruce, B., and J.K. Peyton. 1993. "A Situated Evaluation of ENFI." In *Networked-Based Classrooms: Promises and Realities,* B. Bruce, J.K. Peyton, and T. Batson, editors. New York: Cambridge University Press.

Bush, M., and R. Terry, editors. 1997. *Technology-Enhanced Language Learning.* Lincolnwood, IL: National Textbook Co.

Byram, M. 1997. *Teaching and Assessing Intercultural Competence.* Clevedon, UK: Multilingual Matters.

Byram, M., and V. Esarte-Sarries. 1991. *Investigating Cultural Studies in Foreign Language Teaching: A Book for Teachers.* Clevedon, UK: Multilingual Matters.

Carrell, P.L. 1984. "The Effects of Rhetorical Organization on ESL Readers." *TESOL Quarterly* Vol. 18: 441-469.

Carrell, P., and T. Wise. 1998. "The Relationship Between Prior Knowledge and Topic Interest in Second Language Reading." *Studies in Second Language Acquisition* Vol. 20, No. 3: 285-310.

Celce-Murcia, M. 1991. "Grammar Pedagogy in Second and Foreign Language Teaching." *TESOL Quarterly* Vol. 25, No. 3: 459-480.

Celce-Murcia, M., Z. Dörnyei, and S. Thurrell. 1995. "Communicative Competence: A Pedagogically Motivated Model with Content Specifications." *Issues in Applied Linguistics* Vol. 6, No. 2: 5-35.

Chamot, A.U., and L. Kupper. 1989. "Learning Strategies in Foreign Language Instruction." *Foreign Language Annals* Vol. 22: 13-24.

Chamot, A.U., J.M. O'Malley, L. Kupper, and M.V. Impink-Hernández. 1987. *A Study of Learning Strategies in Foreign Language Instruction: First Year Report.* Rosslyn, VA: InterAmerica Research Associates.

Chastain, K. 1990. "Characteristics of Graded and Un-graded Compositions." *Modern Language Journal* Vol. 74: 10-14.

Christian, D., C. Montone, K. Lindholm, and I. Carranza. 1997. *Profiles in Two-Way Immersion Education.* Washington, DC: Center for Applied Linguistics and Delta Systems, Inc.

Cooper, T. 1981. "Sentence Combining: An Experiment in Teaching Writing." *Modern Language Journal* Vol. 65: 158-165.

Curtain, H., and C.A. Pesola. 1994. *Languages and Children: Making the Match.* New York: Longman, Inc.

Day, E., and S. Shapson. 1996. *Studies in Immersion Education.* Clevedon, UK: Multilingual Matters.

DeGuerrero, M.C.M. and O.S. Villamil. 1994. "Social-Cognitive Dimensions of Interaction in L2 Peer Revision." *Modern Language Journal* Vol. 78, No. 4: 484-496.

DeKeyser, R.M. 1993. "The Effect of Error Correction on L2 Grammar Knowledge and Oral Proficiency." *Modern Language Journal* Vol. 77: 501-514.

DeKeyser, R.M. 1997. "Beyond Explicit Rule Learning." *Studies in Second Language Acquisition* Vol. 19: 195-221.

Devitt, S. 1997. "Interacting with Authentic Texts: Multilayered Processes." *Modern Language Journal* Vol. 81, No. 4: 457-469.

Donato, R. 1998. "Assessing Foreign Language Abilities of the Early Language Learner." In *Critical Issues in Early Second Language Learning*, M. Met, editor. Glenview, IL: Scott Foresman Addison Wesley.

Donato, R. 2000. "Sociocultural Contributions To Understanding The Foreign And Second Language Classroom." In *Sociocultural Theory and Second Language Learning*, J. Lantolf, editor (pp. 29-52). Oxford: Oxford University Press.

Donato, R., and D. McCormick. 1994. "A Sociocultural Perspective On Language Learning Strategies: The Role Of Mediation." *Modern Language Journal* Vol. 78, No. 4: 453-464.

Donato, R., G.R. Tucker, J. Wudthayagorn, and K. Igarashi. 2000. "Attitudes, Achievements, and Instruction in the Later Years of FLES." *Foreign Language Annals* Vol. 33: 377-393.

Dörnyei, Z. 1995. "On the Teachability of Communication Strategies." *TESOL Quarterly* Vol. 29, No. 1: 55-85.

Dörnyei, Z. 1997. "Psychological Processes in Cooperative Language Learning: Group Dynamics and Motivation." *Modern Language Journal* Vol. 81, No. 4: 482-493.

Dörnyei, Z., and J. Kormos. 1998. "Problem-Solving Mechanisms in L2 Communication: A Psycholinguistic Perspective." *Studies in Second Language Acquisition* Vol. 20, No. 3: 349-386.

Doughty, C., and T. Pica. 1986. "'Information Gap' Tasks: Do They Facilitate Second Language Acquisition?" *TESOL Quarterly* Vol. 20: 305-325.

Doughty, C., and E. Varela. 1998. "Communicative Focus on Form." In *Focus on Form in Classroom Second Language Acquisition*, C. Doughty and J. Williams, editors. Cambridge, UK: Cambridge University Press.

Doughty, C., and J. Williams, editors. 1998. *Focus on Form in Classroom Second Language Acquisition*. Cambridge, UK: Cambridge University Press.

Education Commission of the States. 1996. *Bridging the Gap Between Neuroscience and Education*. Denver, CO: Education Commission of the States.

Ellis, R. 1990. *Instructed Language Acquisition*. Oxford, UK: Blackwell Publishers.

Ellis, R. 1993. "The Structural Syllabus and Second Language Acquisition." *TESOL Quarterly* Vol. 27: 91-112.

Ellis, R. 1995. "Interpretation Tasks for Grammar Teaching." *TESOL Quarterly* Vol. 29, No. 1: 87-105.

Ellis, R. 2002. "Does Form-Focused Instruction affect the Acquisition of Implicit Knowledge? A Review of the Research." *Studies in Second Language Acquisition* Vol. 24: 223-236.

Fantini, A. 1999. "Comparisons: Towards the Development of Intercultural Competence." In *Foreign Language Standards: Linking Theory, Research, and Practice*, J. Phillips, editor. Lincolnwood, IL: National Textbook Co.

Fathman, A.K., and E. Whalley. 1990. "Teacher Response to Student Writing: Focus on Form versus Content." In *Second Language Writing: Research Insights for the Classroom*, B. Kroll, editor (pp. 178-190). New York: Cambridge University Press.

Ferris, D. 1999. "The Case for Grammar Correction in L2 Writing Classes: A Response to Truscott (1996)." *Journal of Second Language Writing* Vol. 8:1-11.

Fotos, S. 1994. "Integrating Grammar Instruction And Communicative Language Use Through Grammar Consciousness-Raising Tasks." *TESOL Quarterly* Vol. 28, No. 2: 323-351.

Furstenberg, G., S. Levet, K. English, and K. Maillet. 2001. "Giving a Virtual Voice to the Silent Language of Culture: The Cultura Project." *Language Learning & Technology*. Vol. 5: 55-102.

Garza, T.J. 1991. "Evaluating the Use of Captioned Video Material in Advanced Foreign Language Learning." *Foreign Language Annals* Vol. 24: 239-258.

Gass, S. 1999. "Discussion: Incidental Vocabulary Learning." *Studies in Second Language Acquisition* Vol. 21: 319-333.

Gass, S., and S. Sieloff Magnan. 1993. "Second-Language Production: SLA Research in Speaking and Writing." In *Research in Language Learning*, A.O. Omaggio-Hadley, editor (pp. 156-197). Lincolnwood, IL: National Textbook Company.

Gass, S., and E. Varonis. 1985. "Variation in Native Speaker Speech Modification to Non-Native Speakers." *Studies in Second Language Acquisition* Vol. 7: 37-57.

Genesee, F. 1987. *Learning Through Two Languages*. Rowley, MA: Newbury House.

Genesee, F. 1994. *Integrating Language and Content: Lessons from Immersion*. Santa Cruz, CA: National Center for Research on Cultural Diversity and Second Language Learning.

Genesee, F., and J.A. Upshur. 1996. *Classroom-Based Evaluation in Second Language Education*. New York: Cambridge University Press.

Glisan, E.W. 1988. "A Plan for Teaching Listening Comprehension: Adaptation of an Instructional Reading Model." *Foreign Language Annals* Vol. 31: 9-16.

Glisan, E.W. 1995. "Listening." In *Research Within Reach II*, C. Herron and V. Galloway, editors (pp. 61-83). Valdosta, GA: Southern Conference on Language Teaching.

Gonzalez-Bueno, M. 1998. "The Effects of Electronic Mail On Spanish L2 Discourse." *Language Learning & Technology* Vol. 1: 55-70.

Grabe, W. 1991. "Current Developments in Second Language Reading Research." *TESOL Quarterly* Vol. 25: 375-406.

Haas, M. 1998. "Early vs. Late: The Practitioner's Perspective." In *Critical Issues in Early Second Language Learning*, M. Met, editor (pp. 43-48). Glenview, IL: Scott Foresman Addison Wesley.

Hadley, A.C. 2001. *Teaching Language in Context*. Boston: Heinle & Heinle Publishers.

Hall, J.K. 1999. "The Communication Standards." In *Foreign Language Standards: Linking Theory, Research, and Practice*, J. Phillips, editor (pp. 15-36). Lincolnwood, IL: National Textbook Co.

Hall, J.K., and M. Walsh. 2002. "Teacher-Student Interaction and Language Learning." *Annual Review of Applied Linguistics* Vol. 22: 186-203.

Hanna, B.E., and J. de Nooy. 2003. "A Funny Thing Happened On The Way To The Forum: Electronic Discussion And Foreign Language Learning." *Language Learning & Technology* Vol. 7: 71-85.

Harley, B. 1986. *Age in Second Language Acquisition.* San Diego, CA: College Hill Press.

Harley, B. 1998. "The Outcomes of Early and Later Language Learning." In *Critical Issues in Early Second Language Learning,* M. Met, editor (pp. 26-30). Glenview, IL: Scott Foresman Addison Wesley.

Heilenman, L.K. 1995. "Grammar Research Within Reach." In *Research Within Reach II,* C. Herron and V. Galloway, editors (pp. 129-148). Valdosta, GA: Southern Conference on Language Teaching.

Herron, C. 1994. "An Investigation of the Effectiveness of Using an Advance Organizer to Introduce Video in the Foreign Language Classroom." *Modern Language Journal* Vol. 78: 190-198.

Hillocks, G., Jr. 1986. *Research on Written Composition: New Directions for Teaching.* Urbana, IL: ERIC Clearinghouse on Reading and Communication Skills and the National Conference on Research in English. (ED 265 552)

Huebener, T., and A. Jensen. 1992. "A Study of Foreign Language Proficiency-Based Testing in Secondary Schools." *Foreign Language Annals* Vol. 25: 105-115.

Joiner, E. 1997. "Teaching Listening: How Technology Can Help." In *Technology-Enhanced Language Learning,* M. Bush and R. Terry, editors (pp. 77-120). Lincolnwood, IL: National Textbook Co.

Kaplan, R.B. 1966. "Cultural Thought Patterns in Intercultural Education." *Language Learning* Vol. 16: 1-20.

Kern, R.G. 1995. "Restructuring Classroom Interaction With Networked Computers: Effects On Quantity And Characteristics Of Language Production." *Modern Language Journal* Vol. 79, No. 4: 457-476.

Kinginger, C. 1998. "Videoconferencing as Access to Spoken French." *Modern Language Journal* Vol. 82, No. 4: 502-513.

Klee, C.A. 1998. "Communication as an Organizing Principle in the National Standards: Sociolinguistic Aspects of Spanish Language Teaching." *Hispania* Vol. 81, No. 2: 339-351.

Krapels, A. 1990. "An Overview of Second Language Writing Process Research." In *Second Language Writing: Research Insights for the Classroom,* B. Kroll, editor (pp. 37-56). New York: Cambridge University Press.

Krashen, S. 1982. *Principles and Practice in Second Language Acquisition.* Oxford: Pergamon Press.

Krashen, S. 1984. *Writing, Research, Theory and Applications.* Oxford: Pergamon Press.

Krashen, S.D., R.C. Scarcella, and M.H. Long. 1982. *Child-Adult Differences in Second Language Acquisition.* Rowley, MA: Newbury House.

Lafford, P.A., and B.A. Lafford. 1997. "Learning Language and Culture with Internet Technologies." In *Technology-Enhanced Language Learning,* M. Bush and R. Terry, editors (pp. 215-262). Lincolnwood, IL: National Textbook Co.

Lalande, J. 1982. "Reducing Composition Errors: An Experiment." *Modern Language Journal* Vol. 66: 140-49.

Lange, D. 1999. "Planning for and Using the New National Culture Standards." In *Foreign Language Standards: Linking Theory, Research, and Practice,* J. Phillips, editor (pp. 57-136). Lincolnwood, IL: National Textbook Co.

Larsen-Freeman, D., and M. Long. 1991. *An Introduction to Second Language Acquisition Research.* New York: Longman, Inc.

Lee, J., and B. VanPatten. 1995. *Making Communicative Language Teaching Happen.* New York: McGraw Hill.

Lee, L. 1997. "Using Internet Tools as an Enhancement of C2 Teaching and Learning." *Foreign Language Annals* Vol. 30, No. 3: 410-427.

Lee, L. 2002. "Enhancing Learner's Communication Skills through Synchronous Electronic Interaction and Task-Based Instruction." *Foreign Language Annals* Vol. 35: 18-24.

Lee, P. 1996. "Cognitive Development in Bilingual Children: A Case for Bilingual Instruction in Early Childhood Education." *Bilingual Research Journal* Vol. 20, No. 3-4: 499-522.

Leow, R. 1999. "Attention, Awareness, and Focus on Form Research: A Critical Overview." In *Meaning and Form: Multiple Perspectives,* J.F. Lee and A. Valdman, editors (pp. 69-98). Boston: Heinle & Heinle.

Lightbown, P.M. 1992. "Can They Do It Themselves? A Comprehension-Based ESL Course for Young Children." In *Comprehension-based Second Language Teacher/L'Enseignment des Langues Secondes axé sur la Compréhension,* R. Courchêne, J. Glidden, J. St. John, and C. Therien, editors (pp. 353-370). Ottawa: University of Ottawa Press.

Long, M.H., and P.A. Porter. 1985. "Group Work, Interlanguage Talk, and Second Language Acquistion." *TESOL Quarterly* Vol. 19: 207-227.

Long, M., S. Inagaki, and L. Ortega. 1998. "The Role of Implicit Negative Feedback in SLLA: Models and Recasts in Japanese and Spanish." *Modern Language Journal* Vol. 82, No. 3: 357-371.

Long, M., and P. Robinson. 1998. "Focus on Form: Theory, Research and Practice." In *Focus on Form in Classroom and Second Language Acquisition,* C. Doughty and J. Williams, editors. Cambridge: Cambridge University Press.

Lyster, R., and L. Ranta. 1997. "Corrective Feedback and Learner Uptake: Negotiation of Form in Communicative Classrooms." *Studies in Second Language Acquisition* Vol. 19, No. 1: 37-66.

Mantle-Bromley, C. 1992. "Preparing Students for Meaningful Culture Learning." *Foreign Language Annals* Vol. 25: 117-127.

Markham, P., L. Peter, and T. McCarthy. 2001. "The Effects of Native Language vs. Target Language Captions on Foreign Language Students' DVD Video Comprehension." *Foreign Language Annals* Vol. 34: 439-445.

Martinez-Lage, A. 1997. "Hypermedia Technology for Teaching Reading." In *Technology-Enhanced Language Learning*, M. Bush and R. Terry, editors (pp. 121-164). Lincolnwood, IL: National Textbook Co.

Met, M. 1995. "Speaking." In *Research Within Reach II*, C. Herron and V. Galloway, editors (pp. 97-113). Valdosta, GA: Southern Conference on Language Teaching.

Met, M., and V. Galloway. 1991. "Research in Foreign Language Curriculum." In *Handbook of Research on Curriculum*, P. Jackson, editor. New York: Macmillan.

Mings, R.C. 1993. "Changing Perspectives on the Utility of Error Correction in Second Language Acquisition." *Foreign Language Annals* Vol. 26: 171-179.

Müller-Hartmann, A. 2000. "The Role Of Tasks In Promoting Intercultural Learning In Electronic Learning Networks." *Language Learning & Technology* Vol. 4: 129-147.

Nunan, D. 1991. "Communicative Tasks and the Language Curriculum." *TESOL Quarterly* Vol. 25: 279-295.

Olshtain, E. 1993. "Language in Society." In *Research in Language Learning*, A.O. Omaggio- Hadley, editor (pp. 47-65). Lincolnwood, IL: National Textbook Company.

O'Malley, J.M., and A.U. Chamot. 1990. *Learner Strategies in Second Language Acquisition*. Cambridge, MA: Cambridge University Press.

O'Malley, J.M., and A.U. Chamot. 1993. "Language Learner Characteristics in Second Language Acquisition." In *Research in Language Learning*, A.O. Omaggio-Hadley, editor (pp. 96-123). Lincolnwood, IL: National Textbook Company.

O'Malley, J.M., and L. Valdez-Pierce. 1996. *Authentic Assessment For English Language Learners: Practical Approaches For Teachers*. New York: Addison-Wesley Publishing Co.

Ottawa Board of Education. 1996. *Comparative Outcomes and Impacts of Early, Middle and Late Entry French Immersion Options: Review of Recent Research and Annotated Bibliography*. Ottawa: Ottawa Board of Education.

Oxford, R. 1990. *Language Learning Strategies: What Every Teacher Should Know*. Rowley, MA: Newbury House.

Oxford, R. 1997. "Cooperative Learning, Collaborative Learning, and Interaction: Three Communicative Strands in the Language Classroom." *Modern Language Journal* Vol. 81, No. 4: 443-456.

Oxford, R., Y. Park-Oh, S. Ito, and M. Sumrall. 1993. "Japanese via Satellite: Effect of Motivation, Language Learning Styles and Strategies, Gender, Discourse Level, and Previous Language Learning Experience on Japanese Language Achievement." *Foreign Language Annals* Vol. 26: 359-371.

Padilla, A.M., J.C. Aninao, and H. Sung. 1996. "Development and Implementation of Student Portfolios in Foreign Language Programs." *Foreign Language Annals* Vol. 29, No. 3: 429-438.

Paribakht, T.S., and M. Wesche. 1999. "Reading and 'Incidental' L2 Vocabulary Acquisition." *Studies in Second Language Acquisition* Vol. 21: 195-224.

Pertusa-Seva, I., and M. Stewart. 2000. "Virtual Study Abroad 101: Expanding the Horizons of the Spanish Curriculum." *Foreign Language Annals* Vol. 33: 438-442.

Phillips, J.K. 1984. "Practical Implications of Recent Research in Reading." *Foreign Language Annals* Vol. 17: 285-296.

Phillips, J.K. 1995. "Testing." In *Research Within Reach II*, C. Herron and V. Galloway, editors (pp. 161-174). Valdosta, GA: Southern Conference on Language Teaching.

Pica, T. 1994. "Research On Negotiation: What Does It Reveal About Second-Language Learning Conditions, Processes, And Outcomes?" *Language Learning* Vol. 44: 493-527.

Pinker, S. 1994. *The Language Instinct*. New York: Morrow.

Platt, E., and F. Brooks. 1994. "The 'Acquisition-Rich Environment' Revisited." *Modern Language Journal* Vol. 78, No. 4: 497-511.

Pusack, J.P., and S.K. Otto. 1995. "Instructional Technologies." In *Research Within Reach II*, C. Herron and V. Galloway, editors (pp. 23-41). Valdosta, GA: Southern Conference on Language Teaching.

Reichelt, M. 2001. "A Critical Review of Foreign Language Writing Research on Pedagogical Approaches." *Modern Language Journal* Vol. 85: 578-598.

Rieken, E.G. 1991. *The Effect of Feedback on the Frequency and Accuracy of Use of the Passé Composé by Field-Independent and Field-Dependent Students of Beginning French*. Unpublished Ph.D. dissertation, University of Illinois at Urbana-Champaign.

Robinson, D.W. 1998. "The Cognitive, Academic, and Attitudinal Benefits of Early Language Learning." In *Critical Issues in Early Second Language Learning*, M. Met, editor. Glenview, IL: Scott Foresman Addison Wesley.

Robinson, G. 1981. *Issues in Second Language and Cross-Cultural Education: The Forest Through the Trees*. Boston: Heinle & Heinle Publishers.

Rubin, J. 1981. "Study of Cognitive Processes in Second Language Learning." *Applied Linguistics* Vol. 11: 117-131.

Rubin, J. 1990. "Improving Foreign Language Listening Comprehension." In *Georgetown University Round Table on Languages and Linguistics*, J.E. Alatis, editor. Washington, DC: Georgetown University Press.

Rubin, J. 1995. "Learning Processes and Strategy." In *Research Within Reach II*, C. Herron and V. Galloway, editors (pp. 11-22). Valdosta, GA: Southern Conference on Language Teaching.

Savignon, S. 1997. *Communicative Competence: Theory And Classroom Practice*. 2nd Ed. New York: McGraw Hill.

Savignon, S.J. 1991. "Communicative Language Teaching: State of the Art." *TESOL Quarterly* Vol. 25: 261-77.

Schmidt, R., and S. Frota. 1986. "Developing Basic Conversational Ability in a Second Language: A Case Study of an Adult Learner of Portuguese." In *Talking to Learn: Conversation in Second Language Acquisition*. R. Day, editor (pp. 237-326). Rowley, MA: Newbury House.

Scott, V. 1995. "Writing." In *Research within Reach II*, C. Herron and V. Galloway, editors (pp. 115-128). Valdosta, GA: Southern Conference on Language Teaching.

Secules, T., C. Herron, and M. Tomasello. 1992. "The Effect of Video Context on Foreign Language Learning." *Modern Language Journal* Vol. 76: 480-490.

Seelye, H.N. 1993. *Teaching Culture: Strategies for Intercultural Communication*. Lincolnwood, IL: National Textbook Co.

Shohamy, E. 1984. "Does the Testing Method Make a Difference? The Case of Reading Comprehension." *Language Testing* Vol. 1: 147-170.

Shohamy, E. 1991. "Connecting Testing and Learning in the Classroom and on the Program Level." In *Building Bridges and Making Connections*, J.K. Phillips, editor. South Burlington, VT: Northeast Conference.

Shohamy, E. 1994. "The Validity of Direct vs. Semi-direct Oral Tests." *Language Testing* Vol. 11: 99-123.

Shrum, J., and E. Glisan. 2000. *Teacher's Handbook. Contextualized Language Instruction*. Boston: Heinle & Heinle Publishers.

Standards for Foreign Language Learning: Preparing for the 21st Century. 1996. Yonkers, NY: National Standards in Foreign Language Education Project.

Swaffar, J., and A. Vlatten. 1997. "A Sequential Model for Video Viewing in the Foreign Language Curriculum." *Modern Language Journal* Vol. 81, No. 2: 175-188.

Swain, M. 1985. "Communicative Competence: Some Roles of Comprehensible Input and Comprehensible Output in Its Development." In *Input in Second Language Acquisition*. S. Gass and C. Madden, editors. Rowley, MA: Newbury House.

Swain, M., L. Brooks, and A. Tocalli-Beller. 2002. "Peer-Peer Dialogue As A Means of Second Language Learning." *Annual Review of Applied Linguistics* Vol. 22: 171-185.

Swain, M., and S. Lapkin. 1982. *Evaluating Bilingual Education: A Canadian Case Study*. Clevedon, UK: Multilingual Matters.

Swain, M., and S. Lapkin. 1991. "Additive Bilingualism and French Immersion Education: The Roles of Language Proficiency and Literacy." In *Bilingualism, Multiculturalism, and Second Language Learning: The McGill Conference in Honour of Wallace E. Lambert*, H.G. Reynolds, editor. Hillsdale, NJ: Lawrence Erlbaum.

Swain, M., and S. Lapkin. 1998. "Interaction And Second Language Learning: Two Adolescent French Immersion Students Working Together." *Modern Language Journal* Vol. 82, No. 3: 320-337.

Thomas, W.P., V. Collier, and M. Abbott. 1993. "Academic Achievement through Japanese, Spanish, or French: The First Two Years of Partial Immersion." *Modern Language Journal* Vol. 77, No. 2: 170-179.

Truscott, J. 1996. "The Case Against Grammar Correction In L2 Writing Classes." *Language Learning* Vol. 46: 327-369.

Truscott, J. 1999. "The Case For 'The Case Against Grammar Correction In L2 Writing Classes': A Response To Ferris." *Journal of Second Language Writing* Vol. 8:111-122.

Underhill, N. 1987. *Testing Spoken Language*. Cambridge, UK: Cambridge University Press.

Vandergrift, L. 1997. "The Cinderella of Communication Strategies: Reception Strategies in Interactive Listening." *Modern Language Journal* Vol. 81, No. 4: 494-505.

Van Lier, L. 1996. *Interaction in the Language Curriculum*. New York: Longman.

VanPatten, B. 1993. "Grammar Teaching for the Acquisition-Rich Classroom." *Foreign Language Annals* Vol. 26: 435-450.

VanPatten, B. 1996. *Input Processing and Grammar Instruction in Second Language Acquisition*. Greenwich, CT: Ablex Publishing Co.

VanPatten, B. 1998. "Perceptions of and Perspectives on the Term 'Communicative.'" *Hispania* Vol. 81: 925-932.

VanPatten, B. 2000. "Processing Instruction as Fork-Meaning Connections: Issues in Theory and Research." In *Meaning and Form: Multiple Perspectives*, J.F. Lee and A. Valdman, editors (pp. 43-68). Boston: Heinle & Heinle.

Warschauer, M., editor. 1995. *Virtual Connections*. Manoa, HI: University of Hawaii.

Warschauer, M. 1997. "Computer-Mediated Collaborative Learning: Theory and Practice." *Modern Language Journal* Vol. 81, No. 4: 470-481.

Wenden, A. 1991. *Learner Strategies for Learner Autonomy*. Englewood Cliffs, NJ: Prentice-Hall International.

White, L., N. Spada, P. Lightbown, and L. Ranta. 1991. "Input Enhancement and L2 Question Formation." *Applied Linguistics* Vol. 12, No. 4: 416-432.

Wiggins, G.P. 1998. *Educative Assessment: Designing Assessments to Inform and Improve Student Performance*. San Francisco: Jossey-Bass.

Wolf, D. 1993. "A Comparison of Assessment Tasks Used to Measure L1 Reading Comprehension." *Modern Language Journal* Vol. 77: 473-488.

Chapter 5. Health Education

Robin G. Sawyer

Health education historically has held a somewhat unique position in school settings. Unlike most other traditional subjects that anticipate a measurable increase in knowledge levels, health education is often expected to affect a more complicated construct, that of behavior change. Compounding this difficulty of being held to a higher standard than other subjects is the reality that health education typically is viewed as being peripheral to the overall academic goals of the school. This often results in less class time and fewer resources being allocated to health education. Therefore, teachers need to maximize their limited contact time with students in order to have any hope of achieving their educational objectives.

The eight practices discussed in this chapter have a common thread based on many years of research, indicating clearly and emphatically that simply teaching *facts* about health does *not* change behavior. Although cognitive information can help provide a basis for decision making, affective and skills-based components are necessary to facilitate behavior change. Much classroom instruction continues to be predominantly cognitive, but this past decade has seen a major shift in health education strategy, with teachers being much more willing to include affective and skills-based methodologies in their classroom repertoire.

Factual information should continue to be part of the curriculum, but unless students are able to apply this knowledge to enhance their own lives, the usefulness of this cognitive approach is questionable. Teaching for positive, permanent behavior change requires that students think critically and reflectively about the consequences of health decisions, practice skills that

will facilitate positive health behaviors, and experience consistent, positive reinforcement for their choices.

Health education's peripheral status is somewhat ironic when it is considered in light of the alarming national data on the health status of youth and adolescents. With regard to sexuality, although teen unintended pregnancy rates have recently declined, American teenagers continue to become pregnant at a substantially higher rate than their counterparts in any Western, industrialized nation, a situation reflecting a birthrate in the United States of 64 per 1,000 women 15-19 years of age, compared with rates of 13 in Germany, 9 in France, and 5.2 in Holland (Advocates for Youth 1998). In addition, teens have a higher rate of sexually transmitted diseases such as gonorrhea and chlamydia than adult age groups (Centers for Disease Control and Prevention 1992).

Alcohol is widely used and abused by American youth, with more than 80 percent of 12th-graders reporting having had at least one drink in their lifetime, and more than 30 percent stating they had more than five drinks on one occasion in the past 30 days (Johnston et al. 1998). The consequences of youth drinking can be catastrophic, with one study indicating individuals who begin drinking before 15 years of age are four times more likely to develop alcohol dependence, and more than twice as likely to develop alcohol abuse than those who do not begin drinking until 21 (Grant and Dawson 1997). The combination of drinking and driving is a major cause of adolescent fatality, with high rates of teenage vehicular deaths related to alcohol use (National Highway Traffic Safety Administration 1998). Youth and adolescence is clearly a crucial time to influence life-long health behaviors. In addition to alcohol and other drug activity, the pressure to smoke cigarettes becomes acute in the adolescent years, with the majority of cigarette smokers beginning to smoke before the age of 18 (American Lung Association 2002).

The Centers for Disease Control and Prevention (1992) reports a high percentage of morbidity and mortality is caused by six categories of risk behaviors: 1) use of alcohol and other drugs; 2) participation in behaviors that result in sexually transmitted diseases including HIV; 3) use of tobacco; 4) poor nutrition; 5) physical inactivity; and 6) intentional and unintentional injury (Dalis 1993, 9.15). These behaviors are often learned by children and youth and carried into adulthood. For these reasons, a comprehensive and effective health education curriculum is not only critically important to the health and well-being of every school-age child, it is also a viable means of addressing the escalating costs of health care.

The Joint Committee on National Health Education Standards (1995) developed seven standards that should be addressed in health education. Students should be able to:

- comprehend health promotion and disease prevention concepts;

- access valid health information and appropriate health products and services;

- practice health-enhancing behaviors and reduce health risks;

- analyze the impact of culture, media, technology, and other societal factors on health;

- use interpersonal communication skills that enhance health;

- use goal-setting and decision-making skills that enhance health; and

- advocate for personal, family, and community health.

The Committee's report defines health literacy as "the capacity of individuals to obtain, interpret, and understand basic health information and services and the competence to use such information and services in ways which enhance health" (1995, 5). The health-literate person, according to the report, is: 1) a critical thinker and problem solver; 2) a responsible, productive citizen; 3) a self-directed learner; and 4) an effective communicator (1995, 5). Use of these standards and characteristics can provide structure and guidance for the content of school health education programs.

A synthesis of research related to the delivery of effective school health education would suggest the most effective way to deliver programming is within the context of a comprehensive school health education program. Further, although factual information about health issues is important, if educators truly seek to initiate positive behavioral change in their students, then a shift toward teaching at affective and behavioral levels is essential. It is hoped that the eight methodologies presented in this chapter will assist the classroom teacher in striving to achieve such positive changes in health behavior.

The author wishes to express appreciation to the following scholars who reviewed this chapter for the revised edition of the *Handbook*: Dr. Glen Gilbert, dean, School of Health and Human Performance, East Carolina University; Dr. Jerrold Greenberg, professor in the Department of Health Education, University of Maryland; and Dr. Deitra Wengert, associate professor in the Department of Health Sciences, Towson University, Maryland.

5.1. Developing Personal Competence: Students who develop personal competence are more likely to make a commitment to positive health behaviors.

Research findings:

The body of research surrounding the concept of personal competence focuses on the efficacy of personal skill development. These strategies are aimed at developing the student's self-esteem, self-management skills, and internal locus of control.

In research conducted in a range of settings with heterogeneous target populations, personal competence training has proven successful in reducing unhealthy choices such as teenage pregnancy and tobacco, alcohol, and drug abuse.

In the classroom:

Personal competence includes the ability to make logical and rational decisions without being unduly influenced by others. After students have been made aware of alternative modes of behavior, they need to understand that they do, in fact, control decisions that lead to positive health behaviors. Commitment to healthy living can occur only when the individual understands the controlling factors involved in a decision and is willing to practice self-management even when decisions prove unpopular with peers. Students should learn coping skills to manage stress and anxiety and increase their own sense of personal control.

Coping skills can be taught in a variety of health education units. They can be integrated, for example, within units on tobacco, alcohol, and family skills. Caring for self, both physically and psychologically, is a primary objective of these units. Some students, unfortunately, may never have experienced feelings of care. They may not have been cared for by others. Teachers should provide role modeling of caring behaviors and articulate explicit aspects of caring to assist all students to learn to care for themselves. Service learning is a fairly new methodology that could be useful in developing the concept of "caring" (see Practice 5.7).

Sources:

Botvin 1992; Botvin, Baker, Dusenbury, Tortu, and Botvin 1990; Botvin, Baker, Filazzola, and Botvin 1990; Botvin and Dusenbury 1992; Braun 1992; Elias et al. 1986; Elias et al. 1991; Elias and Kress 1994; Flay 1985; Pentz 1985; Pentz and Kazdin 1982; Schinke 1984; Spivack and Shure 1982; Weissberg et al. 1981.

5.2. Developing Social Competence: Students who develop effective interpersonal communication skills can withstand peer pressure to engage in unhealthy practices.

Research findings:

Researchers are using social learning and behavior theories as the basis for assessing strategies to develop social competence. Although the application of this work to the development of teaching strategies is relatively recent in health education, it appears to hold promise for structuring a range of strategies that are effective in making students: 1) aware of negative peer influences; 2) cognizant of strategies to confront and reject peer pressures; and 3) able to select and engage in positive health behaviors.

In the classroom:

Interpersonal skills include the ability to communicate with others, listen attentively, demonstrate consideration, and respect others. Students gain these skills through the opportunity to practice social interactions in situations with varying levels of conflict. Teaching strategies can be used to structure the environment from that of low conflict (friends discussing an issue about which they all agree) to high conflict (individuals from different neighborhoods discussing issues that are sources of conflict). Teachers need to help students to develop and demonstrate effective interpersonal and communication skills to resolve conflicts peacefully instead of fighting.

Social skills curricula and teaching strategies are based on the development of communication skills (verbal and nonverbal), avoidance of misunderstandings, overcoming shyness, initiating conversations, receiving compliments, and acquiring skills needed to maintain close interpersonal relationships. Assertiveness training is also part of these curricula as students learn when to refuse and when to initiate actions. They learn to seek out situations conducive to healthy practices while avoiding those dangerous to themselves and others. Strategies are taught using role playing or behavioral rehearsal between two or more individuals to provide practice in performing these skills.

Sources:

Botvin 1992; Botvin et al. 1989; Botvin, Baker, Dusenbury, Tortu, and Botvin 1990; Botvin, Baker, Filazzola, and Botvin 1990; Coombs and Slaby 1977; Elias et al. 1986; Elias et al. 1991; Elias and Kres 1994; Flay 1985; Spivack and Shure 1982; Weissberg et al. 1981.

5.3. Practice in Goal Setting and Decision Making: Instruction that enhances students' goal-setting and decision-making skills will contribute to their ability to make positive health decisions.

Research findings:

Research results show goal setting and decision making are critical to behavioral change, and substantive changes in behavior are unlikely to occur without conscious effort. Findings suggest students must be: 1) aware of the problem and acknowledge it; 2) nurtured in their efforts to make a commitment to the behavioral change; and 3) able to use effective strategies to make the desired change. Strategies that are most effective involve individual ownership of the goal-setting and decision-making process. Individuals are more likely to attain goals that are consistent with their lifestyles. Research also indicates individuals commonly make a number of "false starts" in their efforts to set and meet goals for behavioral change.

In the classroom:

Students need opportunities to transfer health knowledge into decisions about their personal health needs. Individuals often make decisions that over- or underestimate their ability to reach a goal. They need assistance to set and work toward their goals using a reasonable timeframe. Behavioral changes take time. Saying you want to stop smoking does not often translate into immediately reaching this goal. Students need to be helped to understand the strategies involved in effectively setting and meeting realistic goals, and to realize goals may need to be set in stages that lead progressively to behavioral change.

Decision-making skills involve evaluating factual information about health issues as well as one's own personal lifestyle to select a reasonable course of action that will lead to success. Students need opportunities to set personally meaningful goals and to strive to reach them. They need to experience the consequences of success and failure in situations that are safe and supportive.

Goal-setting and decision-making strategies are part of a larger curricular focus on learning for understanding that originates in constructivist education. Constructivism asserts that knowledge and courses of action are based on reasoned decisions that are personally and socially constructed by the individual. Although knowledge can be useful in formulating a plan, it is the student's values and beliefs that ultimately determine the course of action (see Practice 5.4). A constructivist approach to health education focuses on the learner's reasons for learning and his/her need to make sense of knowledge. It requires thought-demanding experiences that lead students to ask pertinent questions, and that motivate them to consider culturally and intellectually challenging solutions to difficult problems.

Sources:

Botvin et al. 1995; Botvin and Tortu 1988; Brooks and Brooks 1993; Dalis 1994; Duffy and Jonassen 1992; Elias and Kress 1994; Tobler 1986.

5.4. Development of Values Awareness: Students who understand their own values and those of others can associate values with positive and productive courses of action.

Research findings:

Values are internally controlled and subject to personal adjustment. Research supports the importance of helping students to equate their reasons for their feelings or actions with their values.

Values clarification, used extensively in many health education programs, is one of the most researched strategies in health education. Researchers have found the development of a supportive, neutral environment is a critical factor in the success of values clarification, and this is also the most difficult factor for teachers to manage when using this strategy.

In the classroom:

The primary goal of instruction in values awareness is to help young people develop their own value structure, and to heighten students' awareness of their own values and the role values play in decision making related to positive health behaviors. Teachers begin by selecting an activity or question for discussion requiring students to make judgments or propose courses of action. They are asked to share their rationales for their decisions with a partner, a small group, or the class. Teachers help students to link these reasons to values, and may encourage them to analyze their values

based on personal or community expectations. Teachers should avoid influencing or judging students' responses. They should establish and maintain a non-judgmental environment encouraging open, responsible communication.

Values awareness depends on the use of active strategies that encourage students to become involved in their own learning. Rather than imposing external values on students, teachers encourage students to examine their own values and compare them to good health practices.

Educating students to be supportive of each other while simultaneously asking thought-provoking questions takes time and careful planning. Encouraging students to analyze and critique their own values can be challenging, particularly in situations in which students have acquired and value unhealthy courses of action. Health educators need to be skillful in structuring the discussion to lead students to evaluate their actions as they impact their own lives and those of others.

Sources:

Association for the Advancement of Health Education 1992; Braun 1992; Dalis 1994; Dalis and Strasser 1981; Duffy and Jonassen 1992; Morrow 1987; Raths, Harmin, and Simon 1966; Read, 1997; Wallerstein and Bernstein 1998.

5.5. Practice in Critical Analysis of Health Information: Instruction that increases students' ability to analyze and critically examine the health messages promoted in the media and culture helps them to make informed health choices.

Research findings:

Research has confirmed the influence of the media and advertising in glamorizing negative health messages. Advertising messages sometimes portray smoking as "cool" in an effort to sell cigarettes, and communicate the message that sex is a right without responsibilities or consequences. Although some attempts have been made to limit both negative forms of advertising and the portrayal of unsafe and unhealthy practices in movies and videos, the fact remains that the excitement and intuitive appeal of risk-taking is tremendously powerful and compelling for adolescents.

Research suggests the process of helping students reflect on and critically examine these media messages requires long time periods and intensive interactions with strategies in order to effect change. Researchers are continuing to identify strategies that are sufficiently powerful to combat the alluring messages that pervade the consciousness of adolescents.

In the classroom:

It is essential that students learn to analyze and evaluate a variety of positive and negative health messages to determine the credibility of the information and the extent to which it should influence their lives. Students should learn to analyze the role of cultural beliefs in determining positive health practices. Awareness of cultural diversity may both enrich and challenge anecdotal and research-based information.

As consumers, students need to acquire the critical thinking skills of information gathering, synthesis of concepts and ideas, and analysis and evaluation of the messages within their lives.

Further, the development of a critical perspective that includes strategies to question long-held beliefs may be instrumental in encouraging some individuals to consider alternative and more positive health behaviors. Teachers can teach and use divergent questioning models, such as brainstorming and involvement (placing oneself in a hypothetical situation), to help students develop critical thinking skills.

Negative health messages often originate in glitzy presentations on television, videos, movies, and most recently the Internet. These messages are powerful and persuasive, often incorporating misleading interpretations of statistics. Instructional methods that incorporate analysis and critique teach students to use critical thinking skills to recognize false information and develop personally satisfactory alternatives.

Increased access to one of the most powerful information tools in history, the Internet, only reinforces the importance of the classroom teacher in training students to access information, and then evaluate the accuracy and validity of the source. Classroom assignments could first include accessing a health-related site, and then examining important issues such as the intended audience for the information, the site's author, and the accuracy, currency, and objectivity of the information.

Sources:

Cinelli et al. 1995; Elias et al. 1986; Ennett et al. 1994; Gregory 1991; Joint Committee on National Health Education Standards 1995; McCormack Brown, 1998; Owston, 1997; Pentz 1985; Schinke 1984; Spivack and Shure 1982; Wallerstein and Bernstein 1998.

5.6. Activity-Oriented, Interactive Learning: Interactive teaching strategies are more likely to result in student examination of alternative courses of action, leading to the development of positive lifestyle choices.

Research findings:

A solid base of research and experience indicates an activity-oriented health education program that encourages students to think, explore, and investigate health topics for themselves is more effective in encouraging students to make wise health decisions than a program depending mainly on lecture or textbooks. The U.S. Public Health Service recommends an instructional approach that includes activity-oriented curricula, participatory classroom activities, small-group work, and peer interaction. Other specific instructional approaches found to be effective include role-playing and cooperative learning.

Overall, teaching strategies need to be varied and stimulating, ensuring high levels of interest and student involvement in a subject too many young people consider boring and irrelevant. In addition, information and skills learned through this type of interactive education should be reinforced continuously, if possible. Interventions performed on a limited basis, without reinforcement, are unlikely to be effective.

In the classroom:

Students need opportunities to examine both positive and negative

lifestyle choices through interaction with curriculum materials, peers, and teachers. Rather than simply lecturing students on positive choices, teachers should provide opportunities for students to consider the consequences of several courses of action. Activity-oriented teaching strategies include vignettes, values clarification exercises, role-playing, debates, discussion, games, and simulation. These strategies often require students to get out of their chairs and interact with peers in the decision-making process. Because reinforcement is necessary to optimize the likelihood of positive health behavior change, refreshers or reminders of previously covered skills and information should be included in the health education curriculum.

Sources:

Allensworth 1993; Black, Tobler, and Sciacca 1998; Botvin, Baker, Dusenbury, Tortu, and Botvin 1990; Botvin, Baker, Filazzola, and Botvin 1990; Cinelli et al. 1994; Donnermeyer and Davis, 1998; Gilbert and Sawyer 1995; Gold 1994; Marr 1997; National Commission on the Role of the School and Community in Improving Adolescent Health 1990; Pentz and Kazdin 1982; Spivack and Shure 1982; Tobler 1996; U.S. Department of Health and Human Services 1993.

5.7. Using the Student as Teacher: Students who are trained to act as surrogate teachers show evidence of increased self-esteem, self-efficacy, and social and personal responsibility. In addition, young learners are often more receptive to information from their peer group rather than from an older adult.

Research findings:

Research strongly suggests two forms of "surrogate teaching" are likely to enhance the effectiveness of health education—*peer education*, which has been commonly used for several years, and a more recent methodology that is becoming increasingly popular, *service learning*. Peer education has been shown to be an effective means to disseminate information, because young individuals often give more credence to their peers than to figures of authority. In addition, recent research suggests the effects of the peer experience may have a profoundly positive influence on the peers themselves.

Service learning is a fairly recent development and involves the student as a teacher/mentor in a service environment (an environment where a need for help exists). Research suggests this methodology can increase the participating students' problem-solving skills, open-mindedness, social and personal responsibility, self-efficacy, self-esteem, and empathy, as well as decrease discipline problems.

In the classroom:

Peer education can occur on a limited basis within a single classroom, where students simply prepare and present information to each other. This can be expanded to presentations to other classes within the same grade, other classes in all grades, and perhaps students at other schools. Obviously,

as the scope of the presentation increases so must the preparation. Equal attention should be paid to the process and style of the presentation as to the information and content. Peer education has also been found to be an effective strategy with special needs populations, such as individuals who are deaf or hard of hearing.

Service learning involves the development of a project idea, followed by the planning and implementation of the service with a population of identified need. Grade levels will obviously influence the extent and complexity of the service. For example, third- and fourth-graders might use the expertise of several individuals within their school to develop a service plan to feed individuals who are homeless; middle school students might tutor elementary school children; and high school students might develop a stress management program for staff at a local nursery school. Many school districts have incorporated a service component into their graduation requirements, thus making service learning an attractive proposition.

Sources:

Black, Tobler, and Sciacca 1998; Boss 1994; Calabrese and Schumer 1986; Cognetta and Sprinthall 1978; Conrad and Hedin 1982, 1991; Fennell 1993; Giles and Eyler 1994; Gould and Lomax 1993; Greenberg 1997; Joseph 1993; Markus, Howard, and King 1993; Sawyer, Pinciaro, and Bedwell 1997; Sloane and Zimmer 1993; Wilson 1974.

5.8. Encouraging and Developing Parental Involvement: Parental support is crucial to both optimizing curriculum effectiveness and increasing the likelihood that positive health behaviors might be maintained. Additionally, parental support will enhance the probability for the continuation of comprehensive health education programming in the school system.

Research findings:

Research indicates parental involvement in education can increase student achievement, student self-esteem, and community support for schools. Specific to health education, research also demonstrates family involvement can positively influence children's health behavior in several areas.

In a more political vein, parental and family involvement is of paramount importance in maintaining the existence of comprehensive school health education and the integrity of its curriculum. Because several facets of health education are deemed to be controversial, this subject tends to be scrutinized very closely by parents and community. School administrators have become very sensitive to parental complaints, and by actively involving parents in the health education curriculum, teachers can potentially reduce the number of parental concerns, in addition to developing a critical mass of community support for the program.

In the classroom:

Parents can be actively involved in the development of new programs by serving on committees that examine curricula and available materials. For existing programs, teachers should be prepared to share materials and discuss/advocate for the health education curriculum at open houses or "back to school" evenings. Activities that involve the parent/family in the learning process should be developed, utilizing parent(s), sibling(s), or even grandparents. Using nutrition as an example, suggested activities could include tracking a family's favorite food sources for various vitamins; reviewing food labels or discussing television advertising with a parent; comparing today's eating habits with those of previous generations with a grandparent; and examining the role played by food in family or social rituals.

Given that most students spend much more time in the home than they do in the classroom, ignoring this important influence on an individual's health behavior would not be sensible. Involving parents in health-related activities along with their children is an excellent way to positively involve the very people who inevitably play an important role in influencing their children's behaviors.

Sources:

Birch 1994; Botvin, Baker, Dusenbury, Tortu, and Botvin 1990; Botvin, Baker, Filazzola, and Botvin 1990; Cinelli et al. 1994; Gold 1994; National Commission on the Role of the School and Community in Improving Adolescent Health 1990; Pentz and Kazdin 1982; Perry, Luepker, and Murray 1988; Spivack and Shure 1982; U.S. Department of Health and Human Services 1993.

Bibliography

Advocates for Youth. October 1998. *Major Data Comparisons* (Press Release October 1998). Washington DC: Author.

Allensworth, D. 1993. "Health Education: 'State of the Art.'" *Journal of School Health* Vol. 63, No. 1: 14-20.

American Lung Association. 2002. *Tobacco Use—Fact Sheet*. June Update. Retrieved from www.lungusa.org/tobacco/teenager_factsheet99.html.

Association for the Advancement of Health Education. 1992. "A Point of View for Health Education." *Journal of Health Education* Vol. 23, No. 1: 4-6.

Birch, D.A. 1994. "Involving Families in School Health Education: Implications for Professional Preparation." *Journal of School Health* Vol. 64, No. 7: 296-299.

Black, D.R., N.S. Tobler, and J.P. Sciacca. 1998. "Peer Helping/Involvement: An Effective Way to Meet the Challenge of Reducing Alcohol, Tobacco, and Other Drug Use Among Youth?" *Journal of School Health* Vol. 68, No. 3: 87-93.

Boss, J.A. 1994. "The Effects of Community Service Work on the Moral Development of College Ethics Students." *Journal of Moral Education* Vol. 23: 183-198.

Botvin, G.J. 1992. "Personal and Social Skills Training: Applications for Substance Abuse Prevention." In *Strengthening Health Education for the 1990s* (pp. 29-38). Reston, VA: Association for the Advancement of Health Education.

Botvin, G.J., E. Baker, L. Dusenbury, S. Tortu, and E. Botvin. 1990. "Preventing Adolescent Drug Abuse Through a Multimodal Cognitive-Behavioral Approach: Results of a Three-Year Study." *Journal of Consulting and Clinical Psychology* Vol. 58, No. 4: 437-445.

Botvin, G.J., E. Baker, A.D. Filazzola, and E. Botvin. 1990. "A Cognitive-Behavioral Approach to Substance Abuse Prevention: A One-Year Follow-up." *Addictive Behaviors* Vol. 15: 47-63.

Botvin, G.J., and L. Dusenbury. 1992. "Substance Abuse Prevention: Implications for Reducing the Risk of HIV Infection." *Psychology of Addictive Behaviors* Vol. 6, No. 2: 70-80.

Botvin, G.J., L. Dusenbury, E. Baker, D. James-Ortiz, and J. Kerner. 1989. "A Skills Training Approach to Smoking Prevention in Hispanic Youth." *Journal of Behavior Medicine* Vol. 12: 279-296.

Botvin, G.J., L. Dusenbury, E.M. Botvin, and T. Diaz. 1995. "Long-Term Follow-Up Results of a Randomized Drug Abuse Prevention Trial in a White, Middle-Class Population." *Journal of the American Medical Association* Vol. 273, No. 14: 1106-1112.

Botvin, G.J., and S. Tortu. 1988. "Preventing Adolescent Substance Abuse Through Life Skills Training." In

Fourteen Ounces of Prevention: A Casebook for Practitioners. R.H. Price, E.L. Cowen, R.P. Lorion, and J. Ramos-Mckay, editors. Washington, DC: American Psychological Association.

Braun, J.A. 1992. "Caring, Citizenship, and Conscience: The Cornerstones of a Values Education Curriculum for Elementary Schools." *International Journal of Social Education* Vol. 7, No. 2: 47-56.

Brooks, J.G., and M.G. Brooks. 1993. *The Case for Constructivist Classrooms.* Alexandria, VA: Association for Supervision and Curriculum Development.

Calabrese, R., and H. Schumer. 1986. "The Effects of Service Activities on Adolescent Alienation." *Adolescence* Vol. 21: 675-687.

Centers for Disease Control and Prevention. 1992. *Chronic Disease and Health Promotion Reprints.* Atlanta, GA: Author.

Children's Defense Fund. 1990. *Children* [Pamphlet]. Washington, DC: Author.

Cinelli, B., C.W. Symons, L. Bechtel, and M.R. Colley. 1994. "Applying Cooperative Learning in Health Education Practice." *Journal of School Health* Vol. 64, No. 3 (March): 99-102.

Cinelli, B., L.J. Bechtel, M.R. Colley, and R. Nye. 1995. "Critical Thinking Skills in Health Education." *Journal of Health Education* Vol. 26, No. 2 (March/April): 119-120.

Cognetta, P.V., and N.A. Sprinthall. 1978. "Students as Teachers: Role Taking as a Means of Promoting Psychological and Ethical Development During Adolescence." In *Valued Development as the Aim of Education*, N.A. Sprinthall and R.L. Mosher, editors (pp. 53-68). Schenectady, NY: Character Research Press.

Conrad, D., and D. Hedin. 1982. "The Impact of Experiential Education on Adolescent Development." *Child and Youth Services* Vol. 4: 57-76.

Conrad, D., and D. Hedin. 1991. "School-Based Community Service: What We Know From Research and Theory." *Phi Delta Kappan* Vol. 72: 743-749.

Coombs, M.L., and D.A. Slaby. 1977. "Social Skills Training with Children." In *Advances in Clinical Child Psychology, I*, B.B. Lakey and A.E. Kazdin, editors (pp. 161-201). New York: Plenum Press.

Dalis, G.T. 1993. "Health Education/Healthy, Active Living." In *The Curriculum Handbook.* Alexandria, VA: Association for Supervision and Curriculum Development.

Dalis, G.T. 1994. "Effective Health Instruction: Both a Science and an Art." *Journal of Health Education* Vol. 25: 289-294.

Dalis, G.T., and B.B. Strasser. 1981. "Teach Values in Health Education." In *Education in the 80s: Health*

Education, R. Russell, editor (pp. 116-122). Washington, DC: National Educational Association.

Donnermeyer, J.F., and R.R. Davis. 1998. "Cumulative Effects of Prevention Education on Substance Abuse Among 11th-Grade Students in Ohio." *Journal of School Health* Vol. 68, No. 4: 151-158.

Duffy, T.M., and D.H. Jonassen. 1992. *Constructivism and the Technology of Instruction: A Conversation.* Hillsdale, NJ: Laurence Erlbaum.

Elias, M., M. Gara, M. Ubriaco, P.A. Rothbaum, J.F. Clabby, and T. Schuyler. 1986. "Impact of a Preventive Social Problem Solving Intervention on Children's Coping with Middle School Stress." *American Journal of Community Psychology* Vol. 14: 259-275.

Elias, M.J., M.A. Gara, T. Schuyler, L.R. Branden-Muller, and M.A. Sayette. 1991. "The Promotion of Social Competence: Longitudinal Study of a Preventive School-Based Program." *American Journal of Orthopsychiatry* Vol. 61, No. 3: 409-417.

Elias, M.J., and J.S. Kress. 1994. "Social Decision-Making and Life Skills Development: A Critical Thinking Approach to Health Promotion in the Middle School." *Journal of School Health* Vol. 64, No. 2 (February): 62-66.

Ennett, S.T., M.S. Tobler, C.L. Ringwalt, and R.L. Flewelling. 1994. "How Effective is Drug Abuse Resistance Education? A Meta-Analysis of Project DARE Outcome Evaluations." *American Journal of Public Health* Vol. 84, No. 9: 1394-1401.

Fennell, R. 1993. "A Review of Evaluations of Peer Education Programs." *Journal of American College Health* Vol. 41, No. 6: 251-253.

Flay, B.R. 1985. "Psychosocial Approaches to Smoking Prevention: A Review of the Findings." *Health Psychology* Vol. 4, No. 5: 449-488.

Gilbert, G.G., and R.G. Sawyer. 1995. *Health Education: Creating Strategies for School and Community Health.* Boston: Jones and Bartlett.

Giles, D.E., and J. Eyler. 1994. "The Impact of a College Community Service Laboratory on Students' Personal, Social and Cognitive Outcomes." *Journal of Adolescence* Vol. 17: 327-339.

Gold, R.S. 1994. "The Science Base for Comprehensive Health Education." In *The Comprehensive School Health Challenge (Volume 2),* P. Cortese and K. Middleton, editors (pp. 545-573). Santa Cruz, CA: ETR Associates.

Gould, J.M., and A.R. Lomax. 1993. "The Evolution of Peer Education: Where Do We Go from Here?" *Journal of American College Health* Vol. 41, No. 6: 235-240.

Grant, B.F., and D.A. Dawson. 1997. "Age at Onset of Alcohol Use and its Association with DSM-IV Alcohol Abuse and Dependence." *Journal of Substance Abuse* Vol. 9: 103-110.

Greenberg, J.S. 1997. "Service-Learning in Health Education." *Journal of Health Education* Vol. 28, No. 6: 345-349.

Gregory, R. 1991. "Critical Thinking for Environmental Health Risk Education." *Health Education Quarterly* Vol. 18, No. 3: 273-284.

Hicks, B.A., J.A. Morris, S.M. Bass, G.W. Holcomb, and W.W. Neblett. 1990. "Alcohol and the Adolescent Trauma Population." *Journal of Pediatric Surgery* Vol. 25, No. 9: 944-949.

Johnston, L., P. O'Malley, and J. Bachman. 1998. "National Survey Results on Drug Use from the Monitoring the Future Study, 1975-1997 Vol. 1." National Institute on Drug Abuse, U.S. Department of Health and Human Services. Public Health Service. Rockville, MD: National Institutes of Health.

Joint Committee on National Health Education Standards. 1995. *Health Education Standards.* Reston, VA: Association for the Advancement of Health Education. Also available from American School Health Association and American Cancer Society.

Jones, E.F. 1986. *Teenage Pregnancy in Industrialized Countries.* New Haven: Yale University Press.

Joseph, J.M. 1993. "Peer Education and the Deaf Community." *Journal of American College Health* Vol. 41, No. 6: 264-266.

Markus, G.B., J.P.F. Howard, and D.C. King. 1993. "Integrating Community Service and Classroom Instruction Enhances Learning: Results From an Experiment." *Educational Evaluation and Policy Analysis* Vol. 15: 410-419.

Marr, M.B. 1997. "Cooperative Learning: A Brief Review." *Reading and Writing Quarterly: Overcoming Learning Difficulties* Vol. 13, No. 1: 7-20.

McCormack Brown, K. 1998. "Designing Web-Based Experiences for Health Educators: A Teaching Idea for Professional Preparation." *Journal of Health Education* Vol. 29, No. 6: 373-375.

Morrow, S.R. 1987. "Values and Moral Education: Revisited." *Counciler* Vol. 47: 31-33.

National Commission on the Role of the School and Community in Improving Adolescent Health. 1990. *Code Blue: Uniting for Healthier Youth.* Alexandria, VA: National Association of State Boards of Education and American Medical Association.

National Highway Traffic Safety Administration (NHTSA). 1998. *Youth Fatal Crash and Alcohol Facts.* June 30, 1998.

Owston, R.D. 1997. "The World Wide Web: A Technology to Enhance Learning and Teaching?" *Educational Research* (March): 27-33.

Pentz, M.A. 1985. "Social Competence Skills and Self-Efficacy as Determinants of Substance Use in Adolescence." In *Coping and Substance Abuse,* S. Shiffman and T.A. Willis, editors. New York: Academic Press.

Pentz, M.A., and A.E. Kazdin. 1982. "Assertion Modeling and Stimuli Effects on Assertive Behavior and Self-Efficacy in Adolescents." *Behavioral Research and Therapy* Vol. 20: 365-371.

Perry, C.L., R.V. Luepker, and D.M. Murray. "Parental Involvement with Children's Health Promotion: The Minnesota Home Team." *American Journal of Public Health* Vol. 78, No. 9: 1156-1160.

Raths, L.E., M. Harmin, and S.B. Simon. 1966. *Values and Teaching.* Columbus, OH: Charles E. Merrill.

Read, D. 1997. *Health Education: A Cognitive-Behavioral Approach.* Boston: Jones and Bartlett.

Sawyer, R.G., P. Pinciaro, and D. Bedwell. 1997. "How Peer Education Changed Peer Sexuality Educators' Self-Esteem, Personal Development, and Sexual Behavior." *Journal of American College Health* Vol. 45, No. 5: 211-217.

Schinke, S.P. 1984. "Preventing Teenage Pregnancy." In *Progress in Behavior Modification, 16,* M. Hersen, R.M. Eisler, and P.M. Miller, editors (pp. 31-63). New York: Academic Press.

Sloane B.C., and C.G. Zimmer. 1993. "The Power of Peer Health Education." *Journal of American College Health* Vol. 41, No. 6: 241-245.

Spivack, G., and M.D. Shure. 1982. "The Cognition of Social Adjustment: Interpersonal Cognitive Problem-Solving Thinking." In *Advances in Child Clinical Psychology, 5,* B.B. Lakey and A.E. Kazdin, editors (pp. 323-372). New York: Plenum Press.

Tobler, N.S. 1986. "Meta-Analysis of 143 Adolescent Drug Prevention Programs: Quantitative Outcome Results of Program Participants Compared to a Control or Comparison Group." *Journal of Drug Issues* Vol. 16: 537-567.

Tobler, N.S. May 1996. Adolescent Drug Programs. Congressional Forum on Drug Education sponsored by the Drug Policy Foundation, Washington, DC.

U.S. Department of Health and Human Services. 1990. *Prevention '89/'90: Federal Programs and Progress.* Washington, DC: Author.

U.S. Department of Health and Human Services. 1993. *School Health: Findings from Evaluated Programs.* Washington, DC: Author.

Wallerstein, N., and E. Bernstein. 1998. "Empowerment Education: Freire's Ideas Adapted to Health Education." *Health Education Quarterly* Vol. 15, No. 4: 379-394.

Weissberg, R.P., E.L. Gesten, C.L. Carnrike, P.A. Toro, B.D. Rapkin, E. Davidson, and E.L. Cowen. 1981. "Social Problem-Solving Skills Training: A Competence Building Intervention With Second to Fourth Grade Children." *American Journal of Community Psychology* Vol. 9: 419-423.

Wilson, T.C. 1974. *An Alternative Community-Based School Education Program and Student Political Development.* Doctoral dissertation, University of Southern California.

Chapter 6a. Language Arts

James R. Squire

Reading, writing, and oral language are the bedrock subjects of the curriculum, for they develop the competencies on which virtually all subsequent instruction and learning depend. Together with literature, which introduces young people to the ideas and values of their own and other cultures, these subjects constitute a segment of the curriculum occupying from about 60 percent of school time at the primary school level to about 17 percent of school time at the secondary level. Unless boys and girls develop competence in using language, they will be handicapped throughout schooling and life.

The 12 practices identified in this chapter deal with the language arts as a whole, including the three major components of reading, writing, and oral language. A separate sub-chapter by Carolyn Dunkle Perry follows dealing with specific practices relating only to oral language.

For almost all of the 20th century, teaching strategies and learning practices effective in the language arts have been vigorously researched. Yet, over these decades, the profession has continuously debated the desirability of various approaches. Disagreements have focused on the need for carefully controlled instruction versus the benefits of more open-ended, creative, and exploratory approaches. Many maintain learners must be taught the needed skills and strategies; others, that learners will develop the needed competencies as they are engaged in meaningful language activities. Yet it seems clear learners reap benefits from both kinds of teaching, and the most desirable overall approach combines instruction on key skills and strategies within a rich learning environment that stimulates reading, writing, and talking. Such a consensus now appears to be emerging among professional leaders.

A review of the literature related to teaching and learning of the language arts also makes clear the interrelationships between many of the practices discussed in the following pages. Research points to the positive connection between extensive reading and improved reading comprehension. Providing opportunities for students to discuss what they have read—to become active participants in making meaning from written text—has also been proven to help students' reading skills to grow. This second approach also has positive effects on the first, because students who are provided with time and opportunity to share their thoughts about reading tend to read more.

The teaching of strategies to help students comprehend what they are reading is another approach that results in more than one positive outcome. Students not only understand more of what they are reading; again, they tend to read more. This linkage has a commonsense base. As reading becomes easier and more understandable, it becomes more enjoyable, and students are likely to do more of it.

Similar relationships can be found among many of the 12 research-based approaches discussed in this section on the language arts. Instruction that effectively integrates them in the daily life of the classroom will be a strong force both for improving the reading and writing skills of students and for encouraging them to make reading part of their lives outside as well as inside school.

The author wishes to thank Dr. Roselmina Indrisano, professor of education, Boston University, and Dr. Julie Jensen, professor of education, University of Texas, for their comments and suggestions regarding this chapter.

6a.1. Extensive Reading: Extensive reading of material of many kinds, both in school and outside, results in substantial growth in vocabulary and comprehension abilities and in the information base of students.

Research findings:

Research has demonstrated that time spent reading, both inside and outside of school, is essential to developing cognitive abilities such as comprehension and vocabulary development. Reading of many different types of material also has benefits, because students see words in a variety of contexts. The meanings of these words are then more readily accessible during future reading. Students with both low- and high-level literacy skills benefit from time spent reading, with vocabulary learned from context and comprehension improved if the difficulty of the material presented is appropriate to the current reading level.

Yet studies demonstrate that many children spend no more than a few minutes a day reading in school or outside, on either assigned or independent reading. In addition, students with low reading skill levels are found to spend even less classroom time reading and more working on skill-based approaches.

Research has also found an increase in the amount and breadth of independent reading, when paired with the presentation of strategies for improving comprehension, is associated with instruction that provides opportunities for students to discuss and share what they read.

In the classroom:

Young people need large blocks of time within the school day to read, with time for text reading

considered an essential aspect of comprehension instruction. Students should be helped to select material of a suitable level of difficulty, so that the text can be comprehended but the reading activity will also result in new learning.

An atmosphere that encourages reading outside as well as inside the classroom can be provided by teachers who schedule time for students to talk with each other about the books they have read, to engage in shared reading, and to give personal reactions and interpretations of text.

School resources can be allocated to encourage reading of many types by students. Books in classrooms and in the school library should be of different types and cover a variety of topics. In addition, school time should be organized to encourage reading activities not only in language arts but also in other subject areas, such as social studies and science. To help teachers decide what balance of activities is appropriate, schools need to be explicit about the dimensions of cognitive growth to be considered essential aspects of the educational program. These might include language concepts and the ability to analyze, synthesize, and make informed judgments based on valid criteria, all skills strengthened by reading and discussing what was read.

Sources:

Allington 1994; Anderson et al. 1985; Anderson, Wilson, and Fielding 1988; Fielding and Pearson 1994; Guthrie et al. 1995; LaBrant 1961; Nagy, Anderson, and Herman 1987.

6a.2. Interactive Learning: Learning in which children and young people are interactive produces far more effective growth than instruction in which they are passive.

Research findings:

John Dewey (1933) emphasized that we learn from experience, and that activities become experience only as we think about and act upon them. Vgotsky (1978), Piaget (1959), and Britton (1970) reported similar observations. Reading, characterized as "highly interactive and reciprocal," fits well within this context. Part of the experience involves the reader-author connection, but research also stresses the importance of student-student and student-teacher interaction; discussing what has been read adds another dimension to the experience and expands the reader's understanding.

Research in strategic teaching and learning is becoming increasingly specific about what can be learned through cooperative activity or interactive processes. It demonstrates that such social processes, when compared with individual study, can stimulate greater growth for learners. In the area of the language arts, this can result in both an expanded vocabulary and higher levels of comprehension.

In addition, social time spent talking about reading—sharing, asking questions, explaining—has been demonstrated to increase the amount of reading students do, and so contributes in an additional way to improving reading skills.

In the classroom:

Language learning comes not from the activity itself but from thinking about, writing about, or talking about the activity. As the great linguist C.C. Fries observed, "There is no language save for the speaker active in expression." Readers and writers must be encouraged to think about and discuss what they are reading, writing, and doing if they are to learn. Talking about ideas also helps young people think through the ideas. When Purves stressed "it takes two to read a book," he was referring to research that indicates learning from reading comes from writing about and talking about what is read. Hence, classrooms in which young people are active in using language are essential in teaching the language arts.

The sharing opportunities can take many forms: reading partners, cooperative learning groups, reading journals passed back and forth between student and teacher, whole-class discussions, or presentation of reports. What is more important than the type of activity is that students are actively engaged rather than passive.

When time is provided to discuss reading done outside as well as inside class, students are also encouraged to read more and to read more widely than would be possible in the time available in class.

Sources:

Britton 1970; Dewey 1933; Dole et al. 1991; Goodman, Hood, and Goodman 1991; Johnson, Johnson, and Holobec 1991; Piaget 1959; Pressley et al. 1990; Purves and Beach 1972; Vgotsky 1978.

6a.3. Extension of Background Knowledge: Reading comprehension is enhanced when readers extend their experience and background knowledge and develop their sensitivity to increasingly difficult concepts and complex patterns of language.

Research findings:

Recent research emphasizes the significance of background knowledge in reading comprehension. The more a reader knows about a topic, the better his or her comprehension of newly encountered writing about the topic, and the less that has to be "filled in" by someone who may be unclear about the intent of the author. Background knowledge combines with basic skills such as vocabulary growth in order to make the text understandable. Thus, students who have low basic skills but high background knowledge about the topic being discussed may be able to understand what the author intended even if the words used are difficult.

In the process of comprehending the text, the reader gains more background knowledge to be used in understanding future texts. A reader's background knowledge can include either general issues related to the text or subject-matter knowledge relevant to the text. The combination of available background knowledge allows a reader to make inferences about meanings in a text, and thus to comprehend it. Extensive reading, another of the research-based factors shown to improve reading comprehension and vocabulary, is an important factor in increasing the bank of background knowledge available to a reader.

In the classroom:

Each reading experience both benefits from and enhances back-ground knowledge; new words and meanings are added to background knowledge through reading. Schools and teachers can help with the critical need to expand background knowledge by providing time for students to read and supplying books that are both interesting and varied.

Teachers can also supply background knowledge in other ways: preteaching vocabulary before it is presented in text, enriching background knowledge through previews or by highlighting background knowledge students are known to have, or assessing students' present level of background knowledge and then selecting additional resources that can help to fill gaps in areas that would hinder comprehension.

Methods of linking background knowledge to the text might include using advance organizers, providing students with objectives or purposes for the text, and using pretests or prequestioning. Direct instruction in how to use background knowledge to make inferences about unfamiliar text may also help students. For example, having students predict what will happen in a story requires them to draw on both their understanding of the text and their background knowledge.

Sources:

Anderson and Pearson 1984; McCabe and Peterson 1991; Nagy 1988; Strickland 1962; Strickland and Strickland 1998; Tierney and Cunningham 1984.

6a.4. Instruction in Strategic Reading and Writing: Activities that enable students to apply meaning-making skills and strategies such as summarizing, questioning, and interpreting contribute to improved reading comprehension and written composition.

Research findings:

Research on strategic reading and writing has been a primary focus of studies during recent years, as cognitive psychologists (those concerned about the development of thinking abilities) have turned their attention to the learning of language. Studies of good and poor readers have provided especially important insights. Specifically, good readers spontaneously use a wide range of strategies when unfamiliar text or tasks are encountered, while poor readers are unlikely to do so. A number of cognitive strategies useful to readers and writers have been developed and can be taught to students.

In the classroom:

Teachers should become familiar with the variety of cognitive strategies students can use to improve their reading comprehension and writing ability. Strategies that have been identified include using background knowledge, previewing, setting goals, determining importance, evaluating content, generating questions, predicting, and summarizing, as well as many others. These strategies may take place before, during, or after an event of reading or writing, and can be applied over a number of subject areas. The challenge for teachers is getting students to understand and apply the strategies during reading and writing.

Modeling of the strategy for students is an important component of instruction. Other important components are explaining how the strategy will help with learning, selecting strategies appropriate to the learner and the context, and providing feedback and encouragement as the student learns to use them. Group activities can be used to introduce and implement cognitive strategies. For example, students in a group may develop predictions about a story after having read part of it, identify strategies they each used to understand unfamiliar words, and develop a group summary of the story.

The most significant learning occurs after the act of reading, as the individual thinks about the ideas themselves and the ways in which they are presented. Thus, strategies focusing on this aspect of the reading-writing process are critical. Teachers' conferences with their students offer an effective way to encourage young people to reflect on what they have been reading or writing. Other instructional strategies also help readers elaborate on the ideas they are reading or writing about, and thus promote higher thought processes and the ability to think more critically. Children consistently demonstrate improved understanding after engaging in such activities.

Sources:

Cazden 1991; Dahl and Farnan 1998; Flood and Lapp 1991; Freedman 1987; Haller, Child, and Walberg 1988; Hill 1991; McLain 1991; Palincsar and Brown 1985; Paris, Wasik, and Turner 1991; Wittrock 1990.

6a.5. Interrelated Activities: Organizing instruction into broad, thematically based clusters of work through which reading, writing, and speaking activities are interrelated promotes understanding of the connections among activities and ideas.

Research findings:

Although individuals have long advocated interrelating reading, writing, speaking, and listening in the classroom, research demonstrating the power of such approaches has begun to appear only during the last decade: first, with respect to preschool and early language development; more recently, with respect to teaching in the upper grades.

In the classroom:

Thematic instruction provides an ideal framework for the classroom teacher who wants students to make the connection between reading, writing, and speaking. Activities designed around a unifying theme build on each other rather than remain as fragmented disciplines. A connection of ideas as well as of related skills provides opportunities for reinforcement. For example, students who are learning to identify the main points in a story can, as a prewriting strategy, develop main points for their own stories.

When concepts are developed over a period of time so that one day's reading prepares students for discussion or writing, and the discussion of that writing in turn leads to more reading and writing, young people are more likely to grasp the connections among ideas and to develop and understand broad generalizations. If each day's reading, writing, and discussion relates to that done on earlier days and foreshadows upcoming activities, students will begin to see precedents as well as consequences and transitions from one version to another.

Skill development can also be an important outcome of this integrated approach. The spelling and structure of beginning writers improve as more reading experience is provided. As they begin to write and realize the purpose of writing is to convey an idea, they better understand that authors are creating messages for them.

Sources:

Allington 1994; Burke 1999; Chall and Jacobs 1996; Freedman and McLeod 1988; Goodman, Hood, and Goodman 1991; Harste and Short 1988; Hartman 1995; Maguire 1994; Moffett and Wagner 1983; Pressley et al. 1990; Shaughnessy 1977.

6a.6. Teaching Critical Reading/Writing Skills: The teaching of critical skills such as word attack or grammar in reading and writing helps students develop competence in such skills within a reasonable period of time. Such instruction may be embedded in the total context of language learning or may be presented directly by the teacher.

Research findings:

Research has consistently demonstrated that many children will not automatically acquire all the basic skills needed for reading and writing, and so may have to be taught some of them through direct instruction. Thus, poor readers, who read less and so have fewer opportunities to successfully practice skills such as word identification, remain poor decoders unless they receive specific skills instruction.

Research, however, has also pointed to the need for a balance between instruction in basic skills and instruction in context even for poor readers or writers. For example, when instruction for children with reading problems provides skills-based instruction to the exclusion of ample opportunities to read for meaning, the development of both vocabulary and reading comprehension skills suffer.

In the classroom:

There are many effective ways to teach reading and writing skills to young people. The skills may be embedded in a total language context or taught directly by the teacher.

If taught directly, however, such instruction must include both time for young people to learn skills and ample experience applying them. For example, if children are taught the sounds of words, opportunities to identify the words in a meaningful context should also be available.

Sources:

Adams 1990; Allington 1994; Chall 1967, 1983; Clay 1991; Farrell 1991; Indrisano and Paratore 1991; Lyons, Pinnell, and Deford 1993; Palincsar and Brown 1985; Rosenshine and Stevens 1984, Snow; Burns, and Griffin 1998.

6a.7. Discussion and Analysis: Instruction emphasizing discussion and analysis rather than rote memory contributes most effectively to development of students' thinking abilities.

Research findings:

Research has consistently demonstrated that most young people will reach their potential in developing higher thought processes only if these processes are taught and practiced. Ability to recall information may also improve as the student creates a context in which to remember facts.

In the classroom:

Teachers should avoid excessive reliance on questions that require no more than recall of information. Frequent use of true-false, multiple-choice, and short-answer questions may teach students to respond quickly to certain kinds of tests, but it does not help them think while they read. Instead, guided questions that focus on skills such as developing inferences or analyzing the content should predominate. In order to help students think through more complex ideas and practice building thought-frameworks of written material, opportunities should be provided for reading and then discussing relatively long selections.

Writing and reading are so closely related that they are most effectively taught together. This instruction can also be structured so that a primary focus is on higher-order skills. For example, the process of composing can be presented to students as a way to construct and communicate their own ideas, while the process of reading comprehension helps them to reconstruct the ideas first communicated by another. Reading/writing assignments in which this theme of communication predominates provide a framework for discussion and analytic thinking.

Sources:

Armbruster, Anderson, and Ostertag 1987; Chall 1983; Jensen 1984; Pearson 1985; Tierney and Shanahan 1991.

6a.8. Emphasis on the Writing Process: Stressing the processes of composing (planning, drafting, revising, sharing, and publishing) contributes to improved competence in writing.

Research findings:

Extensive research on the composing processes of young people began about 25 years ago and has continued to this day. The research has helped to identify both the various stages of writing and the ways in which attention to process can effectively inform classroom instruction.

Some research is also available about the effects of word processing on composition, but it is often contradictory. Aspects of writing studied include motivation toward writing, frequency of revision, and quality of writing. Results are generally small, although in the positive direction.

In the classroom:

The complete process of written composition involves a series of recursive and interlocking stages, each of which should be discussed with students so that they understand its value and place in the process. Composing processes may vary with individuals, but long-range improvement in writing competence depends in good measure on students' understanding of the processes in which they engage.

Frequent practice is also necessary if writing is to improve, and such practice requires devoting time to writing in class. Particularly useful are occasional double periods or writing workshops during which the teacher is free to provide guidance to individuals as they engage in the writing process. Also useful are conferences to discuss the processes with individuals or to help students apply a point made during instruction to their work.

Whole-class or small-group discussion that provides time for students to talk about their work and ask for feedback from other students can also be used as a way to focus on process. For example, a student may share his/her thoughts about a possible revision from the perspective of his/her original plans for the written piece, as well as where it currently stands.

Sources:

Bangert-Drowns 1993; Bereiter and Scardanalia 1987; Burke 1999; Dahl and Farnan 1998; Dyson and Freedman 1991a, 1991b; Emig 1971; Freedman 1987; Graves 1983; Jensen 1993.

6a.9. Balanced Reading and Writing: Programs that provide balanced attention to both imaginative and informative reading, writing, and speaking promote competence in handling discourse of many kinds.

Research findings:

Beginning with Rosenblatt's definitive study of literary response in 1978 and the work by Britton (1975) and his associates in defining the various modes of writing, researchers have been increasingly concerned about the need for balanced attention to the different modes of reading and writing.

Researchers agree that the writing process, as generally presented in classrooms, should be considered only a general guide to writing. Different types of writing require variations of the process. Thus, students engaged in producing different styles of writing learn not only new modes but also different approaches to developing a finished product. Recent studies indicate schools are failing to have students practice the skills associated with expository writing.

In the classroom:

The curriculum must help children develop competence in comprehending and composing prose of many kinds. Literary selections can engage children's interest as they begin to read, but experience with factual and scientific prose is also important. Similarly, over-emphasis on personal writing to the neglect of informative or factual writing can limit students' overall growth in their ability to compose.

This suggests teachers should provide instruction in a variety of forms as well as variations of the writing process. The differences among the types of writing should be explicitly presented, and students should be given assistance while they practice. The role for the teacher in this process is an active one; extensive guidance will be needed by many students as they attempt to comprehend and demonstrate mastery of the distinctions among the many different types of writing.

Regular opportunities to engage in activities that use different modes of discourse are also important to student growth. For example, the processes involved in responding to literature differ from those used in seeking information from texts and then presenting it to others. These modes must be taught, modeled, and practiced.

Sources:

Britton et al. 1975; Dyson and Freedman 1991a, 1991b; Olson 1995; Probst 1988; Rosenblatt 1978; Squire 1984; Tompkins 1997; Venezky et al. 1987.

6a.10. Early Intervention: Carefully designed early intervention for children who experience difficulty in learning to read and write can produce significant long-term improvement.

Research findings:

For 50 years, research has pointed to the importance of early intervention to help children who experience difficulty in learning to read and write. Today's studies warn, however, against extensively isolating children for remedial instruction, and suggest new ways in which tutoring and other support activities can be provided without permanently assigning children to "special" classrooms. The need to provide extensive opportunities to read, rather than merely drill and practice skills in isolation, has been documented as important for students with early reading difficulties.

In the classroom:

Early intervention occurs most effectively within the total classroom, with special support provided as needed. Pull-out programs that permanently isolate children in order to cater to special needs contribute less to their learning than does mainstream classroom instruction with provision for flexible grouping of students. Moreover, such mainstream grouping gives students with reading difficulties the opportunity to observe and learn from students who have moved to the next stage of development and to benefit from the social aspects of reading.

Pull-out programs have often had the additional disadvantage of making less rather than more time for reading instruction available to students with reading problems. Two widely emulated programs—the Reading Recovery program developed by Marie Clay and the Success for All program of Robert Slavin—have been carefully structured to ensure this does not happen. Both involve early diagnosis and treatment, one-to-one tutoring by certified teachers, varied use of flexible grouping in the basic classroom, a print-rich environment with opportunities for reading, and personal instruction on word attack skills with students scheduled for special help in addition to rather than as a substitute for regular reading instruction.

Opportunities to read for meaning and experience success with reading are as important for students having difficulty as for students without problems—perhaps even more important. To address these needs, Reading Recovery uses a series of little books, carefully selected to be both interesting and accessible, that can be read by the students in the program.

Sources:

Allington 1994; Cazden 1988; Indrisano and Paratore 1991; Lyons, Pinnell, and Deford 1993; Slavin and Madden 1987; Slavin et al. 1992; Snow, Burns, and Griffin 1998.

6a.11. Exposure to a Range of Literature: Reading and reflecting on a range of selected literary works can help young people learn about the ideas and values of their own and diverse cultures as well as about the experiences of different groups.

Research findings:

Recent studies of the types of literary works taught in many schools agree that the school curriculum has changed over recent decades, but there is no universal agreement about the extent to which it has changed or whether the changes made are all for the better. Controversy exists over the mix taught, over possible inadequate representation of some minority groups, and over whether efforts to include material from many cultures have resulted in a decline in student knowledge about writers traditionally considered to be important. The degree of change that has actually occurred appears to vary by community.

In the classroom:

The traditional literary canon conveys many of the values on which our country is based. In addition, young people need to understand the values conveyed in the literary heritages of varied cultural groups, with this need increasingly critical because of dramatically changing demographics. Schools should develop curricular programs that contain both traditional and nontraditional literature of high quality.

Although balance in the types of literature taught is important, local communities will continue to resolve, sometimes through controversy, what will be taught locally.

Sources:

Applebee 1991; Burke 1999; Cullinan 1987; Galda, Cullinan, and Strickland 1997; Purves 1994; Ravitch and Finn 1987; Stotsky 1995.

6a.12. Appropriate Assessment: Assessment focusing on what is being taught in a school's curriculum and on the modes of instruction used in the curriculum promotes learners' growth toward curricular goals.

Research findings:

Studies of assessment have identified a misalignment between many of the assessment instruments and approaches used and instructional goals and programs. For example, while instructional attention in the area of writing has shifted from a focus on specific skills to the processes involved in learning to write, few assessment instruments address this new emphasis. Many reading tests ignore assessment of competence in comprehending longer selections, a task receiving increased attention in schools.

In the classroom:

Assessments should measure what teachers teach and students learn. Such assessments help teachers to discover what is working in the teaching-learning interaction. Too often, assessment instruments focus on content that is not central to a school's program. When schoolwide, local, and especially high-stakes state assessments are unrelated to classroom instruction, students' test scores may be low, but the data generated tell little about what should be done to improve instruction. Additional classroom-based assessment may have to be conducted for this purpose.

An alternative scenario may be one that currently exists in some states: Interest in improving higher-order skills of students is intense, and state assessments are being developed and administered that focus on these skills. In cases such as these, changes in assessment may actually precede changes in instruction and provide direction about new curricular goals.

Sources:

Farr 1992; Farr and Beck 1991; Geneshi 1994; Johnston 1984; Strickland and Strickland 1998.

Bibliography

Adams, M. 1990. *Beginning to Read: Thinking and Learning About Print.* Cambridge, MA: The MIT Press.

Allington, R.L. 1994. "The Schools We Have, the Schools We Need." *Reading Teacher* Vol. 48, No. 1 (September 1994): 14-28.

Anderson, R.C., E.H. Hiebert, J.A. Scott, and I.A.G. Wilkinson. 1985. *Becoming a Nation of Readers.* Washington, DC: National Academy of Education.

Anderson, R.C., and D.D. Pearson. 1984. "A Schema-Theoretic View of Basic Process in Reading Comprehension." In *Handbook of Reading Research,* D. Pearson et al., editors (pp. 255-291). New York: Longman.

Anderson, R.C., P.T. Wilson, and L.G. Fielding. 1988. "Growth in Reading and How Children Spend Their Time Outside of School." *Reading Research Quarterly* Vol. 23: 285-303.

Applebee, A.N. 1991. *A Study of High School Literary Anthologies.* Albany, NY: Literature Center, University of New York at Albany.

Armbruster, B., T. Anderson, and D. Ostertag. 1987. "Does Test Structure/Summarization Instruction Facilitate Learning from Expository Text?" *Reading Research Quarterly* Vol. 21: 331-346.

Bangert-Drowns, R.L. 1993. "The Word Processor as an Instructional Tool: A Meta-analysis of Word Processing in Writing Instruction." *Review of Educational Research* Vol. 63, No. 1 (Spring 1993): 69-93.

Bereiter, C., and M. Scardanalia. 1987. *The Psychology of Written Composition.* Hillsdale, NJ: Lawrence Erlbaum Associates, Publishers.

Britton, J. 1970. *Language and Learning.* Coral Gables, FL: University of Miami Press.

Britton, J., T. Burgess, T. Martin, A. McLeod, and H. Rosen. 1975. *The Development of Writing Abilities.* London and Basingstoke, England: McMillan Ltd.

Burke, J. 1999. *The English Teacher's Companion.* Portsmouth, NH: Heinemann.

Cazden, C. 1988. *Classroom Discourse: The Language of Teaching and Learning.* Portsmouth, NH: Heinemann.

Cazden, C. 1991. *Whole Language Plus.* New York: Teachers College, Columbia University.

Chall, J.S. 1967 (revised 1983). *Learning to Read: The Great Debate.* New York: McGraw-Hill Book Company.

Chall, J.S. 1983. *Stages of Reading Development.* New York: McGraw-Hill Book Company. 1996.

Chall, J.S., and V.A. Jacobs. 1996. *The Reading, Writing, and Language Connection.* In *Education and Literacy,* J. Shimron, editor (pp 33-48). Creskill, NJ: Hampton Press.

Claggett, I. 1996. *A Measure of Success: From Assignment to Evaluation.* Portsmouth, NH: Heinemann.

Clay, M. 1991. *Becoming Literate: The Construction of Inner Control.* Portsmouth, NH: Heinemann.

Cullinan, B., editor. 1987. *Children's Literature in the Reading Program.* Newark, DE: International Reading Association.

Dahl, K., and N. Farnan. 1998. *Children's Writing: Perspectives from Research.* Newark, DE: International Reading Association.

Dewey, J. 1933. *How We Think: A Restatement of the Relation of Reflective Thinking to the Educative Process (revised).* Boston: D.C. Heath.

Dole, J., G. Duffy, L. Roehler, and P. Pearson. 1991. "Moving from the Old to the New: Research on Reading Comprehension Instruction." *Review of Educational Research* Vol. 61, No. 2: 239-264.

Dyson, A.H., and S.W. Freedman. 1991a. *Critical Challenges for Research on Writing and Literacy: 1990-1995.* Berkeley, CA: Center for the Study of Literacy and Pittsburgh, PA: Center for the Study of Writing.

Dyson, A.H., and S.W. Freedman. 1991b. "Writing." In *Handbook of Research on Teaching the English Language Arts,* J. Flood, J.M. Jensen, D. Lapp, and J.R. Squire, editors (pp. 754-774). New York: Macmillan Publishing Company.

Emig, J. 1971. *The Composing Processes of Twelfth Graders.* Urbana, IL: National Council of Teachers of English.

Farr, R. 1992. "Putting It All Together: Solving the Reading Assessment Puzzle." *The Reading Teacher* Vol. 46, No. 1: 26-37.

Farr, R., and M. Beck. 1991. "Formal Methods of Evaluation." In *Handbook of Research on Teaching the English Language Arts,* J. Flood, J.M. Jensen, D. Lapp, and J.R. Squire, editors (pp. 489-501). New York: Macmillan Publishing Company.

Farrell, E.J. 1991. "Instructional Models for English Language Arts, K-12." In *Handbook of Research on Teaching the English Language Arts,* J. Flood, J.M. Jensen, D. Lapp, and J.R. Squire, editors (pp. 63-84). New York: Macmillan Publishing Company.

Fielding, L.G., and P.D. Pearson. 1994. "Reading Comprehension: What Works." *Educational Leadership* Vol. 51, No. 5: 62-68.

Flood, J., and D. Lapp. 1991. "Reading Comprehension Instruction." In *Handbook of Research on Teaching the English Language Arts,* J. Flood, J.M. Jensen, D. Lapp, and J.R. Squire, editors (pp. 732-742). New York: Macmillan Publishing Company.

Freedman, S.W. 1987. *Response to Student Writing.* Urbana, IL: National Council of Teachers of English.

Freedman, S.W., and A. McLeod. 1988. *National Surveys of Successful Teachers of Writing and Their Students.* Berkeley, CA: National Center for the Study of Writing, University of California at Berkeley.

Galda, L., B. Cullinan, and D. Strickland. 1997. *Language, Literature, and the Child.* Newark, DE: International Reading Association.

Geneshi, C. 1994. "Assessment and Achievement Testing in the Early Grades." In *Encyclopedia of English Studies and Language Arts,* A. Purves, editor (pp. 72-76). New York: Scholastic.

Goodman, Y., W. Hood, and K. Goodman. 1991. *Organizing for Whole Language.* Portsmouth, NH: Heinemann Educational Books.

Graves, D. 1983. *Writing: Teachers and Children at Work.* Portsmouth, NH: Heinemann Educational Books.

Guthrie, J.T., W. Schafer, Y.Y. Wang, and P. Afflerbach. 1995. "Relationships of Instruction to the Amount of Reading: An Exploration of Social, Cognitive, and Instructional Connections." *Reading Research Quarterly* Vol. 30, No. 1: 8-25.

Haller, E., D. Child, and H. Walberg. 1988. "Can Comprehension Be Taught? A Quantitative Synthesis of Metacognitive Studies." *Educational Researcher* Vol. 17, No. 9: 5-8.

Harste, J.C., and K.G. Short. 1988. *Creating Classrooms for Authors: The Reading-Writing Connection.* Portsmouth, NH: Heinemann Educational Books.

Hartman, D. 1995. "The Intertextual Links of Proficient Readers Reading Multiple Passages." *Reading Research Quarterly.*

Hill, M. 1991. "Writing Summaries Promotes Thinking and Learning Across the Curriculum, But Why Are They So Difficult to Write?" *Journal of Reading* Vol. 34, No. 7 (April 1991): 536-539.

Indrisano, R., and J.R. Paratore. 1991. "Classroom Contexts for Literacy Learning." In *Handbook of Research on Teaching the English Language Arts,* J. Flood, J.M. Jensen, D. Lapp, and J.R. Squire, editors (pp. 477-488). New York: Macmillan Publishing Company.

Jensen, J., editor. 1984. *Composing and Comprehending.* Urbana, IL: National Council of Teachers of English.

Jensen, J.M. 1993. "What Do We Know About the Writing of Elementary School Children?" *Language Arts* Vol. 70: 290-294.

Johnson, D., R. Johnson, and E. Holobec. 1991. *Cooperation in the Classroom.* Edina, MN: Interaction Book Company.

Johnston, P.H. 1984. "Assessment in Reading." In *Handbook of Reading Research,* D. Pearson et al., editors (pp. 147-184). New York: Longman.

LaBrant, L. 1961. "The Uses of Communication Media." In *The Guinea Pigs Grow Up,* M. Willis, editor. Columbus, OH: Ohio State University Press.

Lyons, C.A., G.S. Pinnell, and D.E. Deford. 1993. *Partners in Learning: Teachers and Children in Reading Recovery.* New York: Teachers College Press.

Maguire, M. 1994. "Integration of Learning." In *Handbook of Research on Teaching the English Language Arts,* J. Flood, J. M. Jensen, D. Lapp, and J.R. Squire, editors (pp. 638-639). New York: Macmillan Publishing Company.

McCabe, A., and C. Peterson. 1991. *Developing Narrative Structure.* Hillsdale, NJ: Lawrence Erlbaum Associates, Publishers.

McLain, K.V. 1991. "Metacognition in Reading Comprehension: What Is It and Strategies for Instruction." *Reading Improvement* Vol. 28, No. 3: 169-172.

Moffett, J., and B.J. Wagner. 1983. *Student-Centered Language Arts and Reading: A Handbook for Teachers,* 3rd edition. Boston: Houghton-Mifflin.

Nagy, W.E. 1988. *Teaching Vocabulary to Improve Reading Comprehension.* Urbana, IL: National Council of Teachers of English.

Nagy, W., R. Anderson, and P. Herman. 1987. "Learning Word Meanings from Context During Normal Reading." *American Educational Research Journal* Vol. 24, No. 2: 237-270.

Olson, L. 1995. "Students' Best Writing Needs Work, Study Shows." *Education Week* Vol. 14, No. 20 (February 8, 1995): 5.

Palincsar, A.S., and A.L. Brown. 1985. "Reciprocal Teaching Activities to Promote Reading with Your Mind." In *Reading, Thinking, and Concept Development: Strategies for the Classroom,* T.L. Harris and E.J. Cooper, editors (pp. 147-159). New York: The College Board.

Paris, S.G., B.A. Wasik, and J.C. Turner. 1991. "The Development of Strategic Readers." In *Handbook of Reading Research, Volume 2,* D. Pearson et al., editors (pp. 609-640). New York: Longman.

Pearson, P.D. 1985. "Changing the Face of Reading Comprehension Instruction." *The Reading Teacher* Vol. 38, No. 8: 724-738.

Pearson, P.D. 1993. "Teaching and Learning Reading: A Research Perspective." *Language Arts* Vol. 70, No. 6: 502-511.

Piaget, J. 1959. *The Language and Thought of the Child,* 3rd edition. London: Routledge and Kegan Paul.

Pressley, M. et al. 1990. *Cognitive Strategy Instruction that Really Improves Children's Academic Performance.* Cambridge, MA: Brookline Books.

Probst, R. 1988. *Response and Analysis: Teaching Literature in Junior and Senior High School.* Portsmouth, NH: Heinemann.

Purves, A. 1994. "Response to Literature." In *Encyclopedia of English Studies and Language Arts,* A.C. Purves et al., editors (pp. 1043-1046). New York: Scholastic.

Purves, A.C., and R. Beach. 1972. *Literature and the Reader.* Urbana, IL: National Council of Teachers of English.

Ravitch, D., and C. Finn, Jr. 1987. *What Do Our 17-Year Olds Know? A Report on the First National Assessment of History and Literature.* New York: Harper and Row.

Rosenblatt, L.M. 1978. *The Reader, the Text, the Poem: The Transactional Theory of the Literary Work.* Carbondale, IL: Southern Illinois University.

Rosenshine, R., and B. Stevens. 1984. "Classroom Instruction in Reading." In *Handbook of Reading Research,* D. Pearson et al., editors (pp. 745-798). New York: Longman.

Shaughnessy, M.P. 1977. *Errors and Expectations: A Guide for the Teacher of Basic Writing.* New York: Oxford University Press.

Slavin, R.E., and N.A. Madden. 1987. *Effective Classroom Programs for Students At Risk.* Baltimore: Center for Research on Elementary and Middle Schools, Johns Hopkins University.

Slavin, R.E., N.A. Madden, L.J. Dolan, and B.A. Wasik. 1992. *Success for All: A Relentless Approach to Prevention and Early Intervention in Elementary Schools.* Arlington, VA: Educational Research Service.

Snow, C.E., M.S. Burns, and P.J. Griffin, editors. 1998. *Preventing Reading Difficulties in Young Children.* Washington, DC: National Academy Press.

Squire, J.R. 1984. "Composing and Comprehending, Two Sides of the Same Coin." In *Composing and Comprehending,* J. Jensen, editor. Urbana, IL: National Council of Teachers of English.

Stotsky, S. 1995. "Changes in America's Secondary School Literature Programs: Good News and Bad." *Phi Delta Kappan* Vol. 76, No. 8 (April 1995): 605-612.

Strickland, R. 1962. *The Language Development of Children, Its Relationship to the Language of Reading Textbooks, and the Quality of Reading of Selected School Children.* Bloomington, IN: School of Education, Indiana University.

Strickland, K., and J. Strickland. 1998. *Reflections on Assessment.* Portsmouth, NH: Heinemann.

Tierney, R., and J. Cunningham. 1984. "Research on Teaching Reading Comprehension." In *Handbook of Reading Research,* D. Pearson et al., editors (pp. 609-655). New York: Longman.

Tierney, R., and T. Shanahan. 1991. "Research on the Reading-Writing Relationship: Interactions, Transactions, and Outcomes." In *Handbook of Reading Research, Volume 2,* D. Pearson et al., editors (pp. 246-280). New York: Longman.

Tompkins, G. 1997. *Literacy for the 21st Century: A Balanced Approach.* New York: Prentice-Hall.

Venezky, R. et al. 1987. *The Subtle Danger: Reflections on the Literacy Abilities of America's Young Adults.* Princeton, NJ: Educational Testing Service.

Vgotsky, L.S. 1978. *Mind in Society: The Development of Higher Psychological Processes.* Cambridge, MA: Harvard University Press.

Wittrock, M. 1990. "Generative Processes of Comprehension." *Educational Psychologist* Vol. 24: 345- 376.

Chapter 6b. Oral Communication

Carolyn Dunkle Perry

Oral communication is fundamental to all other learning, but the lack of communicative abilities and training among today's students has been recognized nationally (U.S. Department of Labor 1995; Vangelisti and Daly 1989). Yet, while most state departments of education promote broad sets of language arts objectives, classroom instruction still focuses predominately on reading and writing, and many of our schools are still not effectively educating students in speaking, listening, and media literacy.

A student who cannot communicate cannot learn even the most basic concepts of any other academic discipline. Those who would succeed in social, economic, or academic circumstances must be able to fully express ideas and information and to comprehend the messages around them. Educators, the public, and the business community now recognize communication tools such as speaking skills, rhetorical strategies, and listening skills as critical for success in academic, social, and business settings (Dauphinais 1997; Geddes 1993; Harper 1987; Ridley 1996; Rooff-Steffen 1991). Rankin's classic study, cited in *Guidelines for Developing Oral Communication Curricula* (Speech Communication Association 1991), indicates 75 percent of the average person's day is spent communicating as a listener or as a speaker. Corporate managers report they spend 60 percent of their days communicating orally in face-to-face contexts. It is estimated Americans spend more than 42 hours per week involved with some form of media—more time than some spend at their jobs. There should be no question of the importance of learning how to communicate competently.

The National Communication Association (NCA) has collected and annotated nearly 100 articles, commentaries, and publications, all of which call attention to the importance of communication in contemporary society, with particular attention to the development of the whole person; the improvement of the educational enterprise; being a responsible citizen of the world, both socially and culturally; and succeeding in one's career and in the business enterprise (Morreale, Osborn, and Pearson 2000). Moreover, research on human communication states communication education is essential to addressing four grand challenges facing U.S. society in the 21st century:

1. maintaining and enhancing a vigorous, self-renewing democracy;

2. promoting the health and well-being of all citizens;

3. helping organizations and institutions change in ways that enable society to prosper in the emerging global economy; and

4. enabling people to live happy, meaningful lives and to have fulfilling relationships.

The ability to communicate is learned, but the assumption exists that because students can talk and hear, as well as watch television, listen to the radio, and spend time on computers, they don't need direct instruction in speaking, listening, and media literacy. Nothing, however, could be further from the truth. Writing and reading skills, the typical focus of K-12 instruction, do not automatically translate into competent communication knowledge, behaviors, and attitudes. Listening and speaking knowledge and skills, as well as media literacy, are developed through exposure to systematic training in well-conceived techniques and from appropriate modeling.

Teachers in all subject areas can (and should) easily integrate speaking, listening, and media literacy instruction into their content curriculum. The National Communication Association's (1998) K-12 standards and competencies for listening, speaking, and media literacy provide an outline of the oral communication knowledge, behaviors, and attitudes that students should master by high school graduation. It is a helpful resource for integrating communication skills into the K-12 curriculum.

In order to ensure literacy and lifelong learning, a communicative perspective must be part of educational standards. The practices in this chapter discuss specific activities for teaching oral and listening competency and enhancing students' media literacy.

The author wishes to thank Sherwyn P. Morreale, associate director of the National Communication Association, for her contributions to and review of this section.

6b.1. Improving Oral Communication Competence: Students who are given opportunities to improve their oral communication competence demonstrate improvement in their speaking presentation, as well as in vocabulary, organization, and writing skills.

Research findings:

While most students enter the classroom able to talk, all students benefit from instruction in oral communication. Studies have found the following practices tend to result in improvement in speaking skills: 1) giving students the opportunity to prepare for and practice formal speeches; 2) encouraging students to prepare visual aids for their speeches; and 3) providing students with time to rehearse. Moreover, research indicates students who are taught the basic orders of idea development (for example, chronological, spatial, topical, problem/solution, cause/effect, and compare/contrast) better illustrate organizational skills in prepared speeches as well as in writing.

In the classroom:

Competent speakers appropriately and effectively adapt their oral communication strategies according to the needs of the situation and setting and communicate to inform, persuade, and/or entertain, while also respecting differences in listeners' backgrounds. Students benefit from direct feedback on their use of speaking skills in interpersonal, small group, and public situations. They also need instruction in evaluating the speaking skills of others.

Teachers in all K-12 subject areas can easily integrate oral communication instruction into their curricula. In order to help students improve their communication competence, teachers should provide large amounts of time in the classroom for students to practice competent speaking skills in various situations and with opportunities for evaluative or corrective feedback, either by peers or by the instructor. For example, if a project requires students to present information to the class, the teacher should provide some speaking tips to the students before the speaking situation and include speaking in the evaluation criteria.

Other instructional activities for improving speaking skills include variations of reconstructing experience, such as role-plays and interviews. These may or may not be graded, but all role-plays and other similar situations should be practiced before the evaluation stage and approached as a speaking as well as a subject-specific exercise.

Another way to integrate speech instruction and practice is through impromptu speeches as sponge activities at the beginning or end of class. When a teacher has extra time in class, he or she can call on a student at random to speak on a subject appropriate to the class. In English, the student may be asked to speak for 30 seconds to a minute on the book he is currently reading. In science, a student may be asked to explain in her own words the lab experiment she did that period. Teachers should prepare students for this activity by providing examples of what is expected and take care to allow students an opportunity to decline the speaking situation.

Sources:

Boyd and Renz 1985; Buerkel-Rothfuss, Gray, and Yerby 1993; Burleson 1987; Clinton 1992; Fryar 1981; Galvin, Cooper, and Gordon 1988; Hay and Zboray 1992; Maratsos 1973; McMahan and Rogers 1994; Menig-Peterson 1975; Menzel and Carrell 1994; National Communication Association 1998; Osborn and Osborn 1988; Reisch and Ballard-Reisch 1985; Robinson and Robinson 1983; Rubin and Kantor 1984; Schloff and Yudkin 1991; Shatz and Gelman 1973; Sonnenschein and Whitehurst 1984; Whitehurst and Sonnenschein 1985.

6b.2. Addressing Voice and Articulation: Providing students with instruction in how the vocal mechanism works and in methods of pronunciation and articulation will help students: 1) develop awareness of the need for appropriate articulation and pronunciation; and 2) learn to fit their language to match the context of the communication situation.

Research findings:

Research shows a speaker's voice and articulation affect the reception of his/her message by listeners. All speakers should understand the influence of the vocal elements—pitch, volume, rate, quality, animation, and pause—on their oral presentation, whether in interpersonal, small group, or public speaking situations. Moreover, while a number of researchers and scholars have argued for the inherent value of all dialects of spoken American English, the Standard American English dialect is preferred for business and formal interactions. Indeed, research has shown clearly speakers of dialects other than Standard American English are at a disadvantage in some professional and social environments. As a result, many K-12 teachers promote the use of code-switching, the ability of a speaker to analyze an audience and context and to use the dialect (whether standard or regional) most effective for the purposes of the communication interaction.

In the classroom:

A teacher can introduce the topic of voice and articulation into a K-12 class by encouraging students to discuss times when others judged them by the way they talked. Then the teacher may help students understand how the vocal mechanism works by introducing the functions of respiration, phonation, resonation, and articulation, and encouraging students to notice their own and others' use of these processes. At this time, students should be introduced to the vocal elements of oral communication in order to begin to see the effects of those elements on an oral presentation. One of the most efficient ways to help students improve their use of these elements is to tape record them while speaking in various situations. Students may then evaluate their own oral communication skills and set goals for personal improvement.

Students also benefit from instruction in differences in dialect, why dialects occur, and when dialects are and should be used. Students must hear examples of Standard American English and then be given opportunities to practice those pronunciation patterns. Tape-recorded narratives and speeches can provide students with excellent examples of Standard American English and various dialects in order to distinguish similarities and differences. After students hear examples of other speakers, perhaps from television programs, movies, or popular songs, it is often helpful to tape record the students as they read sample passages so that they can hear their own speech patterns. Care must be taken to ensure various dialects and/or accents are not ridiculed but recognized as equally valuable.

Many activities can easily be integrated into all K-12 subject-area instruction to provide students opportunities to practice their use of pitch, volume, rate, quality, animation, and standard pronunciation. Students can practice oral reading of poetry, literature, textbooks, newspaper articles, and transcripts of television shows or commercials. In addition, students can create their own skits in which they role-play situations using dialects and Standard American English.

Sources:

Anderson 1977; Berko, Bostwick, and Miller 1989; Berko, Wolvin, and Wolvin 1995; Crannell 1987; Devito, Giattino, and Schon 1975; Dreher and Gervase 1976; Eisenson 1985; Fairbanks 1960; Fisher 1975; Galvin, Cooper, and Gordon 1988; Glenn, Glenn, and Forman 1993; Hopper and Naremore 1978; King and DiMichael 1991; Lessac 1967; Mayer 1988; Modisett and Luter 1988; Sarnoff 1971; Wilder 1956; Williams, Hopper, and Natgalicio 1977.

6b.3. Reducing Oral Communication Anxiety: Students who are provided with methods for overcoming anxiety about oral communication demonstrate improved coherence and confidence when giving a speech and in other oral communication situations.

Research findings:

It is commonly understood that many people, including students, experience some degree of anxiety regarding oral communication; yet, teachers often ignore this anxiety and forget that students who experience anxiety tend to perform poorly in oral communication tasks and may perform poorly all around. Most treatments of oral communication anxiety are designed for individual or small-group sessions that occur over an extended period of time. Many, however, can be modified for use in a classroom setting and can be used in conjunction with content instruction.

In the classroom:

Because much activity in classroom instruction is communicated orally through discussions, question-and-answer sessions, and presentations, the effective classroom teacher should implement strategies to minimize students' oral communication anxiety so that the students can perform to the best of their abilities. In an ideal situation, the teacher could identify a student's communication problem and send him or her to a specialist for specific treatment of the problem. This, however, is rarely an option. Instead, the problem frequently must be handled within the classroom and solved while the teacher is attempting to meet other instructional goals.

A number of specific approaches can be used in content-area classes to reduce communication anxiety:

- *Visualization* is used prior to the oral communication activity that is causing anxiety. Students are encouraged to think positively about all aspects of the communication act,

from the moment the student gets up in the morning of the presentation until after the presentation has been completed. Students can write out the most perfect scenario they can envision and re-read it after the presentation to note differences between their vision of the situation and the reality. Visualization, which can be used in normal classroom settings and does not require special arrangements for training or application, reduces communication apprehension over both short and extended periods of time.

- *Cognitive restructuring* is based on the premise that students have irrational thoughts about themselves and their behaviors; these thoughts increase their anxiety about communicating with others. Students are encouraged to identify irrational beliefs they have about communication. The teacher and students then attempt to logically refute these beliefs in an attempt to change the students' ways of thinking. Finally, the teacher helps the students formulate new, more appropriate beliefs to replace their illogical beliefs.

- *Instructional intervention* is based on the teacher's ability to manipulate the situational variables of context, motivation, and acquaintance. Oral communication anxiety tends to increase in direct proportion to the formality and importance of the student's role in the communication situation; therefore, the teacher can reduce anxiety by decreasing the formality of the situation. Students also appear more willing to tolerate certain degrees of communication anxiety if there is ample motivation to do so; such motivating factors are greater grade emphasis or greater perceived legitimacy of the communication situation. In addition, students communicate with less anxiety when they speak with friends than with strangers; therefore, the teacher can reduce anxiety by increasing the amount of familiarity between students in the class or group with whom the students will be participating.

- *Skills training* assumes anxiety can be a result of ambiguity or lack of knowledge; thus, any instruction in how to communicate automatically decreases the amount of apprehension or anxiety students feel about communicating. An effective skills training program allows apprehensive students to identify specific deficiencies; establish goals; observe models of the desirable skill; practice the new skill in a controlled, nonthreatening environment; and practice the new skill in a natural environment. Skills training can address verbal as well as nonverbal communication behaviors. Reticent communicators often display nonverbal behaviors others may interpret as detachment and submissiveness. Teachers can counteract such displays by encouraging communication-reticent students to become involved with their listeners through eye contact, speaking tempo, and facial expressions and gestures.

Sources:

Ayres and Hopf 1985, 1990; Booth-Butterfield 1988; Brownell and Katula 1984; Burgoon, Pfau, Birk, and Manusov 1987; Hay and Zboray, 1992; Hopf, Ayres, Ayres, and Baker 1995; Kelly, Duran, and Stewart 1990; Motley and Molloy 1994; Neer and Kircher 1990; Richmond and McCroskey 1995; Rubin, Rubin, and Jordan, 1997; Vicker 1982; Watson 1986.

6b.4. Emphasizing Communication Ethics: Instruction in standards for ethical communication, as well as the role of culture in the communication process, will provide students with the necessary strategies for maximizing competent communication and avoiding *mis*communication in today's culturally and technologically complex world.

Research:

The roots of communication ethics can be traced to ancient Greece, but contemporary students—on the whole—are only exposed to implicit suggestions, rather than explicit instructions about being ethical communicators. In addition, a growing body of evidence suggests an increase in unethical communication behaviors and attitudes evidenced by reports of students cheating on tests and plagiarizing the work of others. While these trends are alarming, research also supports the notion that modeling ethical communication and emphasizing a set of standards for ethical communication can positively influence the communication behaviors of students.

A contemporary issue influencing the need for ethical communication is the rising multicultural nature of society. Young people frequently give little thought to the role of varying perspectives in the communication process, and most do not realize each culture has its own unwritten rules for communicating. Similarly, young people are often physically skilled in using new technologies to communicate but often aren't aware of the ethical responsibilities inherent in their use. The increase in ways of communicating—email, cellular phones, the Internet with chat rooms and discussion lists—mandates that more attention be paid to instruction in communication ethics. Without intending to do so, students may communicate disrespectfully or offensively.

In the classroom:

The National Communication Association's (NCA) Professional Code of Ethics (1999) states: "Our obligation to behave as ethical communicators and to model ethical communication behavior endures as long as we call ourselves members of the communication discipline." Teachers, by nature of their responsibilities, are *de facto* members of the communication discipline and therefore should also hold themselves to high ethical communication standards as models for their students.

In addition to serving as communication models for their students, teachers should provide students with clear standards for communicating ethically. One example is NCA's Credo for Ethical Communication (1999) that could be used as a base for students and teachers to collaboratively create their own lists of ethical communication behaviors. Schools with existing honor codes or character education programs could also apply those standards to communication behavior.

Serving as models and supplying guidelines, however, are only the first steps toward ethical communication instruction. Students must have guided practice in communication skills in order to grow into ethical communicators. Strategies that can be used across the curriculum include:

- providing time for student-generated, teacher-assisted dialogue on the topic of ethical communication;

- respecting ethnic and cultural differences in communication and valuing both native and standard systems of language use;

- analyzing the elements of communication: topic, audience, message, and purpose with an emphasis on the ethical dimensions of each element;

- emphasizing critical thinking skills as an essential ethical responsibility of any communicator; and

- focusing on the ethical responsibility of comprehension as a shared goal of communication.

Teachers in all subject areas are responsible for guiding students in their awareness of and sensitivity to cultural differences. When students learn about and respect the social norms, linguistic habits, and knowledge systems of alternative cultures, they are better prepared to value their multicultural peers, prevent miscommunication, and communicate ethically with others unlike themselves. Teachers and students can collaborate to identify sensitive and respectful ways to communicate in an increasingly diverse and technological world.

Sources:

Andersen 2000; Broome 1991; Calloway-Thomas and Garner 2000; Chesebro, Berko, Hopson, Cooper, and Hodges 1995; Gudykunst, Ting-Toomey, and Wiseman 1991; Maney 1995; McCroskey and Richmond 1990; Morreale, Osborn, and Pearson 2000; Whitehurst and Sonnenschein 1985.

6b.5. Facilitating Interpersonal and Small-Group Communication: Providing students with models of competent interpersonal and small-group communication behaviors, as well as opportunities to practice these behaviors, will help them become more effective learners across the curriculum.

Research findings:

Numerous surveys clearly indicate the need for students to enter the work force with competent interpersonal and small-group communication skills. Studies indicate that simply putting students into groups to complete a task has very little impact on their growth as communicators or on their learning in the content area. However, students have shown great gains when assigned to cooperative learning groups that create positive interdependence through individual and group accountability. In particular, cooperative learning, compared with competitive or individual efforts, results in higher achievement and greater productivity; more caring, supportive, and committed relationships; and greater psychological health, social competence, and self-esteem. The gains are even more significant when teachers allow time in class for students to model and practice competent skills for these group and interpersonal interactions.

In the classroom:

Teachers in any content area can use cooperative groups or dyads (interpersonal teams of two) at any part of the instructional process: learning, practice, or assessment. No matter where in the pedagogical process the interpersonal or group interaction occurs, however, teachers should complete the following steps:

- *Model behaviors.* Early in the school year, before pairing and grouping become a norm, teachers should set aside time to model competent interpersonal and group behaviors.

These models can occur as teacher examples or in scripts that students perform.

- *Reflect upon and practice behaviors.* During the early interpersonal and group interactions, teachers should occasionally take time to stop the process and allow students to ask questions about the process and reflect on how well they are practicing their communication skills. Moreover, teachers should be familiar with the stages of group development. One popular description of these stages is forming, storming, norming, and performing. Students who understand these stages and know what to expect at each stage will be more productive than students who are not similarly informed.

- *Provide handouts or signs with communication expectations.* All expectations for communication behaviors in dyads or groups should be clearly indicated in writing, whether in a handout students keep in their notebooks or on posters displayed prominently in the classroom. Teachers and students should regularly refer to these resources.

- *Determine if the task can be completed through a group process.* Not every classroom activity is appropriate for interpersonal or group activity. A genuine cooperative activity requires interdependence and cannot be completed independently.

- *Define task.* All dyads and groups should have a clear understanding of the task they are to complete. Moreover, students should know in what part of the instructional process—learning, practice, assessment—they are participating.

- *Define group member roles.* Each group member should have a role in the completion of the task. Some common roles include chairman or taskmaster, secretary or recorder, presenter, encourager, supply manager, and timekeeper. Roles and their descriptions can be posted or included with handouts for group communication expectations.

- *Assign groups.* Teachers should assign groups based on the objectives of the task. Self-selected or random groups are appropriate in some circumstances, but teacher-assigned groups are usually more effective. Heterogeneous groups are often more suitable than homogeneous groups. Bases for selecting group members include students' learning styles, ability levels, and interests.

- *Monitor group process.* During long dyadic or small-group activities, teachers should monitor the process. Teachers can do this in a number of ways, during or after the activity. During the activity, teachers can conduct impromptu checks by circulating throughout the room. After the activity, teachers can confer with students or ask students to complete a self-assessment regarding their contributions to the group effort.

- *Evaluate product.* Products of paired or group work should be evaluated in some manner. If the students are still learning new knowledge or skills, then the product should provide evidence that at least some learning has occurred. If the students are practicing new knowledge or skills, then the product should provide evidence that the knowledge or skill is being practiced. If the students are being assessed in their mastery of new knowledge or skills, then the product should be evaluated for evidence of that mastery.

- *Assess process.* Typically, the group process ends when the product has been turned in for evaluation. However, providing students with time to assess their behaviors throughout the interpersonal or group process adds to their development as communicators. Various assessment forms are available, and most include some type of scale on which students can judge how well they stayed on task, contributed to the work of the group, and listened to the contributions of others.

Sources:

Argyle 1985; Broome 1991; Cohen 1994; Cragan and Shields 1999; Cragan and Wright 1990; Galvin and Book 1990; Geddes 1993; Johnson and Johnson 1989, 1996, 1999; Kagan 1985; Putnam 1994; Putnam and Stohl 1990; Sharan and Sharan 1992; Slavin 1986.

6b.6. Increasing Listening Effectiveness: Students who are provided with instruction in listening skills and opportunities to practice effective and appropriate listening demonstrate improvement in listening as well as in speaking, reading, and learning.

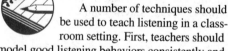

Research findings:

Listening is the process of receiving, constructing meaning from, and responding to spoken and/or nonverbal messages. Of the major verbal communication skills (listening, speaking, reading, and writing), listening is the skill first experienced (by a fetus), most required (at all levels of education), and most fundamental for mastery of all other communication skills and cognitive processes. While research reveals students receive numerous opportunities to "practice" habituated listening behaviors in the classroom, it also reveals most students are not competent listeners. Studies further indicate most students do not receive direct listening instruction, although listening instruction also results in improved communication and other cognitive behaviors, including speaking, reading, and learning.

In the classroom:

A number of techniques should be used to teach listening in a classroom setting. First, teachers should model good listening behaviors consistently and continually. Once shown a competent example of a desired listening practice, students are better able to adopt the behavior to their own use.

Teachers should direct students' attention to the importance of listening. Significant facts about listening and examples of costly listening errors can be found in various sources, including *Teaching Effective Listening: A Practical Guide for the High School Classroom, Vols. 1 and 2* (Coakley 1997) and *Understanding and Developing the Skills of Oral Communication: Speaking and Listening, 2nd Edition* (Hunsaker 1990).

In order to provide both students and teachers with some evidence of improvement in listening as a result of classroom instruction and correct practice, teachers should assess their students' listening knowledge, behaviors, attitudes, and improvement. Teachers may choose to use a standardized test such as the *Brown-Carlsen (BC) Listening Comprehension Test (Revised)* or the *Watson-Barker Listening Test: High School Version*, or to create their own listening assessment instrument, although this requires quite a bit of time and research. Another option is to have students describe and analyze their own listening behaviors through a survey or diary.

Next, teachers should inform students of the steps in the listening process: receiving a spoken and/or nonverbal message, constructing meaning from that message, and responding to it. Students should learn about listening barriers and be provided with strategies to overcome or manage such barriers. After students understand the details of the listening process, teachers should provide students with a list of ways to improve listening skills. Students can also generate their own lists of ways to improve their listening skills. Suggestions include, but are not limited to, the following:

- minimize or eliminate distractions;
- maintain focused attention;
- identify the speaker's purpose and adapt to it;
- listen for main ideas and significant details;
- identify useful information;
- plan to share the content of the message with someone else within eight hours;
- develop note-taking skills; and

- take responsibility for the success of the communication interaction.

Finally, students should have opportunities to practice competent listening to various types of information, including instructions, organization and order, main ideas, facts, opinions, and implied ideas. In addition, students should be given opportunities to practice overcoming various listening barriers. The classroom is an ideal situation for students to talk and listen correctly to one another, whether in classroom discussions, small groups, or interpersonal (dyadic) interactions. Teachers can easily select and present oral text selections to provide students with both content-specific information and correct practice in listening.

Teachers across the curriculum can help students be more effective listeners during content-area presentations by providing students with pre-listening strategies and cues.

Just as a list of objectives at the beginning of a written text chapter provides students with clues about what to look for while they are reading, a pre-listening guide can help students focus on the important points in a lecture or other oral presentation.

Sources:

Adler 1983; Barker 1988; Berko, Bostwick, and Miller 1989; Brown 1987; Coakley 1997; Coakley and Wolvin 1989; Cooper 1985; Fitch-Hauser and Hughes 1992; Galvin and Book 1990; Galvin, Cooper, and Gordon 1988; Gilbert 1988; Goodlad 1983; Hunsaker 1990; International Listening Association 1995; Lundsteen 1979; Nichols and Stevens 1957; O'Hair, O'Hair, and Wooden 1988; Roach and Wyatt 1988; Steil 1980; Swanson 1993; West 1983.

6b.7. Developing Media Literacy: Helping students improve their awareness of how various media affect them will give them the control they need to reach higher levels of media literacy.

Research findings:

Ours is a media-saturated culture. Research shows Americans spend an average of 3,297 hours with the media each year, including watching television; reading newspapers, books and magazines; and listening to the radio. In addition, computers are rapidly becoming an everyday part of our media intake. Over 40 million personal computers are in U.S. homes, and more than 97 percent of U.S. schools have computers in them. Yet, while most American students are media familiar and aware, many operate at low levels of media literacy—the understanding of how words, images, and sounds influence the way meanings are created and shared in society.

Studies show media messages are very powerful. They can give us ideas and information; create and shape our opinions, beliefs, and values; influence our automatic bodily systems; and trigger actions. Media literacy is a goal, however, and not an end. All students can improve their level of media literacy. While much of this change occurs as a natural process of maturation as students gain skills and knowledge of their world, teachers can employ many techniques to help students increase their media literacy.

In the classroom:

Teachers from all content areas can help students improve their media literacy by providing them with hands-on activities and specific opportunities for learning. Students begin thinking critically about their own beliefs and attitudes about media when they examine their own use of media or after they take an informal pretest about media. They

also benefit from identifying the parts of media messages, if only in the context of the particular media being used in a classroom activity. A common approach to improving students' media literacy is to remind students media deserve the same critical scrutiny as all sources of information. In particular, teachers should give students time to review a media message, reflect on its content and format, and react to it.

When reviewing a media presentation, students should be given time to consider several aspects of it, including the degree of realism of the presentation; the moral, if any; the language used; the accuracy; the entertainment value; and the timeliness of the message. After reviewing the content of the presentation, students should then be provided with the opportunity to reflect on the content and format. Both the review and the reflection may be done in journals, class discussions, small groups, or in peer dyads. In terms of content, students should consider such issues as how they feel about the message, their level of agreement with the message, the possible effects viewing the presentation will have on their lives, and to what degree the characters represent the students and people they know. In terms of format, students may reflect upon the audience to which the media presentation was directed, the source of the presentation, the reliability of the material included in the presentation, and the possibility of bias in the presentation.

After any instruction involving media, teachers should allow students time to react to the media presentation. Students must realize they can decide to do something, change the way they think about something, or do nothing. Teachers can guide students as they explore the list of possible reactions to a media presentation, helping them weigh pros and cons of various responses.

Sources:

Berko, Wolvin, and Wolvin 1995; Considine and Haley 1992; Hay and Zboray 1992; Haynes 1988; Intelligence Infocorp 1996; Maney 1995; Mastrolia 1997; Potter 1998; Rosen, Quesada, and Summers 1998; Summers 1997; U.S. Department of Commerce 1995; Wood, Bradac, Barnhart, and Kraft 1970.

Bibliography

Adler, M.J. 1983. *How to Speak, How to Listen.* New York: Macmillan.

Andersen, K.E. 2000. "Developments in Communication Ethics: The Ethics Commission, Code of Professional Responsibilities, Credo for Ethical Communication." *Journal of the Association for Communication Administration* Vol. 29, 131-144.

Anderson, V.A. 1977. *Training the Speaking Voice* (3rd edition). London: Oxford University.

Argyle, M. 1985. *The Psychology of Interpersonal Behavior.* Baltimore: Penguin.

Ayres, J., and T.S. Hopf. 1985. "Visualization: A Means of Reducing Speech Anxiety." *Communication Education* Vol. 34: 318-323.

Ayres, J., and T.S. Hopf. 1990. "The Long-Term Effect of Visualization in the Classroom: A Brief Research Report." *Communication Education* Vol. 39: 75-78.

Barker, L.L. 1988. *Listening Skills: Objectives and Criterion References Exercises for Grades K-12.* Auburn, AL: Spectra.

Berko, R., F. Bostwick, and M. Miller. 1989. *Basically Communicating: An Activity Approach* (2nd edition). Dubuque, IA: Wm. C. Brown.

Berko, R., A. Wolvin, and D. Wolvin. 1995. *Communicating: A Social and Career Focus* (6th edition). Boston: Houghton Mifflin.

Booth-Butterfield, S. 1988. "Instructional Interventions for Reducing Situational Anxiety and Avoidance." *Communication Education* Vol. 37: 214-223.

Boyd, S., and M.A. Renz. 1985. *Organization and Outlining: A Workbook for Students in a Basic Speech Course.* Indianapolis, IN: Bobbs-Merrill.

Broome, B.J. 1991. "Building Shared Meaning: Implication of a Relational Approach to Empathy for Teaching Intercultural Communication." *Communication Education* Vol. 40: 235-250.

Brown, J.I. 1987. "Listening—Ubiquitous, Yet Obscure." *Journal of the International Listening Association* Vol. 1: 3-14.

Brownell, W.W., and R.A. Katula. 1984. "The Communication Anxiety Graph: A Classroom Tool for Managing Speech Anxiety." *Communication Quarterly* Vol. 32: 243-249.

Buerkel-Rothfuss, N.L., P.I. Gray, and J. Yerby. 1993. "Meta-Analysis Between Communication Apprehension and Cognitive Performance." *Communication Education* Vol. 41: 68-76.

Burgoon, J.K., M. Pfau, T. Birk, and V. Manusov. 1987. "Nonverbal Communication Performance and Perceptions Associated with Reticence: Replications and Classroom Implications." *Communication Education* Vol. 36: 119-130.

Burleson, B.R. 1987. "Cognitive Complexity." *Personality and Interpersonal Communication,* J.C. McCroskey and J.A. Daly, editors (pp. 305-349). Newbury Park, CA: Sage.

Calloway-Thomas, C., and T. Garner. 2000. "A Confrontation with Diversity: Communication and Culture in the 21st Century." *Journal of the Association for Communication Administration* Vol. 29: 145-154.

Chesebro, J., R. Berko, C. Hopson, P. Cooper, and H. Hodges. 1995. "Effective Strategies for Increasing Achievement in Oral Communication." *Educating Everybody's Children,* R.W. Cole, editor. Alexandria, VA: Association for Supervision and Curriculum Development.

Clinton, B.L. 1992. "Informative Communication Instruction: An Application of Theory and Research to the Elementary School Classroom." *Communication Education* Vol. 41: 54-67.

Coakley, C.G. 1997. *Teaching Effective Listening: A Practical Guide for the High School Classroom,* Vol. 1. Sonoma, CA: Coakley Communication Connection.

Coakley, C.G., and A. Wolvin, editors. 1989. *Experiential Training: Tools for Teachers and Trainers.* New Orleans, LA: Spectra.

Cohen, E. 1994. *Designing Groupwork: Strategies for the Heterogeneous Classroom.* New York: Teachers College Press.

Considine, D.M., and G.E. Haley. 1992. *Visual Messages: Integrating Imagery into Instruction.* Englewood, CO: Teacher Ideas Press.

Cooper, P.J. 1985. *Activities for Teaching Speaking and Listening: Grades 7-12.* Urbana, IL: ERIC/SCA.

Cragan, J.F., and D.C. Shields. 1999. "Translating Scholarship into Practice: Communication Studies Reflecting the Value of Theory-Based Research to Everyday Life." *Journal of Applied Communication Research* Vol. 27.

Cragan, J.F., and D.W. Wright. 1990. "Small Group Communication Research of the 1980s: A Synthesis and Critique." *Communication Studies* Vol. 41: 212-236.

Crannell, K.C. 1987. *Voice and Articulation.* Belmont, CA: Wadsworth.

Dauphinais, W. 1997. "Forging the Path to Power." *Security Management,* 41: 21-23.

Devito, J.A., J. Giattino, and T.D. Schon. 1975. *Articulation and Voice: Effective Communication.* Indianapolis, IN: Bobbs-Merrill.

Dreher, B.B., and C.J. Gervase. 1976. *Phonetics: Instruction Aid in Language Arts.* Dubuque, IA: Wm. C. Brown.

Ecroyd, D.H. 1973. "The Relevance of Oral Language Development to Classroom Teaching." *Communication Quarterly* Vol. 21: 1-17.

Eisenson, J. 1985. *Voice and Diction: A Program for Improvement* (5th edition). New York: Macmillan.

Fairbanks, G. 1960. *Voice and Articulation Drillbook* (2nd edition). New York: Harper.

Fisher, H. 1975. *Improving Voice and Articulation* (2nd edition). Boston: Houghton-Mifflin.

Fitch-Hauser, M., and M.A. Hughes. 1992. "The Conceptualization and Measurement of Listening." *Journal of the International Listening Association* Vol. 6: 6-22.

Fryar, M. 1981. *Coaching for Individual Events*. Paper presented at the annual meeting of the Southern Speech Communication Association, Austin, TX.

Galvin, K., and C. Book. 1990. *Person to Person*. Lincolnwood, IL: National Textbook.

Galvin, K., P. Cooper, and J.M. Gordon. 1988. *The Basics of Speech*. Lincolnwood, IL: National Textbook.

Geddes, D.S. 1993. "Empowerment Through Communication: Key People-to-People and Organizational Success." *People and Education* Vol. 1: 76-104.

Gilbert, M.B. 1988. "Listening in School: I Know You Can Hear Me—But Are You Listening?" *Journal of the International Listening Association* Vol. 2: 121-132.

Glenn, E.C., P. J. Glenn, and S. Forman. 1993. *Your Voice and Articulation* (3rd edition). Englewood Cliffs, NJ: Prentice Hall.

Goodlad, J. 1983. "A Study of Schooling: Some Findings and Hypotheses." *Phi Delta Kappan* Vol. 64, No. 7 (March 1983): 465-470.

Goulden, N.R. 1998. "The Roles of National and State Standards in Implementing Speaking, Listening, and Media Literacy." *Communication Education* Vol. 47: 194-208.

Gudykunst, W., S. Ting-Toomey, and R.L. Wiseman. 1991. "Taming the Beast: Designing a Course in Intercultural Communication." *Communication Education* Vol. 40: 272-285.

Hall, B., S. Morreale, and J.L. Gaudino. "A Survey of the Status of Oral Communication in the K-12 Public Educational System in the United States." *Communication Education* Vol. 49: 139-148.

Harper, S.C. 1987. "Business Education: A View from the Top." *Business Forum* Vol. 12: 24-27.

Hay, L., and R. Zboray. 1992. *Complete Communication Skills Activities Kit*. West Nyack, NY: Center for Applied Research in Education.

Haynes, W.L. 1988. "Of That Which We Cannot Write: Some Notes on the Phenomenology of Media." *Quarterly Journal of Speech* Vol. 74, No. 1 (February 1988): 71-101.

Hopf, T., F. Ayres, T. Ayres, and B. Baker. 1995. "Does Self-Help Material Work? Testing a Manual Designed to Help Trainers Construct Public Speaking Apprehension Reduction Workshops." *Communication Research Reports* Vol. 12: 34-38.

Hopper, R., and R.J. Naremore. 1978. *Children's Speech: A Practical Introduction to Communication Development* (2nd edition). New York: Harper Collins.

Hunsaker, R.A. 1990. *Understanding and Developing the Skills of Oral Communication: Speaking and Listening* (2nd edition). Englewood, CO: Morton.

Intelligence Infocorp. 1996. *Nando.net.release*. LaJolla, CA: Author.

International Listening Association. 1995. "An ILA Definition of Listening." *ILA Listening Post*, Vol. 53: 4.

Johnson, D.W., and R. Johnson. 1989. *Cooperation and Competition: Theory and Research*. Edina, MN: Interaction Book Company.

Johnson, D.W., and R. Johnson. 1999. *Learning Together and Alone: Cooperative, Competitive, and Individualistic Learning*. Boston: Allyn and Bacon.

Johnson, D.W., and R.T. Johnson. 1996. The Role of Cooperative Learning in Assessing and Communicating Student Learning. In 1996 ASCD Yearbook: *Communicating Student Learning*. T. R. Guskey, editor. Alexandria, VA: Association for Supervision and Curriculum Development.

Kagan, S. 1985. *Cooperative Learning Resources for Teachers*. Riverside, CA: University of California at Riverside.

Kelly, L., R.L. Duran, and J. Stewart. 1990. "Rhetoritherapy Revisited: A Test of Its Effectiveness as a Treatment for Communication Problems." *Communication Education* Vol. 39: 207-226.

King, R.K., and E.M. DiMichael. 1991. *Voice and Diction Handbook*. Prospect Heights, IL: Waveland.

Lessac, A. 1967. *The Use and Training of the Human Voice* (2nd edition). Mountain View, CA: Mayfield.

Lundsteen, S. 1979. *Listening: Its Impact on Reading and the Other Language Arts, 2nd Edition*. Urbana, IL: NCTE ERIC.

Maney, K. 1995. *Megamedia Shakeout: The Inside Story of the Leaders and the Losers in the Exploding Communications Industry*. New York: Wiley.

Maratsos, M.P. 1973. "Nonegocentric Communication Abilities in Preschool Children." *Child Development* Vol. 44: 697-700.

Mastrolia, B.A. 1997. "The Media Deprivation Experience: Revealing Mass Media as Both Message and Massage." *Communication Education* Vol. 46, No. 6: 203-210.

Mayer, L.V. 1988. *Fundamentals of Voice and Diction* (8th edition). Dubuque, IA: Wm. C. Brown.

McCroskey, J.C., and V.P. Richmond. 1990. "Willingness to Communicate: Differing Cultural Perspectives." *The Southern Communication Journal* Vol. 56.

McMahan, E.M., and K.L. Rogers. 1994. *Interactive Oral History Interviewing*. Hillsdale, NJ: Lawrence Erlbaum.

Menig-Peterson, C.L. 1975. "The Modification of Communication Behavior in Preschool-Aged Children as a Function of the Listener's Perspective." *Child Development* Vol. 46: 1015-1018.

Menzel, K.E., and L.J. Carrell. 1994. "The Relationship Between Preparation and Performance in Public Speaking." *Communication Education* Vol. 43: 17-26.

Modisett, N.F., and J.G. Luter. 1988. *Speaking Clearly: The Basics of Voice and Articulation* (3rd edition). Edina, MN: Burgess.

Morreale, S.P., M.M. Osborn, and J.C. Pearson. 2000. Why communication is important: A rationale for the centrality of the study of communication. *Journal of the Association for Communication Administration*, Vol. 29: 1-25.

Motley, M.T., and J.L. Molloy. 1994. "An Efficacy Test of a New Therapy (Communication-Orientation Motivation) for Public Speaking Anxiety." *Journal of Applied Communication Research* Vol. 22: 48-58.

National Communication Association. 1998. *Competent Communicators: K-12 Speaking, Listening, and Media Literacy Standards and Competency Statements*. Annandale, VA: Author.

National Communication Association. 2002. *Communication: Ubiquitous, Complex, Consequential*. Washington, DC: Author.

Neer, M.R., and W.F. Kircher. 1990. *Classroom Interventions for Reducing Public Speaking Anxiety*. Paper presented at the Speech Communication Association 76th Annual Meeting, Chicago, IL.

Nichols, R.G., and L.A. Stevens. 1957. *Are You Listening?* New York: McGraw-Hill.

Osborn, M., and S. Osborn. 1988. *Public Speaking*. Boston: Houghton Mifflin.

O'Hair, M., D. O'Hair, and S.L. Wooden. 1988. "Enhancement of Listening Skills as a Prerequisite to Improved Study Skills." *Journal of International Listening Association* Vol. 2: 113-120.

Potter, W.J. 1998. *Media Literacy*. Thousand Oaks, CA: Sage.

Putnam, L. 1994. "Revitalizing Small Group Communication: Lessons Learned from a Bona Fide Group Perspective." *Communication Studies* Vol. 45: 97-102.

Putnam, L.L., and C. Stohl. 1990. "Bona Fide Groups: A Reconceptualization of Groups in Context." *Communication Studies* Vol. 41: 248-265.

Reisch, R.J., and D.S. Ballard-Reisch. 1985. *Coaching Strategies in Contest Persuasive Speaking: A Guide to Coaching the Novice*. Paper presented at the annual meeting of the Speech Communication Association, Denver, CO.

Richmond, V.P., and J.C. McCroskey. 1995. *Communication: Apprehension, Avoidance, and Effectiveness*. Scottsdale, AZ: Gorsuch, Scarisbrick.

Ridley, A.J. 1996. "A Profession for the Twenty-First Century." *Internal Auditor* Vol. 53: 20-25.

Roach, C., and N.J. Wyatt. 1988. *Successful Listening*. New York: Harper and Row.

Robinson, E.J., and W.P. Robinson. 1983. "Communication and Meta-Communication: Quality of Children's Instructions in Relation to Judgments About the Adequacy of Instructions and the Locus of Responsibility for Communication Failure." *Journal of Experimental Child Psychology* Vol. 35: 305-320.

Rooff-Steffen, K. 1991. "The Push Is on for People Skills." *Journal of Career Planning and Employment* Vol. 52: 61-63.

Rosen, E.Y., A.P. Quesada, and S.L. Summers. 1998. *Changing the World through Media Education*. Golden, CO: Fulcrum Resources.

Rubin, D.L., and K.J. Kantor. 1984. "Talking and Writing: Building Communication Competence." In *Speaking and Writing K-12*, C. Thaiss and C. Suhor, editors (pp. 29-73). Urbana, IL: National Council of Teachers of English.

Rubin, R.B., A.M. Rubin, and F.F. Jordan. 1997. "Effects of Instruction on Communication Apprehension and Communication Competence." *Communication Education* Vol. 46: 104-114.

Sarnoff, D. 1971. *Speech Can Change Your Life*. New York: Dell.

Schloff, L., and M. Yudkin. 1991. *Smart Speaking*. New York: Holt.

Sharan, S., and Y. Sharan. 1992. *Group Investigation: Expanding Cooperative Learning*. New York: Teachers College Press.

Shatz, M., and R. Gelman. 1973. "The Development of Communication Skills: Modifications in the Speech of Young Children as a Function of Listener." *Monographs of the Society for Research in Child Development* Vol. 38 (5, Serial No. 152).

Slavin, R. 1986. *Using Student Team Learning* (3rd edition). Baltimore: Johns Hopkins University Press.

Sonnenschein, S., and G.J. Whitehurst. 1984. "Developing Referential Communication: A Hierarchy of Skills." *Child Development* Vol. 48: 993-1001.

Speech Communication Association. 1991. *Guidelines for Developing Oral Communication Curricula in Kindergarten Through Twelfth Grade*. Annandale, VA: Author.

Spitzberg, B.H. 2000. "What is Good Communication?" *Journal of the Association for Communication Administration* Vol. 29: 103-119.

Steil, L.K. May 26, 1980. "Secrets of Being a Better Listener." *U.S. News and World Report*, pp. 65-67.

Summers, S.L. 1997. *Media Alert! 200 Activities to Create Media Savvy Kids*. Castle Rock, CO: Hi Willow Research and Publishing.

Swanson, C.H. 1993. "Empower Your Teaching by Meeting Your Listeners' Needs." *Journal of the International Listening Association* (Special issue): 17-26.

U.S. Department of Commerce. 1995. *Statistical Abstract of the United States.* Washington, DC: U.S. Government Printing Office.

U.S. Department of Labor. 1995. *Fastest Growing Careers.* Chevy Chase, MD: U.S. Government Printing Office.

Vangelisti, A.L., and J.A. Daly. 1989. "Correlates of Speaking Skills in the United States: A National Assessment." *Communication Education* Vol. 38: 122-143.

Vicker, L.A. 1982. *The Speech Anxiety Reduction Program: Implementation of a Large-Scale Program for Reducing Fear of Public Speaking.* Paper presented at the annual convention of the Eastern Communication Association, Hartford, CT.

Watson, A.K. 1986. *Communication Apprehension: Alleviation Through a Semester Basic Speech Course.* Paper presented at the annual convention of the Eastern Communication Association, Atlantic City, NJ.

West, B.F. 1983. "The Most Used Communication Method Receives the Least Instruction Time." *Listening Post Supplement,* pp. 3-19.

Whitehurst, G.J., and S. Sonnenschein. 1985. "The Development of Communication: A Functional Analysis." In *Annals of Child Development, 2,* G.J. Whitehurst, editor (pp. 1-48). Greenwich, CT: JAI.

Wilder, L. 1956. *Professionally Speaking.* New York: Simon and Schuster.

Williams, F., R. Hopper, and D.S. Natgalicio. 1977. *The Sounds of Children.* Englewood Cliffs, NJ: Prentice Hall.

Wood, R.V., J.J. Bradac, S.A. Barnhart, and E. Kraft. 1970. "The Effect of Learning About Techniques of Propaganda on Subsequent Reaction to Propagandistic Communication." *The Speech Teacher* Vol. 19: 49-53.

Chapter 7. Mathematics

Douglas A. Grouws

The number of research studies conducted in mathematics education over the past three decades has increased dramatically (Kilpatrick 1992). The resulting research base spans a broad range of content, grade levels, and research methodologies. The results from these studies, along with relevant findings from research in other domains, such as cognitive psychology, are used to identify the successful teaching strategies and practices described in this chapter.

Teaching and learning mathematics are complex tasks. The effect on student learning of changing a single teaching practice may be difficult to discern because of the simultaneous effects of both the other teaching activities surrounding it and the context in which the teaching takes place.

Thus, as teachers seek to improve their teaching effectiveness by changing their instructional practices, they should carefully consider the teaching context, giving special consideration to the types of students they teach. And, further, they should not judge the results of their new practices too quickly. Judgments about the appropriateness of their decisions must be based on more than a single outcome. If the results are not completely satisfactory, then teachers should consider the circumstances that may be diminishing the impact of the practices they are implementing. For example, the value of a teacher focusing more attention on teaching for meaning may not be demonstrated if student assessments concentrate on rote recall of facts and proficient use of isolated skills.

The quality of the implementation of a teaching practice also greatly influences its impact on student learning. The value of using manipulative materials to investigate a concept, for example, depends not only on *whether* manipulatives are used, but also on *how* they are used with the students. Similarly, small-group instruction will benefit students only if the teacher knows when and how to use this teaching practice. Hence, as a teacher implements any of the recommendations in this section, it is essential that he or she constantly monitors and adjusts the way the practice is implemented to optimize improvements in quality.

These cautions not withstanding, the research findings indicate certain teaching strategies and methods are worth careful consideration as teachers strive to improve their mathematics teaching practices. As readers examine the suggestions that follow, it will become clear many of the practices are interrelated. There is also considerable variety in the practices found to be effective, and so most teachers should be able to identify ideas they would like to try in their classrooms. The practices are not mutually exclusive; indeed, they tend to be complementary. The logical consistency and variety in the suggestions from research make them both interesting and practical.

The author wishes to acknowledge the following colleagues who reviewed this section and made helpful suggestions: Tim Cooney, professor of mathematics, University of Georgia; James Hiebert, professor of mathematics education, University of Delaware; Judy Sowder, professor of mathematics, San Diego State University; and Terry Wood, professor of mathematics education, Purdue University.

The author was a visiting scholar at the Pacific Mathematics and Science Regional Consortium at Pacific Resources for Education and Learning (PREL) when this chapter was written, and the consortium's support is gratefully acknowledged.

7.1. Opportunity to Learn: The extent of students' opportunity to learn mathematics content bears directly and decisively on student mathematics achievement.

Research findings:

The term "opportunity to learn" (OTL) refers to what is studied or embodied in the tasks students do. Hence, in mathematics, OTL includes the scope of the mathematics presented, how the mathematics is taught, and the match between students' entry skills and new material.

The strong relationship between OTL and student performance in mathematics has been documented in many research studies. The concept was studied in the First International Mathematics Study (Husén 1967), where teachers were asked to rate the extent of student exposure to particular mathematical concepts and skills. Strong correlations were found between student OTL scores and mean student achievement scores in mathematics, with high OTL scores associated with high achievement. The link between student mathematics achievement and OTL was also found in subsequent international studies. McKnight and colleagues (1987) reported OTL was strongly related to student mathematics achievement in the Second International Mathematics Study (SIMS). Schmidt and colleagues (1997) also reported a strong relationship in the curriculum analyses component of the Third International Mathematics and Science Study (TIMSS).

As might be expected, there is also a positive relationship between total time allocated to mathematics and general mathematics achievement. Suarez et al. (1991), in a review of research on instructional time, found strong support for the link between allocated instructional time and student performance. Internationally, Keeves (1976) found a significant relationship across Australian states between achievement in mathematics and total curriculum time spent on mathematics.

In spite of these research findings, many students still spend only minimal amounts of time in mathematics class. For instance, Grouws and Smith (2000), in an analysis of data from the 1996 NAEP mathematics study, found 20 percent of eighth-grade students had teachers who allocated 2.5 hours or less for mathematics instruction per week—30 minutes or less for mathematics instruction each day.

The importance of student OTL is also attested to by the strong relationship between mathematics course-taking at the secondary school level and student achievement. Reports from the National Assessment of Educational Progress (NAEP) in mathematics showed that for both 13-year-olds and 17-year-olds more advanced mathematics course work was associated with higher scores (Campbell, Hombo, and Mazzeo 2000).

Textbooks are also related to student OTL, because many textbooks do not contain much content that is new to students. The lack of attention to new material and heavy emphasis on review in many textbooks is of particular concern at the elementary and middle school levels. Flanders (1987) examined several textbook series and found less than 50 percent of the pages in textbooks for grades two through eight contained any material new to students. In a review of a dozen middle-grades mathematics textbook series, Kulm, Morris, and Grier (1999) found most traditional textbook series lack many of the content recommendations made in recent standards documents such as those of the National Council of Teachers of Mathematics.

U.S. data from TIMSS showed important differences in the content taught to students in different mathematics classes or tracks. For example, students in remedial classes, typical eighth-grade classes, and pre-algebra classes were exposed to very different mathematics content, and their achievement levels varied accordingly.

The achievement tests used in international studies and in NAEP assessments measure important mathematical outcomes and have commonly provided a broad and representative coverage of mathematics. Moreover, the tests have generally served to measure what even the most able students know and do not know. Consequently, they provide reasonable outcome measures for research examining the importance of OTL as a factor in student mathematics achievement.

In the classroom:

The findings about the relationship between OTL and student achievement have important implications for teachers. In particular, it seems prudent to allocate sufficient time for mathematics instruction at every grade level. Short class periods in mathematics, instituted for whatever practical or philosophical reason, should be seriously questioned. Of special concern are the 30- to 35-minute class periods for mathematics being implemented in some middle schools. Although there certainly is a point of diminishing returns when adding more class time for mathematics, this is not a problem most American teachers will need to be concerned with in the near future, given current time allocation levels.

Textbooks that devote major attention to review and that address little new content each year should be avoided, or their use should be heavily supplemented in appropriate ways. Teachers should use textbooks as just one instructional tool among many, rather than feel duty bound to go through the textbook on a one-section-per-day basis.

Teachers must ensure students are given the opportunity to learn important content and skills. If students are to compete effectively in a global, technologically oriented society, then they must be taught the mathematical skills needed to do so. Thus, if problem solving is essential, explicit attention must be given to problem solving on a regular and sustained basis. If we expect students to develop number sense, then it is important to attend to mental computation and estimation as part of the curriculum. If proportional and deductive reasoning are important, then attention must be given to them in the curriculum implemented in the classroom.

It is important to note OTL is related to equity issues. Some educational practices differentially affect the OTL of particular groups of students. For example, a recent American Association of University Women study showed boys' and girls' use of technology is markedly different. Girls take fewer computer science and computer design courses than do boys. Furthermore, boys often use computers to program and solve problems, whereas girls tend to use the computer primarily as a word processor. This suggests, as technology is used in the mathematics classroom, teachers must assign tasks and responsibilities to students in such a way that both boys and girls have active learning experiences with the technological tools employed.

OTL is also affected when low-achieving students are tracked into special "basic skills" curricula, oriented toward developing procedural skills, with little opportunity to develop problem solving and higher-order thinking abilities. The impoverished curriculum frequently provided to these students is an especially serious problem because the ideas and concepts frequently untaught or de-emphasized are the very ones needed in everyday life and in the workplace.

Sources:

American Association of University Women 1998; Atanda 1999; Campbell, Hombo, and Mazzeo 2000; Flanders 1987; Grouws and Smith 2000; Hawkins, Stancavage, and Dossey 1998; Husén 1967; Keeves 1976, 1994; Kulm, Morris, and Grier 1999; McKnight et al. 1987; Mullis, Jenkins, and Johnson 1994; National Center for Education Statistics 1996, 1997, 1998; Schmidt, McKnight, and Raizen 1997; Secada 1992; Suarez, Torlone, McGrath, and Clark 1991.

7.2. Focus on Meaning: Focusing instruction on the meaningful development of important mathematical ideas increases student learning.

Research findings:

There is a long history of research on the effects of teaching for meaning and understanding in mathematics— research going back to the 1940s and the work of William Brownell. Investigations consistently have shown an emphasis on teaching for meaning has positive effects on student learning, including better initial learning, greater retention, and increased likelihood the ideas will be used in new situations. These results have also been found in studies conducted in classrooms in high-poverty areas.

In the classroom:

As might be expected, the way "teaching for meaning" has been conceptualized has varied somewhat from study to study, and the concept has evolved over time. Teachers will want to consider how various interpretations of this concept can be incorporated into their classroom practice. These variations include:

- *Emphasis on the mathematical meanings of ideas, including how the idea, concept, or skill is connected in multiple ways to other mathematical ideas in a logically consistent and sensible manner.* Thus, for subtraction, the inverse, or "undoing," relationship between it and addition is emphasized. Careful development of the relationship between fractions and decimals as two ways to name rational numbers is another example. In general, this emphasis was common in early research in this area in the late 1930s, and its purpose was to ensure the mathematical meaningfulness of the ideas taught was not relegated to minor attention due to a heavy emphasis on the social uses and utility of mathematics in everyday life, practices prevalent at the time.

- *Focus on the critical role of the classroom learning context in which students construct their meanings.* There is evidence that students can learn important mathematics in contexts that are both closely connected to real-life situations and those that are purely mathematical. This suggests the abstractness of a learning environment and how students relate to it must be carefully regulated, closely monitored, and thoughtfully chosen. Furthermore, consideration should be given to students' interests and backgrounds. This does *not* mean, however, every learning context must be grounded in a real-life situation, or abstract settings are always appropriate. Rather, the mathematics taught and learned must seem reasonable to the students and make sense to them. An important factor in teaching for meaning is connecting the new ideas and skills to the student's past knowledge and experience.

- *Emphasis on making explicit the connections between mathematics and other subject matter areas.* For example, instruction could relate data-gathering and data-representation skills to public opinion polling in social studies. Or it could relate the mathematical concept of direct variation to the concept of force in physics to help establish a real-world referent for the idea. Relating the notion of an isoperimetric relationship to cost effectiveness in packaging in business achieves a similar purpose.

- *Attend to student meanings and student understanding in instruction.* Student conceptions of the same idea will vary from student to student, as will their methods of solving problems and performing procedures. Teachers should build on students' intuitive notions and methods in designing and implementing instruction.

Sources:

Aubrey 1997; Brownell 1945, 1947; Carpenter et al. 1998; Cobb et al. 1991; Corwin 2002; Fuson 1992; Good, Grouws, and Ebmeier 1983; Hiebert and Carpenter 1992; Hiebert et al. 1997; Hiebert and Wearne 1996; Kamii 1985, 1989, 1994; Knapp, Shields, and Turnbull 1995; Koehler and Grouws 1992; Skemp 1978; Van Engen 1949; Wood and Sellers 1996, 1997.

7.3. Learning New Concepts and Skills While Solving Problems: Students can learn both concepts and skills by solving problems.

Research findings:

Research suggests students who develop conceptual understanding early perform best on procedural knowledge later. Students with good conceptual understanding are able to perform successfully on near-transfer tasks and to develop procedures and skills they have not been taught. Students without conceptual understanding are able to learn procedural knowledge when the skill is taught, but research suggests students with low levels of conceptual understanding need more practice to acquire procedural knowledge.

Research by Heid (1988) suggests students are able to understand concepts without prior or concurrent skill development. In her research with calculus students, instruction was focused almost entirely on conceptual understanding. Skills were taught briefly at the course's end. On procedural skills, the students in the conceptual-understanding approach performed as well as those taught with a traditional approach. Furthermore, these students significantly outperformed traditional students on conceptual understanding.

Mack (1990) demonstrated students' rote (and frequently faulty) knowledge often interferes with their informal (and usually correct) knowledge about fractions. She successfully used students' informal knowledge to help them understand symbols for fractions and develop algorithms for operations. Fawcett's (1938) research with geometry students suggests students can learn basic concepts, skills, and the structure of geometry through problem solving and a conjecturing/verifying approach to instruction.

In the classroom:

There is evidence that students can learn new skills and concepts while they are working out solutions to problems. For example, armed with only a knowledge of basic addition, students can extend their learning by developing informal algorithms for addition of larger numbers. Similarly, by solving carefully chosen non-routine problems, students can develop an understanding of many important mathematical ideas, such as prime numbers and perimeter/area relations.

Development of more sophisticated mathematical skills can also be approached by treating their development as a problem for students to solve. Teachers can use students' informal and intuitive knowledge in other areas to develop other useful procedures. Instruction can begin with an example for which students intuitively know the answer. From there, students are allowed to explore and develop their own algorithm. For instance, most students understand that starting with four pizzas and then eating one-half of one pizza will leave three and one-half pizzas remaining. Teachers can use this knowledge to help students develop an understanding of subtraction of fractions and the associated procedures for computing such differences.

Research suggests it is not necessary for teachers to focus first on skill development and then move on to problem solving. Both can be done together. Skills can be developed on an as-needed basis, or their development can be supplemented through the use of technology. In fact, there is evidence that if students are initially drilled too much on isolated skills, they have a harder time making sense of them later.

Sources:

Cognition and Technology Group 1997; Fawcett 1938; Heid 1988; Hiebert and Wearne 1996; Mack 1990; Resnick and Omanson 1987; Wearne and Hiebert 1988.

7.4. Opportunities for Invention and Practice: Giving students both an opportunity to discover and invent new knowledge and an opportunity to practice what they have learned improves student achievement.

Research findings:

Data from the TIMSS video study show more than 90 percent of mathematics class time in U.S. eighth-grade classrooms is spent practicing routine procedures, with the remainder of the time generally spent applying procedures in new situations. Virtually no time is spent inventing new procedures and analyzing unfamiliar situations. In contrast, students at the same grade level in typical Japanese classrooms spend approximately 40 percent of instructional time practicing routine procedures, 15 percent applying procedures in new situations, and 45 percent inventing new procedures and analyzing new situations.

Research evidence suggests students need opportunities for both practice and invention. The findings from a number of research studies show that when students discover mathematical ideas and invent mathematical procedures, they have a stronger conceptual understanding of connections between mathematical ideas.

Many successful reform-oriented programs include time for students to practice what they have learned and discovered. Students need opportunities to practice what they are learning and to experience performing the kinds of tasks in which they are expected to demonstrate competence. For example, if teachers want students to be proficient in problem solving, then students must be given opportunities to practice problem solving. If strong deductive reasoning is a goal, then student work must include tasks that require such reasoning. And, of course, if competence in procedures is an objective, then the curriculum must include attention to such procedures.

In the classroom:

This "Opportunities for Invention and Practice" section is closely related to the "Opportunity to Learn" section (7.1). Clearly, a balance is needed between the time students spend practicing routine procedures and the time devoted to students inventing and discovering new ideas. Teachers need not choose between them; indeed, they must not make such a choice if students are to develop the mathematical power they need. Teachers must strive to ensure both are included in appropriate proportions and in appropriate ways. The research cited above suggests attention to these two activities is currently out of balance and too frequently there is an overemphasis on skill work, with few opportunities for students to engage in sense-making and discovery-oriented activities.

To increase opportunities for invention, teachers should frequently use non-routine problems, periodically introduce a lesson involving a new skill by posing it as a problem to be solved, and regularly allow students to build new knowledge based on their intuitive knowledge and informal procedures.

Sources:

Boaler 1998; Brownell 1945, 1947; Carpenter et al. 1998; Cobb et al. 1991; Cognition and Technology Group 1997; Resnick 1980; Stigler and Hiebert 1997; Wood and Sellers 1996, 1997.

7.5. Openness to Student Solution Methods and Student Interaction: Teaching that incorporates students' intuitive solution methods can increase student learning, especially when combined with opportunities for student interaction and discussion.

Research findings:

Recent results from the TIMSS video study have shown that Japanese classrooms use student solution methods extensively during instruction. The same teaching technique appears in many successful American research projects. Findings from American studies clearly demonstrate two important principles associated with the development of students' deep conceptual understanding of mathematics. First, when teachers are aware of how students construct knowledge and are familiar with the intuitive solution methods students use when they solve problems, and then if the teachers use this knowledge when planning and conducting instruction in mathematics, student achievement and understanding are significantly improved. These results have been clearly demonstrated in the primary grades and are beginning to be shown at higher grade levels.

Second, structuring instruction around carefully chosen problems, allowing students to interact when solving these problems, and then providing opportunities for them to share their solution methods result in increased achievement on problem-solving measures. Importantly, these gains come without an achievement loss in the skills and concepts measured on standardized achievement tests.

Research has also demonstrated that when students have opportunities to develop their own solution methods, they are better able to apply mathematical knowledge in new problem situations.

In the classroom:

Research results suggest teachers should concentrate on providing opportunities for students to interact in problem-rich situations. These situations can include those where students are asked to compute with numbers that are larger than or different from those they have already developed procedures to process.

Besides providing appropriate problem-rich situations, teachers must encourage students to find their own solution methods and provide opportunities for them to share and compare their solution methods and answers. One way to organize such instruction is to have students initially work in small groups (see section 7.6) and then share ideas and solutions in a whole-class discussion (see section 7.7).

One useful teaching technique is for teachers to assign an interesting problem for students to solve and then circulate about the room as they work, keeping track of which students are using which strategies (taking notes if needed). In a whole-class setting, the teacher can then call on students to discuss their solution methods in a predetermined and carefully considered order, often from the most basic methods to the more formal or sophisticated methods. This teaching structure is used successfully in many Japanese mathematics lessons.

Sources:

Boaler 1998; Carpenter et al. 1988; Carpenter et al. 1989; Carpenter et al. 1998; Cobb et al. 1991; Cobb, Yackel, and Wood 1992; Cognition and Technology Group 1997; Fennema et al. 1993; Fennema et al. 1996; Fennema, Carpenter, and Peterson 1989; Hiebert and Wearne 1993, 1996; Kamii 1985, 1989, 1994; Kersaint 2002; Stigler et al. 1999; Stigler and Hiebert 1997; Verschaffel, DeCorte, and Vierstraete, 1999; Wood et al. 1993; Wood, Cobb, and Yackel 1995; Yackel, Cobb, and Wood 1991.

7.6. Small-Group Learning: Using small groups of students to work on activities, problems, and assignments can increase student mathematics achievement.

Research findings:

There is considerable research evidence within mathematics education indicating that using small groups of various types for different classroom tasks has positive effects on student learning. Davidson (1985), for example, reviewed almost 80 studies in mathematics that compared student achievement in small-group settings with traditional whole-class instruction. In more than 40 percent of these studies, students in the classes using small-group approaches significantly outscored control students on measures of student performance. In only two of the 79 studies did control-group students perform better than the small-group students, and in these studies there were some design irregularities.

From a review of 99 studies of cooperative group-learning methods at the elementary and secondary school levels, Slavin (1990, 1995) concluded cooperative methods were effective in improving student achievement. The most effective methods emphasized both group goals and individual accountability.

In a review of studies examining peer interaction and achievement in small groups (17 studies, grades 2-11), Webb (1991) found several consistent findings. First, giving an explanation of an idea, method, or solution to a teammate in a group situation was positively related to achievement. Second, receiving "non-responsive" feedback (no feedback or feedback that is not pertinent to what one has said or done) from teammates was negatively related to achievement. Webb's review also showed group work was most effective when students were taught how to work in groups and how to give and receive help. Received help was most effective when it was in the form of elaborated explanations (not just the answer) and then

applied by the student to either the present problem or a new problem.

Qualitative investigations have shown other important and often unmeasured outcomes beyond improved general achievement can result from small-group work. In one such investigation, Yackel, Cobb, and Wood (1991) studied a second-grade classroom in which small-group problem solving followed by whole-class discussion was the primary instructional strategy for the entire school year. They found this approach created many learning opportunities that do not typically occur in traditional classrooms, including opportunities for collaborative dialogue and resolution of conflicting points of view.

Slavin's research has also shown positive effects of small-group work on cross-ethnic relations and student attitudes toward school.

In the classroom:

Research findings clearly support the use of small groups as part of mathematics instruction. This approach can result in increased student learning as measured by traditional achievement measures as well as other important outcomes, such as improvement in student ability to communicate, resolve differences, and get along with others.

When using small groups for mathematics instruction, teachers should:

- Choose tasks that deal with important mathematical concepts and ideas.

- Select tasks that are appropriate for group work.

- Consider having students initially work individually on a task and then follow this with group work where students share and build on their individual ideas and work.

- Give clear instructions to the groups and set clear expectations for each group.

- Emphasize both group goals and individual accountability—for example, indicate that an individual from each group will report for the group, but withhold the name of the individual until group work has been completed.

- Choose tasks that students find interesting.

- Ensure there is closure to the group work, where key ideas and methods are brought to the surface either by the teacher, the students, or both.

Finally, as several research studies have shown, teachers should not think of small groups as something that must always be used or never be used. Rather, small-group instruction should be thought of as an instructional practice appropriate for certain learning objectives, and as a practice that can work well with other organizational arrangements including whole-class instruction.

 Sources:

Cohen 1994; Davidson 1985; Laborde 1994; Slavin 1990, 1995; Webb 1991; Webb, Troper, and Fall 1995; Yackel, Cobb, and Wood 1991.

7.7. **Whole-Class Discussion:** Whole-class discussion following individual and group work improves student achievement.

Research findings:

Research suggests whole-class discussion can be effective when it is used for sharing and explaining the variety of solutions by which individual students have solved problems. It allows students to see the many ways to examine a situation and the variety of appropriate and acceptable solutions.

Wood (1999) found whole-class discussion works best when discussion expectations are clearly understood. Students should be expected to evaluate each other's ideas and reasoning in ways that are not critical of the sharer. This helps to create an environment in which students feel comfortable sharing ideas and discussing each other's methods and reasoning. Furthermore, students should be expected to be active listeners who participate in the discussion and feel a sense of responsibility for each other's understanding.

Cognitive research suggests conceptual change and progression of thought result from the mental processes involved in the resolution of conflict and contradiction. Thus, confusion and conflict during whole-class discussion hold considerable potential for increasing student learning when carefully managed by the teacher. As students address challenges to their methods, they strengthen their understanding of concepts and procedures by working together to resolve differences in thinking or confusions in reasoning. In a sense, the discussion becomes a collaborative problem-solving effort. Each individual, then, is contributing to the total outcome of the problem-solving situation. This discussion helps produce the notion of commonly held knowledge (public knowledge).

In the classroom:

It is important that whole-class discussion follow student work on problem-solving activities. The discussion should be a summary of individual work in which key ideas are brought to the surface. This can be accomplished through students presenting and discussing their individual solution methods, or through other methods of achieving closure led by the teacher, the students, or both.

Whole-class discussion can also be an effective diagnostic tool for determining depth of student understanding and identifying existing misconceptions. Teachers can identify areas of difficulty for particular students as well as ascertain areas of student success or progress.

Whole-class discussion can be an effective and useful instructional practice. Some of the instructional opportunities offered in whole-class discussion do not occur in small group or individual settings. Thus, whole-class discussion has an important place in the classroom along with other instructional practices.

Sources:

Ball 1993; Cobb, Wood, Yackel, and McNeal 1992; Wood 1999.

7.8. Number Sense: Teaching mathematics with a focus on number sense encourages students to become problem solvers in a wide variety of situations and to view mathematics as a discipline where thinking is important.

Research findings:

"Number sense" is a construct that relates to having an intuitive feel for number size and combinations as well as the ability to flexibly work with numbers in problem situations in order to make sound decisions and reasonable judgments. Number sense involves being able to flexibly use the processes of mentally computing, estimating, sensing number magnitudes, moving between representation systems for numbers, and judging the reasonableness of numerical results.

Markovits and Sowder (1994) studied seventh-grade classrooms where special units on number magnitude, mental computation, and computational estimation were taught. From individual interviews, they determined students were more likely after this special instruction to use strategies that reflected sound number sense, and this was a long-lasting change.

Other important research in this area involves the integration of the development of number sense with the teaching of other mathematical topics, as opposed to teaching separate lessons on aspects of number sense. In a study of second-graders, Cobb and his colleagues (1991) found students' number sense was improved as a result of a problem-centered curriculum emphasizing student interaction and self-generated solution methods. Almost every student developed a variety of strategies to solve a wide range of problems. Students also demonstrated other desirable affective outcomes, such as increased persistence in solving problems.

Kamii (1985, 1989, 1994) worked with primary-grades teachers as they attempted to implement an instructional approach rooted in a constructivist theory of learning based on the work of Piaget. Central to the instructional approach was providing situations for students to develop their own meanings, methods, and number sense.

Interview data with students showed the treatment group demonstrated greater autonomy, conceptual understanding of place value, and ability to do estimation and mental computation than did students in comparison classrooms.

In the classroom:

Attention to number sense when teaching a wide variety of mathematical topics tends to enhance the depth of student ability in this area. Competence in the many aspects of number sense is an important mathematical outcome for students. More than 90 percent of the computation done outside the classroom is done without pencil and paper, using mental computation, estimation, or a calculator. Yet in many classrooms, efforts to instill number sense are given insufficient attention.

As teachers develop strategies to teach number sense, they should strongly consider moving beyond a unit-skills approach (i.e., a focus on single skills in isolation) to a more integrated approach encouraging the development of number sense in all classroom activities, from the development of computational procedures to mathematical problem solving. Although more research is needed, an integrated approach to number sense likely will result not only in greater number sense but also in other equally important outcomes as well.

Sources:

Cobb et al. 1991; Greeno 1991; Kamii 1985, 1989, 1994; Markovits and Sowder 1994; Reys et al. 1991; Reys and Barger 1994; Sowder 1992a, 1992b.

7.9. Concrete Materials: Long-term use of concrete materials is positively related to increases in student mathematics achievement and improved attitudes toward mathematics.

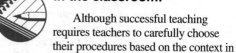

Research findings:

Many studies show the use of concrete materials can produce meaningful use of notational systems and increase student concept development. In a comprehensive review of activity-based learning in mathematics in kindergarten through grade eight, Suydam and Higgins (1977) concluded using manipulative materials produces greater achievement gains than not using them. In a more recent meta-analysis of 60 studies (kindergarten through postsecondary) that compared the effects of using concrete materials with the effects of more abstract instruction, Sowell (1989) concluded the long-term use of concrete instructional materials by teachers knowledgeable in their use increased student achievement and improved student attitudes toward mathematics.

In spite of generally positive results, there are some inconsistencies in the research findings. As Thompson (1992) points out, the research results concerning concrete materials vary, even among closely controlled and monitored treatments involving the same concrete materials. For example, in studies by Resnick and Omanson (1987) and Labinowicz (1985), the use of base-ten blocks showed little impact on children's learning. In contrast, Fuson and Briars (1990) reported positive results from the use of base-ten blocks. The value of conceptually based instruction when using base-ten blocks was also demonstrated in a study by Hiebert and Wearne (1992), who found important learning gains in first grade.

The differences in results among these studies might be due to the nature of the students' engagement with the concrete materials and their orientation toward the materials in relation to notation and numerical values. The results might also be due to different orientations in the studies, with regard to the role of computational algorithms and how they should be developed in the classroom. In general, however, the ambiguities in some of the research findings do not undermine the general consensus that concrete materials are valuable instructional tools.

In the classroom:

Although successful teaching requires teachers to carefully choose their procedures based on the context in which they will be used, available research suggests teachers should more regularly use manipulative materials in mathematics instruction in order to give students hands-on experience that helps them construct useful meanings for the mathematical ideas they are learning. Use of the same material to teach multiple ideas over the course of schooling has the advantages of shortening the amount of time it takes to introduce the material and also helps students to see connections between mathematical ideas.

The use of concrete material should not be limited to demonstrations. It is essential that children use materials in meaningful ways rather than in a rigid and prescribed way focusing on remembering rather than on thinking. Thus, as Thompson (1992) says, "before students can make productive use of concrete materials, they must first be committed to making sense of their activities and be committed to expressing their sense in meaningful ways. Further, it is important that students come to see the two-way relationship between concrete embodiments of a mathematical concept and the notational system used to represent it."

Sources:

Fuson and Briars 1990; Hiebert and Wearne 1992; Labinowicz 1985; Leinenbach and Raymond 1996; Resnick and Omanson 1987; Sowell 1989; Suydam and Higgins 1977; Thompson 1992; Varelas and Becker 1997.

7.10. Student Use of Calculators: Using calculators in the learning of mathematics can result in increased achievement and improved student attitudes.

Research findings:

The impact of calculator use on student learning has been a popular research area in mathematics education. The many studies conducted have quite consistently shown thoughtful use of calculators in mathematics classes improves student mathematics achievement and attitudes toward mathematics.

From a meta-analysis of 79 non-graphing calculator studies, Hembree and Dessart (1986, 1992) concluded the use of hand-held calculators improved student learning. In particular, they found improvement in students' understanding of arithmetical concepts and in their problem-solving skills. Their analysis also showed students using calculators tended to have better attitudes toward mathematics and much better self-concepts in mathematics than did their counterparts who did not use calculators. They also found there was no loss in student ability to perform paper-and-pencil computational skills when calculators were used as part of mathematics instruction.

Research on the use of scientific calculators with graphing capabilities has also shown positive effects on student achievement. Most studies have found positive effects on students' graphing ability, conceptual understanding of graphs, and their ability to relate graphical representations to other representations, such as tables and symbolic representations. Other content areas where improvement has been shown when these calculators have been used in instruction include function concepts and spatial visualization. Other studies have found students are better problem solvers when using graphing calculators. In addition, students are more flexible in their thinking with regard to solution strategies, have greater perseverance, and focus more on trying to conceptually understand the problem rather than simply focus on computa-

tions. However, with increased use of graphing calculators students are more likely to rely on graphical procedures than on other procedures such as algebraic methods. Most studies of graphing calculators have found no negative effect on basic skills, factual knowledge, or computational skills.

In general, research has found the use of calculators changes the content, methods, and skill requirements in mathematics classrooms. Studies have shown teachers ask more high-level questions when calculators are present, and students become more actively involved through asking questions, conjecturing, and exploring when they use calculators.

In the classroom:

Research strongly supports the call of the National Council of Teachers of Mathematics' *Curriculum and Evaluation Standards for School Mathematics* for the use of calculators at all levels of mathematics instruction. Using calculators in carefully planned ways can result in increases in student problem-solving ability and improved affective outcomes without a loss in basic skills.

One valuable use for calculators is as a tool for exploration and discovery in problem-solving situations and when introducing new mathematical content. By reducing computation time and providing immediate feedback, calculators help students to focus on understanding their work and justifying their methods and results. The graphing calculator is particularly useful in helping to illustrate and develop graphical concepts and in making connections between algebraic and geometric ideas.

In order to accurately reflect students' meaningful mathematics performance, students should probably be allowed to use their calculators on achievement tests. To not do so is a major disruption in many students' usual way of doing mathematics, and an unrealistic restriction, because when they are away from the school setting, they will certainly use a calculator in their daily lives and in the workplace. Another factor arguing for calculator use is that students are permitted to use calculators on the SAT and ACT tests. Furthermore, the Advanced Placement Calculus examination of the College Board requires the use of a graphing calculator.

Sources:

Davis 1990; Drijvers and Doorman 1996; Dunham and Dick 1994; Flores and McLeod 1990; Giamati 1991; Groves and Stacey 1998; Harvey 1993; Hembree and Dessart 1986, 1992; Mullis, Jenkins, and Johnson 1994; National Council of Teachers of Mathematics 1989; Penglase and Arnold 1996; Rich 1991; Ruthven 1990; Slavit 1996; Smith 1996; Stacey and Groves 1994; Wilson and Krapfl 1994.

Bibliography

American Association of University Women. 1998. *Gender Gaps: Where Schools Still Fail Our Children*. Washington, DC: Author.

Atanda, D. 1999. *Do Gatekeeper Courses Expand Education Options?* (NCES 1999-303). Washington, DC: National Center for Education Statistics.

Aubrey, C. 1997. *Mathematics Teaching in the Early Years: An Investigation of Teachers' Subject Knowledge*. London: Falmer Press.

Ball, D. 1993. "With an Eye on the Mathematical Horizon: Dilemmas of Teaching Elementary School Mathematics." *Elementary School Journal* Vol. 93: 373-397.

Boaler, J. 1998. "Open and Closed Mathematics: Student Experiences and Understandings." *Journal for Research in Mathematics Education* Vol. 29: 41-62.

Brownell, W.A. 1945. "When Is Arithmetic Meaningful?" *Journal of Educational Research* Vol. 38: 481-498.

Brownell, W.A. 1947. "The Place of Meaning in the Teaching of Arithmetic." *Elementary School Journal* Vol. 47: 256-265.

Campbell, J.R., C.M. Hombo, and J. Mazzeo. 2000. *NAEP Trends in Academic Progress: Three Decades of Student Performance*. Washington, DC: Office of Education Research Improvement, U.S Department of Education.

Carpenter, T.P., E. Fennema, P.L. Peterson, and D. Carey. 1988. "Teachers' Pedagogical Content Knowledge of Students' Problem Solving in Elementary Arithmetic." *Journal for Research in Mathematics Education* Vol. 19: 385-401.

Carpenter, T.P., E. Fennema, P.L. Peterson, C.P. Chiang, and M. Loef. 1989. "Using Knowledge of Children's Mathematics Thinking in Classroom Teaching: An Experimental Study." *American Educational Research Journal* Vol. 26: 499-531.

Carpenter, T.P., M.L. Franke, V.R. Jacobs, E. Fennema, and S.B. Empson. 1998. "A Longitudinal Study of Invention and Understanding in Children's Multidigit Addition and Subtraction." *Journal for Research in Mathematics Education* Vol. 29: 3-20.

Cobb, P., T. Wood., E. Yackel, and B. McNeal. 1992. "Characteristics of Classroom Mathematics Traditions: An Interactional Analysis." *American Educational Research Journal* Vol. 29: 573-604.

Cobb, P., T. Wood, E. Yackel, J. Nicholls, G. Wheatley, B. Trigatti, and M. Perlwitz. 1991. "Assessment of a Problem-Centered Second-Grade Mathematics Project." *Journal for Research in Mathematics Education* Vol. 22: 3-29.

Cobb, P., E. Yackel, and T. Wood. 1992. "A Constructivist Alternative to the Representational View of Mind in Mathematics Education." *Journal for Research in Mathematics Education* Vol. 23: 2-23.

Cognition and Technology Group. 1997. *The Jasper Project: Lessons in Curriculum, Instruction, Assessment, and Professional Development*. Mahwah, NJ: Erlbaum.

Cohen, E.G. 1994. "Restructuring the Classroom: Conditions for Productive Small Groups." *Review of Educational Research* Vol. 64: 1-35.

Corwin, R.B. 2002. "Assessing Children's Understanding: Doing Mathematics to Assess Mathematics." *Teaching Children Mathematics* Vol. 9: 229-233.

Davidson, N. 1985. "Small Group Cooperative Learning in Mathematics: A Selective View of the Research." In *Learning to Cooperate, Cooperating to Learn*, R. Slavin, editor (pp. 211-230). New York: Plenum Press.

Davis, M. November 1990. *Calculating Women: Precalculus in Context*. Paper presented at Third Annual Conference on Technology in Collegiate Mathematics, Columbus, OH.

Drijvers, P. and M. Doorman. 1996. "The Graphics Calculator in Mathematics Education." *Journal of Mathematical Behavior* Vol. 15: 425-440.

Dunham, P.H. and T.P. Dick. 1994. "Research on Graphing Calculators." *Mathematics Teacher* Vol. 87: 440-445.

Fawcett, H.P. 1938. *The Nature of Proof: A Description and Evaluation of Certain Procedures Used in Senior High School to Develop an Understanding of the Nature of Proof*. 1938 Yearbook of the National Council of Teachers of Mathematics. New York: Columbia University, Teachers College.

Fennema, E., T.P. Carpenter, M.L. Franke, L. Levi, V.R. Jacobs, and S.B. Empson. 1996. "A Longitudinal Study of Learning to Use Children's Thinking in Mathematics Instruction." *Journal for Research in Mathematics Education* Vol. 27: 403-434.

Fennema, E., T.P. Carpenter, and P.L. Peterson. 1989. "Learning Mathematics with Understanding: Cognitively Guided Instruction." In *Advances in Research on Teaching*, J. Brophy, editor (pp. 195-221). Greenwich, CT: JAI Press.

Fennema, E., M.L. Franke, T.P. Carpenter, and D.A. Carey. 1993. "Using Children's Mathematical Knowledge in Instruction." *American Educational Research Journal* Vol. 30: 555-583.

Flanders, J.R. 1987. "How Much of the Content in Mathematics Textbooks Is New?" *Arithmetic Teacher* Vol. 35: 18-23.

Flores, A. and D.B. McLeod. November 1990. *Calculus for Middle School Teachers Using Computers and Graphing Calculators*. Paper presented at Third

Annual Conference on Technology in Collegiate Mathematics, Columbus, OH.

Fuson, K.C. 1992. "Research on Whole Number Addition and Subtraction." In *Handbook of Research on Mathematics Teaching and Learning*, D.A. Grouws, editor (pp. 243-275). New York: Macmillan.

Fuson, K.C. and D.J. Briars. 1990. "Using a Base-Ten Blocks Learning/Teaching Approach for First- and Second-Grade Place-Value and Multidigit Addition and Subtraction." *Journal for Research in Mathematics Education* Vol. 21: 180-206.

Giamati, C.M. 1991. *The Effect of Graphing Calculator Use on Students' Understanding of Variations of Their Graphs.* Doctoral dissertation, University of Michigan. *Dissertation Abstracts International* Vol. 52: 103A. (University Microfilms No. AAC 9116100)

Good, T.L., D.A. Grouws, and H. Ebmeier. 1983. *Active Mathematics Teaching.* New York: Longman.

Greeno, J.G. 1991. "Number Sense as Situated Knowing in a Conceptual Domain." *Journal for Research in Mathematics Education* Vol. 22: 170-218.

Grouws, D.A. and M.S. Smith. 2000. "Findings from NAEP on the Preparation and Practices of Mathematics Teachers." In *Results from the Seventh Mathematics Assessment of the National Assessment of Educational Progress,* E.A. Silver and P.A. Kenney, editors. Reston, VA: National Council of Teachers of Mathematics.

Groves, S. and K. Stacey. 1998. "Calculators in Primary Mathematics: Exploring Numbers Before Teaching Algorithms." In *The Teaching and Learning of Algorithms in School Mathematics,* L.J. Morrow, editor (pp. 120-129). Reston, VA: National Council of Teachers of Mathematics.

Harvey, J.G. September 1993. *Effectiveness of Graphing Technology in a Precalculus Course: The 1988-89 Field Test of the C3PC Materials.* Paper presented at the Technology in Mathematics Teaching Conference, Birmingham, England.

Hawkins, E.F., F.B. Stancavage, and J.A. Dossey. 1998. *School Policies and Practices Affecting Instruction in Mathematics: Findings from the National Assessment of Educational Progress.* NCES 98-495. Washington, DC: National Center for Education Statistics.

Heid, M.K. 1988. "Resequencing Skills and Concepts in Applied Calculus Using the Computer as a Tool." *Journal for Research in Mathematics Education* Vol. 19: 3-25.

Hembree, R. and D.J. Dessart. 1986. "Effects of Hand-Held Calculators in Pre-College Mathematics Education: A Meta-analysis." *Journal for Research in Mathematics Education* Vol. 17: 83-99.

Hembree, R. and D.J. Dessart. 1992. "Research on Calculators in Mathematics Education." In *Calculators in Mathematics Education, 1992 Yearbook of the National Council of Teachers of Mathematics,* J.T. Fey, editor (pp. 22-31). Reston, VA: National Council of Teachers of Mathematics.

Hiebert, J. and T.L. Carpenter. 1992. "Learning and Teaching with Understanding." In *Handbook of Research on Mathematics Teaching and Learning,* D.A. Grouws, editor (pp. 65-97). New York: Macmillan.

Hiebert, J., T.P. Carpenter, E. Fennema, K.C. Fuson, D. Wearne, H. Murray, A. Olivier, and P. Human. 1997. *Making Sense: Teaching and Learning Mathematics with Understanding.* Portsmouth, NH: Heinemann.

Hiebert, J. and D. Wearne. 1992. "Links Between Teaching and Learning Place Value with Understanding in First Grade." *Journal for Research in Mathematics Education* Vol. 22: 98-122.

Hiebert, J. and D. Wearne. 1993. "Instructional Tasks, Classroom Discourse, and Students' Learning in Second-Grade Arithmetic." *American Educational Research Journal* Vol. 30: 393-425.

Hiebert, J. and D. Wearne. 1996. "Instruction, Understanding, and Skill in Multidigit Addition and Subtraction." *Cognition and Instruction* Vol. 14: 251-283.

Husén, T. 1967. *International Study of Achievement in Mathematics* (Volume 2). New York: Wiley.

Kamii, C. 1985. *Young Children Reinvent Arithmetic: Implications of Piaget's Theory.* New York: Teachers College Press.

Kamii, C. 1989. *Young Children Continue to Reinvent Arithmetic: Implications of Piaget's Theory.* New York: Teachers College Press.

Kamii, C. 1994. *Young Children Continue to Reinvent Arithmetic-3rd Grade: Implications of Piaget's Theory.* New York: Teachers College Press.

Keeves, J.P. 1976. "Curriculum Factors Influencing School Learning." *Studies in Educational Evaluation* Vol. 2: 167-184.

Keeves, J.P. 1994. *The World of School Learning: Selected Key Findings from 35 Years of IEA Research.* The Hague, Netherlands: International Association for the Evaluation of Educational Achievement (IEA).

Kersaint, G. 2002. "The Pool Problem." *Mathematics Teaching in the Middle School* Vol. 8: 190-192.

Kilpatrick, J. 1992. "A History of Research in Mathematics Education." In *Handbook of Research on Mathematics Teaching and Learning,* D.A. Grouws, editor (pp. 3-38). New York: Macmillan.

Knapp, M.S., P.M. Shields, and B.J. Turnbull. 1995. "Academic Challenge in High-Poverty Classrooms." *Phi Delta Kappan* Vol. 77: 770-776.

Koehler, M. and D.A. Grouws. 1992. "Mathematics Teaching Practices and Their Effects." In *Handbook of Research on Mathematics Teaching and Learning,* D.A. Grouws, editor (pp. 115-126). New York: Macmillan.

Kulm, G., K. Morris, and L. Grier. 1999. *Middle Grade Mathematics Textbooks: A Benchmarks-based Evaluation.* Washington, DC: American Association for the Advancement of Science.

Labinowicz, E. 1985. *Learning from Students: New Beginnings for Teaching Numerical Thinking.* Menlo Park, CA: Addison-Wesley.

Laborde, C. 1994. "Working in Small Groups: A Learning Situation?" In *Didactics of Mathematics as a Scientific Discipline,* R. Biehler, R.W. Scholz, R. Strasser, and B. Winkelmann, editors (pp. 147-158). Dordrecht, The Netherlands: Kluwer.

Leinenbach, M. and A.M. Raymond. 1996. "A Two-Year Collaborative Action Research Study on the Effects of a 'Hands-On' Approach to Learning Algebra." In *Proceedings of the Annual Meeting of the North American Chapter of the International Group for the Psychology of Mathematics Education,* E. Jakubowski, editor. Panama City, FL. (ERIC Document Reproduction; Service No. ED 400 178)

Mack, N.K. 1990. "Learning Fractions with Understanding: Building on Informal Knowledge." *Journal for Research in Mathematics Education* Vol. 21: 16-32.

Markovits, Z. and J. Sowder. 1994. "Developing Number Sense: An Intervention Study in Grade 7." *Journal for Research in Mathematics Education* Vol. 25: 4-29.

McKnight, C.C., F.J. Crosswhite, J.A. Dossey, E. Kifer, J.O. Swafford, K.J. Travers, and T.J. Cooney. 1987. *The Underachieving Curriculum.* Champaign, IL: Stipes.

Mullis, I.V.S., F. Jenkins, and E.G. Johnson. 1994. *Effective Schools in Mathematics: Perspectives from the NAEP 1992 Assessment.* Washington, DC: U.S. Department of Education, Office of Educational Research and Improvement (Report No. 23-RR-01).

National Center for Education Statistics. 1996. *Pursuing Excellence: A Study of U.S. Eighth-Grade Mathematics and Science Teaching, Learning, Curriculum, and Achievement in International Context* (NCES 97-198). Washington DC: U.S. Department of Education.

National Center for Education Statistics. 1997. *Pursuing Excellence: A Study of U.S. Fourth-Grade Mathematics and Science Achievement in International Context* (NCES 97-255). Washington DC: U.S. Department of Education.

National Center for Education Statistics. 1998. *Pursuing Excellence: A Study of U.S. Twelfth-Grade Mathematics and Science Achievement in International Context* (NCES 98-049). Washington DC: U.S. Department of Education.

National Council of Teachers of Mathematics. 1989. *Curriculum and Evaluation Standards for School Mathematics.* Reston, VA: Author.

Penglase, M. and S. Arnold. 1996. "The Graphics Calculator in Mathematics Education: A Critical Review of Recent Research." *Mathematics Education Research Journal* Vol. 8: 58-90.

Resnick, L.B. 1980. "The Role of Invention in the Development of Mathematical Competence." In *Developmental Models of Thinking,* R.H. Kluwe and H. Spada, editors (pp. 213-244). New York: Academic Press.

Resnick, L.B. and S.F. Omanson. 1987. "Learning to Understand Arithmetic." In *Advances in Instructional Psychology,* R. Glaser, editor (Vol. 3, pp. 41-95). Hillsdale, NJ: Lawrence Erlbaum Associates.

Reys, B.J. and R.H. Barger. 1994. "Mental Computation: Issues from the United States Perspective." In *Computational Alternatives for the Twenty-first Century,* R.E. Reys and N. Nohda, editors, (pp. 31-47). Reston, VA: National Council of Teachers of Mathematics.

Reys, B.J., R. Barger, B. Dougherty, L. Lembke, A. Parnas, R. Sturdevant, M. Bruckheimer, J. Hope, Z. Markovits, S. Reehm, and M. Weber. 1991. *Developing Number Sense in the Middle Grades.* Reston, VA: National Council of Teachers of Mathematics.

Rich, B.S. 1991. *The Effects of the Use of Graphing Calculators on the Learning of Function Concepts in Precalculus Mathematics.* Doctoral dissertation, University of Iowa. *Dissertation Abstracts International* Vol. 52: 835A. (University Microfilms No. AAC 9112475)

Ruthven, K. 1990. "The Influence of Graphic Calculator Use on Translation from Graphic to Symbolic Forms." *Educational Studies in Mathematics* Vol. 21: 431-450.

Schmidt, W.H., C.C. McKnight, and S.A. Raizen. 1997. *A Splintered Vision: An Investigation of U.S. Science and Mathematics Education.* Dordrecht, Netherlands: Kluwer Academic Publishers.

Secada, W.G. 1992. "Race, Ethnicity, Social Class, Language, and Achievement in Mathematics." In *Handbook of Research on Mathematics Teaching and Learning,* D.A. Grouws, editor (pp. 623-660). New York: Macmillan.

Skemp, R.R. 1978. "Relational Understanding and Instrumental Understanding." *Arithmetic Teacher* Vol. 26: 9-15.

Slavin, R.E. 1990. "Student Team Learning in Mathematics." In *Cooperative Learning in Math: A Handbook for Teachers,* N. Davidson, editor, (pp. 69-102). Reading, MA: Addison-Wesley.

Slavin, R.E. 1995. *Cooperative Learning: Theory, Research, and Practice* (2nd edition). Boston: Allyn and Bacon.

Slavit, D. 1996. "Graphing Calculators in a 'Hybrid' Algebra II Classroom." *For the Learning of Mathematics* Vol. 16: 9-14.

Smith, B.A. 1996. *A Meta-Analysis of Outcomes from the Use of Calculators in Mathematics Education.* Doctoral dissertation, Texas A&M University at Commerce. *Dissertation Abstracts International* Vol. 58: 03.

Sowder, J. 1992a. "Estimation and Number Sense." In *Handbook of Research on Mathematics Teaching and Learning,* D.A. Grouws, editor (pp. 371-389). New York: Macmillan.

Sowder, J. 1992b. "Making Sense of Numbers in School Mathematics." In *Analysis of Arithmetic for Mathematics Education,* G. Leinhardt, R. Putnam, and R. Hattrup, editors (pp. 1-51). Hillsdale, NJ: Lawrence Erlbaum Associates.

Sowell, E.J. 1989. "Effects of Manipulative Materials in Mathematics Instruction." *Journal for Research in Mathematics Education* Vol. 20: 498-505.

Stacey, K. and S. Groves. April 1994. *Calculators in Primary Mathematics*. Paper presented at Annual Meeting of National Council of Teachers of Mathematics, Indianapolis, IN.

Stigler, J.W., P. Gonzales, T. Kawanaka, S. Knoll, and A. Serrano. 1999. *The TIMSS Videotape Study: Methods and Findings From an Exploratory Research Project on Eighth Grade Mathematics Instruction in Germany, Japan, and the United States* (NCES 99-130). Washington, DC: National Center for Education Statistics.

Stigler, J.W. and J. Hiebert. 1997. "Understanding and Improving Classroom Mathematics Instruction." *Phi Delta Kappan* Vol. 79: 14-21.

Suarez, T.M., T.J. Torlone, S.T. McGrath, and D.L. Clark. 1991. "Enhancing Effective Instructional Time: A Review of Research." *Policy Brief* Vol. 1, No. 2. Chapel Hill, NC: North Carolina Educational Policy Research Center.

Suydam, M.N. and J.L. Higgins. 1977. *Activity-based Learning in Elementary School Mathematics: Recommendations from Research*. Columbus, OH: ERIC Center for Science, Mathematics, and Environmental Education.

Thompson, P.W. 1992. "Notations, Conventions, and Constraints: Contributions of Effective Uses of Concrete Materials in Elementary Mathematics." *Journal for Research in Mathematics Education* Vol. 23: 123-147.

Van Engen, H. 1949. "An Analysis of Meaning in Arithmetic." *Elementary School Journal* Vol. 48: 395-400.

Varelas, M. and J. Becker. 1997. "Children's Developing Understanding of Place Value: Semiotic Aspects." *Cognition and Instruction* Vol. 15: 265-286.

Verschaffel, L., E. DeCorte, and H. Vierstraete. 1999. "Upper Elementary School Pupils' Difficulties in Modeling and Solving Nonstandard Additive Word Problems Involving Ordinal Numbers." *Journal*

for Research in Mathematics Education Vol. 30: 265-285.

Wearne, D. and J. Hiebert. 1988. "A Cognitive Approach to Meaningful Mathematics Instruction: Testing a Local Theory Using Decimal Numbers." *Journal for Research in Mathematics Education* Vol. 19: 371-384.

Webb, N.M. 1991. "Task-Related Verbal Interaction and Mathematics Learning in Small Groups." *Journal for Research in Mathematics Education* Vol. 22: 366-389.

Webb, N.M., J.D. Troper, and R. Fall. 1995. "Constructive Activity and Learning in Collaborative Small Groups." *Journal of Educational Psychology* Vol. 87: 406-423.

Wilson, M.R. and C.M. Krapfl. 1994. "The Impact of Graphics Calculators on Students' Understanding of Function." *Journal of Computers in Mathematics and Science Teaching* Vol. 13: 252-264.

Wood, T. 1999. "Creating a Context for Argument in Mathematics Class." *Journal for Research in Mathematics Education* Vol. 30: 171-191.

Wood, T., P. Cobb, and E. Yackel. 1995. "Reflections on Learning and Teaching Mathematics in Elementary School." *Constructivism in Education*, L.P. Steffe and J. Gale, editors (pp. 401-422). Hillsdale, NJ: Lawrence Erlbaum Associates.

Wood, T., P. Cobb, E. Yackel, and D. Dillon. 1993. "Rethinking Elementary School Mathematics: Insights and Issues." *Journal for Research in Mathematics Education Monographs, 6*.

Wood, T. and P. Sellers. 1996. "Assessment of a Problem-Centered Mathematics Program: 3rd Grade." *Journal for Research in Mathematics Education* Vol. 27: 337-353.

Wood, T. and P. Sellers. 1997. "Deepening the Analysis: Longitudinal Assessment of a Problem-Centered Mathematics Program." *Journal for Research in Mathematics Education* Vol. 28: 163-186.

Yackel, E., P. Cobb, and T. Wood. 1991. "Small-Group Interactions as a Source of Learning Opportunities in Second-Grade Mathematics." *Journal for Research in Mathematics Education* Vol. 22: 390-408.

Chapter 8. Physical Education

Catherine D. Ennis

This chapter consists of seven practices that contribute to effective physical education programs. These practices have widespread support from physical education professionals across the United States and are backed by extensive research examining the teaching-learning environment in urban, suburban and rural schools. Also included are preliminary findings from brain/cognitive research regarding the relationship between physical activity and cognitive ability that hold promise to contribute to student achievement. Practices incorporate standards and guidelines for physical education and physical activity approved by the National Association for Sport and Physical Education (NASPE 1995, 1998), the Centers for Disease Control and Prevention (1997, 1998a, 1998b), and the U. S. Department of Health and Human Services (1992, 1996).

NASPE (1995) has established seven content standards for school physical education that can be used to guide program development and restructuring:

- Students should demonstrate competency in many and proficiency in a few movement forms.

- Students should apply movement concepts and principles to the learning and development of motor skills. This includes the understanding of physiological, biomechanical, psychological, and sociological aspects of learning and performing.

- Students should achieve and maintain fitness (see specific guidelines below).

- Students should participate in and understand the costs and benefits of health-enhancing physical activity. They should have opportunities to make decisions about their own fitness needs and gain a greater understanding of the benefits and consequences of their decisions.

- Students should demonstrate responsible personal and social behavior in physical activity settings.

- Students should understand and respect differences among people in physical activity settings. They should learn to appreciate differences in performance based on body size, strength, coordination, and prior experience.

- Students should understand physical activity provides opportunities for enjoyment, challenge, self-expression, and social interaction. Students should be encouraged to think about physical activity as a source of enjoyable and rewarding experiences both during the school years and throughout one's life.

Quality physical education is an essential element in the total school program. It involves a structured program permitting students to experience a variety of moderate to vigorous physical activities, make decisions about the benefits of physical activity, and learn to perform skillfully in physical activities of their choice. Students learn skills, concepts, and knowledge necessary to appreciate the benefits of regular moderate to vigorous physical activity. They learn to participate safely and effectively and to create personalized programs that are interesting and meaningful to them. Learning occurs in an atmosphere that is enjoyable and entices students to develop positive attitudes toward active, healthy living.

Health Benefits of Physical Activity

Research now provides very strong support for the multiple health benefits of regular physical activity. For example, engaging in regular physical activity relieves tension and stress, helps in weight management, lowers the rate of many diseases, including heart disease and some forms of cancer, and increases life expectancy while improving independence and quality of life. Conversely, a sedentary lifestyle has been identified by the American Heart Association and the U.S. Department of Health and Human Services (1996) as a primary factor in coronary heart disease, nearly doubling a person's risk.

Because more people in the United States are at risk for coronary heart disease due to physical inactivity than to any other single risk factor (i.e., smoking, high blood pressure, high cholesterol), regular physical activity has an especially important health impact. Specifically, physical activity is inexpensive, available to most individuals, and supported by compelling research evidence associated with disease, stress and depression reduction, weight management, and positive self-perceptions (e.g., personal pride, feelings of self-efficacy, persistence, positive goal-setting).

Further, the 1996 U.S. surgeon general's Report *Physical Activity and Public Health* (U.S. Department of Health and Human Services 1996) emphasized people who are physically active tend to show patterns linked with better mental health. When compared with inactive individuals, active individuals scored higher on indicators of positive self-concept and self-esteem and had more positive "moods" and "affects." These trends were reported to be similar in youth and adults. The surgeon general's report suggested active older individuals also appear to score higher on perceived ability to perform activities of daily living, physical well-being, and other measures related to quality of life.

Today, there is increasing evidence that active lifestyles and regular, moderate to vigorous physical activity also may be linked to higher levels of student alertness and mental ability, including the ability to learn. For example, a growing body of evidence within the brain research literature suggests important relationships between physical activity, brain development, and cognitive performance. Although additional research is still needed to understand the full scope of these relationships, this research presents very promising connections between the mind and the body.

Academic Achievement and Physical Activity

Findings from brain research suggest moderate to vigorous physical activity, like that found in quality physical education programs, contributes to children's ability to learn by enhancing the development of brain synapses (i.e., synaptogenesis), synaptic reinforcement, and the relationship between the motor-related functioning of the cerebellum. Spatial learning tasks, selective attention, and manipulation of information and language processing also appear to benefit from regular physical activity.

Evidence from research on synaptogenesis suggests, from birth to age 10, sensory and motor experiences play a significant role in stimulating the growth of a proliferation of synapses between neurons. From age two to 10, the brain functions with a maximum number of synapses. During this time, particular synapses undergo dramatic changes. Specific synapses are developed and reinforced through the growing child's experiences with a variety of sensory and motor events. Motor experiences such as cross-lateral movement patterns, tracking of objects such as balls, and the development of gross and fine-motor patterns appear to contribute to children's success in reading and writing. These tasks contribute to visual focusing and tracking across a written page and to the control of manual reaching patterns across the body's midline in left to right pathways used when writing. Additionally, vestibular balance contributes to visual focusing and tracking skills that can be refined using a variety of enjoyable movement tasks. Children who experience delayed development in reading often demonstrate difficulty when tracking and catching balls, hesitancy in crossing the midline of their bodies (dribbling balls, catching with non-dominant hand), and instability in static and dynamic balance tasks.

At about age 10, the period of synaptogenesis comes to a close and the brain begins a period of "synaptic downsizing." The strongest synapses, or those that have been reinforced most effectively, are preserved, while the weakest synapses are sacrificed and undergo atrophy. Contemporary research points to the fact that sensory and motor experiences play a prominent role in reinforcing or strengthening particular synaptic connections and neural pathways. By the end of adolescence, at about age 18, the "plasticity" or ability of the brain to reshape the synaptic wiring has declined. At this point, the complex foundation of motor skills and associated pathways in the brain has been created. While it is relatively easy to learn new physical skills before age 10 or 11, adults who attempt to learn golf, skiing, or snowboarding for the first time can vouch for the challenge required to create new neural pathways and synapses for these activities. Physical skills are best learned early and practiced often.

The same is true for a variety of life skills—such as reading, writing, language development, and manipulation of objects—which benefit from early instruction in an active, physical environment. Thus, although skills that facilitate and enhance movement can be learned throughout life, prior to age 18 the synaptic wiring of the brain is most receptive to changes driven, in part, by motor experience. This appears to be the most effective time period for establishing academic and motor skills and acquiring the broadest range of new and advanced skills (Caine and Caine 1991; Jensen 1998).

An area of brain research examining the contribution of the cerebellum to learning also is documenting links to motor performance. Historically, the cerebellum has been viewed as having a strictly motor-related function. Currently, however, a growing body of research suggests the cerebellum may also play a signifi-

cant role in sensory and cognitive functioning. Studies of individuals with brain injuries suggest the cerebellum may be involved in spatial learning tasks, such as reading and writing, selective attention between sensory modalities, manipulation of information in the association cortex, and possibly a role in some types of language processing. Because most areas of the brain integrate their functional activities, there is good reason to expect an interactive relationship between motor and cognitive activities of the cerebellum.

Further, multiple studies now demonstrate aerobic exercise— activity that causes your heart to beat faster and your body to perspire—can also improve cognitive performance. It appears that increased cerebrovascular circulation is responsible for this effect. Research has demonstrated that regularly performed aerobic exercise produces an increase in the number of capillaries servicing tissues and organs, including the brain. This effect enhances brain functioning and performance and continues across the lifespan, benefiting everyone from infants to elders.

It stands to reason that school-age children benefit in numerous ways from regular moderate to vigorous physical activity. Programs promoting exercise and physical activity, such as quality physical education, are a very important component of the school curriculum and can contribute in many ways to the academic mission of the school.

Windows of Opportunity

There are two "Windows of Opportunity" during the school years to harness physical activity to support and reinforce academic achievement in reading, writing, and general forms of language development. The first window occurs from preschool through elementary school. Brain research suggests children need a variety of daily, moderate to vigorous physical activities that develop the basic motor skills associated with human movement, such as basic motor patterns (e.g., walking, running, and jumping), maintaining balance with changes in body position, changing the speed of movement, and changing the direction of movement. The emphasis at this age is on the development of fundamental or basic motor skills, such as throwing and catching, chasing, fleeing and dodging, and striking with hands and feet. These skills not only support the development of synapses; they also lay the foundation for the development of new, more complex skills during the second opportunity window, which occurs during middle and high school. The development of basic motor skills is especially important before fifth grade to develop and reinforce as many motor pathway synapses as possible before the synaptic downsizing begins around age 10.

After age 10, the second "window" permits the continued enrichment of motor pathways through moderate to vigorous physical activity requiring children to develop new skills. From middle school through high school, the child should now be challenged with a variety of novel physical activities requiring the development of complex skills beyond the basic motor skills they currently possess. Additionally, regularly performed moderate to vigorous aerobic or cardio-vascular exercise produces an increase in the number of capillaries servicing many tissues and organs, including the brain. Increased capillary density in the brain corresponds to greater and more efficient capillary exchange of nutrients and waste products, optimizing brain functioning and performance. Preschool through high school children (as well as adults) clearly benefit from moderate to vigorous physical activities performed on a regular basis.

Physical Activity Guidelines for Children and Adolescents

Several organizations have issued guidelines to translate this research into concrete recommendations for students' health and optimal physical performance. These guidelines are strongly supported by research and are accepted nationally and internationally for children's programs. The following guidelines appear to promote both academic achievement and cognitive engagement leading to a higher quality of life and enhanced academic performance. In

addition to the National Standards for Physical Education listed at the beginning of this chapter, NASPE (1998) proposes specific guidelines for elementary children:

- Elementary school-aged children should accumulate *at least 30 to 60 minutes* of age-appropriate physical activity from a variety of physical activities on all, or most, days of the week.

- An accumulation of *more than 60 minutes and up to several hours per day* of age-appropriate, developmentally appropriate activity is encouraged for elementary school children.

- Some of the child's physical activity each day should be in periods lasting 10 to 15 minutes or more and include moderate to vigorous physical activity. This activity will typically be intermittent in nature, involving alternating moderate to vigorous activity with *brief periods* of rest and recovery.

- Extended periods of inactivity are inappropriate for children.

- A variety of physical activities is recommended for elementary school children.

In 1994, an international conference was held to establish physical activity guidelines for adolescents (Sallis, Patrick, and Long 1994). These guidelines emphasized:

- All adolescents should be physically active daily, or nearly every day, as part of play, games, sports, work, transportation, recreation, physical education, or planned exercise, in the family, school and community activities.

- Adolescents should engage in three or more sessions per week of activities lasting 20 minutes or more at a time and requiring moderate to vigorous levels of exertion.

The Role of a Quality Physical Education Program

Participation in school physical education is a valuable way to meet these physical activity guidelines. The Centers for Disease Control and

Prevention assert "Schools should implement physical education programs that emphasize enjoyable participation in physical activity and that help students develop the knowledge, attitudes, motor skills, behavioral skills, and confidence needed to adopt and maintain a physically active lifestyle." This is particularly important for adolescents, because time spent in regular moderate to vigorous physical activity outside of school declines as students become older, with particularly sharp declines for all individuals during the late fall and winter months. Daily, quality physical education programs can play an important role in helping children and youth maintain a high level of physical activity year round (U.S. Department of Health and Human Services 1996, 248).

Contribution of a Quality Physical Education Program to the Mission of the School

School reform initiatives in physical education (e.g., Corbin 2002; Corbin and Lindsey 1997; Ennis 1999b; Maryland State Department of Education 2001; Mohnson 1998; Siedentop 1996) have focused on four major areas of program quality:

- increasing the level of moderate to vigorous activity for every student within a positive enjoyable environment;

- enhancing the quality of the physical education content through an emphasis on disciplinary knowledge from exercise physiology, biomechanics, motor learning, and social psychology to enhance natural connections between physical education and other subjects;

- emphasizing commonalities in the learning processes, such as decision making and problem solving, used in performance-based physical education and classroom teaching; and

- providing opportunities for student choice, personal goal setting, and meaningful decision making essential to active, healthy living and integral to all aspects of the school and community.

Physical education can contribute to the mission of the school by helping students develop a "readiness" to learn through optimal physical health and stimulated brain activity. On a daily basis, a quality physical education program ensures moderate to vigorous physical activity to enhance students' abilities to concentrate and focus on academic tasks. Many academic process skills, such as comparing two activities, predicting performance, and solving tactical problems, are a natural part of physical education. Students frequently engage in tasks that include reading directions, writing about activity experiences in journals, and using thinking skills. Content in a quality physical education program draws from many different disciplines and can be used to reinforce and extend these experiences. For example, students can integrate knowledge from:

- life sciences, as they learn how the body responds to exercise;

- physical science, as they explain how the body can generate and absorb force and can act as a powerful machine utilizing concepts such as torque and leverage;

- mathematics, as they calculate angles of force, performance statistics, and algebraic relationships between movers and objects; and

- language skills, as they express the value of meaningful physical experiences through poetry and short stories.

In each of these experiences, students have the opportunity to integrate an alert mind in a healthy body as they gain the tools and habits of mind to enhance productivity and function as healthy members of their school and life community.

8.1. Time for Practice: Time provided in the school day for moderate to vigorous physical activity and motor skill development during both recess and physical education contributes to both academic and movement goals.

Research findings:

Brain research suggests physical activity enhances the development of brain synapses that facilitate cognitive processing. From birth to age 10, the brain creates and utilizes large numbers of synapses to learn new tasks, creating complex neural pathways. Between ages 10 and 18, the brain selects from the available synapses to maintain those used most frequently and effectively.

Additionally, physical activity increases blood flow to the brain, stimulating brain functioning. Regular to moderate physical activity nurtures the development of brain synapses and enhances blood flow during critical growth and learning periods. Physical education programs focusing on the development of new skills and emphasizing physical activity for all children can support and enhance learning.

A large body of pedagogical and motor learning research exists to support the importance of focused, appropriate practice in physical education. The research was initiated in the 1970s and 1980s, and continues to serve as a foundation for physical education reform. This research confirms a direct link between the time students spend practicing specific motor skills and participating in moderate to vigorous physical activity and their level of achievement.

When learning motor skills, for example, there is a direct relationship between the amount of time a student spends practicing a specific skill and the degree of learning that occurs. Academic learning time in physical education is defined as time in which each student is performing or cognitively engaged in reflecting, analyzing, or evaluating performance. Students need to be physically active throughout the class period at an appropriate level of difficulty. High student time on task occurs when *each* student has a piece of equipment, a place to practice, and an interesting and challenging activity to perform.

Inappropriate practices are characterized by students waiting in line for a turn, sitting out of games, and engaging in off-task or disruptive behaviors. These behaviors signal that the content has not been modified to address students' physical abilities, interests, or emotional needs. Creating a positive learning environment in physical education begins with the effective use of class time.

In the classroom:

An educational physical education program requires high levels of appropriately meaningful practice time to enhance student learning. The first step in creating an effective program is to ensure students spend as much of the available class time in appropriate practice as possible.

Research suggests three components of skill practice are essential for student learning. First, the student must spend enough time engaged in practicing the task to learn and refine the movement. Second, the difficulty of the task must match the student's current ability (see Principle 8.2) so that the student can experience frequent, yet challenging, success. Third, the student must mentally concentrate on performing the task correctly (see Principle 8.3). This assumes each student has a piece of equipment with which to practice and the class size reflects that of a typical classroom so that the teacher can work with individual students to provide specific, corrective feedback to improve performance.

It is important to point out that student practice alone is insufficient to enhance achievement. The practice must be at an appropriate level of difficulty and focused on the attainment of an educationally sound objective. For students who have low skills or cognitive or physical disabilities, the use of peer tutors has been shown to assist them in focusing on the task and to increase the quality and meaningfulness of the practice, thus enhancing achievement. Peer tutors may help students follow directions, complete the movement correctly, and socially engage in classroom interactions.

Likewise, when the physical education curriculum focuses on health benefits associated with physical activity, all students need to participate in moderate to vigorous physical activity for 30 to 60 minutes for most days of the week. Beginning early in the elementary grades, students should understand and monitor levels of exercise intensity relative to target heart rates and perceived exertion, using pedometers and heart rate monitors. Even young children can learn to adjust their levels of intensity in response to increases or decreases in heart rate. Middle and high school students use heart rate monitors to examine the relationships between exercise intensity, frequency, duration, and type of activity. As students analyze each component of fitness, they learn to synthesize information to develop a personal fitness program consistent with their interests and lifestyles.

Sources:

Behets 1997; Centers for Disease Control and Prevention 1997, 1998a, 1998b; Clark 1995; Corbin and Lindsey 1997; Houston-Wilson, Dunn, and van der Mars 1998; Ignico and Mahon 1995; Johnson and Ward 2001; LaMaster et al. 1998; McKenzie et al. 1995; McKenzie et al. 1998; Mitchell 1996; Nevitt, Rovegno and Babiarz 2001; Nevitt, Rovegno, Babiarz, and McCauhtry 2001; Pate et al. 1995; Perron and Downey 1997; Prusak and Darst 2002; Rink 2001; Sallis et al. 1997; Sallis, Patrick, and Long 1994; Silverman 1990, 1991, 1993, 1994; Silverman, Tsangaridou, and O'Sullivan 2003; Silverman, Tyson, and Morford 1988; Stone et al.1998; van der Mars, Vogler, Darst, and Cusimano 1998.

8.2. Appropriate, Meaningful Practice: Tasks consistent with the learning objective and the ability of the learner, and perceived by the learner to be relevant, increase student interest and motivation and lead to the development of skillful, active movers.

Research findings:

Research supporting the nature and specificity of tasks to meet certain objectives has greatly contributed to our understanding of class structures that promote student achievement. Likewise, task difficulty and task relevance have been found to be critical variables in the learning process, enhancing student interest and engagement. This research suggests either multiple tasks or tasks with multiple levels of difficulty should be used to accommodate the wide range of skill, motivation, and energy levels present in most physical education classes. Task multiplicity is also necessary to challenge learners as their ability increases.

A growing body of research is focusing on achievement motivation and student engagement in physical education. Achievement motivation researchers examine ego-involved and task-involved learning environments to identify situations that both facilitate and constrain learning. Ego-oriented environments often place students in competitive situations in which their success may come at the expense of others. Students focus, not on learning the content, but on placing other students at a disadvantage. Some physical educators critical of this practice describe it as "teaching students to lose." It is not surprising that an ego-involved environment in physical education can foster dominant, aggressive behaviors and lead to embarrassment and harassment of low-skilled students.

Conversely, task-involved environments encourage all students to focus on the criteria for "good" performance. Instead of comparing their performance with that of others, students set individual goals and compare their performance to their goals. Both high-skilled and low-skilled students are challenged to improve their perfor-

mance in a positive, nurturing environment. Students report a higher level of interest and enjoyment in physical activity and physical education. Results of achievement motivation research suggest students experience improvements in self-concept, goal setting, and feelings of competency. They also are more motivated to perform, resulting in enhanced achievement.

In the classroom:

A quality physical education program is characterized by a task-involved climate that adequately addresses the needs and interests of students with varied abilities, motivations, skills, and prior experiences. Each student should be engaged at a level of difficulty providing frequent success. Tasks are modified to include several "built-in" levels of difficulty so that every student can participate successfully. This is most easily accomplished when students are encouraged to assess and compare their own abilities with teacher-provided (e.g., wall charts, teacher instruction, video or CD-ROM models) or student-constructed criteria. These criteria increase the relevance of the activity for students and help them to engage meaningfully in physical activity.

The first step in creating appropriate, meaningful practice is to provide opportunities for students to make *choices* about the equipment to be used, the task to be performed, and the students with whom they would like to cooperate. For example, students may be permitted to select among several pieces of equipment to find one that is consistent with their body size and developing abilities. Students can complete the same ball-throwing activity using different size, weight, or shaped balls. They can choose to throw to a target that is large or small, high or low, moving or stationary. When they are encouraged to assess their own skill, strength, accuracy, or form, they are able to select from teacher-designed tasks or, better, construct their own tasks, games, fitness activities, or problem-solving experiments in which they can find frequent, yet challenging, success. In physical activity situations, they can use heart rate monitors to provide knowledge of their personal target heart rate as an effective guide to determine when they need to work harder (increase their intensity) or slow down because their heart rate is above the target zone.

Numerous computer programs are now available to guide students in making personalized decisions. Pedometers that are inexpensive and fit on a student's waistband or personal heart rate monitors that consist of a chest strap and a wrist monitor make physical activity a personal and private matter. Students with disabilities, those who are overweight, or those who have not had positive experiences in traditional physical education programs often find personalized

programs provide physical activities that are appropriate and meaningful to them.

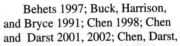

Sources:

Behets 1997; Buck, Harrison, and Bryce 1991; Chen 1998; Chen and Darst 2001, 2002; Chen, Darst, and Pangrazi 2001; Clark 1995; Corbin and Lindsey 1997; Darst, Chen, van der Mars, and Cusimano 2001; Ennis, Solmon, Satina, Loftus, Mensch, and McCauley 1999; Gibbons, Ebbeck, and Weiss, 1995; Graham, Holt-Hale, and Parker 2002; Halas 2002; Hare and Graber 2000; Hebert, Landin, and Solmon 1996; Ignico and Mahon 1995; Johnson and Ward 2001; Oslin, Stroot, and Siedentop 1997; Prusak and Darst 2002; Rink 1994, 1996a, 2001; Silverman, Kulinna, and Crull 1995; Silverman, Subramaniam, and Woods 1998; Silverman, Woods and Subramaniam 1998; Solmon 1996; Solmon and Boone 1993; Solmon and Lee 1996; Treasure and Roberts 1995; Xiang and Lee 1998.

8.3. Cognitive Engagement: Students should be challenged to think about their own movement; understand the science-based principles from biomechanical, physiological, motor learning, and social-psychological principles, and those that facilitate effective performance; and learn to analyze, synthesize, and apply these across a wide range of human movement.

Research findings:

Research suggests, for many students, interest in physical activity increases when they understand scientific principles and concepts that facilitate effective, injury-free performance. Research examining student disengagement in physical education has suggested students find traditional physical education to lack value and meaning when compared with other subject areas. Students acknowledge that physical education can be enjoyable and fun, but see little value in game play, especially when they are unskilled. Conversely, these students respond quite differently to physical education programs in which they are asked to use both their minds and their bodies.

Students should be provided with opportunities to learn the fundamental concepts and principles that enhance effective, safe, and injury-free performance. Research in motor learning, for example, has suggested when beginner-level and intermediate-level students learn skills, they attempt to attend to a few critical factors that contribute to effective performance. As learners become more skilled, their cognitive focus shifts from performing the isolated skill to monitoring the environment to determine contextual factors that influence temporal and spatial parameters essential to success.

Research examining the influence of specific context factors on learning has concluded contextual interference during early stages of learning, such as distractions or frequently changing practice conditions, require the learner to concentrate much harder to attend to these factors and to adjust their performances as they learn. Although it initially takes performers longer to learn when and how to perform under these conditions, their ability to adapt and adjust their performance to a variety of unanticipated or unpracticed events or situations is enhanced during the later stages of learning.

These programs also focus on scientific principles and concepts that provide the foundation for effective, safe movement. Not surprisingly these concepts are the same ones taught in life science (e.g., biology and physiology, especially as they relate to bodily systems and the human body's responses to stressors such as physical activity), physics (e.g., generation of power and forces associated with acceleration, torque, gravity, balance, etc.), psychology and sociology (e.g., self and social responsibility, goal setting, positive self-concept, self-esteem and self-efficacy, cooperation with others through active listening), and across the academic curriculum associated with learning theories (e.g., development of proficiency, characteristics of effective practice, etc.).

In the classroom:

A number of school districts, schools, and individual teachers have experimented with concept-based curricula in physical education over the last two decades. We now have a growing body of practical knowledge for teaching that can assist physical educators in organizing their content based on principles and concepts, rather than around traditional sports activities. Teachers find this particularly helpful when sequencing content (see Principle 8.4) to build across units and grades.

Teachers in the state of Maryland, for example, are currently creating concept-oriented content standards based on four disciplinary principles associated with exercise physiology, biomechanics, motor learning, and social psychology. The biomechanics principle states, "Students will improve their movement effectiveness and safety by applying the principles of biomechanics to generate and control force." Master physical education teachers have developed exit indicators for students in grades three, five, eight, and 12. One biomechanical subconcept focusing on the "physics" of rotational actions takes students from simple rolling movements in third grade to the investigation of complex principles of rotation and torque in their high school physical education class:

- **Third-Grade Exit Standard:** Students should be able to identify and demonstrate rolling, turning, twisting, rotating actions and use these effectively to stop and change direction.

- **Fifth-Grade Exit Standard:** Students should be able to demonstrate or explain axial rotation (horizontal, vertical, and transverse axes) and the principle that increasing the length of the rotating body part (axis of rotation) decreases the speed of rotation.

- **Eighth-Grade Exit Standard:** Students should be able to explain various types of anatomical joints and the range of motion for each, the result of eccentric (off-center) forces, and compare angular/rotary motion with linear motion and the effect on human movements.

- **Twelfth-Grade Exit Standard:** Students should be able to analyze and explain the relationship between torque and angular motion, joint movement, and the Magnus force.

Curricula such as these encourage students to synthesize knowledge across several traditionally separate subject areas and to explore and experiment with scientific principles as they affect their bodies. Teachers create problem-based learning experiences that challenge students to apply their knowledge from the classroom into the gymnasium and other parts of their lives. Excellent opportunities exist for cross-curricular connections and content integration between teachers in different subject areas. Often, experimenting with scientific concepts in the gymnasium can make a significant difference in student motivation and understanding.

Sources:

Allison and Thorpe 1997; Burrows, Wright, and Jungensen-Smith 2002; Chen 1998; Chen and Cone 2003; Cothran and Ennis 1997, 1999, 2000; Douthitt 1994; Ennis 1996, 1998a; Ennis et al. 1997, 1999; Gibbons and Ebbeck 1997; Gibbons, Ebbeck, and Weiss 1995; Gréhaigne and Godbout 1995; Griffin, Dodds, Placek, and Tremino 2001; Griffin, Mitchell, and Oslin 1997; Halas 2002; Harrison, Preece, Blakemore, Richards, Wilkinson, and Fellingham 1999; Hastie 1998; Hellison 1996; Langley 1995; Lee 1997; Maryland State Department of Education 2001; McBride and Bonnette 1995; Mohnson 1998; Placek 1996; Placek, Griffin, Dodds, Raymond, Tremino, and James 2001; Rink 1996b; Rovegno, Nevitt, and Babiarz 2001; Siedentop 1996, Solmon and Lee 1997.

8.4. Content Sequencing: Progressive sequencing of concepts and tasks across units and grade levels permits students to build new knowledge on a solid foundation of existing knowledge.

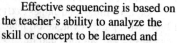

Research findings:

Research on sequencing suggests achievement is enhanced when skills are presented in a progressive order. Researchers have examined many different sequencing progressions for skill and fitness concepts and themes. Simple to complex, part to whole, and whole to part sequencing all are effective in presenting foundational knowledge in physical education and building progressive, complex additions to that knowledge. Skills and concepts sequenced using a simple to complex format can be taught across units and grade levels to help students understand how to perform and why a movement is effective. Conversely, when instruction consists only of a review of foundational knowledge in short units, students may become bored and believe a low level of performance is adequate. It is important that sequences in physical education include the increasingly more complex information necessary to enhance achievement.

In the classroom:

Effective sequencing is based on the teacher's ability to analyze the skill or concept to be learned and place it in simple to complex or part to whole sequences to enhance student understanding and learning. Sequencing of tasks within the lesson helps the teacher adjust the lesson to the student's level of interest and ability.

For example, task series are effective sequencing strategies that provide both structure and flexibility for teachers. Task series often begin with a *basic* task presented to students as an open activity. The tasks can be taught directly or presented using a problem-based format challenging students to examine movement or compare tactics and make choices relevant to their own performance. As students engage in the activity, teachers offer refining cues to help students improve on their specific performance.

If the basic tasks prove to be too difficult for some students, the teacher may select simplifying tasks to decrease the level of difficulty. *Refining* cues and additional appropriate practices often assist the student to move back to the original basic task. For students who effectively perform the basic and refining tasks, the teacher offers one or more *extending* tasks to encourage the student to perform the skill or examine the concept under different game or environmental conditions. Adaptations might be required to perform in a more complex environment in which the students are moving more rapidly, the physical boundaries are increased or decreased, or the equipment is changed to make it more challenging. Under these situations, teachers help students adjust their movements to the new demands of the task, enhancing both their understanding of movement and their ability to perform.

Teachers may also provide *application* tasks that encourage students to apply their newly learned skills within a game, movement sequence, or exercise plan. This helps students realize the functional application of the skill or concept, connecting it to valued personal goals or functional activities in their lives.

Developmental analyses of skills and concepts that are useful when planning several classes or several weeks of classes may use a developmentally appropriate framework sensitive to the physical, cognitive, emotional, and social needs and abilities of the child. *It is clear that students do not learn skills or concepts by simply being involved in game play.* Instead, an understanding and ability to perform skills, use strategies, and apply scientific concepts should be developed through instructional tasks that use progressively more complex activities, beginning with the most fundamental concepts and then adding other components as the child learns.

A frequent concern in physical education occurs when students continue year after year to be involved in the same sports and games, yet perform at a very low level of skill and conceptual understanding. Efforts to disrupt this process require teachers to refocus the content on skills, concepts, and corresponding criteria for performance. Progressive sequencing in these activities helps all students refine their skills and apply newly learned

concepts to activities they find interesting and enjoyable. Appropriate sequencing and the ability to match students' abilities to the level of task difficulty greatly enhance the learning environment and students' opportunities to learn.

 Sources:

Barrett et al. 1997; Ennis et al. 1999; Gibbons, Ebbeck, and Weiss 1995; Harrison et al. 1999; Jewett, Bain and Ennis 1995; Rink 1996a, 1996b, 2001; Rink et al. 1992.

8.5. Spiral Curriculum: Revisiting important topics at increasing levels of difficulty and complexity, both several times during each grade and at different grades, provides multiple opportunities for students to develop a deeper understanding of movement concepts and principles and the ability to perform competently.

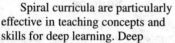

Research findings:

Spiral curricula are particularly effective in teaching concepts and skills for deep learning. Deep learning is described as a person's ability to think reflectively about the concept and its influence in many different situations. Most concepts that influence movement and physical activity also can be found in many different parts of our lives. As students progress through their school years, their ability to understand and perform can be challenged by revisiting the concepts and extending them to more complex levels.

Research suggests it is important to help students develop a solid knowledge foundation as early as possible. Teachers who employ a spiral curriculum revisit the concept throughout the school year and in successive years. Each time they spiral to the concept, they review the information learned previously, check for understanding, and remind students of relevant concept applications. Once satisfied that students are ready to move to the next level, teachers then expand, extend, and elaborate the concept as it applies in new situations or as it relates to other concepts recently studied. This continuous revisiting of the concepts within the spiral not only builds student knowledge progressively, it also reconfirms the importance of the concept and its generalizability to a variety of meaningful aspects of their lives.

In the classroom:

A spiral curriculum is based on the idea that there are a limited number of broad concepts that are central to the discipline. Once identified, teachers decide at what point the concepts should be introduced in the curriculum and then designate opportunities in which the concepts can be revisited and expanded.

For example, the concept of balance is important not only in physical education but across our lifespan. It is a concept students realize immediately as relevant in their lives. They can watch younger brothers and sisters master upright, dynamic balancing as they learn to walk. They themselves must think about balance as they jump across puddles or gingerly slide across an icy sidewalk. They also have the opportunity to watch grandparents and other older adults who may feel insecure in their footing. Learning to balance is a lifelong activity. It flows through our lives and is an example of a concept that can be spiraled effectively through the physical education curriculum.

In physical education, the concept of balance can be taught first as the concept of "stillness." Stillness is achieved by tightening muscles, focusing on a fixed point, and aligning body parts. Later students learn the relationship between the center of gravity and base of support. This can be followed in later years by the concepts of counter balance and counter tension that elaborate and extend our understanding of balance beyond those earlier conceptualizations. By revisiting concepts—such as cardiovascular fitness; muscular strength, endurance and flexibility; creating and absorbing forces; and self-regulation and goal setting—students realize the value of the concept and watch it grow in complexity as they themselves grow. The spiraling of concepts adds meaning and value to the content and to the physical education curriculum.

Sources:

Belka 1994; Dyson and O'Sullivan 1998; Ennis et al. 1999; Griffin, Mitchell, and Oslin 1997; Jewett, Bain, and Ennis 1995; National Association for Sport and Physical Education 1993, 1995; Rink 1996b, 2001.

8.6. Developmental Program Focus: Programs focused on the development and assessment of fundamental knowledge of movement, fitness, and scientific concepts and principles and their application to physical activity are essential to the development of physically educated persons.

Research findings:

Motor development research indicates learners are most successful in acquiring new motor skills during the preschool and elementary years. Students' coordinative structures and neurological pathways are developing rapidly during this period and are receptive to the development of fundamental movement patterns and basic skills. They can then refine, extend, and apply these patterns to more complex skills during adolescence.

Developmentally appropriate physical education programs reflect students' current abilities and provide tasks to challenge them to the next level of performance. Tasks are sequenced carefully to enhance student success while providing new opportunities that are just beyond the student's current abilities. Task sequencing within effective curriculum "spirals" contribute to student learning and feelings of success (see Principles 8.4 and 8.5).

Performance assessment is critical to students' ability to self-evaluate and compare their performance to criteria. Assessment informs students of their current levels of ability and provides concrete benchmarks against which to measure future improvement. Criteria help students to focus on critical aspects of the movement and modify their movements to enhance performance.

In the classroom:

Although students are typically grouped by age in schools, they are certainly diverse in many other ways. Students of the same chronological age typically include a variety of body sizes and shapes and varied interests, motivations, skills, abilities, and fitness levels. As students grow and mature, their needs and interests change based on their past experiences as well as on their size and strength.

Creating physical education lessons that are developmentally appropriate for all students in a single class requires the teacher to build several levels of difficulty into each task and activity. This is made easier when students are: a) permitted to set their own goals for an activity; b) taught to select tasks consistent with their current ability; and c) encouraged to improve on their own performance to meet their goals. Students can assess their own performance against student- or teacher-designed criteria.

In skills associated with speed and strength, nesting several different experiences within one task can be used to increase the developmental appropriateness of the activity (task multiplicity). By providing children with several options, we permit them to select the task that is developmentally appropriate for them. Students can evaluate their skills based on the level in which they are currently working and then decide whether their performance was successful, signaling their readiness to move to a more challenging level. Peers can assist in this process by using check sheets based on the criteria for a successful performance. Peer-mediated accountability is an effective tool when teaching large numbers of students in complex teaching environments. Students enjoy the responsibility and help the teacher maintain a positive teaching-learning environment.

193

Most tasks can be made developmentally appropriate by building in several levels of difficulty. This is true in fitness activities in which students wear pedometers and heart rate monitors that help them evaluate the intensity of the exercise. This is particularly important for overweight students who may appear to be moving slowly, but actually may be working at a *higher* heart rate or level of intensity than some of their "speedy" classmates. By focusing on developmentally appropriate activities, teachers add an additional element of sensitivity to students and assist them in motivating and challenging themselves based on personalized goals.

Sources:

Clark 1995; Ennis 1998a, 1999a; Ennis et al. 1999; Gibbons, Ebbeck, and Weiss 1995; Graham, Holt-Hale, and Parker 2002; Houston-Wilson, Dunn, and van der Mars 1998; Naper-Owens, Kovar, Ermler, and Mehrhof 1999; Oslin, Stroot and Siedentop 1997; Taylor, Baranowski, and Young 1998; Ward, Smith, Makasci, and Crouch 1998.

8.7. Administrative Support: Administrative support of an equitable, academic, learning-oriented approach to physical education is critical to children's development and to the implementation of a quality physical education program that contributes directly to the academic mission of the school.

Research findings:

Research suggests many teachers work very hard to create a quality physical education program for their students. They depend on the principal and the school management team to support their programs with ongoing, reasonable expenditures for equipment and by providing indoor and outdoor spaces for students to move equitably, safely, and effectively.

Studies in motivational theory confirm that when individuals do not receive regular support and constructive critiques of their work, their motivation declines and their job performance suffers. In the current educational environment, in which principals are focusing on test score improvements in traditional academic subjects, physical education teachers may not receive either the resources or the emotional support they need to continue to strive for quality. Administrators' support for physical education contributes directly to teachers' perceptions of status, their satisfaction with their job, and their willingness to give effort in a demanding environment. It is a key component for enhancing and maintaining a quality physical education program.

In the classroom:

It is important for administrators to hold high expectations for *learning* in physical education. This expectation transfers for teachers into a sense of importance and pride essential to quality programs. Physical education can contribute to the academic and social missions of the school through a focus on problem solving, decision making, critical and creative thinking, equity,

cooperation, and moral development. Students can collaborate, analyze, classify, evaluate, compare, predict, design, and calculate in physical education. They can learn thinking processes in physical education necessary for focused and disciplined study in any subject area.

The physical education class can become a laboratory in which students test principles associated with the social, psychological, and biological systems such as those experienced through team play, intrinsic and extrinsic motivation, physiological effects of exercise on the body, power and force production, and the interaction of multiple scientific factors that facilitate or constrain performance.

There are numerous cross-disciplinary connections that occur daily in physical education. As physical educators are invited to become members of grade-level and subject-oriented teams of teachers, they become aware of how their content reinforces and extends knowledge typically confined to the classroom. Students benefit greatly from opportunities to apply knowledge in multiple venues. They discard compartmentalized notions of science or math and begin to experience the interrelationships that contribute to deep learning.

Administrators who have been disillusioned by traditional physical education should encourage traditional physical educators to extend their knowledge and create individualized approaches to physical education for their students. Students who are developing knowledge, fitness, and skill are more likely to engage in an active, healthy lifestyle. They are often more willing and able to be good citizens of the school and the community. With administrator support for physical education, students quickly learn that physical education is an

A Checklist for Quality Physical Education: Is It Time for a Change?	No	Yes
Is the physical education curriculum consistent with the NASPE National Standards?		
Do students participate in moderate to vigorous physical activity during the school day?		
Do students wait in long lines for a turn, sit out of games, and engage in off-task or disruptive behaviors? (see Principle 8.1)		
Is the physical education program structured in short units that do not permit adequate time for students to learn skills or cognitive concepts? (8.1)		
Do students become bored, disruptive, or believe a low level of performance is adequate? (8.1)		
Are students always involved in game play? (8.2)		
Do students frequently participate in overly competitive situations in which their success may come at the expense of others? Do students focus, not on learning the content, but on placing other students at a disadvantage? (8.2)		
Do some students engage in dominant, aggressive behaviors that lead to embarrassment and harassment of low-skilled students? (8.2)		
Do students acknowledge that physical education can be enjoyable and fun, but see little value in game play, especially when they lack physical skills? (8.3)		
Are students engaged both cognitively and physically in learning? (8.3)		
Do students continue year after year to practice the same sports and games, yet perform at a very low level of skill and conceptual understanding? (8.4)		
Are skills and tasks sequenced effectively and matched to students' level of ability to enhance learning? (8.4)		
Are all students in physical education doing the same task, in the same way, and at the same time regardless of their diverse interests, body sizes, strength, and physical abilities? (8.5)		
Do a few key concepts spiral effectively through the physical education curriculum? (8.5)		
Are students assessed frequently in a positive and supportive environment? (8.6)		
Do students with disabilities and overweight students receive an individual, developmentally appropriate program in physical education? (8.6)		
Do physical education teachers receive the instructional resources and the emotional support they need to continue to strive for quality? (8.7)		
Are classes scheduled so that physical educators rarely have an opportunity to collaborate with academic grade-level or subject-matter "teams"? (8.7)		
Do principals hold high expectations for student *learning* in physical education? (8.7)		

integral part of the school curriculum and a class in which they learn in an enjoyable and intellectually stimulating environment.

Sources:

Allison and Thorpe 1997; Behets 1997; Donnelly, Helion, and Fry 1999; Dyson and O'Sullivan 1998; Ennis 1998b, 1999a; Fejgin and Hanegby 1999; Gibbons and Ebbeck 1997; Gibbons, Ebbeck, and Weiss 1995; Hastie, Saunders, and Rowland 1999; Hellison 1996; Ignico and Mahon 1995; Jensen 1998; LaMaster et al. 1998; McBride and Bonnette 1995; McKenzie et al. 1997; Mitchell 1996; Naper-Owens et al. 1999; Papaioannou 1998; Rink 2001; Satina et al. 1998; Taylor, Baranowski, and Young 1998.

Bibliography

Allison, S. and R. Thorpe. 1997. "A Comparison of the Effectiveness of Two Approaches to Teaching Games within Physical Education: A Skills Approach versus a Games for Understanding Approach." *The British Journal of Physical Education* Vol. 28: 9-13.

Barrett, K.R., K. Williams, J. McLester, and S. Ljungkvist. 1997. "Developmental Sequences for the Vertical Cradle in Lacrosse: An Exploratory Study." *Journal of Teaching in Physical Education* Vol. 16: 469-489.

Behets, D. 1997. "Comparison of More and Less Effective Teaching Behaviors in Secondary Physical Education." *Teaching and Teacher Education* Vol. 13: 215-224.

Belka, D.E. 1994. *Teaching Children Games: Becoming a Master Teacher.* Champaign, IL: Human Kinetics.

Buck, M., J. Harrison, and G.R. Bryce. 1991. "An Analysis of Learning Trials and Their Relationship to Achievement." *Journal of Teaching in Physical Education* Vol. 10: 134-152.

Burrows, L., J. Wright, and J. Jungersen-Smith. 2002. "Measure Your Belly." New Zealand Children's Constructions Of Health And Fitness. *Journal of Teaching in Physical Education* Vol. 22: 39-48.

Caine, R.N., and G. Caine. 1991. *Making Connections: Teaching and the Human Brain.* Alexandria, VA: Association for Supervision and Curriculum Development.

Centers for Disease Control and Prevention. 1997. "Guidelines for School and Community Programs to Promote Lifelong Physical Activity among Young People." *Morbidity and Mortality Weekly Report* Vol. 46, No. RR-6: 1-36.

Centers for Disease Control and Prevention. 1998a. *Strengthening Physical Education in Schools: Process Evaluation Manual.* Atlanta: U.S. Department of Health and Human Services, Centers for Disease Control and Prevention.

Centers for Disease Control and Prevention. 1998b. "Youth Risk Behavior Surveillance—United States, 1997." *Morbidity and Mortality Weekly Report* Vol. 47, No. SS-3: 1-89.

Chen, A. 1998. "Meaningfulness in Physical Education: A Description of High School Students' Conceptions." *Journal of Teaching in Physical Education* Vol. 17: 285-306.

Chen, A., and P.W. Darst. 2001. "Situational Interest in Physical Education: A Function of Learning Task Design." *Research Quarterly for Exercise and Sport* Vol. 72: 150-164.

Chen, A., and P.W. Darst. 2002. "Individual and Situational Interest: The Role of Gender and Skill." *Contemporary Educational Psychology* Vol. 27: 250-269.

Chen, A., P.W. Darst, and R.P. Pangrazi. 2001. "An Examination of Situational Interest and its Sources in Physical Education." *British Journal of Educational Psychology* Vol. 71: 383-400.

Chen, W. and T. Cone. 2003. "Links Between Children's Use of Critical Thinking and an Expert Teacher's Teaching of Creative Dance." *Journal of Teaching in Physical Education* Vol. 22: 169-185.

Clark, J.E. 1995. "On Becoming Skillful: Patterns and Constraints." *Research Quarterly for Exercise and Sport* Vol. 66: 173-183.

Corbin, C.B. 2002. "Physical Activity for Everyone: What Every Physical Educator Should Know About Promoting Lifelong Physical Activity." *Journal of Teaching in Physical Education* Vol. 21: 128-144.

Corbin, C.B. and R. Lindsey. 1997. *Fitness for Life* (4th edition). Glenview, IL: Scott, Foresman Publishers.

Cothran, D.J. and C.D. Ennis. 1997. "Students and Teachers' Perceptions of Conflict and Power." *Teaching and Teacher Education* Vol. 13: 541-553.

Cothran, D.J. and C.D. Ennis. 1999. "Alone in a Crowd: Meeting Students' Needs for Relevance and Connection in Urban High School Physical Education." *Journal of Teaching in Physical Education* Vol. 18: 234-247.

Cothran, D.J. and C.D. Ennis. 2000. "Building Bridges to Student Engagement: Communicating Respect and Care for Students in Urban High Schools." *Journal of Research and Development in Education* Vol. 23: 106-117.

Darst, P.W., A. Chen, H. van der Mars, and B.E. Cusimano. 2001. "Teacher, Class Size, and Situational Interest: Student Responses to Fitness Routines." *Journal of Sport Pedagogy* Vol. 7: 43-66.

Donnelly, F.C., J. Helion, and F. Fry. 1999. "Modifying Teacher Behaviors to Promote Critical Thinking in K-12 Physical Education." *Journal of Teaching in Physical Education* Vol. 18: 199-215.

Douthitt, V.L. 1994. "Psychological Determinants of Adolescent Exercise Adherence." *Adolescence* Vol. 29: 711-722.

Dyson, B. and M. O'Sullivan. 1998. "Innovation in Two Alternative Elementary School Programs: Why it Works." *Research Quarterly for Exercise and Sport* Vol. 69: 242-253.

Ennis, C.D. 1996. "When Avoiding Confrontation Leads to Avoiding Content: Disruptive Students' Impact on Curriculum." *Journal of Curriculum and Supervision* Vol. 11: 145-162.

Ennis, C.D. 1998a. "The Context of Culturally Unresponsive Curriculum." *Teaching and Teacher Education* Vol. 14: 749-760.

Ennis, C.D. 1998b. "Shared Expectations: Creating a Joint Vision for Urban Schools." In Jere Brophy (Ed.), *Advances in Research on Teaching* Vol. 7: 151-182, New York: JAI Press.

Ennis, C.D. 1999a. "Creating a Culturally Relevant Curriculum for Disengaged Girls." *Sport, Education, and Society* Vol. 4: 31-49.

Ennis, C.D. 1999b. "Communicating the Value of Active, Healthy Lifestyles to Urban Students." *Quest* Vol. 51: 164-169.

Ennis, C.D. 2000. "Canaries in the Coal Mine: Responding to Disengaged Students using Theme-Based Curricula. *Quest* Vol. 52: 119-130.

Ennis, C.D., D.J. Cothran, K.D. Stockin, L.M. Owens, S.J. Loftus, L. Swanson, and P. Hopsicker. 1997. "Implementing Curriculum within a Context of Fear and Disengagement." *Journal of Teaching in Physical Education* Vol. 17: 58-72.

Ennis, C.D., M.A. Solmon, B. Satina, S.J. Loftus, J. Mensch, and M.T. McCauley. 1999. "Creating a Sense of Family in Urban Schools using the 'Sport for Peace' Curriculum." *Research Quarterly for Exercise and Sport* Vol. 70: 273-285.

Fejgin, N. and R. Hanegby. 1999. "Physical Educators' Participation in Decision-making Processes in Dynamic Schools." *Journal of Teaching in Physical Education* Vol. 18: 141-158.

Gibbons, S.L. and V. Ebbeck. 1997. "The Effect of Different Teaching Strategies on the Moral Development of Physical Education Students." *Journal of Teaching in Physical Education* Vol. 17: 85-98.

Gibbons, S.L., V. Ebbeck, and M.R. Weiss.1995. "Fair Play for Kids: Effects on the Moral Development of Children in Physical Education." *Research Quarterly for Exercise and Sport* Vol. 66: 247-254.

Graham, G., S. Holt-Hale, and M. Parker. 2002. *Children Moving*. Palo Alto, CA: Mayfield.

Gréhaigne, J.F. and P. Godbout. 1995. "Tactical Knowledge in Team Sports from a Constructivist and Cognitive Perspective." *Quest* Vol. 47: 490-505.

Griffin, L.L., P. Dodds, J.H. Placek, and F. Tremino. 2001. "Middle School Students Conceptions of Soccer: Their Solutions to Tactical Problems. *Journal of Teaching in Physical Education* Vol. 20: 324-340.

Griffin, L.L., S.A. Mitchell, and J.L. Oslin. 1997. *Teaching Sport Concepts and Skills: A Tactical Games Approach*. Champaign, IL: Human Kinetics.

Halas, J. 2002. "Engaging Alienated Youth in Physical Education: An Alternative Program with Lessons for the Traditional Class." *Journal of Teaching in Physical Education* Vol. 21: 267-286.

Hare, M.K. and K.C. Graber. 2000. "Student Misconceptions during Two Invasion Game Units in Physical Education: A Qualitative Investigation of Student Thought Processes." *Journal of Teaching in Physical Education* Vol. 20: 55-57.

Harrison, J.M., L.A. Preece, C.L. Blakemore, R.P. Richards, C. Wilkinson, and G.W. Fellingham. 1999. "Effects of Two Instructional Models—Skill Teaching and Mastery Learning—On Skill Development, Knowledge, Self-Efficacy, and Game Play in Volleyball." *Journal of Teaching in Physical Education* Vol. 19: 34-57.

Hastie, P.A. 1998. "Skill and Tactical Development during a Sport Education Season." *Research Quarterly for Exercise and Sport* Vol. 69: 368-379.

Hastie, P.A., J.E. Saunders, and R.S. Rowland. 1999. "Where Good Intentions Meet Harsh Realities: Teaching Large Classes in Physical Education." *Journal of Teaching in Physical Education* Vol. 18: 277-289.

Hebert, E.P., D. Landin, and M.A. Solmon. 1996. "Practice Schedule Effects on the Performance and Learning of Low- and High-Skilled Students: An Applied Study." *Research Quarterly for Exercise and Sport* Vol. 67: 52-58.

Hellison, D. 1996. "Teaching Physical Education and Social Responsibility in Physical Education." In *Student Learning in Physical Education: Applying Research to Enhance Instruction*, S.J. Silverman and C.D. Ennis, editors (pp. 269-286). Champaign, IL: Human Kinetics.

Houston-Wilson, C., J.M. Dunn, and H. van der Mars. 1998. "The Effect of Peer Tutors on Motor Performance in Integrated Physical Education Classes." *Adapted Physical Activity Quarterly* Vol. 14: 298-313.

Ignico, A.A., and A.D. Mahon. 1995. "The Effects of a Physical Fitness Program on Low-fit Children." *Research Quarterly for Exercise and Sport* Vol. 66: 85-90.

Jensen, E. 1998. *Teaching with the Brain in Mind*. Alexandria, VA: Association of Supervision and Curriculum Development.

Jewett, A.E., L.L. Bain, and C.D. Ennis. 1995. *The Curriculum Process in Physical Education*. Dubuque, IA: Wm. C. Brown.

Johnson, M. and P. Ward. 2001. "Effects of Classwide Peer Tutoring on Correct Performance of Striking Skills in Third-grade Physical Education." *Journal of Teaching in Physical Education* Vol. 20: 247-263.

LaMaster, K., K. Gall, G. Kinchin, and D. Siedentop. 1998. "Inclusion Practices of Effective Elementary Specialists." *Adapted Physical Education Quarterly* Vol. 15: 64-81.

Langley, D.J. 1995. "Student Cognition in the Instructional Setting." *Journal of Teaching in Physical Education* Vol. 15: 25-52.

Lee, A.M. 1997. "Contributions of Research on Student Thinking in Physical Education." *Journal of Teaching in Physical Education* Vol. 16: 162-277.

Maryland State Department of Education. 2001. *Student Standards for Physical Education: Report of the Physical Education Study Group.* Baltimore: Author.

McBride, R.E. and R. Bonnette. 1995. "Teacher and At-Risk Students' Cognitions during Open-ended Activities: Structuring the Environment for Critical Thinking." *Teaching and Teacher Education* Vol. 11: 373-388.

McKenzie, T.L., J.E. Alcaraz, J.F. Sallis, and F.N. Faucette. 1998. "Effects of a Physical Education Program on Children's Manipulative Skills." *Journal of Teaching in Physical Education* Vol. 17: 327-341.

McKenzie, T.L., H. Feldman, S.E. Woods, K.A. Romero, V. Dahlstrom, E.J. Stone, P.K. Strikmiller, J.M. Williston, and D.W. Harsha. 1995. "Children's Activity Levels and Lesson Context during Third-grade Physical Education." *Research Quarterly for Exercise and Sport* Vol. 66: 184-193.

McKenzie, T.L., J.F. Sallis, B. Kolody, and F.N. Faucette. 1997. "Long Term Effects of a Physical Education Curriculum and Staff Development Program: SPARK." *Research Quarterly for Exercise and Sport* Vol. 68: 1-14.

Mitchell, S.A. 1996. "Relationship between Perceived Learning Environment and Intrinsic Motivation in Middle School Physical Education." *Journal of Teaching in Physical Education* Vol. 15: 369-383.

Mohnson, B. (Ed.). 1998. *Concepts of Physical Education: What Every Student Should Know.* Reston, VA: NASPE Publications.

Naper-Owens, G.E., S.E. Kovar, K.L. Ermler, and J.H. Mehrhof. 1999. "Curricular Equity in Required Ninth-grade Physical Education." *Journal of Teaching in Physical Education* Vol. 19: 2-21.

National Association for Sport and Physical Education. 1993. *Quality Physical Education.* Reston, VA: NASPE Publications.

National Association for Sport and Physical Education. 1995. *Content Standards and Assessment Guide for School Physical Education.* Reston, VA: NASPE Publications.

National Association for Sport and Physical Education. 1998. *Physical Activity for Children: A Statement of Guidelines.* Reston, VA: NASPE Publications.

Nevitt, M., I. Rovegno, and M. Babiarz. 2001. "Fourth Grade Children's Knowledge of Cutting, Passing and Tactics in Invasion Games after a 12-Lesson Unit of Instruction." *Journal of Teaching in Physical Education* Vol. 20: 389-401.

Nevitt, M., I. Rovegno, M. Babiarz, and N. McCauhtry. 2001. "Changes in Basic Tactics and Motor Skills in an Invasion-type Game after a 12-Lesson Unit of Instruction." *Journal of Teaching in Physical Education* Vol. 20: 352-369.

Oslin, J.L., S. Stroot, and D. Siedentop. 1997. "Use of Component-specific Instruction to Promote Development of the Over-arm Throw." *Journal of Teaching in Physical Education* Vol. 16: 340-356.

Papaioannou, A. 1998. "Students' Perceptions of the Physical Education Class Environment for Boys and Girls and the Perceived Motivational Climate." *Research Quarterly for Exercise and Sport* Vol. 69: 267-275.

Pate, R.R., M.L. Small, J.G. Ross, J.C. Young, K.H. Flint, and C.W. Warren. 1995. "School Physical Education." *Journal of School Health* Vol. 65: 312-318.

Perron, J. and P.J. Downey. 1997. "Management Techniques Used by High School Physical Education Teachers." *Journal of Teaching in Physical Education* Vol. 17: 72-84.

Placek, J.H. 1996. "Integration as a Curriculum Model in Physical Education: Possibilities and Problems." In *Student Learning in Physical Education: Applying Research to Enhance Instruction,* S.J. Silverman and C.D. Ennis, editors (pp. 287-311). Champaign, IL: Human Kinetics.

Placek, J.H., L.L. Griffin, P. Dodds, C. Raymond, F. Tremino, and A. James. 2001. "Middle School Students' Conceptions of Fitness: The Long Road to a Healthy Lifestyle." *Journal of Teaching in Physical Education* Vol. 20: 314-323.

Prusak, K.A. and P.W. Darst. 2002. "Effects of Type of Walking Activities on Actual Choices by Adolescent Female Physical Education Students." *Journal of Teaching in Physical Education* Vol. 21: 230-241.

Rink, J. 1994. "Task Presentation in Pedagogy." *Quest* Vol. 46: 270-280.

Rink, J.E. 1996a. "Effective Instruction in Physical Education." In *Student Learning in Physical Education: Applying Research to Enhance Instruction,* S. J. Silverman and C.D. Ennis, editors (pp. 171-198). Champaign, IL: Human Kinetics.

Rink, J.E. 1996b. "Tactical and Skill Approaches to Teaching Sport and Games: Introduction." Monograph. *Journal of Teaching in Physical Education* Vol. 15: 395-396.

Rink, J.E. 2001. *Teaching Physical Education for Learning.* St. Louis, MO: Times/Mirror Mosby.

Rink, J.E., K. French, P. Werner, S. Lynn, and A. Mays. 1992. "The Influence of Content Development on the Effectiveness of Instruction." *Journal of Teaching in Physical Education* Vol. 11: 139-149.

Rovegno, I., M. Nevitt, and M. Babiarz. 2001. "Learning and Teaching Invasion Game Tactics in Fourth Grade: Introduction and Theoretical Perspective." *Journal of Teaching in Physical Education* Vol. 20: 341-351.

Sallis, J.F., T.F. McKenzie, J.E. Alcaraz, B. Kolody, N. Faucette, and M.F. Hovell. 1997. "The Effects of a 2-year Physical Education Program (SPARK) on Physical Activity and Fitness in Elementary School Students." *American Journal of Public Health* Vol. 87: 1328-1334.

Sallis, J.F., K. Patrick, and B.L. Long. 1994. "An Overview of International Consensus Conference on Physical Activity Guidelines for Adolescents." *Pediatric Exercise Science* Vol. 6: 299-301.

Satina, B., M.A. Solmon, D.J. Cothran, S.J. Loftus, and K. Stockin-Davidson. 1998. "Patriarchal Consciousness: Middle School Students and Teachers' Perceptions of Motivational Practices." *Sport, Education, and Society* Vol. 3: 181-200.

Siedentop, D. 1996. "Physical Education and Educational Reform: The Case of Sport Education." In *Student Learning in Physical Education: Applying Research to Enhance Instruction,* S. J. Silverman and C.D. Ennis, editors (pp. 247-268). Champaign, IL: Human Kinetics.

Silverman, S. 1990. "Linear and Curvilinear Relationships between Student Practice and Achievement in Physical Education." *Teaching and Teacher Education* Vol. 6: 305-314.

Silverman, S. 1991. "The Validity of Academic Learning Time—Physical Education (ALT-PE) as a Process Measure of Student Achievement." *Research Quarterly for Exercise and Sport* Vol. 62: 319-325.

Silverman, S. 1993. "Student Characteristics, Practice and Achievement in Physical Education." *Journal of Educational Research* Vol. 87: 54-61.

Silverman, S. 1994. "Communication and Motor Skill Learning: What We Learn from Research in the Gymnasium." *Quest* Vol. 46: 345-355.

Silverman, S., P. Kulinna, and G. Crull. 1995. "Skill Related Task Structures Explicitness and Accountability: Relationships with Student Achievement." *Research Quarterly for Exercise and Sport* Vol. 66: 32-41.

Silverman, S., P.R. Subramaniam, and A.M. Woods. 1998. "Task Structures, Student Practice and Student Skill Level in Physical Education." *Journal of Educational Research* Vol. 91: 298-306.

Silverman, S., N. Tsangaridou, and M. O'Sullivan. 2003. "Physical Education Teachers' Theories of Action and Theories-in-use." *Journal of Teaching in Physical Education* Vol. 22: 132-152.

Silverman, S., L.A. Tyson, and L.M. Morford. 1988. "Relationships of Organization, Time, and Student Achievement in Physical Education." *Teaching and Teacher Education* Vol. 4: 247-257.

Silverman, S., A.M. Woods, and P.R. Subramaniam. 1998. "Task Structures, Feedback to Individual Students and Student Skill Level in Physical Education." *Research Quarterly for Exercise and Sport* Vol. 69: 420-424.

Solmon, M.A. 1996. "Impact of Motivational Climate on Students' Behaviors and Perceptions in a Physical Education Setting." *Journal of Educational Psychology* Vol. 88: 731-738.

Solmon, M.A. and J. Boone. 1993. "The Impact of Student Goal Orientation in Physical Education Classes." *Research Quarterly for Exercise and Sport* Vol. 64: 418-424.

Solmon, M.A. and A. Lee. 1996. "Entry Characteristics, Practice Variables, and Cognition: Student Mediation of Instruction." *Journal of Teaching in Physical Education* Vol. 15: 136-150.

Solmon, M.A. and A. Lee. 1997. "Development of an Instrument to Assess Cognitive Processes in Physical Education Classes." *Research Quarterly for Exercise and Sport* Vol. 68: 152-160.

Stone, E.J., T.L. McKenzie, G.J. Welk, and M.L. Booth. 1998. "Effects of Physical Activity Interventions in Youth: Review and Synthesis." *American Journal of Preventive Medicine* Vol. 15: 298-315.

Taylor, W.C., T. Baranowski, and D.R. Young. 1998. "Physical Activity Interventions in Low-income, Ethnic Minority, and Populations with Disability." *American Journal of Preventive Medicine* Vol. 15: 334-344.

Treasure, D.C., and G.C. Roberts. 1995. "Applications of Achievement Goal Theory to Physical Education: Implications for Enhancing Motivation." *Quest* Vol. 47: 475-489.

U.S. Department of Health and Human Services. 1992. *Healthy People 2000: National Health Promotion and Disease Prevention Objectives.* Washington, DC: Author.

U.S. Department of Health and Human Services. 1996. *Physical Activity and Health: A Report of the Surgeon General.* Atlanta, GA: U.S. Department of Health and Human Services, Centers for Disease Control and Prevention, National Center for Chronic Disease Prevention and Health Promotion.

van der Mars, H., B. Vogler, P. Darst, and B. Cusimano. 1998. "Students' Physical Activity Levels and Teachers' Active Supervision During Fitness Instruction." *Journal of Teaching in Physical Education* Vol. 18: 57-75.

Ward, P., S. Smith, K. Makasci, and D.W. Crouch. 1998. "Differential Effects of Peer-Mediated Accountability on Task Accomplishments in Elementary Physical Education." *Journal of Teaching in Physical Education* Vol. 17: 442-452.

Xiang, P. and A. Lee. 1998. "The Development of Self-perceptions of Ability and Achievement Goals and their Relations in Physical Education." *Research Quarterly for Exercise and Sport* Vol. 69: 231-241.

Chapter 9. Science

Dorothy Gabel

The science education research literature of the past decade confirms the findings of studies reported in the first edition of this *Handbook*. Hence, the recommendations for teaching remain unchanged. At the present time, studies are more likely to be qualitative rather than quantitative, control-group comparisons. This has resulted in more limited generalizability.

As might be expected, there has been an increase in the number of studies related to the use of technology in the classroom. Another area of instruction (and associated research studies) beginning to expand is "problem-based learning." This might be considered to be a hybrid of students working on real-life situations (Practice 9.11) and collaborative learning (Practice 9.2), both of which are included in the *Handbook*. In problem-based learning, students solve real-world problems that have relevance for them, usually in a collaborative group setting. Very few studies have been reported at the present time, and frequently there are so many variables within a given study that it is difficult to ascertain which variables are essential to produce positive outcomes.

The science education research literature of the last 20 years is replete with studies indicating students at all levels possess many inaccurate scientific conceptions. Although this may be due in part to the rapid growth of scientific knowledge, it may also have been caused by the textbooks used by students.

In the first edition of the *Handbook*, it was reported that analyses of textbooks indicated they contained many more concepts than they had in the past, with fewer pages devoted to explaining or describing each particular concept. In addition, the science curriculum had shifted down, so that rather complex topics that 20 years ago were thought too difficult for students at particular grade levels were being taught at those levels. Today, however, the recent publication of the *National Science Education Standards* appears to be influencing the content of many textbooks. Alternative textbooks have recently appeared in the marketplace that endorse the recommendation of the *Standards* to cover less content but in greater depth and to use a more inquiry-based orientation to learning.

Whether this change of content coverage will actually take place is yet to be seen. Teachers may still feel compelled to teach as they have in the past because of state and international assessments. Hence the result may be the same. Students have little time to think about what they are learning, rarely see individual concepts taught in a multitude of contexts, do not see the relevance of what they are learning, frequently have negative attitudes toward science, and resort to memorizing facts and solving problems algorithmically in order to survive.

The teaching strategies and practices research has shown to be effective in improving achievement in the teaching and learning of science all have one thing in common: they keep students' attention focused on learning. Whether this is done by pausing after asking a question before calling on a student to answer the question (wait-time), by involving students in decision making (computer simulations), or by having students make comparisons with familiar situations (using analogies), all of these strategies require active learning. Many involve creating situations that challenge students' assumptions by having them make observations that are in conflict with their beliefs (cognitive conflict), and then resolving the conflict. It is only when instruction involves or at least begins with topics of interest to students, and is related to their world, that students will learn in more authentic ways. That is, they will see the relationship between what they are learning and what they already know; they will *think* instead of memorize.

Although several of the strategies included in this review can be used by teachers and students on an individual basis, there is a growing body of evidence that learning is a social endeavor, and strategies that include interactions between students (collaborative learning) are more effective than activities in which students work alone. This appears to be true even when students work at a computer using probeware or computer simulations. Interactions among students help them clarify their own ideas and those of their peers.

All of the teaching strategies (with the exception of using computer simulations) also require additional time to implement in the classroom. This increase of instructional time per concept will require educators to carefully consider which of many important concepts should be taught at particular grade levels and which should be delayed or even omitted from the curriculum. One way this can be accomplished is to integrate science instruction across the disciplines as suggested by the American Association for the Advancement of Science's recommendations in *Benchmarks for Science Literacy, Project 2061*. As indicated earlier, a reduction of the science content included at the pre-college level has also been recommended by the National Research Council in the *National Science Education Standards*.

The author wishes to thank the following individuals for their valuable assistance in reviewing this section: Dr. Michael R. Abraham, professor of chemistry, University of Oklahoma, Norman, Okla.; Dr. Diane M. Bunce, professor of chemistry, Catholic University of America, Washington, D.C.; Dr. Anita Roychoudhury, professor of education, Miami University, Hamilton, Ohio; Dr. Robert D. Sherwood, professor of education, Vanderbilt University, Nashville, Tenn.; Dr. David F. Treagust, professor of education, Curtin University of Technology, Perth, Australia; and Dr. Robert E. Yager, professor of education, University of Iowa, Iowa City.

9.1. **Learning Cycle Approach:** The use of the learning cycle approach (exploration, invention, and application) results in better content achievement, improved thinking skills, and more positive attitudes toward science.

Research findings:

Numerous studies beginning in the 1960s and continuing today indicate the learning cycle approach is effective in promoting conceptual understanding as well as positive attitudes toward science and process skill acquisition for students at the elementary, middle school, and high school levels. Positive outcomes occur when laboratory experiences (exploration and application) are combined with concept introduction (invention). However, research on the effectiveness of laboratory instruction by itself, without concept introduction, does not support its effectiveness in improving student achievement in science.

In the classroom:

The learning cycle approach, as originally envisioned in the early 1960s for the teaching of elementary science, included three phases: exploration, invention, and discovery. During the exploration phase, students explore new materials and ideas with minimum guidance. This helps students to raise questions about the phenomena being explored that cannot be resolved by their accustomed way of thinking and to identify patterns of regularity in the phenomena. The invention phase is more teacher centered. Terms and concepts are introduced to explain the patterns discovered in the exploration phase. In the application phase, students apply the terms and concepts to new situations, thus helping them generalize in a broader context.

The learning cycle approach has been incorporated into a variety of science curricula and programs, particularly at the elementary level. These include *Science Curriculum Improvement Study* (SCIS) and *Biological Sciences Curriculum Study* (BSCS). Recent studies have shown using the learning cycle approach is an effective way to determine and correct students' misconceptions, and it can aid in improving young students' reasoning abilities. Studies indicate all three phases are necessary, although in some instances an in-depth laboratory experience may substitute for some phases.

Current research indicates modifications of the learning cycle can make it an even more effective instructional strategy. Helping students to focus their exploration by adding an engagement or prediction/discussion phase and following the application phase with evaluation appear to promote conceptual understanding. A monograph by Lawson, Abraham, and Renner (1989) provides a rich description of the use and possible modifications of the learning cycle approach.

Sources:

Abraham 1989; Bybee and Landes 1990; Campbell 1977; Carlson 1975; Davis 1977; Davison 1989; Glassen and Lalik 1993; Good and Lavoie 1986; Jackman, Moellenberg, and Brabson 1990; Lavoie 1989; Lawson, 1988, 1995; Lawson, Abraham, and Renner 1989; Lawson and Weser 1990; Lawson and Wollman 1976; Marek and Methven 1991; McKinnon and Renner 1971; Purser and Renner 1983; Renner, Abraham, and Birnie 1985; Renner and Marek 1988; Rubin and Norman 1989, 1992; Scharmann 1992; Schneider and Renner 1980; Ward and Herron 1980; Westbrook and Rogers 1994.

9.2. Collaborative Learning: Using collaborative learning for classroom and laboratory instruction increases student achievement, attitudes, and on-task behavior.

Research findings:

Collaborative learning refers to situations where students work with others in a group setting to learn concepts and skills. Two specific types of collaborative learning (the jigsaw approach and a laboratory, investigative approach) are described below. A considerable number of research studies on the effectiveness of collaborative learning indicate its usefulness for the teaching of science. Although studies in the early 1980s focused on the elementary school level, studies from the mid-1980s show middle school and high school science students also profit from the use of these collaborative learning approaches.

In the classroom:

The use of collaborative learning for the teaching of science has improved science achievement at all grade levels. In the classroom, cooperative groups of about four students frequently use the jigsaw approach, in which each student in a given group takes a particular role or part of a larger task. Students with the same role from each of the other jigsaw groups in the class form a new group in which each member investigates/learns his or her part of the topic. After members of this group have shared ideas and learned the material or performed the task, they return to their original group, where they are responsible for sharing what they have learned and teaching students in that original group the new information.

In most investigative cooperative groups used for laboratory instruction, each member of the group of four takes on a different role, such as recorder, checker, facilitator, or experimenter. Roles rotate with each lab investigation. In almost all studies of effective collaborative learning, there is positive interdependence, face-to-face interaction, individual accountability, interpersonal and small-group interactions, and group processing.

Some of the potential benefits of cooperative learning are increased achievement scores including long-term retention, more positive attitudes toward laboratory work, higher self-esteem, higher laboratory and process skill achievement, and greater on-task behavior. One area where collaborative learning has not been shown to be successful at the secondary level is increasing students' ability to solve problems. The most effective form of cooperative learning appears to occur when students are encouraged to cooperate within their group but to compete with other groups within the class.

More recent collaborative learning studies have included groups of various sizes such as pairs or triads working together, and studies in which no specific roles were assigned to students. Findings indicate the peer interactions enhance science concept development. When roles are not assigned, students assume roles based on their expertise, and this enhances both problem-solving ability and concept development.

Sources:

Bianchini 1997; Hay 1980; Humphreys, Johnson, and Johnson 1982; Johnson and Johnson 1985a, 1985b; Jones and Steinbrink 1989, 1991; Kempa and Ayob 1991; Keys 1996; Lazarowitz 1991; Lazarowitz and Hertz-Lazarowitz 1998; Lazarowitz, Hertz-Lazarowitz, and Baird 1994; Lazarowitz et al. 1985; Lazarowitz et al. 1988; Lazarowitz and Karsenty 1990; Lonning 1993; Lumpe and Staver 1995; Okebukola 1985a, 1985b, 1986a, 1986b, 1986c; Okebukola and Ogunniyi 1984; Richmond and Striley 1996; Rogg and Kahle 1992; Sherman 1989; Slavin 1980, 1984, 1991; Tingle and Good 1990; Walters 1988; Watson 1991; Webb 1985.

9.3. Analogies: Using analogies in the teaching of science results in the development of conceptual understanding by enabling the learner to compare something familiar with something unfamiliar.

Research findings:

Some research studies prior to the 1980s have been conducted on the use of analogies, but a new interest in this area has produced several in-depth studies indicating that using analogies assists in concept development. This is particularly true when students have alternative conceptions about a particular concept. Research in this area tends to be qualitative in nature, and the conceptual change that occurs may not result in higher scores on multiple-choice science tests of facts and concepts.

In the classroom:

Textbooks and teachers sometimes use analogies to help familiarize students with concepts that are abstract and outside their previous experience. To be effective, analogies must be familiar to students, and their features/functions must be congruent with those of the target. Because adult perspectives are not identical with those of adolescents, it is not surprising that, even though students are familiar with the physical phenomena or event that might be used as the analogy, they are not always familiar with those features that provide the similarity to the target. Once a suitable analogy is found, considerable time must be spent by students in discussion of similarities between the analogy and the target.

It is also important for students to understand how the analogy and target differ. Sometimes this can be done by using multiple analogies to teach the same concept. Studies of chemistry and biology instruction show that some students, who are exposed to and who become skilled in the use of multiple analogies, develop a more scientific understanding of particular science concepts than do students who concentrate on one acceptable analogy. Use of multiple analogies in a bridging sequence has been successful in helping students make sense of initially counterintuitive ideas.

Analogies occurring in texts may be simple—based on surface similarities—or more complex (particularly in chemistry and physics)—based on similarities of function. The use of functional analogies appears to be more appropriate at the secondary level, where students have developed appropriate reasoning strategies.

The discussion that occurs when using analogies not only helps students construct their own knowledge but also assists teachers in basing instruction on students' prior knowledge and existing alternative conceptions. Analogies may also motivate students to learn by provoking their interest. Finally, having students create their own analogies also appears to be an effective instructional strategy.

Sources:

Brown 1992; Clement 1993; Dagher 1994; Dagher and Cossman 1992; Duit 1991b; Dupin and Joshua 1989; Flick 1991; Friedel, Gabel, and Samuel 1990; Gabel and Samuel 1986; Garnett and Treagust 1992; Glynn 1991; Griffiths and Preston 1992; Harrison and Treagust 1993; Lawson 1993; Stavy 1991; Stavy and Tirosh 1993; Sutula and Krajcik 1988; Thagard 1992; Thiele and Treagust 1994; Treagust et al. 1992; Venville and Treagust 1997; Wong 1993a, 1993b; Zeitoun 1984.

9.4. Wait Time: Pausing after asking a question in the classroom results in an increase in achievement.

Research findings:

In most classrooms, students are typically given less than one second to respond to a question posed by a teacher. Research shows under these conditions students generally give short, recall responses or no answer at all rather than giving answers involving higher-level thinking. Studies beginning in the early 1970s and continuing through the 1980s show if teachers pause between three and seven seconds after asking higher-level questions, students respond with more thoughtful answers and science achievement is increased. This finding is consistent at the elementary, middle school, and high school levels and across the science disciplines.

Some research studies have suggested, however, that the benefits of increasing wait time may depend on factors such as student expectations and the cognitive level of the questions. In a study of increased wait time in a high school physics class, students became more apathetic in classes where the wait time was increased. This might have occurred because this strategy did not match students' expectations of how a high school physics course should be conducted. In a study at the elementary level, a decrease in achievement was attributed to waiting *too* long for responses to low-level questions.

In the classroom:

Increasing the wait time from three to seven seconds results in an increase in: 1) the length of student responses; 2) the number of unsolicited responses; 3) the frequency of student questions; 4) the number of responses from less capable children; 5) student-student interactions; and 6) the incidence of speculative responses. In addition to pausing after asking questions, research shows many of these same benefits result when teachers pause after the student's response to a question and when teachers do not affirm answers immediately.

Increasing wait time also increases science achievement and students' participation in inquiry. Research indicates when teachers increase their wait time to more than three seconds in class discussions, achievement on higher-cognitive-level science test items increases significantly. This holds for test items involving content, the process skills, and items involving probabilistic reasoning.

However, care must be taken in applying wait time judiciously. The optimal wait time for a given question should be adjusted to the cognitive level of the question, and student responses should be carefully monitored.

Sources:

Altiere and Duell 1991; Anderson 1978; Fowler 1975; Garigliano 1972; Jegede and Olajide 1995; Lake 1973; Mansfield 1996; Riley 1986; Rowe 1974a, 1974b, 1986; Samiroden 1983; Tobin 1985, 1986, 1987; Tobin and Capie 1982.

9.5. Concept Mapping: The use of student-generated and teacher-generated concept maps for teaching science concepts results in improved student achievement and more positive student attitudes.

Research findings:

More than 150 studies on concept mapping have been reported since the late 1970s. A careful meta-analysis conducted by Horton et al. (1993) of 19 studies that qualified out of 133 reported by 1990 indicates positive effects on student achievement and attitudes. (The analysis included only studies that occurred in actual classrooms using control groups and in which sufficient quantitative data were reported.) One hundred references related to concept mapping were reported by Al-Kunifed and Wandersee (1990). More recently, the usefulness of concept maps as an assessment technique for evaluating changes in student understanding of science concepts and the connections among them has been reported.

In the classroom:

A concept map is a schematic diagram or semantic network that includes concepts arranged in a hierarchical order linked by words forming propositions. Teachers or students can make concept maps either individually or in a group. They are used in a variety of situations, such as in an overview at the beginning of a unit, during instruction to assess conceptual understanding, and at the end of a unit to review for a test or evaluate learning.

Concept mapping in the science classroom, particularly for biology instruction, improves science achievement and attitudes. The use of concept maps appears to be more beneficial at the end of a unit than at the beginning. Although there appears to be no difference in student achievement whether the maps are constructed by the teacher or by the students, there are greater gains in achievement when students supply the key terms to construct the maps.

If concept maps are used as an assessment tool to measure students' conceptual understanding, several different approaches can be used. Care must be taken to ensure accuracy and consistency, as recommended by Ruiz-Primo and Shavelson (1996).

In addition to their direct use in classroom instruction, concept maps also have other educational benefits for students. They can help teachers become more effective by assessing students' conceptual understanding before instruction and can be used as a heuristic in curriculum development.

Sources:

Al-Kunifed and Wandersee 1990; Beyerbach and Smith 1990; Fisher 1990; Fleer 1996; Horton et al. 1993; Hoz, Tomer, and Tamir 1990; Novak and Gowin 1984; Novak and Musonda 1991; Odom and Kelly 1998; Pankratius 1990; Roth 1994; Roth and Roychoudhury 1992; Ruiz-Primo and Shavelson 1996; Shymansky et al. 1997; Starr and Krajcik 1990; Wallace and Mintzes 1990; White and Gunstone 1992; Willerman and Mac Harg 1991; Wilson 1994.

9.6. Computer Simulations: Using computer simulations to represent real-world situations enables students to become more reflective problem-solvers and to increase their conceptual understanding.

Research findings:

Data from a survey of secondary science departments in the fall of 1992 indicate 49 percent of those surveyed used computers in teaching science at least occasionally. Although the most common use of computers was for simulations, only 18 percent of the schools surveyed indicated computers were used once or twice per week.

While more research studies need to be undertaken on the use of simulations in science instruction at the middle and secondary levels, many of the studies currently reported show evidence that students' conceptual understanding can be improved by the use of simulation software.

In the classroom:

Many scientific models are difficult or impossible to observe, or are so complex they are difficult to study in the laboratory. In chemistry, for example, students cannot observe the motion of atoms in solids, liquids, and gases because of their size. In physics, the study of velocity and acceleration becomes difficult in the laboratory because the observer has to account for friction. In biology, studies of genetics might have to extend over a prolonged time period.

Computer simulations can overcome these obstacles by simplifying complex systems and then incorporating the various complexities to show their effect on the system. Use of simulations tends to result in increased achievement on complex and difficult concepts in less time than conventional instruction. Simulations (sometimes referred to as microworlds) can be used by instructors in classroom settings; however, the most effective use is by students either alone or in small groups. This permits students' guided exploration of the variations of the system, leads to better conceptual understanding and achievement, and appears to increase students' problem-solving and process skills. Recent microworld software allows students to "build" their own models of situations and then test them in a simulated environment.

As with analogies, the use of simulations may create misconceptions, and so requires careful attention to the understandings (or misunderstandings) produced. They should not be used exclusively in place of laboratory activities, and teachers must take care to help students identify the limitations of the simulated models.

Sources:

Berge 1990; Berger 1982, 1984; Choi and Gennaro 1987; diSessa 1988; Faryniarz and Lockwood 1992; Geban, Askar, and Ozkan 1992; Hakerem, Dobrynina, and Shore 1993; Jungck and Calley 1986; Kinnear 1983; Krajcik 1989; Lehman 1994; Linn 1988; Njoo and de Jong 1993; Rivers and Vockell 1987; Schecker 1998; Simmons 1989; Soloway et al. 1997; Spitulnik et al. 1998; Wells and Berger 1986; White 1984, 1993, 1998; White and Frederiksen 1989; White, Frederiksen, and Spoehr 1993; White and Horowitz 1987, 1988; Williamson and Abraham 1995; Wiser and Kipman 1988; Zeitsman and Hewson 1986.

9.7. Microcomputer-Based Laboratories: Using computers to collect and display data from science experiments enables students at the secondary level to understand science concepts and learn to use science process skills.

Research findings:

Although the research in this area remains somewhat limited, several studies indicate the value of students' participation in microcomputer-based laboratories (MBLs); these outweigh other studies showing no improvement over traditional laboratory approaches. The use of MBLs in conjunction with dynamic model-building systems (MBS) in the science classroom shows promise in fostering scientific understanding. Unfortunately, the use of this technology is not widely used in science courses at the current time.

In the classroom:

In a microcomputer-based laboratory (MBL) experiment, students use electronic probes interfaced with a microcomputer that directly records and graphs data being collected. This enables students to immediately see the trends in the data as they are being collected and to focus on the meaning of the experiment rather than on completing a data table or making a graph. This may enable students to question their prior beliefs and to ask new questions related to the experiment. Use of the MBL probes extends experimental possibilities beyond standard laboratory apparatus and enables students to investigate phenomena previously not accessible. The effectiveness of using these scientific probes depends greatly on the instructional sequence in which they are used.

The computer software that processes the data (MBS) allows students to modify settings and design their own experiments. Hence, the use of MBLs in conjunction with the MBS provides opportunities for students to perform "mental experiments." In addition, they permit students to perform mathematical operations that are inordinately time-consuming and sometimes beyond the mathematical competence of the user.

In comparisons with traditional instruction, MBL use frequently results in a different set of outcomes. For example, students using MBLs are better able to interpret graphs, whereas students with conventional laboratory experiences are better able to construct graphs. Because both are important instructional outcomes, MBLs should be interspersed with conventional laboratory experiences, rather than used exclusively.

Sources:

Adams and Shrum 1990; Beichner 1990; Berger 1987; Brasell 1987; Friedler, Nachmias, and Linn 1990; Grayson and McDermott 1989; Jackson, Edwards, and Berger 1993; Krajcik and Layman 1989; Lewis and Linn 1989; Linn 1998; Linn and Songer 1988; Mokros and Tinker 1987; Nakhleh and Krajcik 1994; Schecker 1998; Thornton 1987; Tinker 1985; Wise 1988; Wiser and Kipman 1988.

9.8. Systematic Approaches in Problem Solving: Planning the solutions to mathematical chemistry and physics problems in a systematic way enables students to more frequently solve the problems correctly.

Research findings:

Most of the studies on mathematical problem solving in the sciences have examined processes students use to solve chemistry and physics problems. Mathematical problem solving in biology focuses on genetics, and research on using a systematic approach in solving these types of problems is lacking. Polya (1945) in the 1940s suggested the four-step approach described below, which researchers have modified over the years.

In the classroom:

Expert problem-solvers take a considerable length of time in planning and analyzing a given problem before using mathematics for its solution. Novice problem-solvers appear to use cues in the problem to search their memory for a formula or algorithm they can use to solve the problem. Unfortunately, if superfluous information is given in a problem, this frequently causes them to use an incorrect formula.

Even though it is recognized that students use different types of strategies in solving problems, novice problem-solvers can improve their problem-solving skills if they do so in an organized way. Such a systematic approach includes: 1) understanding the problem; 2) devising a plan; 3) carrying out the plan; and 4) looking back. In order to understand the problem, students must identify what information is given in the problem and what is sought. Sometimes drawing a picture (such as a force diagram in physics or a picture of what is happening on the molecular level in chemistry) aids in understanding the problem. Using this information, students then formulate plans for the problem solution. Helping students categorize problems into specific types enhances the planning stage. The final step, looking back, involves checking the mathematics used, the execution of the plan, and the reasonableness of the answer.

These steps are not necessarily sequential in nature. For example, during the planning stage it may be necessary to revert to the understanding phase to recall additional information needed or eliminate superfluous information. The steps do not come naturally to students and need to be illustrated and practiced when students are taught to solve problems. In addition, because using a systematic approach requires more time than simply using a formula, care must be taken to assign fewer, but more varied, problems for practice and to allow more time for problem solving on tests.

Sources:

Bhaskar and Simon 1977; Bunce et al. 1990; Bunce, Gabel, and Samuel 1991; Bunce and Heikkinen 1986; Cameron 1985; Chi, Feltovich, and Glaser 1981; de Jong and Ferguson-Hessler 1986; Frank and Herron 1987; Hegarty 1991; Heller and Hollabaugh 1992; Heller, Keith, and Anderson 1992; Heller and Reif 1984; Kramers-Pals, Lambrechts, and Wolff 1982; Larkin 1980; Lesgold and Lajoie 1991; Mettes et al. 1980; Niaz, 1996; Polya 1945; Reif 1983; Reif and Heller 1982; Schoenfeld 1978; Stiff 1988; Van Heuvelen 1991; Wright and Williams 1986.

9.9. Conceptual Understanding in Problem Solving: Understanding concepts qualitatively enables students to solve quantitative problems in biology, physics, and chemistry more effectively.

Research findings:

Research at the secondary and even postsecondary level on understanding of basic concepts involved in solving biology, chemistry, and physics problems indicates students do not understand the concepts. This is confirmed by many research studies on problem solving in which students solve problems aloud. Research shows even though students frequently solve mathematical problems correctly, they are unable to answer conceptual questions on which the problems are based.

Although there is a limited amount of research to indicate understanding basic concepts qualitatively improves mathematical problem solving, it appears this would be the case, especially for solving higher-level problems. Problem-solving research has led to the identification of commonly held scientific misconceptions and to the conclusion that addressing these misconceptions in instruction may help to improve students' problem-solving ability.

In the classroom:

Many secondary students use algorithms to solve biology, chemistry, and physics problems requiring the use of mathematics. They substitute data given in a problem into a formula (use the factor-label method or a Punnett Square), perform appropriate mathematical operations, and arrive at a correct solution. However, when asked about the meaning of what they have done or requested to describe the variables and the relationship among the variables involved, they are unable to do so.

There is some evidence that having students perform numerous problems in this manner does not necessarily lead to conceptual understanding. If conceptual understanding is an expected outcome of science instruction, a more reasonable approach would be to first emphasize a qualitative understanding of the underlying concepts, including clarification of related student misconceptions. Then the use of mathematical problem solving should help provide students with deeper insight into the concepts.

For example, many students can calculate the density of a solid, yet when shown samples of identical mass but different volumes, they are unable to serial order the samples by density. It is unlikely that having students solve numerous density problems by substituting values into the density formula will help them distinguish between density and volume.

Sources:

Anamuah-Mensah 1986; Bhaskar and Simon 1977; Bunce, Gabel, and Samuel 1991; Cavallo 1996; Chi, Feltovich, and Glaser 1981; de Jong and Ferguson-Hessler 1986; Finegold and Mass 1985; Friedel and Maloney 1995; Gabel 1981; Gabel and Bunce 1994; Gabel, Sherwood, and Enochs 1984; Gorodetsky and Hoz 1980; Griffiths, Pottle, and Whelan 1983; Hegarty 1991; Heller, Keith, and Anderson 1992; Herron and Greenbowe 1986; Hobden 1998; Larkin 1980, 1983; Larkin et al. 1980; Lythcott 1990; Maloney 1994; Mason, Shell, and Crawley 1997; McMillan and Swadener 1991; Niaz and Robinson 1989; Reif and Heller 1982; Robertson 1990; Sawrey 1990; Schmidt 1990, 1997; Stewart and Hafner 1994; Sumfleth 1988; Sweller 1988; Ward and Sweller 1990.

9.10. Science-Technology-Society: Using a Science-Technology-Society approach in the teaching of science results in an increase in the number of students taking additional science courses and advanced-level courses, as well as changing students' attitudes toward science and their understanding of the nature of science and its relationship to technology and societal issues.

Research findings:

Studies in this area have become much more numerous in the past few years. Although most comparative studies have been performed by one major researcher and his graduate students for children in grades four through nine, the National Research Council's *National Science Education Standards* endorse the inclusion of science, technology, and society (STS) issues in the curriculum at all grade levels. Furthermore, AAAS's *Project 2061* is a national effort illustrating the use of the STS approach in the United States, and curriculum developers in Canada and the United Kingdom include this approach in widely used national curriculum projects at the secondary level. In the United States, new curricula have been developed by the American Chemistry Society in chemistry at the middle school and high school levels.

There is little evidence that STS increases students' knowledge of facts, concepts, or principles, but also no evidence that it decreases it. When STS is integrated into the curriculum as a major thrust (not as vignettes), positive outcomes occur. These include an increase in understanding the processes of science, such as analyzing experimental data, designing and testing the validity of proposed explanations, offering more possible explanations, communicating experimental results, and using them for evidence for their explanations. Students' creativity and attitude toward science improve as well. An additional benefit in Canada was improving students' understanding science as a way of knowing. In the United Kingdom, STS was found to dramatically increase the number of students taking additional science courses.

In the classroom:

Educators should consider using Science-Technology-Society approaches as a way to make science more relevant to students' lives. Although STS issues can be included as vignettes as a small part of the curriculum, recent studies have shown a more effective approach is to use STS as an entire course that has as its objectives the development of an appreciation of the interactive nature of science, technology, and society; knowledge of technology as applications of science; the ability to respond critically to technology issues; or a combination of these later goals with teaching science concepts and principles.

Sources:

Aikenhead and Ryan 1992; American Association for the Advancement of Science 1993; Barker 1993a, 1993b; Ben-Zvi and Gai 1994; Bybee 1987; Campbell et al. 1994; Hart and Robottom 1990; McFadden 1991; Myers 1988; National Research Council 1994; National Science Teachers Association 1982, 1991; Ramsden 1992, 1994; Rosenthal 1989; Rubba, McGuyer, and Wahlund 1991; Sutman and Bruce 1992; Waks and Barchi 1992; Winther and Volk 1994; Yager 1996; Yager and Tamir 1993; Yager, Tamir, and Mackinnu 1993; Yager and Yager 1985; Zoller et al. 1990.

9.11. Real-Life Situations: Using real-life situations in science instruction through the use of technology (films, videotapes, videodiscs, CD-ROMs) or actual observation increases student interest in science, problem-solving skills, and achievement.

Research findings:

Research support for the use of real-life situations (or simulations of these) in classroom instruction continues to increase as the technologies for bringing real-life situations into the classroom become more available to teachers. The leading research group in the United States using anchored instruction to increase students' problem-solving skills is located at Vanderbilt University. Others working in this area include groups led by Linn (1998), Edelson (1998), and Songer (1998).

In the classroom:

Students frequently compartmentalize learning. For example, many students who have studied mathematics are unable to apply it in solving problems in chemistry and physics. Many fail to associate the variable "x" used extensively in algebra problems to letters standing for variable names in physics problems. Even within the science course itself, many students fail to recognize the topics they are studying apply to real-life situations. One reason proposed for this lack of transfer is that problem solving and learning have not taken place in real-world contexts. The use of videotapes, videodiscs and CD-ROMs depicting real-life situations or simulations of these (either alone or in tandem with computers) makes it much more feasible to teach using real-world situations.

Videodiscs using simulations of real-world problem-solving situations, developed to improve students' mathematics and science problem-solving skills, have been used successfully by middle school students at several different sites. Although results indicate no difference in standardized test achievement, this finding was considered to be positive because time normally spent on conventional instruction was reduced to allow for the use of the problem-solving videodiscs, which did have a positive effect on students' problem-solving skills. The instruction surrounding the use of the videodiscs was very carefully structured by classroom teachers, and this appears to be an important factor in the use of technology in the classroom.

The use of interactive video is also proving to be an important instructional strategy. Guidance in using videodiscs and CD-ROMs is programmed and controlled by a computer that directs students' attention and frequently requires students to make decisions about their own learning. Effective programs, particularly at the secondary and college levels, show student achievement and attitudes improve with their use, and in some cases interactive videodiscs are an effective substitute for conventional laboratory experiences, such as dissections in biology.

Sources:

Bereiter and Scardamalia 1989; Bohren 1993; Brown 1992; Brown, Collins, and Duguid 1989; Cobb 1994; Cognition and Technology Group at Vanderbilt 1992, 1993; Dawson 1991; Edelson 1998; Hofmeister, Engelmann, and Carnine 1988; Kinzie, Strauss, and Foss 1993; Leonard 1992; Linn 1998; Lockhart, Lamon, and Gick 1988; Myers 1993; Savenye and Strand 1989; Sherwood et al. 1998; Smith and Jones 1988; Songer 1998.

9.12. Discrepant Events: Using discrepant events in science instruction results in cognitive conflict that enhances students' conceptual understanding and students' attitudes toward critical-thinking activities.

Research findings:

There is little direct research evidence that using discrepant events promotes conceptual understanding. However, two of the practices included in this chapter (Learning Cycle Approach and Real-Life Situations) are thought to be effective because they frequently include discrepant events. Discrepant events are one form of anomalous data that help students focus on their prior conceptions, a step thought to be necessary if students are to alter their conceptions so that they become closer to the accepted scientific view. During the exploration phase of the learning cycle, students may confront anomalous data, or such data may be included in instruction based on real-world situations. Chinn and Brewer (1993) provide the theoretical framework for using anomalous data in science instruction.

In the classroom:

Many science teachers use discrepant events frequently in their teaching, and this practice has been advocated by authors of methods texts over the years. An example of a discrepant event from physics instruction would be to drop a Styrofoam and a steel ball of equal volumes from the same height at the same time and note that both hit the floor at the same time. Because most students think that the heavier ball will hit first, the event is discrepant.

Although discrepant events frequently take the form of demonstrations, all demonstrations do not necessarily include discrepant events. Discrepant events can be built into hands-on activities students actually perform and can be included in computer simulations and on videodiscs.

Just because students view or experience something that is discrepant does not guarantee they will learn from the situation. Students may ignore or reject it. In order to maximize its effectiveness, the anomalous data must be credible and unambiguous. A recommended strategy for effective instruction includes the following steps: 1) consider a physical scenario of unknown outcome; 2) predict the outcome; 3) construct one or more theoretical explanations; 4) observe the outcome; 5) modify the theoretical explanation; 6) evaluate competing explanations; and 7) repeat the previous steps with another discrepant event illustrating the same theory or concept.

Steps one through five may be carried out in various ways. Research on the effective use of discrepant events suggests teachers not confirm or deny students' tentative explanations of the event but provide guidance and cues so that they can make explanations on their own. The social interaction from small-group and whole-group discussions, and from letting children interact with the materials, appears to facilitate conceptual understanding.

Sources:

Appleton 1995, 1996; Butts, Hoffman, and Anderson 1993; Chinn and Brewer 1993; Dreyfus, Jungwirth, and Eliocitch 1990; Duit 1991a; Lawson 1990; Linn and Songer 1991; Zielinski and Sarachine 1994.

Bibliography

Abraham, M.R. 1989. "Research and Teaching: Research on Instructional Strategies." *Journal of College Science Teaching* Vol. 18: 185-187.

Adams, D.D., and J.W. Shrum. 1990. "The Effects of Microcomputer-based Laboratory Exercises on the Acquisition of Line Graph Construction and Interpretation Skills by High School Biology Students." *Journal of Research in Science Teaching* Vol. 27: 777-787.

Aikenhead, G.S., and A.G. Ryan. 1992. "The Development of a New Instrument: Views on Science-Technology-Society." *Science Education* Vol. 76: 477-491.

Al-Kunifed, A., and J.H. Wandersee. 1990. "One Hundred References Relating to Concept Mapping." *Journal of Research in Science Teaching* Vol. 27: 1069-1075.

Altiere, M.A., and O.K. Duell. 1991. "Can Teachers Predict Their Students' Wait Time Preferences?" *Journal of Research in Science Teaching* Vol. 28: 455-461.

American Association for the Advancement of Science. 1993. *Benchmarks for Science Literacy, Project 2061.* New York: Oxford University Press.

Anamuah-Mensah, J. 1986. "Cognitive Strategies Used by Chemistry Students to Solve Volumetric Analysis Problems." *Journal of Research in Science Teaching* Vol. 23: 759-769.

Anderson, B.O. 1978. *The Effects of Long Wait-Time on High School Physics Pupils' Response Length, Classroom Attitudes and Achievement.* Doctoral dissertation, University of Minnesota. *Dissertation Abstracts International* Vol. 39: 3493A. (University Microfilms No. 78-23, 871)

Appleton, K. 1995. "Problem Solving in Science Lessons: How Students Explore the Problem Space." *Research in Science Education* Vol. 4: 383-393.

Appleton, K. April 1996. *Students' Responses during Discrepant Event Science Lessons.* Paper presented at the annual meeting of the National Association for Research in Science Teaching, St. Louis. (ERIC Document Reproduction Service No. Ed 393 696)

Barker, V. 1993a. *16 Year Old Students' Understanding of the Conservation of Matter in Chemical Reactions* (Science Education Research Paper 93/03). York, UK: Department of Educational Studies, University of York.

Barker, V. 1993b. "An Investigation of 16-18 Year Old Students' Understanding of Basic Chemical Ideas." In *European Research in Science Education. Proceedings of the First Ph.D. Summer School,* P. Lijns, editor (pp. 175-183). Utrecht: CD-b Press.

Beichner, R.J. 1990. "The Effect of Simultaneous Motion Presentation and Graph Generation in a Kinematics Lab." *Journal of Research in Science Teaching* Vol. 27: 803-815.

Ben-Zvi, N., and R. Gai. 1994. "Macro- and Micro-Chemical Comprehension of Real World Phenomena." *Journal of Chemical Education* Vol. 71: 730-732.

Bereiter, C., and M. Scardamalia. 1989. "Intentional Learning as a Goal of Instruction." In *Knowing, Learning, and Instruction: Essays in Honor of Robert Glaser,* L.B. Resnick, editor (pp. 361-392). Hillsdale, NJ: Lawrence Erlbaum Associates.

Berge, Z.L. 1990. "Effects of Group Size, Gender, and Ability Grouping on Learning Science Process Skills Using Microcomputers." *Journal of Research in Science Teaching* Vol. 27: 747-759.

Berger, C. 1982. "Attainment of Skill in Using Science Processes, I: Instrumentation, Methodology and Analysis." *Journal of Research in Science Teaching* Vol. 19: 249-260.

Berger, C. 1984. "Learning More than Facts: Microcomputer Simulation in the Science Classroom." In *Intelligent School House: Readings on Computers and Learning,* D. Peterson, editor. Reston, VA: Reston Publishing Company.

Berger, C. April 1987. *Misconceptions and Thin Conceptions of Teachers Using Microcomputer-based Laboratories.* Paper presented at the meeting of the American Educational Research Association, Washington, DC.

Beyerbach, B., and J. Smith. 1990. "Using a Computerized Concept Mapping Program to Assess Preservice Teachers' Thinking About Effective Teaching." *Journal of Research in Science Teaching* Vol. 27: 961-972.

Bhaskar, R., and H.A. Simon. 1977. "Problem Solving in Semantically Rich Domains: An Example from Engineering Thermodynamics." *Cognitive Science* Vol. 1: 193-215.

Bianchini, J.A. 1997. "Where Knowledge Construction, Equity, and Context Intersect: Student Learning in Science in Small Groups." *Journal of Research in Science Teaching* Vol. 34: 1039-1065.

Bohren, J.L. 1993. *Science Learning and Interactive Videodisc Technology.* Paper presented at the annual meeting of the International Visual Literacy Association, Pittsburgh, PA. (ERIC Document Reproduction Service No. ED 363 286)

Brasell, H. 1987. "The Effect of Real-Time Laboratory Graphing on Learning Graphic Representations of Distance and Velocity." *Journal of Research in Science Teaching* Vol. 24: 385-395.

Brown, A.L. 1992. "Design Experiments: Theoretical and Methodological Challenges in Creating Complex Interventions in Classroom Settings." *Journal of the Learning Sciences* Vol. 2: 141-178.

Brown, D.E., and J. Clement. 1992. "Using Examples and Analogies to Remediate Misconceptions in Physics: Factors Influencing Conceptual Change." *Journal of Research in Science Teaching* Vol. 29: 17-34.

Brown, J.S., A. Collins, and P. Duguid. 1989. "Situated Cognition and the Culture of Learning." *Educational Researcher* Vol. 18, No. 1: 32-42.

Bunce, D.M., K. Baxter, A. DeGennaro, B. Jackson, J. Lyman, M. Olive, and B. Yohe. December 1990. *Teaching Students to Solve Chemistry Problems—A Cooperative Research Project.* Paper presented at the annual meeting of the National Science Teachers Association, Washington, DC.

Bunce, D.M., D.L. Gabel, and K.B. Samuel. 1991. "Enhancing Chemistry Problem-Solving Achievement Using Problem Categorization." *Journal of Research in Science Teaching* Vol. 28: 505-521.

Bunce, D.M., and H. Heikkinen. 1986. "The Effects of an Explicit Problem-Solving Approach on Mathematical Chemistry Achievement Using Problem Categorization." *Journal of Research in Science Teaching* Vol. 28: 11-20.

Butts, D.P., H.M. Hoffman, and M. Anderson. 1993. "Is Hands-On Experience Enough? A Study of Young Children's Views of Sinking and Floating Objects." *Journal of Elementary Science Education* Vol. 5: 50-64.

Bybee, R.W. 1987. "Science Education and the Science/ Technology/Society (STS) Theme." *Science Education* Vol. 71: 667-683.

Bybee, R.W., and N.M. Landes. 1990. "Science for Life and Living." *American Biology Teacher* Vol. 52: 92-98.

Cameron, D.L. 1985. "A Pictorial Framework to Aid Conceptualization of Reaction Stoichiometry." *Journal of Chemical Education* Vol. 62: 510-511.

Campbell, B., J. Lazonby, R. Millar, P. Nicolson, J. Ramsden, and D. Waddington. 1994. "Science: The Salters Approach—A Case Study of the Process of Large Scale Curriculum Development." *Science Education* Vol. 78: 415-447.

Campbell, T.C. 1977. "An Evaluation of a Learning Cycle Intervention Strategy for Enhancing the Use of Formal Operational Thought by Beginning College Physics Students." *Dissertation Abstracts International* Vol. 36, No. 7: 3903A.

Carlson, D.A. 1975. "Training in Formal Reasoning Abilities Provided by the Inquiry Rose Approach and Achievement on the Piagetian Formal Operational Level." *Dissertation Abstracts International* Vol. 36, No. 11: 7368A.

Cavallo, A.M.L. 1996. "Meaningful Learning, Reasoning Ability, and Students' Understanding and Problem Solving of Topics in Genetics." *Journal of Research on Problem Solving* Vol. 33: 625-656.

Chi, M.T.H., P.S. Feltovich, and R. Glaser. 1981. "Categorization and Representation of Physics Problems by Experts and Novices." *Cognitive Science* Vol. 5: 121-152.

Chinn, C.A., and W.F. Brewer. 1993. "The Role of Anomalous Data in Knowledge Acquisition: A Theoretical Framework and Implications for Science Instruction." *Review of Educational Research* Vol. 63: 1-49.

Choi, B.S., and E. Gennaro. 1987. "The Effectiveness of Using Computer Simulated Experiments on Junior High Students' Understanding of the Volume Displacement Concept." *Journal of Research in Science Teaching* Vol. 24: 539-552.

Clement, J. 1993. "Using Bridging Analogies and Anchoring Intuitions to Deal with Students' Preconceptions in Physics." *Journal of Research in Science Teaching* Vol. 30: 1241-1257.

Cobb, P. 1994. "Where Is the Mind? Constructivist and Socio-Cultural Perspectives on Mathematical Development." *Educational Researcher* Vol. 23, No. 7: 13-20.

Cognition and Technology Group at Vanderbilt. 1992. "Anchored Instruction in Science and Mathematics: Theoretical Basis, Developmental Projects, and Initial Research Findings." *Educational Researcher* Vol. 19, No. 6: 2-10.

Cognition and Technology Group at Vanderbilt. 1993. "Anchored Instruction and Situated Cognition Revisited." *Educational Technology* Vol. 33: 52-70.

Dagher, Z.R. 1994. "Does the Use of Analogies Contribute to Conceptual Change?" *Science Education* Vol. 78: 601-614.

Dagher, Z.R. 1995. "Analysis of Analogies Used by Teachers." *Journal of Research in Science Teaching* Vol. 32: 259-270.

Dagher, Z., and G. Cossman. 1992. "Verbal Explanations Given by Science Teachers: Their Nature and Implications." *Journal of Research in Science Teaching* Vol. 29: 361-374.

Davis, J.O. 1977. "The Effects of Three Approaches to Science Instruction on the Science Achievement, Understanding, and Attitudes of Selected Fifth and Sixth Grade Students." *Dissertation Abstracts International* Vol. 39: 211A.

Davison, M.A. 1989. *Use of the Learning Cycle to Promote Cognitive Development.* Doctoral dissertation, Purdue University, 1988. *Dissertation Abstracts International* Vol. 49: 3320-A.

Dawson, G. 1991. *Science Vision: An Inquiry-based Videodisc Science Curriculum.* (ERIC Document Reproduction Service No. ED 336 257)

de Jong, T., and M.G.M. Ferguson-Hessler. 1986. "Cognitive Structures of Good and Poor Novice Problem Solvers in Physics." *Journal of Educational Psychology* Vol. 78: 279-288.

diSessa, A.A. 1988. "Knowledge in Pieces." In *Constructivism in the Computer Age,* G. Forman and P. B. Pufal, editors. Hillsdale, NJ: Lawrence Erlbaum Associates.

Dreyfus, A., E. Jungwirth, and R. Eliovitch. 1990. "Applying the 'Cognitive Conflict' Strategy for Conceptual

Change—Some Implications, Difficulties, and Problems." *Science Education* Vol. 74: 555-569.

Duit, R. 1991a. "Students' Conceptual Frameworks: Consequences for Learning Science." In *The Psychology of Learning Science*, S.M. Glynn, R.H. Yeany, and B.K. Britton, editors (pp. 65-85). Hillsdale, NJ: Lawrence Erlbaum Associates, Inc.

Duit, R. 1991b. "On the Role of Analogies and Metaphors in Learning Science." *Science Education* Vol. 75: 649-672.

Dupin, J.J., and S. Joshua. 1989. "Analogies and 'Modeling Analogies' in Teaching: Some Examples in Basic Electricity." *Science Education* Vol. 73: 207-224.

Edelson, D. 1998. "Realising Authentic Science Learning Through the Adaptation of Scientific Practice." In *International Handbook of Science Education*, B.J. Fraser, and K.G. Tobin, editors (pp. 295-315). Dordrecht, Boston, and London: Kluwer Academic Publishers.

Faryniarz, J.V., and L.G. Lockwood. 1992. "Effectiveness of Microcomputer Simulations in Stimulating Environmental Problem Solving by Community College Students." *Journal of Research in Science Teaching* Vol. 29: 453-470.

Finegold, M., and R. Mass. 1985. "Differences in the Process of Solving Physics Problems Between Good Physics Problem Solvers and Poor Physics Problem Solvers." *Research in Science and Technological Education* Vol. 3: 59-67.

Fisher, K. 1990. "Semantic Networking: The New Kid on the Block." *Journal of Research in Science Teaching* Vol. 27: 1001-1018.

Fleer, M. 1996. "Early Learning about Light: Mapping Preschool Children's Thinking about Light Before, During and After Involvement in a Two Week Teaching Program." *International Journal of Science Education* Vol. 18: 819-836.

Flick, L. 1991. "Where Concepts Meet Precepts: Stimulating Analogical Thought in Children." *Science Education* Vol. 75: 215-230.

Fowler, T.W. March 1975. *An Investigation of the Teacher Behavior of Wait Time During an Inquiry Science Lesson.* Paper presented at the annual meeting of the National Association for Research in Science Teaching, Los Angeles.

Frank, D.V., and J.D. Herron. April 1987. *Teaching Problem Solving to University General Students.* Paper presented at the annual meeting of the National Association for Research in Science Teaching, Washington, DC.

Friedel, A.W., D.L. Gabel, and J. Samuel. 1990. "Using Analogs for Chemistry Problem Solving: Does It Increase Understanding?" *School Science and Mathematics* Vol. 90: 674-682.

Friedel, A.W., and D.P. Maloney. 1995. "Those Baffling Subscripts." *Journal of Chemical Education* Vol. 72: 899-905.

Friedler, Y., R. Nachmias, and M.C. Linn. 1990. "Learning Scientific Reasoning Skills in Microcomputer-Based Laboratories." *Journal of Research in Science Teaching* Vol. 27: 173-191.

Gabel, D.L. February 1981. *Facilitating Problem Solving in High School Chemistry.* Bloomington, IN: Indiana University, School of Education. (ERIC Document Reproduction Service No. ED 210 192)

Gabel, D.L., and D.M Bunce. 1994. "Research on Problem Solving: Chemistry." In *Handbook of Research on Science Teaching and Learning.* D.L. Gabel, editor (pp. 301-326). New York: Macmillan.

Gabel, D.L., R.D. Sherwood, and L.G. Enochs. 1984. "Problem-Solving Skills of High School Chemistry Students." *Journal of Research in Science Teaching* Vol. 21: 221-233.

Gabel, D.L., and K.V. Samuel. 1986. "High School Students' Ability to Solve Molarity Problems and Their Analog Counterparts." *Journal of Research in Science Teaching* Vol. 23: 165-176.

Garigliano, L.J. 1972. *The Relation of Wait-Time to Student Behaviors in Science Curriculum Improvement Study Lessons.* Unpublished doctoral dissertation, Columbia University. (ERIC Document Reproduction Service No. ED 080 324)

Garnett, P.J., and D.F. Treagust. 1992. "Conceptual Difficulties Experienced by Senior High School Students of Electrochemistry: Electric Circuits and Oxidation-Reduction Equations." *Journal of Research in Science Teaching* Vol. 29: 121-142.

Geban, O., P. Askar, and I. Ozkan. 1992. "Effects of Computer Simulations and Problem Solving Approaches on High School Students." *Journal of Educational Research* Vol. 86, No. 1: 5-10.

Glasson, G.E., and R.V. Lalik. 1993. "Reinterpreting the Learning Cycle from a Social Constructivist Perspective: A Qualitative Study of Teachers' Beliefs and Practices." *Journal of Research in Science Teaching* Vol. 30: 187-204.

Glynn, S.M. 1991. "Explaining Science Concepts: A Teaching-with-Analogies Model." In *The Psychology of Learning Science*, S. Glynn, R. Yearny, and B. Britton, editors (pp. 219-240). Hillsdale, NJ: Lawrence Erlbaum Associates.

Good, R., and D. Lavoie. 1986. "The Importance of Prediction in Science Learning Cycles." *Pioneer: Journal of the Florida Association of Science Teachers* Vol. 1: 24-35.

Gorodetsky, M., and R. Hoz. 1980. "Use of Concept Profile Analysis to Identify Difficulties in Solving Science Problems." *Science Education* Vol. 64: 671-678.

Grayson, D., and L.C. McDermott. March 1989. *Using the Computer to Identify and Address Student Difficulties with Graphing.* Paper presented at the annual meeting of the American Educational Research Association, San Francisco.

Griffiths, A.K., J. Pottle, and P. Whelan. April 1983. *Application of the Learning Hierarchy Model to the Identification of Specific Misconception for the Two Science Concepts.* Paper presented at the annual meeting of the National Association for Research in Science Teaching, Dallas, TX.

Griffiths, A.K., and K.R. Preston. 1992. "Grade-12 Students' Misconceptions Relating to Fundamental Characteristics of Atoms and Molecules." *Journal of Research in Science Teaching* Vol. 29: 611-628.

Hakerem, G., G. Dobrynina, and L. Shore. 1993. *The Effect of Interactive, Three Dimensional, High Speed Simulations on High School Science Students' Conceptions of the Molecular Structure of Water.* (ERIC Document Reproduction Service No. ED 362 390)

Harrison, A.G. 1995. "Secondary Students' Mental Models of Atoms and Molecules: Implications for Teaching." *Science Education* Vol. 80: 509-534.

Harrison, A.G., and D.F. Treagust. 1993. "Teaching with Analogies: A Case Study in Grade-10 Optics." *Journal of Research in Science Teaching* Vol. 30: 1291-1307.

Hart, E.P., and I.M. Robottom. 1990. "The Science-Technology-Society Movement in Science Education: A Critique of the Reform Process." *Journal of Research in Science Teaching* Vol. 27: 575-588.

Hay, J.A. 1980. *Effects of Cooperative Goal Structuring of Sixth Grade Science Students' Abilities to Initiate Task and Maintenance Group Behaviors.* Doctoral dissertation, Michigan State University, 1980. *Dissertation Abstracts International* Vol. 41: 3857.

Hegarty, M. 1991. "Knowledge and Processes in Mechanical Problem Solving." In *Complex Problem Solving: Principles and Mechanisms,* R. J. Sternberg and P. A. Frensch, editors (pp. 253-285). Hillsdale, NJ: Lawrence Erlbaum Associates.

Heller, J.I., and F. Reif. 1984. "Prescribing Effective Human Problem-Solving Processes: Problem Description in Physics." *Cognition and Instruction* Vol. 1: 177-216.

Heller, P., and M. Hollabaugh. 1992. "Teaching Problem Solving Through Cooperative Grouping. Part 2: Designing Problems and Structuring Groups." *American Journal of Physics* Vol. 60: 637-645.

Heller, P., R. Keith, and S. Anderson. 1992. "Teaching Problem Solving Through Cooperative Grouping. Part 1: Group Versus Individual Problem Solving." *American Journal of Physics* Vol. 60: 627-636.

Herron, J.D., and T.J. Greenbowe. 1986. "What Can We Do About Sue: A Case Study of Competence." *Journal of Chemical Education* Vol. 63: 528-531.

Hobden, P. 1998. "The Role of Routine Problem Solving Tasks in Science Teaching." In *International Handbook of Science Education,* B.J. Fraser, and K.G. Tobin, editors (pp. 219-231). Dordrecht, Boston, and London: Kluwer Academic Publishers.

Hofmeister, A.M., S. Engelmann, and D. Carnine. 1988. *Developing and Validating Science Education Videodiscs.* (ERIC Document Reproduction Service No. ED 297 943)

Horton, P., A. McConney, M. Gallo, A. Woods, G. Senn, and D. Hamelin. 1993. "An Investigation of the Effectiveness of Concept Mapping as an Instructional Tool." *Science Education* Vol. 77: 95-111.

Hoz, R., Y. Tomer, and P. Tamir. 1990. "The Relations Between Disciplinary and Pedagogical Knowledge and the Length of Teaching Experience of Biology and Geography Teachers." *Journal of Research in Science Teaching* Vol. 27: 973-988.

Humphreys, B., R. Johnson, and D. Johnson. 1982. "Effects of Cooperative, Competitive, and Individualistic Learning on Students' Achievement in Science Class." *Journal of Research in Science Teaching* Vol. 19: 351-356.

Jackman, L.E., W.P. Moellenberg, and G.D. Brabson. 1990. "Effects of Conceptual Systems and Instructional Methods on General Chemistry Laboratory." *Journal of Research in Science Teaching* Vol. 27: 699-709.

Jackson, D.F., B.J. Edwards, and C.F. Berger. 1993. "Teaching the Design and Interpretation of Graphs Through Computer Aided Graphical Data Analysis." *Journal of Research in Science Teaching* Vol. 30: 483-501.

Jegede, O.J., and J.O. Olajide. 1995. "Wait-Time, Classroom Discourse, and the Influence of Sociocultural Factors in Science Teaching." *Science Education* Vol. 79: 233-249.

Johnson, D.W., and R.T. Johnson. 1985a. "Classroom Conflict: Controversy Versus Debate in Learning Groups." *American Educational Research Journal* Vol. 22: 237-256.

Johnson, R.T., and D.W. Johnson. 1985b. "Student-Student Interaction: Ignored but Powerful." *Journal of Teacher Education* Vol. 36, No. 4: 22-26.

Jones, R., and J. Steinbrink. 1989. "Using Cooperative Groups in Science Teaching." *School Science and Mathematics* Vol. 89: 541-551.

Jones, R., and J. Steinbrink. 1991. "Home Teams: Cooperative Learning in Elementary Science." *School Science and Mathematics* Vol. 91: 139-143.

Jungck, J., and J. Calley. 1986. *Genetics: Strategic Simulations in Mendelian Genetics.* Wentworth, NH: COMPress.

Kempa, R., and A. Ayob. 1991. "Learning Interactions in Group Work in Science." *International Journal of Science Education* Vol. 13: 341-354.

Keys, C.W. 1996. "Writing Collaborative Lab Reports in Ninth Grade Science: Three Cases of Social Interactions." *School Science and Mathematics* Vol. 96: 178-196.

Kinnear, J. 1983. *Using Computer Simulations to Enhance Problem-Solving Skills and Concept Development in Biology Students.* Paper presented at the Computer ALITE Conference, Brisbane, Australia.

Kinzie, M.B., R. Strauss, and J. Foss. 1993. "The Effects of an Interactive Dissection Simulation on the Performance Achievement of High School Biology Students." *Proceedings of Selected Research and Development Presentations at the Convention of the Association for Educational Communications and Technology.* New Orleans, LA. (ERIC Document Reproduction Service No. ED 362 173)

Krajcik, J.S. November 1989. "Students' Interactions with Science Software Containing Dynamic Visuals." In *Meanings of Science and Technology in Schools and Communities,* M. Eisenhart and J.G. Goetz (Chairs). Symposium conducted at the 88th annual meeting of the American Anthropological Association, Washington, DC.

Krajcik, J.S., and J.W. Layman. March 1989. *Middle School Teachers' Conceptions of Heat and Temperature: Personal and Teaching Knowledge.* Paper presented at the 62nd annual meeting of the National Association for Research in Science Teaching, San Francisco.

Kramers-Pals, H., J. Lambrechts, and P.J. Wolff. 1982. "Recurrent Difficulties: Solving Quantitative Problems." *Journal of Chemical Education* Vol. 59: 509-513.

Lake, J.H. 1973. *The Influence of Wait-Time on the Verbal Dimensions of Student Inquiry Behavior.* Unpublished doctoral dissertation, Rutgers University. (ERIC Document Reproduction Service No. ED 116 897)

Larkin, J.H. 1980. "Skilled Problem Solving in Physics: A Hierarchical Planning Model." *Journal of Structural Learning* Vol. 1: 271-297.

Larkin, J.H. 1983. "The Role of Problem Representation in Physics." In *Mental Models,* D. Gentner and A.L. Stevens, editors (pp. 75-98). Hillsdale, NJ: Lawrence Erlbaum Associates.

Larkin, J.H., J. McDermott, D.P. Simon, and H.A. Simon. 1980. "Models of Competence in Solving Physics Problems." *Cognitive Science* Vol. 4: 317-345.

Lavoie, D. April 1989. *Enhancing the Learning Cycle with Prediction and Level Three Interactive Videodisc Lessons in Science.* Paper presented at the annual meeting of the National Association for Research in Science Teaching, San Francisco.

Lawson, A.E. 1988. "A Better Way to Teach Biology." *American Biology Teacher* Vol. 50: 266-289.

Lawson, A.E. 1990. "Use of Reasoning to a Contradiction in Grades Three to College." *Journal of Research in Science Teaching* Vol. 27: 541-551.

Lawson, A.E. 1993. "The Importance of Analogy: A Prelude to the Special Issue." *Journal of Research in Science Teaching* Vol. 30: 1213-1214.

Lawson, A.E, 1995. *Science Teaching and the Development of Thinking.* Belmont, CA: Wadsworth Publishing Company.

Lawson, A.E., M.R. Abraham, and J.W. Renner. 1989. *A Theory of Instruction: Using the Learning Cycle to Teach Science Concepts and Thinking Skills* (Monograph of the National Association for Research in Science Teaching, No. 1). Cincinnati, OH: NARST.

Lawson, A.E., and J. Weser. 1990. "The Rejection of Nonscientific Beliefs About Life: Effects of Instruction and Reasoning Skills." *Journal of Research in Science Teaching* Vol. 27: 589-606.

Lawson, A.E., and W.T. Wollman. 1976. "Encouraging the Transition from Concrete to Formal Cognitive Functioning—An Experiment." *Journal of Research in Science Teaching* Vol. 13: 413-430.

Lazarowitz, R. 1991. "Learning Biology Cooperatively: An Israeli Junior High School Study." *Cooperative Learning: The Magazine for Cooperating in Education* Vol. 11: 19-21.

Lazarowitz, R., J.H. Baird, R. Hertz-Lazarowitz, and J. Jenkins. 1985. "The Effects of Modified Jigsaw on Achievement, Classroom Social Climate, and Self-Esteem in High School Science Classes." In *Learning to Cooperate, Cooperating to Learn.,* R. Slavin, S. Sharan, S. Kagan, R. Hertz-Lazarowitz, N.M. Webb, and R. Schmuck, editors (pp. 231-253). New York and London: Plenum.

Lazarowitz, R., and R. Hertz-Lazarowitz. 1998. "Cooperative Learning in the Science Curriculum." In *International Handbook of Science Education,* B.J. Fraser, and K.G. Tobin, editors (pp. 449-469). Dordrecht, Boston, and London: Kluwer Academic Publishers.

Lazarowitz, R., R. Hertz-Lazarowitz, and J.H. Baird. 1994. "Learning Science in a Cooperative Setting: Academic Achievement and Affective Outcomes." *Journal of Research in Science Teaching* Vol. 31: 1121-1131.

Lazarowitz, R., R. Hertz-Lazarowitz, J.H. Baird, and V. Bowlden. 1988. "Academic Achievement and On-Task Behavior of High School Biology Students Instructed in a Cooperative Small Investigative Group." *Science Education* Vol. 72: 475-487.

Lazarowitz, R., and G. Karsenty. 1990. "Cooperative Learning and Students' Self-Esteem in Tenth Grade Biology Classrooms." In *Cooperative Learning, Theory and Research,* S. Sharan, editor (pp. 123-149). New York: Praeger.

Lehman, J. 1994. "Secondary Science Teachers' Use of Microcomputers During Instruction." *School Science and Mathematics* Vol. 94: 413-420.

Leonard, W.H. 1992. "A Comparison of Student Performance Following Instruction by Interactive Videodisc Versus Conventional Laboratory." *Journal of Research in Science Teaching* Vol. 29: 93-102.

Lesgold, A., and S. Lajoie. 1991. "Complex Problem Solving in Electronics." In *Complex Problem Solving: Principles and Mechanisms,* R.J. Sternberg and P.A. Frensch, editors (pp. 287-316). Hillsdale, NJ: Lawrence Erlbaum Associates.

Lewis, E.L., and M.C. Linn. April 1989. *Heat Energy and Temperature Concepts of Adolescents and Experts: Implications for Curricular Improvement.* Paper presented at the 62nd annual meeting of the National Association for Research in Science Teaching, San Francisco.

Linn, M. 1988. *Autonomous Classroom Computer Environments for Learning.* Progress report and annotated bibliography. Washington, DC: National Science Foundation. (ERIC Document Reproduction Service No. ED 305 903)

Linn, M. 1998. "The Impact of Technology on Science Instruction: Historical Trends and Current Opportunities." In *International Handbook of Science Education*, B.J. Fraser, and K.G. Tobin, editors (pp. 265-294). Dordrecht, Boston, and London: Kluwer Academic Publishers.

Linn, M.C., and N.B. Songer. April 1988. "Curriculum Reformulation: Incorporating Technology into Science Instruction." In *Conceptual Models of Science Learning and Science Instruction.* Symposium conducted at the annual meeting of the American Educational Research Association, New Orleans.

Linn, M.C., and N.B. Songer. 1991. "Teaching Thermodynamics to Middle School Students: What Are Appropriate Cognitive Demands?" *Journal of Research in Science Teaching* Vol. 28: 885-918.

Lockhart, R.S., M. Lamon, and M.L. Gick. 1988. "Conceptual Transfer in Simple Insight Problems." *Memory and Cognition* Vol. 16: 136-144.

Lonning, R.A. 1993. "Effect of Cooperative Learning Strategies on Student Verbal Interactions and Achievement During Conceptual Change Instruction in 10th Grade General Science." *Journal of Research in Science Teaching* Vol. 30: 1087-1101.

Lumpe, A.T., and J.R. Staver. 1995. "Peer Collaboration and Concept Development." *Journal of Research and Science Teaching* Vol. 32: 71-98.

Lythcott, J. 1990. "Problem Solving and Requisite Knowledge of Chemistry." *Journal of Chemical Education* Vol. 67: 248-252.

Maloney, D.P. 1994. "Research on Problem Solving: Physics." In *Handbook of Research on Science Teaching and Learning.* D. L. Gabel, editor (pp. 327-356). New York: Macmillan.

Mansfield, J.B. 1996. "The Effect of Wait-Time on Issues of Gender Equity, Academic Achievement, and Attitude toward a Course." *Teacher Education and Practice* Vol. 12: 86-93.

Marek, E., and S. Methven. 1991. "Effects of the Learning Cycle Upon Student and Classroom Teacher Performances." *Journal of Research in Science Teaching* Vol. 28: 41-53.

Mason, D.S., D.F. Shell, and F.E. Crawley. 1997. "Difference in Problem Solving by Nonscience Majors in Introductory Chemistry on Paired Algorithmic-Conceptual Problems." *Journal of Research in Science Teaching* Vol. 34: 905-923.

McFadden, C.P. 1991. "Towards an STS School Curriculum." *Science Education* Vol. 75: 457-469.

McKinnon, J.W., and J.W. Renner. 1971. "Are Colleges Concerned with Intellectual Development?" *American Journal of Physics* Vol. 39: 1047-1052.

McMillan, C., and M. Swadener. 1991. "Novice Use of Qualitative Versus Quantitative Problem Solving in Electrostatics." *Journal of Research in Science Teaching* Vol. 28: 661-670.

Mettes, C.T.C.W., A. Pilot, H.J. Roossink, and H. Kramers-Pals. 1980. "Teaching and Learning Problem Solving in Science." *Journal of Chemical Education* Vol. 57: 882-885.

Mokros, J.R., and R.F. Tinker. 1987. "The Impact of Microcomputer-based Labs on Children's Ability to Interpret Graphs." *Journal of Research in Science Teaching* Vol. 24: 369-383.

Myers, L.H. 1988. *Analysis of Student Outcomes in Ninth Grade Physical Science Taught with a Science/Technology/Society Focus Versus One Taught with a Textbook Orientation.* Unpublished doctoral dissertation, The University of Iowa.

Myers, R. 1993. *Interdisciplinary, Anchored Instruction Using Videotape.* Paper presented at the annual conference of the International Visual Literacy Association, Pittsburgh, PA. (ERIC Document Reproduction Service No. ED 363 306)

Nakhleh, M.B., and J.S. Krajcik. 1994. "Influence of Levels of Information as Presented by Different Technologies on Students' Understanding of Acid, Base, and pH Concepts." *Journal of Research in Science Teaching* Vol. 31: 1077-1096.

National Research Council. November 1994. *National Science Education Standards.* Washington, DC: National Academy Press.

National Science Teachers Association. 1982. *Science-Technology-Society: Science Education for the 1980's.* Position paper. Washington, DC: National Science Teachers Association.

National Science Teachers Association. 1991. "Science/Technology/Society: A New Effort for Providing Appropriate Science for All (The NSTA Position Statement)." *NSTA Reports* (April 1991): 36-37.

National Science Teachers Association. 1993. *Scope, Sequence, and Coordination of Secondary School Science (Volume 1). The Content Core* (Revised edition). Washington, DC: National Science Teachers Association.

Niaz, M. 1996. "How Students Circumvent Problem-Solving Strategies that Require Greater Cognitive Complexity." *Journal of College Science Teaching* Vol. 2: 361-363.

Niaz, M., and W.R. Robinson. April 1989. *Teaching Algorithmic Problem Solving or Conceptual Understanding: Role of Developmental Level, Mental Capacity, and Cognitive Style.* Paper presented at the annual meeting of the National Association for Research in Science Teaching, Lake Geneva, WI.

Njoo, M., and T. de Jong. 1993. "Exploratory Learning with a Computer Simulation for Control Theory: Learning Processes and Instructional Support." *Journal of Research in Science Teaching* Vol. 30: 821-844.

Novak, J.D., and D.B. Gowin. 1984. *Learning How to Learn.* New York: Cambridge University Press.

Novak, J.D., and D. Musonda. 1991. "A Twelve-Year Longitudinal Study of Science Concept Learning." *American Educational Research Journal* Vol. 28: 117-153.

Odom, A.L., and P.V. Kelly. 1998. "Making Learning Meaningful." *The Science Teacher* Vol. 65, Issue 4: 33-37.

Okebukola, P.A. 1985a. "Effects of Student-Student Interactions on Affective Outcomes of Science Instruction." *Research in Science and Technological Education* Vol. 3, No. 1: 5-17.

Okebukola, P.A. 1985b. "The Relative Effectiveness of Cooperative and Competitive Interaction Techniques in Strengthening Students' Performance in Science Classrooms." *Science Education* Vol. 69: 501-511.

Okebukola, P.A. 1986a. "Cooperative Learning and Students' Attitudes to Laboratory Work." *School Science and Mathematics* Vol. 86: 582-590.

Okebukola, P.A. 1986b. "The Influence of Preferred Learning Styles on Cooperative Learning in Science." *Science Education* Vol. 70: 509-518.

Okebukola, P.A. 1986c. "Impact of Extended Cooperative and Competitive Relationships on the Performance of Students in Science." *Human Relations* Vol. 39: 673-682.

Okebukola, P.A., and M.B. Ogunniyi. 1984. "Cooperative, Competitive and Individualistic Laboratory Interaction Patterns: Effects on Students' Performance and Acquisition of Practical Skills." *Journal of Research in Science Teaching* Vol. 21: 875-884.

Pankratius, W.J. 1990. "Building an Organized Knowledge Base: Concept Mapping and Achievement in Secondary School Physics." *Journal of Research in Science Teaching* Vol. 27: 315-333.

Polya, C. 1945. *How to Solve It.* Garden City, NY: Doubleday.

Purser, R.K., and J.W. Renner. 1983. "Results of Two Tenth-Grade Teaching Procedures." *Science Education* Vol. 67: 85-98.

Ramsden, J. 1992. "If This Is Enjoyable, Is It Science?" *School Science Review* Vol. 73, No. 265: 65-71.

Ramsden, J. 1994. "Context and Activity-Based Science in Action: Some Teachers' Views of the Effects on Pupils." *School Science Review* Vol. 75, No. 272: 7-14.

Reif, F. 1983. "How Can Chemists Teach Problem Solving?" *Journal of Chemical Education* Vol. 60: 948-953.

Reif, F., and J.I. Heller. 1982. "Knowledge Structures and Problem Solving in Physics." *Educational Psychologist* Vol. 17, No. 2: 102-127.

Renner, J., M. Abraham, and H.H. Birnie. 1985. "The Importance of the Form of Student Acquisition of Data in Physics Learning Cycles." *Journal of Research in Science Teaching* Vol. 22: 303-325.

Renner, J., and E. Marek. 1988. *The Learning Cycle and Elementary School Science Teaching.* Portsmouth, NH: Heinemann.

Richmond, G., and J. Striley. 1996. "Making Meaning in Classrooms." *Journal of Research in Science Teaching* Vol. 33: 839-858.

Riley, J.P., II. 1986. "The Effects of Teachers' Wait-Time and Knowledge Comprehension Questioning on Pupil Science Achievement." *Journal of Research in Science Teaching* Vol. 23: 335-342.

Rivers, R., and E. Vockell. 1987. "Computer Simulations to Stimulate Scientific Problem Solving." *Journal of Research in Science Teaching* Vol. 30: 153-173.

Robertson, W.C. 1990. "Detection of Cognitive Structure with Protocol Data: Predicting Performance on Physics Transfer Problems." *Cognitive Science* Vol. 14: 253-280.

Rogg, S.R., and J.B. Kahle. March 1992. *The Characterization of Small Instructional Work Groups in Ninth-Grade Biology.* Paper presented at the 65th annual meeting of the National Association for Research in Science Teaching (NARST), Boston.

Rosenthal, D.B. 1989. "Two Approaches to STS Education." *Science Education* Vol. 73: 581-589.

Roth, W. 1994. "Student Views of Collaborative Concept Mapping: An Emancipatory Research Project." *Science Education* Vol. 78: 1-34.

Roth, W., and A. Roychoudhury. 1992. "The Social Construction of Scientific Concepts or the Concept Map as Conscription Device and Tool for Social Thinking in High School Science." *Science Education* Vol. 76: 531-557.

Rowe, M.B. 1974a. "Wait-Time and Rewards as Instructional Variables, Their Influence on Language, Logic, and Fate Control: Part I, Fate Control." *Journal of Research in Science Teaching* Vol. 11: 81-94.

Rowe, M.B. 1974b. "Relation of Wait-Time and Rewards to the Development of Language, Logic, and Fate Control: Part II, Rewards." *Journal of Research in Science Teaching* Vol. 11: 291-308.

Rowe, M.B. 1986. "Wait Time: Slowing Down May Be Way of Speeding Up." *Journal of Teacher Education* Vol. 37: 43-50.

Rubba, P.A., M. McGuyer, and T.M. Wahlund. 1991. "The Effects of Infusing STS Vignettes into the Genetics Unit of Biology on Learner Outcomes in STA and Genetics: A Report of Two Investigations." *Journal of Research in Science Education* Vol. 28: 537-552.

Rubin, R.L., and J.T. Norman. March/April 1989. *A Comparison of the Effect of a Systematic Modeling Approach and the Learning Cycle Approach on the Achievement of Integrated Science Process Skills of Urban Middle School Students.* Paper presented at the annual meeting of the National Association for Research in Science Teaching, San Francisco. (ERIC Document Reproduction Service No. ED 308 838)

Rubin, R.L., and J.T. Norman. 1992. "Systematic Modeling Versus the Learning Cycle: Comparative Effects on

Integrating Science Process Skill Achievement." *Journal of Research in Science Teaching* Vol. 29: 715-727.

Ruiz-Primo, M.A., and R.J. Shavelson. 1996. "Problems and Issues in the Use of Concept Maps." *Journal of Research in Science Teaching* Vol. 33: 569-600.

Samiroden, W.D. 1983. *The Effects of Higher Cognitive Level Questions Wait Time Ranges by Biology Student Teachers on Student Achievement and Perception of Teacher Effectiveness.* Unpublished doctoral dissertation, Oregon State University.

Savenye, W.C., and E. Strand. 1989. *Teaching Science Using Interactive Videodisc: Results of the Pilot Year Evaluation of the Texas Learning Technology Group Project.* Proceedings of selected research papers presented at the annual meeting of the Association for Educational Communications and Technology. Dallas, TX. (ERIC Document Reproduction Service No. ED 308 838)

Sawrey, B.A. 1990. "Concept Learning Versus Problem Solving: Revisited." *Journal of Chemical Education* Vol. 67: 253-254.

Scharmann, L. March 1992. *Teaching Evolution: The Influence of Peer Instructional Modeling.* Paper presented at the annual meeting of the National Association for Research in Science Teaching, Boston.

Schecker, H.P. 1998. "Integration of Experimenting and Modeling by Advanced Educational Technology: Examples from Nuclear Physics." In *International Handbook of Science Education*, B.J. Fraser, and K.G. Tobin, editors (pp. 383-398). Dordrecht, Boston, and London: Kluwer Academic Publishers.

Schmidt, H.J. 1990. "Secondary School Students' Strategies in Stoichiometry." *International Journal of Science Education.* Vol. 12: 457-471.

Schmidt, H.J. 1997. "An Alternate Path to Stoichiometric Problem Solving." *Research in Science Education* Vol. 27: 237-249.

Schneider, L.S., and J.W. Renner. 1980. "Concrete and Formal Teaching." *Journal of Research in Science Teaching* Vol. 17: 503-517.

Schoenfeld, A.H. 1978. "Can Heuristics Be Taught?" In *Cognitive Process Instruction,* J. Lochhead and J.J. Clement, editors (pp. 315-338). Philadelphia: Franklin Institute Press.

Sherman, L.W. 1989. "A Comparative Study of Cooperative and Competitive Achievement in Two Secondary Biology Classrooms: The Group Investigative Model Versus an Individually Competitive Goal Structure." *Journal of Research in Science Teaching* Vol. 26: 55-64.

Sherwood, R., A. Petrosino, X.D. Lin, and the Cognition and Technology Group at Vanderbilt. 1998. "Problem-Based Macro Contexts in Science Instruction: Design Issues and Applications." In *International Handbook of Science Education*, B.J. Fraser and K.G. Tobin, editors (pp. 349-362). Dordrecht, Boston, and London: Kluwer Academic Publishers.

Shymansky, J.A., L.D. Yore, D.F. Treagust, R.B. Thiele, A. Harrison, B. Waldrip, S.M. Stocklmayer, and G. Venville. 1997. "Examining the Construction Process: A Study of Changes in Level 10 Students' Understanding of Classical Mechanics." *Journal of Research in Science Teaching* Vol. 34: 571-593.

Simmons, P.E. 1989. *Problem Solving Strategies and Approaches of Successful and Unsuccessful Subjects Interacting with a Genetics Computer Simulation.* Paper presented at the annual meeting of the National Association of Research in Science Teaching, San Francisco.

Slavin, R.E. 1980. "Cooperative Learning." *Review of Education Research* Vol. 50: 315-342.

Slavin, R.E. 1984. "Students Motivating Students to Excel: Cooperative Incentives, Cooperative Tasks, and Student Achievement." *The Elementary School Journal* Vol. 85: 53-63.

Slavin, R.E. 1991. "Synthesis of Research on Cooperative Learning." *Educational Leadership* Vol. 48, No. 5: 71-82.

Smith, S.C., and L.L. Jones. 1988. "Images, Imagination, and Chemical Reality." *Journal of Chemical Education* Vol. 66, No. 1: 8-11.

Soloway, E., A. Pryor, J. Krajcik, S. Jackson, S. Stratford, M. Wisnudel, and J. Klein. 1997. "Science Ware's Model-It: Technology to Support Authentic Science Inquiry." *T. H. E. Journal* Vol. 1: 54-56.

Songer, N. 1998. "Can Technology Bring Students Closer to Science?" In *International Handbook of Science Education*, B.J. Fraser, and K.G. Tobin, editors (pp. 333-347). Dordrecht, Boston, and London: Kluwer Academic Publishers.

Spitulnik, M., S. Stratford, J. Krajcik, and E. Soloway. 1998. "Using Technology to Support Students' Artifact Construction in Science." In *International Handbook of Science Education*, B.J. Fraser and K.G. Tobin, editors (pp. 363-381). Dordrecht, Boston, and London: Kluwer Academic Publishers.

Starr, M., and J. Krajcik. 1990. "Concept Maps as a Heuristic for Science Curriculum Development: Toward Improvement in Process and Product." *Journal of Research in Science Teaching* Vol. 27: 987-1000.

Stavy, R. 1991. "Analogy to Overcome Misconceptions About Conservation of Matter." *Journal of Research in Science Teaching* Vol. 28: 305-313.

Stavy, R., and D. Tirosh. 1993. "When Analogy Is Perceived as Such." *Journal of Research in Science Teaching* Vol. 30: 1229-1239.

Stewart, J., and R. Hafner. 1994. "Research on Problem Solving: Genetics." In *Handbook of Research on Science Teaching and Learning.* D.L. Gabel, editor (pp. 284-300). New York: Macmillan.

Stiff, L.V. 1988. "Problem Solving by Example." *School Science and Mathematics* Vol. 88: 666-675.

Sumfleth, E. 1988. "Knowledge of Terms and Problem-Solving in Chemistry." *International Journal of Science Education* Vol. 10: 45-60.

Sutman, F.X., and M.H. Bruce. 1992. "Chemistry in the Community: A Five Year Evaluation." *Journal of Chemical Education* Vol. 69: 564-567.

Sutula, V., and J.S. Krajcik. September 1988. *The Effective Use of Analogies for Solving Mole Problems in High School Chemistry.* Paper presented at the annual meeting of the National Association of Research in Science Teaching, Lake Ozark, MO.

Sweller, J. 1988. "Cognitive Load During Problem Solving: Effects on Learning." *Cognitive Science* Vol. 12: 257-285.

Thagard, P. 1992. "Analogy, Explanation, and Education." *Journal of Research in Science Teaching* Vol. 29: 537-544.

Thiele, R.B., and D.F. Treagust. 1994. "An Interpretive Examination of High School Chemistry and Teachers' Analogical Explanations." *Journal of Research in Science Teaching* Vol. 31: 227-242.

Thornton, R.K. 1987. "Tools for Scientific Thinking—Microcomputer-Based Laboratories for Teaching Physics." *Physics Education* Vol. 22: 230-238.

Tingle, J.B., and R. Good. 1990. "Effects of Cooperative Grouping on Stoichiometric Problem Solving in High School Chemistry." *Journal of Research in Science Teaching* Vol. 27: 671-683.

Tinker, R.F. 1985. "How to Turn Your Computer into a Science Lab." *Classroom Computer Learning* Vol. 5, No. 6: 26-29.

Tobin, K.G. 1985. "The Effect of an Extended Teacher Wait Time on Science Achievement." *Journal of Research in Science Teaching* Vol. 17: 469-475.

Tobin, K.G. 1986. "Effects of Teacher Wait Time on Discourse Characteristics in Mathematics and Language Arts Classes." *American Educational Research Journal* Vol. 32: 191-200.

Tobin, K.G. 1987. "The Role of Wait Time on Higher Level Cognitive Learning." *Review of Educational Research* Vol. 57: 69-95.

Tobin, K.G., and W. Capie. 1982. "Relationships Between Classroom Process Variables and Middle School Science Achievement." *Journal of Educational Psychology* Vol. 14: 441-454.

Treagust, D.F., R. Duit, P. Joslin, and I. Lindauer. 1992. "Science Teachers' Use of Analogies: Observations from Classroom Practice." *International Journal of Science Education* Vol. 14: 413-422.

Van Heuvelen, A. 1991. "Overview, Case Study Physics." *American Journal of Physics* Vol. 59: 898-906.

Venville, G.J., and D.F. Treagust. 1997. "Analogies in Biology Education: A Contentious Issue." *American Biology Teacher* Vol. 59: 282-287.

Waks, L.J., and B.A. Barchi. 1992. "STS in U. S. School Science: Perceptions of Selected Leaders and Their Implications for STS Education." *Science Education* Vol. 76: 79-90.

Wallace, J., and J. Mintzes. 1990. "The Concept Map as a Research Tool: Exploring Conceptual Change in Biology." *Journal of Research in Science Education* Vol. 27: 1033-1052.

Walters, J. 1988. "Teaching Biological Systems." *Journal of Biological Education* Vol. 22: 87.

Ward, C.R., and J.D. Herron. 1980. "Helping Students Understand Formal Chemical Concepts." *Journal of Research in Science Teaching* Vol. 17: 387-400.

Ward, M., and J. Sweller. 1990. "Structuring Effective Worked Examples." *Cognition and Instruction* Vol. 7: 1-39.

Watson, S.B. 1991. "Cooperative Learning and Group Educational Modules: Effects on Cognitive Achievement of High School Biology Students." *Journal of Research in Science Teaching* Vol. 28: 141-146.

Webb, N. 1985. "Student Interaction and Learning in Small Groups: A Research Summary." In *Learning to Cooperate, Cooperating to Learn*, R. Slavin, S. Sharan, K. Spencer, R. Lazarowitz, C. Webb, and R. Schmuck, editors. Leeds: The University of Leeds.

Wells, C., and C. Berger. 1986. "Teacher/Student-Developed Spreadsheet Simulations: A Population Growth Example." *Journal of Computers in Mathematics and Science Teaching* Vol. 42: 34-40.

Westbrook, S.L., and L.N. Rogers. 1994. "Examining the Development of Scientific Reasoning in Ninth-Grade Physical Science Students." *Journal of Research in Science Teaching* Vol. 31: 65-76.

White, B. 1984. "Designing Computer Activities to Help Physics Students Understand Newton's Laws of Motion." *Cognition and Instruction* Vol. 1: 69-108.

White, B. 1993. "Thinker Tools: Causal Models, Conceptual Change, and Science Education." *Cognition and Instruction* Vol. 10: 1-100.

White, B. 1998. "Computer Microworlds and Scientific Inquiry: An Alternative Approach to Science Education." In *International Handbook of Science Education*, B.J. Fraser and K. G. Tobin, editors (pp. 295-315). Dordrecht, Boston, and London: Kluwer Academic Publishers.

White, B.Y., and J.R. Frederiksen. 1989. *Designing Articulate Microworlds that Facilitate Learning, Understanding, and Problem Solving in Science Education.* Paper presented at the annual meeting of the American Educational Research Association: San Francisco.

White, B., J. Frederiksen, and K. Spoehr. 1993. "Conceptual Models for Understanding the Behavior of Electrical Circuits." In *Learning Electricity and Electronics with Advanced Educational Technology*, M. Caillot, editor (pp. 77-95). New York: Springer Verlag.

White, R., and R. Gunstone. 1992. *Probing Understanding.* New York: Palmer Press.

White, B.Y., and P. Horowitz. 1987. *Thinkertools: Enabling Children to Understand Physical Laws.* Report No. 6470. Cambridge, MA: BBN Laboratories.

White, B.Y., and P. Horowitz. 1988. "Computer Microworlds and Conceptual Change: A New

Approach to Science Education." In *Improving Learning: New Perspectives,* P. Ransden, editor (pp. 69-80). London: Kegan Paul.

Willerman, M., and R.A. Mac Harg. 1991. "The Concept Map as an Advance Organizer." *Journal of Research in Science Teaching* Vol. 28: 705-711.

Williamson, V.M., and M.R. Abraham. 1995. "The Effects of Computer Animation on the Particulate Mental Models of College Chemistry Students." *Journal of Research in Science Teaching* Vol. 32: 521-534.

Wilson, J.M. 1994. "Network Representations of Knowledge About Chemical Equilibrium: Variations with Achievement." *Journal of Research in Science Education* Vol. 31: 1133-1147.

Winther, A.A., and T.L. Volk. 1994. "Comparing Achievement of Inner-City High School Students in Traditional Versus STS-Based Chemistry Courses." *Journal of Chemical Education* Vol. 71: 501-505.

Wise, K.C. 1988. "The Effects of Using Computing Technologies in Science Instruction: A Synthesis of Classroom-Based Research." In *1988 AETSs' Yearbook,* J.D. Ellis, editor (pp. 105-118). Columbus: The Ohio State University.

Wiser, M., and D. Kipman. April 1988. *The Differentiation of Heat and Temperature: An Evaluation of the Effect of Microcomputer Models on Students' Misconceptions.* Paper presented at the annual meeting of the American Educational Research Association, New Orleans, LA.

Wong, D.E. 1993a. "Self-Generated Analogies as a Tool for Constructing and Evaluating Explanations of Scientific Phenomena." *Journal of Research in Science Teaching* Vol. 30: 367-380.

Wong, D.E. 1993b. "Understanding the Generative Capacity of Analogies as a Tool for Explanation." *Journal of Research in Science Teaching* Vol. 30: 1259-1272.

Wright, D.S., and C.D. Williams. 1986. "A Wise Strategy for Introductory Physics." *Physics Teacher* Vol. 24: 211-216.

Yager, R.E., editor. 1996. *Science/Technology/Society as Reform in Science Education.* Albany: State University of New York Press.

Yager, R.E., and P. Tamir. 1993. "STS Approach: Reasons, Intentions, Accomplishments, and Outcomes." *Science Education* Vol. 77: 637-658.

Yager, R.E., P. Tamir, and N. Mackinnu. 1993. "The Effect of a Science/Technology/Society Approach on Achievement and Attitudes of Students Enrolled in Science Classes in Grades 4 Through 9." Manuscript submitted for publication.

Yager, R.E., and S.O. Yager. 1985. "Changes in Perceptions of Science for Third, Seventh, and Eleventh Grade Students." *Journal of Research in Science Teaching* Vol. 22: 347-358.

Zeitoun, H.H. 1984. "Teaching Scientific Analogies: A Proposed Model." *Research in Science and Technological Education* Vol. 2:107-125.

Zielinski, E.J., and D.M. Sarachine. 1994. "An Evaluation of Five Critical/Creative Case Studies for Secondary Science Students." *Rural Education* Vol. 15: 1-6.

Zietsman, A.I., and P.W. Hewson. 1986. "Effect of Instruction Using Microcomputer Simulations and Conceptual Change Strategies on Science Learning." *Journal of Research in Science Teaching* Vol. 23: 27-39.

Zoller, U., J. Ebenezer, K. Morely, S. Paras, V. Sandberg, C. West, T. Wolthers, and S.H. Tan. 1990. "Goal Attainment in Science-Technology-Society S/T/S Education and Reality: The Case of British Columbia." *Science Education* Vol. 74: 19-36.

Chapter 10. Social Studies

James P. Shaver

Social studies has at least two different meanings to those in the field. To some, social studies is a collection of individual courses in U.S. and world history and the social sciences—geography, government, economics, and perhaps sociology, psychology, and anthropology. To others, social studies is a coordinated curriculum that draws on history and the social sciences, as well as other subject areas, with the specific aim of citizenship education. The two definitions are not mutually exclusive, and many social studies teachers identify with both approaches. This chapter does not presume either definition. The practices suggested to improve student learning are appropriate with either one or a combination of both.

A substantial base of research—many studies with rigorous designs or large numbers of cumulative findings—on the teaching of social studies is not available. The findings that do exist, along with relevant research findings from other fields, have been reviewed and synthesized in the *Handbook of Research on Social Studies Teaching and Learning* (Shaver 1991). This chapter relies on several of the handbook chapters, along with other literature reviews. However, it was not often possible to say, "the research clearly indicates . . .," and this author's professional judgment played a role in the selection of the promising practices to be included.

In part because of the scarcity of firm, cumulative findings, research cannot provide mandates for social studies instruction. But there are other reasons that the prescription of classroom practice from research findings should be avoided. Research findings must be applied in specific classroom and school settings. In particular, sound instructional decisions must be based on the educational values of the teacher,

the school, the school district, and the community, as well as on district and state guidelines and requirements. Skilled, thoughtful, and motivated teachers must adapt and implement techniques or approaches suggested by research findings to achieve desired student outcomes.

Research findings can be of assistance in instructional decision making by stimulating thought and suggesting alternatives, and as a source of information on options as teachers consider how to teach. However, the experiences and practical knowledge of the individual teacher and his or her colleagues are crucial in deciding on applications. In addition, each teacher knows his or her students' interests and motivations, their prior experiences, and their expectations, as these will influence each student's reactions to instructional techniques and approaches. Each teacher is also aware of the extent to which his or her students find social studies interesting and challenging, and of the extent to which meaningful learning is occurring. This chapter is intended as a helpful source of instructional alternatives as social studies teachers contemplate how to improve their students' interest and learning.

The suggested promising practices are interrelated rather than mutually exclusive. For example, jurisprudential teaching can contribute to a thoughtful classroom, and the teaching of critical thinking is essential to such classrooms; effective questioning, support for concept development, and establishing an appropriate classroom environment should pervade all instruction; constructivist teaching provides a fundamental context for the effective use of computer technology in instruction and for student community-participation, as well as for concept development and cognitive prejudice reduction. The practices are not presented to be chosen among, but as potential contributors to that complexity of interactions that, over time, constitutes effective social studies instruction.

Comments and suggestions by the following reviewers were helpful in the preparation of this chapter: Dr. Deborah A. Byrnes, professor of elementary education, Utah State University, Logan; Dr. Jack R. Fraenkel, professor of interdisciplinary studies and director, Education Research and Development Center, San Francisco State University, San Francisco; Dr. Richard S. Knight, professor of secondary education, Utah State University, Logan; Dr. John J. Patrick, professor of Education and director, ERIC Clearinghouse for Social Studies/Social Science Education, Indiana University, Bloomington; and Dr. Robert J. Stahl, professor of secondary education, Arizona State University, Tempe.

10.1. Thoughtful Classrooms: Students taught in thoughtful classrooms, with atmospheres that promote higher-order thinking, will find social studies to be challenging and engaging.

Research findings:

An extensive body of literature supports the contributions to motivation and learning when students are engaged in higher-order thinking. Moreover, the development of higher-order thinking is an important element in social studies citizenship education. Standards in history, civics and government, and social studies stress the importance of higher-order thinking outcomes such as analysis, interpretation, and value-conflict resolution.

Thoughtful classrooms counter the lack of student interest in social studies that research indicates is prevalent. The six characteristics of thoughtful classrooms (see classroom section) were used to rate social studies lessons in five high schools; 45 students were interviewed and administered questionnaires. Forty-two percent of the students in thoughtful social studies classrooms reported social studies was their most interesting and worthwhile subject, and more than 35 percent of those students said social studies was their most challenging subject.

In the classroom:

In thoughtful classrooms, students are engaged in higher-order thinking as questions or problems are posed that cannot be dealt with through the routine application of knowledge already learned. Based on an extensive review of the literature, Newmann proposed six characteristics of thoughtful classrooms:

- The in-depth, sustained study of a small number of topics is the mode, not the superficial coverage of many topics.

- Lessons are not fragmented, but each has coherence and continuity, with the parts logically related to the development of one or a few ideas.

- Students are given time to think about their responses during discussions.

- The teacher asks questions or structures tasks that are appropriate for the students' ability and background, and challenging because they call for analysis and interpretation, rather than recall and repetition.

- The teacher models thoughtfulness by revealing how he or she thinks through problems such as those under consideration, acknowledging when a definitive answer is not attainable, and recognizing and respecting alternative approaches, especially student-generated ones, to solving problems.

- Students are encouraged and helped to go beyond stating conclusions to the explication and explanation of their reasoning.

In observations of thoughtful classrooms, Newmann found: a) the teacher responded carefully to the quality of the students' reasons for their ideas and conclusions; b) the teacher often used Socratic-type questioning; and c) primary sources were often used, with less reliance on textbooks.

Sources:

Center for Civic Education 1994; Marker and Mehlinger 1992; National Center for History in the Schools 1994, n.d.; National Council for the Social Studies 1994; Newmann 1990a, 1990b, 1991; Parker 1991; Schug, Todd, and Beery 1984; Shaughnessy and Haladyna 1985; Stevenson 1990; Walsh and Paul 1987.

10.2. Jurisprudential Teaching: Students taught with the jurisprudential approach will gain skills in the analysis of contemporary issues, have greater interest in those issues, and learn as much or more social studies content as students taught in a more traditional manner.

Research findings:

In jurisprudential teaching, students are involved in the in-depth consideration of public policy issues and issues of personal citizenship behavior. Jurisprudential teaching is based on a model that includes several elements:

* A recognition that controversy over public issues is inevitable because people have differing frames of reference, stemming from their different backgrounds (e.g., ethnic, gender, geographic, religious, socioeconomic, familial, urban-rural).

* A conception of values (standards or principles for judging worth) as fundamental elements in each person's frame of reference that conflict with one another (e.g., honesty versus compassion) and that underlie public controversy as persons with differing frames of reference define and weigh common values differently (for example, in defining and prioritizing property rights and environmental responsibility in the development and enforcement of zoning laws).

* An analytic frame for analyzing public issues encompassing the need to:

  * be conscious of differing frames of reference;

  * clarify language, including cognitive meanings and emotive loadings;

  * determine and validate relevant facts;

  * identify, define, and weigh relevant values; and

  * come to a decision that takes into account language problems, factual uncertainties, and value discordance.

* A pedagogical approach that involves intensive dialogue among teachers and students based on specific cases, their historical and social contexts, and their implications for policy.

Research on the jurisprudential approach has included investigation of a two-year U.S. history sequence taught to seventh- and eighth-graders using a jurisprudential framework and investigation of a three-year social studies sequence at the high school level. Outcomes for the experimental students were compared against those for control students in the same school and in other schools. The results indicated the experimental students: 1) used appropriate analytic concepts more frequently in considering and discussing public issues; 2) on average gained as much knowledge of social studies content as did the control students, but gained more historical knowledge when it was studied both in the regular curriculum and as part of an issues unit; and 3) had higher interest in societal issues, especially in areas of controversy that had not been studied.

The use of jurisprudential teaching is supported by national standards in social studies and related areas. The national standards for civics and government emphasize students should learn the intellectual skills necessary to analyze public issues critically, so as to be able to evaluate the positions of others and take and define their own positions. Included is the need to understand and deal with conflicts between values. The standards for U.S. history and world history also emphasize the analysis of value-laden social issues. In addition, the social studies curriculum standards stress students should learn to deal with difficult choices about issues involving value conflicts.

In the classroom:

The systematic identification of issues, gathering of background information, and analysis of definitional, factual, and value questions in arriving at a justified policy decision are at the core of jurisprudential teaching. Whether discussions should involve intense confrontational interchanges or the dispersion of nonemotive questions among class members is a decision for the individual teacher, based on his or her own strengths and preferences and those of the students.

A helpful overview of jurisprudential teaching and a discussion of specific instructional steps is available in Joyce and Weil's *Models of Teaching*. Joyce and Weil (1996) focus their attention on a confrontational, Socratic type of discussion; however, Socratic questioning is not a *sine qua non* of jurisprudential teaching. Recitation discussion can be equally effective.

Jurisprudential teaching is applicable to both contemporary and historical issues. The popularity of the jurisprudential approach has been due in part to the availability of short units that can be interspersed in history courses. Updated unit booklets are available from the Social Science Education Consortium on a number of topics—immigration, the American Revolution, the Civil War, the progressive era and the railroad era, the New Deal, organized labor, religious freedom, and science and public policy. In addition, materials produced by Lockwood and Harris (1985a, 1985b) for teaching ethical issues in

history are helpful. Brief historical cases, such as John Adams' decision to defend the British soldiers after the Boston Massacre, are presented, along with questions to help students review facts and analyze the ethical issues involved.

An outline of concepts for analyzing public issues and suggestions for teaching them were developed by Shaver and Larkins (1973). The concepts encompass psychological and semantic effects on reasoning about public issues; handling factual, definitional, and value disputes; and arriving at a qualified decision that takes into account the assumptions being made and conditions under which the decision would be changed. Materials for concept development and suggestions for their use are provided, along with public issues cases for concept application.

Sources:

Center for Civic Education 1994; Hess 2002; Joyce and Weil 1996; Lockwood and Harris 1985a, 1985b; National Center for History in the Schools 1994, n.d.; National Council for the Social Studies 1994; Oliver and Shaver 1966/1974; Parker 1991; Parker, Mueller, and Wendling 1989; Shaver and Larkins 1973.

Social Science Education Consortium booklets: Giese 1989; Giese and Glade 1988; Glade and Giese 1989; Greenawald 1991; Schott 1991; Singleton 1989, 1990, 1993; Stewart and Giese 1989.

10.3. Appropriate Classroom Environment: When social studies teachers establish appropriate classroom environments, their students will have more positive attitudes toward social studies and will develop more positive political attitudes.

Research findings:

Surveys and interviews of students have repeatedly established both low student interest in social studies and the lack of social studies effects on political knowledge and attitudes. The research indicating classroom environment, or climate, can have positive effects on students' attitudes toward social studies and political attitudes is largely correlational. However, reviewers such as Hahn (1991), Leming (1985), and Patrick and Hoge (1991) have pointed out strategies like those discussed herein are based on consistent, if not strong, research findings with grade school, middle school, and high school students.

In the classroom:

The research indicating students' lack of interest in social studies is of serious concern, as is the evidence indicating social studies courses often have little effect on students' political attitudes and behavior. Establishing an appropriate classroom environment (sometimes referred to as *climate*) can help to counter student apathy toward social studies and improve students' political attitudes.

Environmental factors under the teacher's control that have been shown to improve attitudes toward social studies include:

- the provision of clear expectations and rules for classroom behavior and consistency in dealing with rule infractions;

- the use of diverse teaching strategies and new techniques, and avoidance of repetitious classroom routines;

- teaching techniques that actively involve students in lessons, such as group research projects on civil rights issues in which students interview community members and discuss the results in class;

- cooperative learning activities; and

- positive and supportive communication with students.

When controversial issues are discussed, it is important to establish an open environment, or climate, in which:

- students feel free to express their opinions;

- students feel they are respected and their opinions are valued;

- a wide range of views is expressed; and

- the teacher does not take strong, one-sided stands on issues, but encourages rational discussion and disagreement.

Sources:

Angell 1991; Fouts 1987, 1989; Hahn 1991; Haladyna, Shaughnessy, and Redsun 1982; Harwood 1992; Johnson and Johnson 1979; Leming 1985; Marker and Mehlinger 1992; Patrick and Hoge 1991; Schug, Todd, and Beery 1984; Shaughnessy and Haladyna 1985; Shaver 1987; Shaver, Davis, and Helburn 1979.

10.4. Teaching Critical Thinking: Students will better learn and use critical-thinking skills and strategies if these skills and strategies are taught explicitly in the context of content knowledge and with attention to their appropriate applications.

Research findings:

Research reviews over more than 30 years have attested to a growing body of knowledge about teaching students to think critically. The importance of teaching critical-thinking skills is affirmed by the national standards in civics and government, geography, history, and social studies.

Students can learn critical-thinking skills and strategies appropriate to social studies, if they are taught explicitly. The evidence on the relationship between students' content knowledge and the learning and application of critical-thinking skills is less clear, especially in regard to the most effective mix of in-depth knowledge and specific skills instruction. The efficacy of metacognition—the self-monitoring of one's own thinking activity—in learning is well-established, but less is known about how to teach students to engage in metacognition.

In the classroom:

Students typically will not learn to think critically as an indirect result of exposure to the thinking of others. The critical-thinking concepts, skills, and strategies to be learned must be identified and taught explicitly. Direct instruction and guided application are necessary.

For instruction to be effective, the critical thinking skills and strategies to be learned must be appropriate to the types of problems and issues the students are to confront and must be taught in a substantive context. For example, the adequate consideration of public issues requires the identification and analysis of ethical issues (questions of proper aims and actions), typically not part of instruction in social science or history. Also, students' meaningful application of ethical-issues skills will depend on adequate historical and social science knowledge about the public issue under consideration.

Students must also be helped to reflect on the functions of the critical-thinking skills and strategies, and learn to ask themselves questions about how appropriately and adequately they are applying the skills, rather than relying on the teacher to do so. The encouragement of such metacognition—that is, thinking about thinking—requires several steps. Students must:

- be helped to explicitly conceptualize and verbalize thinking skills and strategies;

- learn to recognize types of problems to which the skills can be applied;

- be involved in the collaborative consideration of the appropriateness with which the skills are being applied during discussions or in their writing; and

- observe the teacher modeling self-thought about the processes and concepts used to think critically about issues (that is, the teacher should think aloud as she or he grapples with the definition of problems and the identification and application of an approach or approaches to solving them).

Sources:

Center for Civic Education 1994; Cornbleth 1985; Geography Education Standards Project 1994; Halpern 1998; National Center for History in the Schools 1994, n.d.; National Council for the Social Studies 1994; Oliver and Shaver 1966/1974; Parker 1991; Parker, Mueller, and Wendling 1989; Shaver 1962.

10.5. Support for Concept Development: Students will develop more adequate concepts when instruction includes appropriate definitions, examples and nonexamples of critical elements, exploration of relations to other concepts, and attention to the students' prior knowledge.

Research findings:

The development of valid concepts (categories for grouping and understanding phenomena) has been the subject of extensive experimental research for the last 25 years or so, but only a limited number of studies have been explicitly in social studies. Synopses of the implications for social studies in the research reviews by Martorella (1990, 1991) and by Stanley and Mathews (1985) are particularly helpful to persons interested in a sound, empirical basis for concept instruction. The central place of concept development in social studies education is supported by the emphasis on knowledge and concepts in statements of national standards.

In the classroom:

Concept development is a central goal in social studies. Instruction for concept development should be carefully planned, including identification of the concept's critical attributes—i.e., whether the concept has a relatively simple, fixed, concrete meaning (such as "arable land") or has a complex, shifting, abstract meaning (such as "ethnicity")—assessment of the students' current understanding, and the corresponding selection of activities and materials.

Several instructional steps will promote valid concept development and use:

- Present examples and nonexamples of the concept in a logical order that expands on the intended meaning, culminating with one best example, if possible.

- Cue students to the critical attributes illustrated by the examples and nonexamples with questions, directions, and activities that not only draw attention to the attributes but also help the students to focus on the similarities among the examples and their dissimilarities with the nonexamples.

- Provide the students with evaluations of their efforts to identify the critical attributes illustrated by the examples and nonexamples.

- If the concept has a clear, fixed definition, either state it for the students or help them to enunciate it, as an introduction to and/or summary of the lesson.

- If the concept's meaning is complex, with multiple, abstract, and/or not clearly identifiable critical elements, specifically tell the students that the concept has fuzzy boundaries and help the students identify salient features through consideration of a few best examples.

- With complex concepts, specifically tell the students during discussions which of the possible definitions you are using.

- Help the students, through discourse or questions, to relate the concept being developed to concepts already part of their knowledge.

- Assess students' comprehension by asking questions to determine if they can correctly determine the applicability of new examples and nonexamples and whether they can think of new examples and apply the concept to new situations.

Sources:

Center for Civic Education 1994; Geography Education Standards Project 1994; Martorella 1990, 1991; National Center for History in the Schools 1994, n.d.; National Council for the Social Studies 1994; Stanley and Mathews 1985.

10.6. Effective Questioning: The appropriate phrasing, pacing, and distribution of questions and responses to student answers will enhance student learning in social studies.

Research findings:

Recitation discussions are a central feature of social studies instruction. How they are conducted can make the difference between bored students who learn little and motivated students who achieve both lower-level and higher-level cognitive outcomes.

There is a substantial body of research on types and frequency of teacher questions, but fewer studies that have investigated the linkages between teacher questions and student achievement. Nevertheless, some clear guidelines for effective questioning have emerged. Brophy and Good (1986) and Wilen and White (1991) have written excellent reviews of the research.

In the classroom:

Effective questioning begins with asking questions appropriate to the students' cognitive level and prior knowledge. Most questions should be phrased to elicit a correct response. Contrary to what is often assumed, questions at a predominately lower cognitive level can also promote higher-level achievement if they are logically structured to lead to that outcome. A high frequency of questions, briskly paced, can maximize student achievement, especially with lower socioeconomic status students.

The clarity of the questions asked is crucial. If questions are unclear, it is difficult for students to respond correctly. Clarity is increased by avoiding the use of vague terms; asking one question at a time; not punctuating questions with false starts; and avoiding redundancies, tangled words, irrelevant content, and interjections such as "uh."

It is important that all students participate. Volunteer and nonvolunteer contributions should be balanced at all grade levels; nonvolunteers who probably know the answer or have a contribution to make should be called on, but in an unpredictable pattern. Students should be expected to respond to all teacher questions, even if only to say, "I don't know."

Teachers should wait about three to five seconds for an answer or answers after posing a question. Wait-time increases achievement by giving students a chance to decide whether to respond, to organize an answer, or to ask for clarification.

Praise should be used sparingly in reacting to student responses. The acknowledgment of a correct answer is usually sufficient reinforcement, and overuse trivializes commendation. If an answer is partly correct, the correct part should be affirmed and the question rephrased or follow-up clues given to elicit a fully correct response. Appropriate responses to an incorrect answer include: a) simply saying it is not right, avoiding personal criticism unless it is called for because the student has been inattentive or is unprepared; b) rephrasing or breaking down the question or providing clues to elicit a better response (but avoiding "hammering" a confused or anxious student with a series of follow-up questions); or c) explaining why the answer is incorrect or how a correct answer could be derived from the available information.

Sources:

Brophy and Good 1986; Wilen and White 1991.

10.7. Cognitive Prejudice Reduction: Prejudice can be reduced by increasing students' cognitive sophistication through emphasis on knowledge about other groups, on the unconscious effects of stereotypes, on reasoning skills for drawing valid inferences about group differences, and on the implications of American values for intergroup relations.

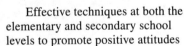

Research findings:

Reviews of research indicate individuals who lack cognitive sophistication and think in either/or terms are more likely to be prejudiced against minority groups. Conversely, those who learn to avoid over-generalizations and stereotypical thinking are less likely to be prejudiced. There is evidence from surveys and interviews by the University of California Research Program on Patterns of American Prejudice that prejudice has a cognitive basis in lack of knowledge, poor reasoning skills, and shallow commitment to basic democratic norms and values. Research also indicates if individuals are helped to confront inconsistencies in their applications of fundamental values to minority groups, they tend to develop more positive attitudes.

The civics and government national standards and the social studies national standards emphasize the importance of students' commitment to and comprehension of basic democratic values, the role of diversity in a democratic society, and reduction in unfair discrimination against those who are different.

In the classroom:

Effective techniques at both the elementary and secondary school levels to promote positive attitudes toward those who are different include contact in cooperative learning groups and simulation situations where prejudice is evoked, analyzed, and discussed. A cognitive approach to prejudice reduction fits particularly well with the academic orientation of secondary-school social studies courses. It can, however, also be an effective complement to elementary teachers' efforts to improve children's self-esteem and develop empathy through fostering positive social interactions among children from different cultural backgrounds and with differing personal characteristics.

Elements in a cognitive approach to prejudice reduction include:

- Providing students with valid knowledge about minorities, including similarities among majority and minority groups, as well as the nature and extent of actual group differences, their roots in social and economic history, and individual diversity within groups.

- Dealing directly with stereotypes and prejudice as concepts, including their basis in partial truths, the unconscious effects of label-based stereotypes, and the commonly negative effects of beliefs and actions based on unexamined prejudgments.

- Developing students' skills in evidence evaluation and logical inference, especially as these apply to caution in drawing conclusions from statements by others about minority groups, from known group differences, and from individual incidents or encounters.

- Developing students' understanding of the nature of democracy and the meanings and implications of basic values such as human worth and dignity, equality, freedom of speech, and religious freedom, as well as the contributions of diversity, and helping students apply basic democratic values in evaluating their own behavior and that of others. (See Avery and Sullivan [1993], and Stephan [1999] for teaching suggestions.)

- Challenging the students to examine their own assumptions and beliefs about persons in other groups, based on sound knowledge, thinking skills, and basic human values.

Sources:

Avery and Sullivan 1993; Banks 1992; Byrnes 1988; Byrnes and Kiger 1992; Center for Civic Education 1994; Curtis 1991; National Council for the Social Studies 1994; Pate 1988; Quinley and Glock 1983; Rokeach 1973; Stephan 1999.

10.8. Computer Technology: Use of computer technology as part of carefully planned instruction can contribute to student interest and motivation and to the attainment of social studies objectives.

Research findings:

Research on the use of computers as instructional media has produced findings of positive effects on student achievement. However, when results are considered only from studies in which the quality of instructional design was controlled—such as having the same instructional designers produce the computer-based instruction and present the live instruction—there are no overall differences in student achievement. It seems evident that the use of computer technology in a classroom will not in itself improve learning. The teacher's curriculum and instructional methodology are crucial, regardless of the medium.

There is evidence that with adequate structuring of the learning environment by teachers, the use of computer databases and simulations can help students develop problem-solving skills. Research also indicates computer use can increase student interest and motivation, enjoyment of and perseverance in their social studies work, and their sense of control over their own learning. However, the control over access to data and to data exploration and manipulation offered by computers is less likely to be used to learning advantage by lower-ability students.

The availability of the Internet and its popular component, the World Wide Web, for classroom use is relatively recent, and the technology is changing so rapidly that there is little research on its instructional effectiveness. Research does confirm use of the Internet in instruction places special demands on teachers and on school resources. In addition, research evidence of an association between socioeconomic status and the availability of computers and Internet access in homes is pertinent to instructional decisions.

Computer technology is not an instructional panacea, and its effective use requires substantial commitment of teacher time, as well as the provision of equipment, infrastructure, and technical and curricular support by the school district. However, computer use in social studies in this technological age is critical for curricular authenticity and for the preparation of students for their future societal roles.

In the classroom:

The use of computer technology in instruction presents many challenges to social studies teachers. At the basic level, they must acquire requisite knowledge to troubleshoot equipment failures in many school districts that do not provide readily available support personnel. Organization of instruction is also challenging if there is not a sufficient number of computers available in the classroom—at least one for each four or five students—or if students must leave the classroom to use computers in a computer lab.

Commercial software to be used in simulations or in database problem-solving activities must be located and evaluated. Then the learning situation must be structured, based on the teacher's objectives, subject-matter knowledge, and analysis of the adequacy of the content, logic, and user friendliness of the software; the capacities of the available computers; the levels of student subject-matter knowledge and reasoning abilities; and student diversity in prior computer use, interest, and expertise.

With computers, regular—often daily—teacher guidance of activities has been found to be more effective than unit-end activities. Helpful activities include group debriefings, interim written products checked by the teacher, clear evaluations of student progress, and assistance to students in deciding on the next steps in the process.

Use of the Internet, including the Web, is even more challenging than the use of computer software. The Internet is a conduit for vast amounts of information, with no mechanisms for controlling who puts information in the stream or for evaluating whether the information is relevant or valid. Although search engines are available, locating Web sites and evaluating their contents for specific instructional purposes can consume a great deal of a teacher's time.

The vast amount of material that is put on the Web without editing or critical review calls for special attention to helping students to be reflective, critical Internet users. Articles by McKenzie (1998) and Risenger (1998) will be useful, as will Practices 2 and 4 of this *Handbook* chapter.

Curricular planning and instruction take on new dimensions with use of the Internet. When students actively interact with the Internet as part of social studies instruction, it is difficult to anticipate the email messages they will exchange, the routes they will take in their Web searches, or the Web sites they will locate. Instruction can no longer be based on the linear introduction of students to resources under control of the teacher. Multiple student-learning routes must be anticipated. Teacher-student roles must be reconfigured, with new and different types of interactions, if electronic technology is to be used to best advantage.

Although the Internet presents social studies teachers with great instructional challenges, it also presents great opportunities. For example, email provides previously unimaginable opportunities for ongoing student exchanges with young people in other societies. Credible Web sites present databases that are not only more comprehensive and interactive, but more up-to-date than is possible with software. Examples, some from a special issue of *Social Education* on technology, include Web addresses for the U.S. Census Bureau (www.census.gov/), the American Psychological Association (www.apa.org), the National Geographic Society (www.nationalgeographic.com/), stock markets (money.cnn.com/markets/), the Library of Congress (lcweb.loc.gov/index.html), and a project to make humanities information available to teachers (edsitement.neh.gov). Regular articles in *Social Education* by Internet editor C. Frederick Risenger (1986a, 1986b) present practical information for social studies teachers, as does his Web site at education.indiana.edu/~socialst.

Sources:

Berson 1996; Braun, Fernlund, and White 1997; Braun and Risenger 1999; Clark 1983, 1994; Clark and Salomon 1986; Clegg 1991; Dillon and Gabbard 1998; Ehman and Glenn 1991; Ehman et al. 1992; Liaw and Huang 2000; Martorella 1997; McKenzie 1998; Risenger 1998a, 1998b; Shaver 1999; Technology 101: Teaching in the Information Age 1998; Windschitl 1998; Zukas 2000.

10.9. Student Participation in the Community: Students who participate actively in the local community as part of the social studies curriculum, performing tasks with real consequences, tend to have a greater sense of social responsibility, increased moral development, enhanced self-esteem, more positive attitudes toward adults, and improved skills and knowledge directly related to the experience.

Research findings:

The evidence on the positive outcomes of community participation as part of the social studies curriculum is tentative. Although a few large studies have been carried out, the difficulties of research control in such settings are great, and the results generally have been small for outcomes such as moral development, anticipated political involvement, self-esteem, thinking skills, and knowledge.

Nevertheless, in every study, the consensus of the participants—not only the students, but also those with whom they worked in the community, their parents, and their teachers—was that community participation is a powerful learning experience that, if structured properly, can be enjoyable and worthwhile.

In the classroom:

The active participation of students in the social and political life of the community gives them opportunities to apply what they have learned and lays a basis for further learning in social studies. Although such real-life involvement fits well with assumptions about how people learn, community participation has not had widespread application in social studies. Programs that have been tried range from public service (such as volunteering in a nursing home or tutoring disadvantaged peers or illiterate adults) to involvement in the political arena (such as

serving an internship with a city or county official). In successful programs, the students are not the recipients of services; rather they perform tasks that they and the community believe are worthwhile and that have observable real-life outcomes, in contrast with most in-class activities.

Community participation is likely to have the greatest effect when the duration is fairly long—for example, a semester or more—and when times are scheduled for the students to meet with other students and teachers or other adults to reflect on the experience. The specific nature of community participation programs varies greatly, however, and students' individual experiences have been found to account for more student learning and growth than do general program characteristics. Among the program elements students have reported as leading to significant experiences are: the freedom to follow personal interests, being allowed to assume adult responsibility for carrying out activities, minimal adult supervision that takes place without negative critiques, the development of personal relationships in the community setting, and the opportunity to discuss the ongoing experience regularly with a knowledgeable, supportive teacher.

Sources:

Conrad 1991; Leming 1985; Newmann 1975; Schug and Beery 1984.

10.10. Constructivist Teaching: When students are involved in actively constructing their knowledge, with teacher guidance based on understanding of the subject matter and the conceptions and misconceptions that the students bring to the learning situation, learning will be both more meaningful and correct.

Research findings:

A constructivist approach to teaching social studies rests on the assumption that meaning, knowledge, or ideas cannot simply be conveyed to students through lectures or reading about a subject-matter area. Individuals construct their own meanings, ideas, and knowledge, and teachers must recognize and guide that process, or inaccurate knowledge or lack of new learning will result. In constructivist teaching, students are given ample opportunities to explore ideas, to think out loud, to develop and share hypotheses, to test their hypotheses and discuss alternative explanations of observed or read-about phenomena, and to revise their thinking in a supportive context.

Constructivist teaching has a solid foundation in the research findings of cognitive psychologists since the 1960s. Much earlier, John Dewey (1933) had clearly articulated the thesis that ideas cannot simply be conveyed from one person to another, but must be developed by individuals as they face quandaries and dilemmas and seek to resolve them based on their own experiences. Most of the recent research has been in science and mathematics education. An educationally significant finding, initially surprising to researchers, is the tenacity of students' "naive" or incorrect beliefs, even when faced with scientifically valid information. The research seems clearly applicable to social studies instruction, whether aimed at teaching social science and historical concepts and knowledge, reducing prejudice, or the analysis of public issues.

In the classroom:

Constructivism as an educational concept is applicable at all learning levels, whether in the involvement of students in production, hands-on projects in the elementary, especially primary, grades or the development of concepts in 12th-grade social science classes. Although focused on the individual student as the developer of his or her own concepts and knowledge, constructivist teaching requires that the teacher play an active instructional role to ensure valid outcomes.

The first teaching step is to decide on the basic ideas, knowledge, and skills to be pursued. Then the students' prior knowledge must be assessed, not only as a base for further learning, but for misunderstandings that might interfere with learning new concepts correctly or developing valid knowledge. Students, for example, may have serious misconceptions about other ethnic groups that will interfere with learning about the dynamics of prejudice or the factors to take into account in debates of public policy.

Once conceptual goals are clearly defined, students' prior knowledge assessed, and any misconceptions identified, the teacher's classroom challenge is to:

- pose the study topic so that it is meaningful to the students, relating it to their prior and ongoing experiences, sometimes through analogy and metaphor (for example, comparing the basic value, "equality of opportunity," to "fairness" in playground team selection);

- engage students in activities (such as Socratic discussions or reading provocative literature) that make them aware of inconsistencies or errors in their thinking;

- propose new ways of viewing the topic (that is, of constructing new schemata) that are not only correct but also meaningful to students (often eliciting the "Oh, now I see!" reaction);

- model and coach appropriate inquiry strategies and skills, while respecting students' often immature efforts at developing meaning;

- encourage students to present their own thinking in discussions with other students;

- assess learning with tests that call for thoughtful analysis and synthesis, not the repetition of memorized bits of information, copying from available sources, or repeating "right" ideas from the teacher or textbook.

Throughout, it is crucial to remember that the students' prior cognitive constructions have been functional and will be resistant to change, whether toward greater accuracy or more complexity. New and accurate meanings that are durable are not likely to be developed quickly, for example, in a one-day lesson. The construction of new meanings that become a part of a student's everyday thought happens over time, with repeated opportunities to think actively about the subject.

 Sources:

Dewey 1933; Halpern 1998; Resnick 1983, 1987; Saunders 1992; Shaver 1977; Windschitl 2002; Zukas 2000.

Bibliography

Angell, A.V. 1991. "Democratic Climates in Elementary Classrooms: A Review of Theory and Research." *Theory and Research in Social Education* Vol. 19: 241-266.

Avery, P., and J. Sullivan. 1993. *Tolerance for Diversity of Beliefs: A Secondary Curriculum Unit.* Boulder, CO: Social Science Education Consortium.

Banks, J.A. 1992. "Reducing Prejudice in Children: Guidelines from Research." *Social Studies and the Young Learner* Vol. 5: 3-5.

Berson, M.J. 1996. "Effectiveness of Computer Technology in the Social Studies: A Review of the Literature." *Journal of Research on Computing Education* Vol. 28: 486-499.

Braun, J.A., Jr., P. Fernlund, and C.W. White. 1997. *Technology Tools in the Social Studies Curriculum.* Wilsonville, OR: Franklin, Beedle & Associates.

Braun, J.A., Jr., and C.F. Risenger, editors. 1999. *Surfing Social Studies: The Internet Book.* Washington, DC: National Council for the Social Studies.

Brophy, J., and T.L. Good. 1986. "Teacher Behavior and Student Achievement." In *Handbook of Research on Teaching* (3rd Edition), M.C. Wittrock, editor (pp. 328-375). New York: Macmillan.

Byrnes, D.A. 1988. "Children and Prejudice." *Social Education* Vol. 52: 267-271.

Byrnes, D.A., and G. Kiger, editors. 1992. *Common Bonds: Anti-Bias Teaching in a Diverse Society.* Wheaton, MD: Association for Childhood Education International.

Center for Civic Education. 1994. *National Standards for Civics and Government.* Calabasas, CA: Center for Civic Education.

Clark, R.E. 1983. "Reconsidering Research on Learning from Media." *Review of Educational Research* Vol. 53: 445-459.

Clark, R.E. 1994. "Media Will Never Influence Learning." *Educational Technology Research and Development* Vol. 42: 21-29.

Clark, R.E., and G. Salomon. 1986. "Media in Teaching." In *Handbook of Research on Teaching* (3rd Edition), M.C. Wittrock, editor (pp. 464-478). New York: Macmillan.

Clegg, A.A., Jr. 1991. "Games and Simulations in Social Studies Education." In *Handbook of Research on Social Studies Teaching and Learning,* J.P. Shaver, editor (pp. 523-529). New York: Macmillan.

Conrad, D. 1991. "School-Community Participation for Social Studies." In *Handbook of Research on Social Studies Teaching and Learning,* J.P. Shaver, editor (pp. 540-548). New York: Macmillan.

Cornbleth, C. 1985. "Critical Thinking and Cognitive Processes." In *Review of Research in Social Studies Education: 1976-1983,* W.B. Stanley, editor (pp. 11-63). Washington, DC: National Council for the Social Studies.

Curtis, C.K. 1991. "Social Studies for Students At-Risk and with Disabilities." In *Handbook of Research on Social Studies Teaching and Learning,* J.P. Shaver, editor (pp. 157-174). New York: Macmillan.

Dewey, J. 1933. *How We Think.* Boston: D.C. Heath.

Dillon, A. and R. Gabbard. 1998. "Hypermedia as an Educational Technology: A Review of the Quantitative Research Literature on Learner Comprehension, Control, and Style." *Review of Educational Research* Vol. 68: 322-349.

Ehman, L.H., and A.D. Glenn. 1991. "Interactive Technology in Social Studies." In *Handbook of Research on Social Studies Teaching and Learning,* J.P. Shaver, editor (pp. 513-522). New York: Macmillan.

Ehman, L.H., A.D. Glenn, V. Johnson, and C.S. White. 1992. "Using Computer Databases in Student Problem Solving: A Study of Eight Social Studies Teachers' Classrooms." *Theory and Research in Social Education* Vol. 20: 179-206.

Fouts, J.T. 1987. "High School Social Studies Classroom Environments and Attitudes: A Cluster Analysis Approach." *Theory and Research in Social Education* Vol. 15: 105-114.

Fouts, J.T. 1989. "Classroom Environments and Student Views of Social Studies: The Middle Grades." *Theory and Research in Social Education* Vol. 17: 136-147.

Geography Education Standards Project. 1994. *Geography for Life: National Geography Standards 1994.* Washington, DC: National Geographic Society.

Giese, J.R. 1989. *The Progressive Era: The Limits of Reform.* Boulder, CO: Social Science Education Consortium.

Giese, J.R., and M.E. Glade. 1988. *The American Revolution: Crisis of Law and Change.* Boulder, CO: Social Science Education Consortium.

Glade, M.E., and J.R. Giese. 1989. *Immigration: Pluralism and National Identity.* Boulder, CO: Social Science Education Consortium.

Greenawald, G.D. 1991. *The Railroad Era: Business Competition and the Public Interest.* Boulder, CO: Social Science Education Consortium.

Hahn, C.L. 1991. "Controversial Issues in Social Studies." In *Handbook of Research on Social Studies Teaching and Learning,* J.P. Shaver, editor (pp. 470-480). New York: Macmillan.

Haladyna, T.M., J. Shaughnessy, and A. Redsun. 1982. "Correlates of Attitudes toward Social Studies." *Theory and Research in Social Education* Vol. 10: 1-26.

Halpern, D.F. 1998. "Teaching Critical Thinking for Transfer Across Domains: Dispositions, Skills, Structure Training, and Metacognitive Monitoring." *American Psychologist* Vol. 53, No. 4: 449-455.

Harwood, A.M. 1992. "Classroom Climate and Civic Education in Secondary Social Studies Research: Antecedents and Findings." *Theory and Research in Social Education* Vol. 20: 47-86.

Hess, D.E. 2002. "Discussing Controversial Public Issues in Secondary Social Studies Classrooms: Learning from Skilled Teachers." *Theory and Research in Social Education* Vol. 30: 10-41.

Johnson, D.W., and R.T. Johnson. 1979. "Conflict in the Classroom: Controversy and Learning." *Review of Educational Research* Vol. 49: 51-70.

Joyce, B., and M. Weil. 1996. *Models of Teaching* (5th Edition). Boston: Allyn and Bacon.

Leming, J.S. 1985. "Research on Social Studies Curriculum and Instruction: Interventions and Outcomes in the Socio-Moral Domain." In *Review of Research in Social Studies Education: 1976-1982,* W.B. Stanley, editor (pp. 123-213). Washington, DC: National Council for the Social Studies.

Liaw, S., and H. Huang. 2000. "Enhancing Interactivity in Web-Based Instruction: A Review of the Literature." *Educational Technology* Vol. 40, No. 3: 41-45.

Lockwood, A.L., and D.E. Harris. 1985a. *Reasoning with Democratic Values: Ethical Problems in United States History, Volume 1: 1607-1876.* New York: Teachers College Press.

Lockwood, A.L., and D.E. Harris. 1985b. *Reasoning with Democratic Values: Ethical Problems in United States History, Volume 2: 1877 to the Present.* New York: Teachers College Press.

Marker, G., and H. Mehlinger. 1992. "Social Studies." In *Handbook of Research on Curriculum,* P.W. Jackson, editor (pp. 830-851). New York: Macmillan.

Martorella, P.H. 1990. "Teaching Concepts." In *Classroom Teaching Skills* (4th Edition), J.M. Cooper, editor. Lexington, MA: D.C. Heath.

Martorella, P.H. 1991. "Knowledge and Concept Development in Social Studies." In *Handbook of Research on Social Studies Teaching and Learning,* J.P. Shaver, editor (pp. 370-384). New York: Macmillan.

Martorella, P.H., editor. 1997. *Interactive Technologies and the Social Studies: Emerging Issues and Applications.* Albany: State University of New York Press.

McKenzie, J. 1998 (Sept.). "Grazing the Net: Raising a Generation of Free-Range Students." *Phi Delta Kappan* Vol. 80: 26-31.

National Center for History in the Schools. (n.d.) *National Standards for United States History: Exploring the American Experience.* Los Angeles: University of California, Los Angeles.

National Center for History in the Schools. 1994. *National Standards for World History: Exploring Paths to the Present.* Los Angeles: University of California, Los Angeles.

National Council for the Social Studies. 1994. *Expectations of Excellence: Curriculum Standards for Social Studies.* Washington, DC: NCSS.

Newmann, F.M. 1975. *Education for Citizen Action: Challenge for Secondary Education.* Berkeley, CA: McCutchan.

Newmann, F.M. 1990a. "Higher Order Thinking in Social Studies: A Rationale for the Assessment of Classroom Thoughtfulness." *Journal of Curriculum Studies* Vol. 22: 41-56.

Newmann, F.M. 1990b. "Qualities of Thoughtful Social Studies Classes: An Empirical Profile." *Journal of Curriculum Studies* Vol. 22: 253-275.

Newmann, F.M. 1991. "Promoting Higher Order Thinking in Social Studies: Overview of a Study of Sixteen High School Departments." *Theory and Research in Social Education* Vol. 19: 324-340.

Oliver, D.W., and J.P. Shaver. 1974. *Teaching Public Issues in the High School.* Logan, UT: Utah State University Press. (Original work published 1966.)

Parker, W.C. 1991. "Achieving Thinking and Decision-Making Objectives in Social Studies." In *Handbook of Research on Social Studies Teaching and Learning,* J.P. Shaver, editor (pp. 345-356). New York: Macmillan.

Parker, W.C., M. Mueller, and L. Wendling. 1989. "Critical Reasoning on Civic Issues." *Theory and Research in Social Education* Vol. 17, No. 1: 7-32.

Pate, G.S. 1988. "Research on Reducing Prejudice." *Social Education* Vol. 52: 287-289.

Patrick, J.J., and J.D. Hoge. 1991. "Teaching Government, Civics, and Law." In *Handbook of Research on Social Studies Teaching and Learning,* J.P. Shaver, editor (pp. 427-436). New York: Macmillan.

Quinley, H.E., and C.Y. Glock. 1983. *Anti-Semitism in America.* New Brunswick, NJ: Transaction Books.

Resnick, L.B. 1983. "Mathematics and Science Learning: A New Conception." *Science* Vol. 220: 470-478.

Resnick, L.B. 1987. *Education and Learning to Think.* Washington, DC: National Academy Press.

Risenger, C.F. 1998a. "Instructional Strategies for the World Wide Web." *Social Education* Vol. 62: 110-111.

Risenger, C.F. 1998b. "Separating the Wheat from the Chaff: Why Dirty Pictures Are Not the Real Dilemma in Using the Internet to Teach Social Studies." *Social Education* Vol. 62: 148-150.

Rokeach, M. 1973. *The Nature of Human Values.* New York: The Free Press.

Saunders, W.L. 1992. "The Constructivist Perspective: Implications and Teaching Strategies for Science." *School Science and Mathematics* Vol. 92, No. 3: 136-141.

Schott, J.C. 1991. *Religious Freedom: Belief, Practice, and the Public Interest.* Boulder, CO: Social Science Education Consortium.

Schug, M.C., and R. Beery. 1984. *Community Study: Applications and Opportunities.* Washington, DC: National Council for the Social Studies.

Schug, M.C., R.J. Todd, and R. Beery. 1984. "Why Kids Don't Like Social Studies." *Social Education* Vol. 48: 382-387.

Shaughnessy, J., and T.M. Haladyna. 1985. "Research on Student Attitude Toward Social Studies." *Social Education* Vol. 49: 692-695.

Shaver, J.P. 1962. "Educational Research and Instruction for Critical Thinking." *Social Education* Vol. 26: 13-16.

Shaver, J.P. 1977. "Needed: A Deweyean Rationale for Social Studies." *The High School Journal* Vol. 60, No. 8: 345-352.

Shaver, J.P. 1979. "The Usefulness of Educational Research in Curricular/Instructional Decision-Making in Social Studies." *Theory and Research in Social Education* Vol. 7, No. 3: 21-46.

Shaver, J.P. 1987. "Implications from Research: What Should Be Taught in Social Studies?" In *Educators' Handbook: A Research Perspective,* V. Richardson-Koehler, editor (pp. 112-138). New York: Longman.

Shaver, J.P., editor. 1991. *Handbook of Research on Social Studies Teaching and Learning.* New York: Macmillan.

Shaver, J.P. 1999. "Electronic Technology and the Future of Social Studies in Elementary and Secondary Schools." *Journal of Education* Vol. 60, No. 3: 13-40.

Shaver, J.P., O.L. Davis, Jr., and S.W. Helburn. 1979. The Status of Social Studies Education: Impressions from the Three NSF Studies. *Social Education* Vol. 43, No. 2: 150-153.

Shaver, J.P., and A.G. Larkins. 1973. *The Analysis of Public Issues Program.* Boston: Houghton Mifflin.

Singleton, L.R. 1989. *The Civil War: Slavery and the Crisis of Union.* Boulder, CO: Social Science Education Consortium.

Singleton, L.R. 1990. *The New Deal: Government and the Economy.* Boulder, CO: Social Science Education Consortium.

Singleton, L.R. 1993. *Science and Public Policy: Uses and Control of Knowledge.* Boulder, CO: Social Science Education Consortium.

Stanley, W.B., and R.C. Mathews. 1985. "Recent Research on Concept Learning: Implications for Social Education." *Theory and Research in Social Education* Vol. 12: 57-74.

Stephan, W. 1999. *Reducing Prejudice and Stereotyping in Schools.* New York: Teachers College Press.

Stevenson, R.B. 1990. "Engagement and Cognitive Challenge in Thoughtful Social Studies Classes: A Study of Student Perspectives." *Journal of Curriculum Studies* Vol. 22: 329-341.

Stewart, J., and J.R. Giese. 1989. *The Rise of Organized Labor: Workers, Employers, and the Public Interest.* Boulder, CO: Social Science Education Consortium.

Technology 101: Teaching in the Information Age. 1998. Special issue of *Social Education* Vol. 62, Number 3.

Walsh, D., and R.W. Paul. 1987. *The Goal of Critical Thinking: From Educational Ideal to Educational Reality.* Washington, DC: American Federation of Teachers.

Wilen, W.W., and J.J. White. 1991. "Interaction and Discourse in Social Studies Classrooms." In *Handbook of Research on Social Studies Teaching and Learning,* J.P. Shaver, editor (pp. 483-495). New York: Macmillan.

Windschitl, M. 1998. "The WWW and Classroom Research: What Path Should We Take?" *Educational Researcher* Vol. 27: 28-33.

Windschitl, M. 2002. "Framing Constructivism in Practice as the Negotiation of Dilemmas: An Analysis of the Conceptual, Pedagogical, Cultural, and Political Challenges Facing Teachers." *Review of Educational Research* Vol. 72: 131-175.

Zukas, A. 2000. "Active Learning , World History, and the Internet: Creating Knowledge in the Classroom." *The International Journal of Social Education* Vol. 15, No. 1: 62-79.

Chapter 11. Focusing Staff Development on Improving the Learning of All Students

Dennis Sparks

High-quality staff development is essential if teachers are to consistently apply in their classrooms the findings of the research described in this *Handbook*. This professional development, however, must be considerably different from that offered in the past. It must not only affect the knowledge, attitudes, and practices of individual teachers, administrators, and other school employees, it must also alter the cultures and structures of the organizations in which those individuals work.

Education leaders who seek to improve student learning must pay attention to organizational change as well as to the learning of individual teachers and administrators so that those activities are coherent and aligned with other reform efforts. "The greatest problem faced by school districts and schools," according to Fullan (1991), is not resistance to innovation, but the fragmentation, overload, and incoherence resulting from the uncritical acceptance of too many different innovations" (197).

Two Basic Assumptions

Two basic assumptions support the staff development recommendations made in this chapter:

- High levels of learning for all students and staff members require deep change in schools and school systems. Structural and cultural factors that surround professional learning can either support or hinder the implementation of staff development efforts.

- Staff development is essential but must be significantly different than the approach taken in the past if it is to produce high levels of learning for students and staff members (Jones 1998; Sparks and Hirsh 1997). This

staff development must have as its core process a "community of learners" whose members accept joint responsibility for the high levels of learning of all students. The teachers in this "community of learners" must meet regularly to learn, plan, and support one another in the process of continuous improvement.

Structural Issues

Someone once noted that every system is specifically designed to produce the results it is getting. The interconnectedness of all parts of the educational enterprise means classrooms, schools, and school districts are tied together in a web of relationships in which decisions and actions in any one part affect the other parts and the system as a whole. Put another way, the systems within which people work (including their cultural dimensions) exert a powerful influence on the performance of schools and individual teachers.

"Systems thinking is a discipline for seeing wholes," Peter Senge (1990) wrote. "It is a framework for seeing interrelationships rather than things" (69). Senge stressed the importance of looking beyond personalities and events and seeing the structures in which employees operate so that the unseen forces limiting progress can be worked with and changed. Because employees do not usually see the structures or realize their power, they often find themselves compelled to act in certain ways.

Without this knowledge of systems, Senge points out "The harder you push, the harder the system pushes back" (1990, 58). He notes that small changes applied at the points of greatest leverage can produce big results, but these points are often the least obvious because of our attention to symptoms rather than underlying causes.

School improvement has often suffered from the very antithesis of systems thinking—a "project mentality" that attempted to isolate parts of the system for special attention while ignoring the remainder of the system. A project might address one particular aspect of the curriculum (for example, elementary mathematics) or of instruction (for example, cooperative learning) without considering how those elements affect and are affected by other parts of the system. For instance, changing the elementary mathematics curriculum without simultaneously considering changes in assessment or instructional skills is likely to lead, at best, to partial implementation of the new curriculum.

Robert Fritz, in *Corporate Tides: The Inescapable Laws of Organizational Structure* (1996), describes how organizational structures influence behavior. He says such structures can either be oscillating or advancing. Oscillating structures occur when the resolution of one tension in an organization produces an opposing tension—movement in one direction precipitates eventual movement in another direction—causing the organization to have a sense of change but no real progress. "Oscillating behavior," Fritz writes, "is that which moves from one place to another, but then moves back toward its original position" (6). The classic example is someone who diets to lose weight, then eats because of the hunger generated by the diet, which in turn causes weight gain.

Problem solving, Fritz says, is bound to be unsuccessful within an oscillating structure because the motivation to continue the problem-solving behavior diminishes as the tension caused by the problem is reduced, and as the problem-solving behavior diminishes, the problems return. The only alternative, according to Fritz, is to design an advancing structure. These structures contain three basic elements: a compelling vision, a thorough assessment of current

reality, and powerful strategies to resolve the tension created by the disparity between the vision and current reality.

Fritz's thoughts on the role of vision within an advancing structure give guidance to schools seeking to improve the learning of all students. "Without vision," he writes, "the organization is left to problem solve its way into an oscillating pattern. But vision cannot be produced by a reaction against what we do not want. It must be a product of what we do want" (177). Aspirations and values, Fritz believes, should be the primary generative force around which we organize our lives and organizations.

Not all visions are equal, Fritz points out, in their ability to move people to positive action. Many vision statements lack power because of their fuzzy language and vagueness. "Authentic vision," he argues, "lives, breathes, and is tangible. The term implies something that we can see well enough to recognize it if it appeared in reality" (184).

"When people share a common vision, they can perform feats that would otherwise be impossible," writes Fritz. "There is something in the human spirit that longs for participation with others, that wants to be involved in a collective endeavor." (202). In that situation, "we not only tolerate change, we actively seek it" (200).

The importance of a compelling vision is also emphasized by Charles Schwahn and William Spady (1998). "Leadership and productive change begin with the creation of a compelling organizational purpose," they write. "... But a compelling purpose alone will not result in *productive change*—change that makes a positive difference in student learning and in how schools operate. What's missing in most cases is a concrete, detailed vision statement that describes what the organization will look like when operating at its ideal best to accomplish its declared purpose" (45).

Deep Change

"Stretch goals" are an aspect of compelling vision that can be a powerful motivator for comprehensive change. Jack Welch, CEO of General Electric, defines stretch goals as those the goal-setter doesn't know how to accomplish when they are set. In his view, these are the kind of goals that many businesses must establish if they are to survive in today's highly competitive marketplace. While public education may or may not be in jeopardy, depending on the eye of the beholder, Welch's notion of stretch goals suggests the depth of change that may be required to create schools in which all students and staff members learn and perform at high levels.

Robert E. Quinn, author of *Deep Change: Discovering the Leader Within* (1996), also wrote about the need for comprehensive change. Incremental change, he argued, does not disrupt past patterns. "Deep change differs from incremental change in that it requires new ways of thinking and behaving. It is change that is major in scope, discontinuous with the past, and generally irreversible" (3).

Compelling Vision

Here is a vision of what is desired that contains sufficient stretch to require deep change in schools. This vision is informed in large degree by *What Matters Most: Teaching for America's Future* (National Commission on Teaching and America's Future 1996):

- All students learn and perform at high levels.

- All students have competent, caring teachers. While competence once was limited to the skills of working in an individual classroom, according to Stephen Anderson, Carol Rolheiser, and Kim Gordon, today it ". . . has shifted from individual teacher expertise toward professional community expertise— teachers jointly defining goals and taking responsibility for all students' progress, engaging in ongoing inquiry and experimentation, and assuming leadership in school development" (1998, 59).

- Teachers are well prepared, provided with ongoing professional development, and receive the appropriate support so they can be competent.

- The vast majority of staff development focuses on the content knowledge, instructional skills, and other classroom-related knowledge and skills required of teachers to be competent and caring. This staff development will improve student learning because it is experiential, grounded in teachers' questions and inquiry, collaborative, linked to and derived from teachers' work with their students, connected to the study of subject matter and teaching methods, sustained and intensive (including coaching, modeling, and problem solving), and connected to other aspects of school change (Darling-Hammond 1998b).

- Educational leaders keep schools focused on the learning processes and organizational/structural changes required to produce high levels of learning and performance for all students and staff members. School leaders who are successful in moving schools to high levels of learning for students and staff members alike see themselves as "system designers" and models of career-long learning. Principals who are designers understand that structures exert a powerful influence on learning and performance and help design a system that produces the desired result. These leaders of change efforts must also be role models, Robert Quinn believes. "When evaluating a vision," Quinn writes, "people watch the behavior of their leaders and quickly recognize if a leader lacks personal discipline and commitment" (1996, 125).

Current Reality

For far too many teachers in the United States, staff development is a demeaning, mind-numbing experience as they passively "sit and get." That staff development is often mandatory in nature, driven by seat-time requirements such as CEUs, and evaluated by "happiness scales." As one observer put it, "I hope I die during an inservice session, because the transition between life and death would be so subtle."

Richard Elmore (1996), a Harvard University professor of education, argues that typical school reform does not affect the "core of educational practice": how teachers understand the nature of knowledge and the student's role in learning, how these ideas are manifested in teaching and classwork, student grouping practices, teachers' responsibilities for groups of students, processes for assessing student learning and communicating it to others, and the physical layout of classrooms. Because staff development is embedded in systems that profoundly affect its effectiveness, school leaders must address structural issues as well as the learning needs of individual school employees. That means principals must see themselves not only as leaders of learning communities and models of career-long learning, but as "school designers" who create structures that support high levels of learning.

Current reality, unfortunately, differs in many important respects from that vision:

- Many students do not learn at high levels.

- Whether students have competent, caring teachers is hit or miss; some kids have the good fortune to have such teachers, but others do not.

- The vast majority of staff development/school improvement activities do not focus on teachers' content knowledge, instructional skills, or other classroom-related knowledge and skills. Too often the focus continues to be on "safe" topics such as student self-esteem, teacher morale, and communication with parents. The small amount of staff development that focuses on teachers' instructional knowledge and skills is often not sufficiently rigorous or sustained to produce lasting on-the-job changes. While there are exceptions to the above, they are far too infrequent to ensure success for all students.

A New Type of Staff Development

A school's compelling vision and stretch goals provide a powerful context for a new kind of staff development. The elements of this new

kind of staff development are outlined in the following pages.

Begins with a clear sense of what students need to learn and be able to do.

That decision, in turn, leads to other decisions about curriculum, instructional practices, and assessment. Ambitious intentions for students—and the changes they require throughout the system—provide a powerful rationale for staff development. Without it, staff development is simply a meaningless requirement rather than a means to an important end. Effective results-driven staff development also requires use of various sources of student-performance data and research in decision making (Schmoker 1996; Wang, Haertel, and Walberg 1998) and program evaluation (Guskey and Sparks 1991).

To be effective, results-driven staff development measures its success in terms of changes in teacher knowledge and skills and improvements in student learning rather than in terms of continuing education units, staff development points earned for attendance at workshops, or other "seat-time" events. That means a larger portion of teachers' pay will be based on demonstrated knowledge and skills rather than longevity and university credits earned (Odden and Kelley 1997). The National Board for Professional Teaching Standards (1997) provides one well-documented means for assessing the knowledge and skills of accomplished teachers. Teacher portfolios, such as the ones used in Robbinsdale, Minn., provide another such process (Bradley 1998).

Is based on standards for student learning, teaching, and staff development.

Standards for student learning provide the rationale for the new forms of staff development described here. Standards for teachers—such as those developed by the National Board for Professional Teaching Standards—provide a benchmark for professional practice and a focus for the things teachers need to learn to be successful. Standards for staff development—such as those developed for elementary, middle schools, and high schools by the National Staff Development Council (1994, 1995a, 1995b)— provide a means for school faculties to assess the quality of their current staff development efforts and make improvement where necessary. These staff development standards insist that these efforts be sustained, rigorous, and focused on high levels of learning for all students.

Focuses on schoolwide goals for student learning that are based on the unique strengths and challenges faced by that particular school community (Renyi 1998; Council of Chief State School Officers 1997).

These goals must reflect high expectations for students and staff members, have as their primary intention the improvement of teachers' content knowledge and instructional skills, and require interdependent effort for their successful accomplishment.

School staff members formed into one or more communities of learners are the center for instructional change efforts, but their work must be supported by the school district. Phil Schlechty argues "only through revitalizing and redirecting the action of district-level operations can the kind of widespread and radical change that must occur become possible" (1997, 79). Elsewhere (Sparks 1998), Schlechty points out school districts must establish a clear focus on a preferred future, maintain that focus by basing it in the system rather than personalities, and have the capacity to behave strategically, particularly the ability to stop doing unnecessary old things that are maintained by constituencies whose interests may be threatened.

District personnel, says Schlechty, need to help principals and teachers become skillful in collecting and analyzing data and using it to inform decisions. "Central office plays a key role in articulating, communicating, and sustaining the beliefs and vision toward which action is expected to be oriented. The idea of each building having its own vision is wrong-headed if we want schools to serve total communities rather

than isolated sets of parents and students" (Sparks 1998, 41).

Is job-embedded and team based.

"My analysis," Milbrey McLaughlin writes, "is based on the view that teachers' professional development of the most meaningful sort takes place not in a workshop or in discrete, bundled convocations but in the context of professional communities—discourse communities, learning communities" (1994, 31). Although workshops and courses have their place in a comprehensive staff development effort, much of the important learning in a school needs to take place as teachers face the day-to-day challenges of their work (Darling-Hammond 1996).

Teacher and principal learning should occur through processes such as study groups (Mohr 1998), coaching, action research (Calhoun 1994), and the joint planning of lessons and critiquing of student work. "Teachers learn best by studying, doing, and reflecting; by collaborating with other teachers; by looking closely at students and their work; and by sharing what they see" (Darling-Hammond 1998b, 8).

Consequently, the core staff development process occurs among a small group of teachers (eight to 12) who share a common responsibility within a school for educating all their students to high levels of learning and who meet several hours each week to refine their lessons, review student work, and discuss ways instruction can be improved (Meier 1998). This team makes its decisions based on data and research (Schmoker 1996). Teams might consist of teachers who share a grade level, who share subject-matter specialization in a secondary school, or who are engaged in interdisciplinary teaching.

While the vast majority of their professional learning occurs in this small-group setting, team members also attend workshops and institutes, participate in various face-to-face and electronic networks, and serve as mentors and coaches. In addition, the team occasionally invites "critical friends" or consultants to meet with their group over an extended period of time to teach a skill, provide feedback, or engage the group in a problem-solving process.

Time for such study is found through changes in the school's schedule (Murphy 1997) or through deeper changes in school organization (National Education Commission on Time and Learning 1994a, 1994b; National Commission on Teaching and America's Future 1996). Such changes will also require new types of labor-management contracts (Kerchner, Koppich, and Weeres 1997).

Is built on a core set of ideas and beliefs.

"Training programs typically function to persuade trainees to change their skill (behavior) rather than their self-concept, beliefs, or work environment," Sally J. Perkins writes. "Yet persuasion research reports that resistance to attitudinal and behavioral change is complicated by the variables of intelligence, locus of control, social norms, time pressure, and degree of vested interest, among others" (1998, 253).

Renate Nummela Caine and Geoffrey Caine agree: "Perhaps the most significant thing we have confirmed for ourselves is that, although actions are important, the thinking that influences and shapes what we do is far more critical," they write. "Changing our thinking is the first thing we have to do both individually and collectively, because without that change we cannot possibly change what we really do on a day-to-day basis" (1997, vi).

Elsewhere, the Caines (1998) describe the importance of "mental models" in shaping school and classroom practice. "Mental models," they write, "are deeply held beliefs, assumptions, and images that influence the way we think and that guide the actions we take. They are so deeply held that they may be invisible to us" (1998, 1). They suggest three elements of the dominant mental model that serve as barriers to reform: 1) experts create knowledge; 2) teachers disseminate this knowledge; and 3) students are graded on how much of this knowledge they have retained.

Ideas and beliefs have a powerful effect on school practice, particularly leadership and instructional practice, but are typically ignored in staff development efforts. For instance, the beliefs that only a small number of students can master rigorous content or that the purpose of schools is to sort and select students for various occupational tracks need to be thoroughly discussed. Ideas about the nature of learning, teaching, and leadership need to be fully explored by teachers, principals, and other members of the school community.

Is matched to the instructional processes desired in the school.

For instance, schools that desire constructivist teaching (in which students are viewed as constructors of their own knowledge systems) require staff development that models constructivist practices. Transmittal forms of staff development will not create constructivist teaching. Likewise, schools that want their students to be involved in more active forms of learning requiring the solving of real-life problems will provide learning opportunities for teachers that involve them in learning through similar means and producing comparable products.

Is focused to a large extent on content and content-specific pedagogy.

Recently developed standards in the various academic disciplines require teachers to lead students to a depth of understanding often not present in their own college courses. Consequently, teachers themselves need opportunities to acquire deeper understanding of the content (Ball and Cohen 1996; Lawton 1998; Darling-Hammond 1998b) and to be taught by teachers who model instructional practices appropriate to that content (for instance, those strategies described in this Handbook). This learning may occur through professional networks (Pennell and Firestone 1998), professional assessment, teacher academies, and peer review (Darling-Hammond 1996, 1998a).

Susan Loucks-Horsley and others (1998) describe the implications of content-focused staff development in the areas of mathematics and science. They recommend learning processes such as action research, case discussions, professional networking, examining student work, and coaching and mentoring.

In comparing teacher development in the United States with that in Japan, James W. Stigler and James Hiebert write, "The approach to improving teaching used in Japan is not based on distributing written reports, or on reforming features of instruction, or on assuming that teachers will change when surrounding elements change. It is based on the direct study of teaching, with the goal of steady improvement in the mathematics learning of students" (1997, 20). Teacher development in Japan, they observe, begins with clearly stated goals for student learning, but is followed by career-long engagement in a " relentless, continuous process of improving their lessons to improve students' opportunities to achieve the learning goals. A key part of this process is their participation in 'lesson study groups.' Small groups of teachers meet regularly, once a week for about an hour, to plan, implement, evaluate, and revise lessons collaboratively" (20). On the other hand, teacher development in the United States, Stigler and Hiebert contend, has no mechanism for teachers to improve gradually over time. This may be because of the U.S. assumption that good teachers are born, not made, and that " good teaching comes through artful and spontaneous interactions with students during lessons" (20).

Changes the organization's structure and culture at the same time individual teachers and administrators are acquiring new knowledge and skills.

It is essential that school leaders recognize the power of the organization—its roles, processes, and structures—to shape the behavior of individuals (Joyce 1990). Senge (1990) argues organizations must continually adapt through the learning of their members or risk failure and extinction. The "learning organizations" he describes possess five "disciplines": systems thinking (described in the following paragraphs),

personal mastery (continually clarifying what is important and continually learning how to see current reality more clearly), mental models (recognizing the power of internal images in shaping practice), shared vision (tapping into people's desire to be connected to an important undertaking), and team learning (using dialogue to help team members suspend their assumptions while at the same time communicating these assumptions freely). In these disciplines, Senge is recognizing the power of collective processes and of the structures to affect individual performance.

School districts and schools are complex organizations whose cultures promote certain behaviors and inhibit others. Staff development focusing exclusively on the behavior of individual teachers without recognizing the influence of the organization in supporting or suppressing new practices is destined for failure.

To become learning organizations, schools must engage in organization development (OD) activities (Schmuck and Runkel 1988). According to Walters (1990), organization development is a process of planned change in which the change is defined and owned by the client organization (in this case the school or school system). It is a long-term, systemic process rather than a one-time intervention. OD is based on continual data collection, analysis, and feedback, and focuses on the development of groups and individual development that would improve group functioning. In addition, organization development improves the organization's capacity to solve future problems.

When training is the learning mode being used, make certain it is well designed and provides a great deal of follow-up support in the classroom over a sustained period of time.

Joyce, Wolf, and Calhoun (1993) point out that poor design of training and follow-up is a primary reason for the low level of implementation of new practices by teachers. They point out that major innovations may require 10-15 days of training rather than the one or two days that are typically provided.

Effective workshops, they argue, provide teachers with a deep understanding of the conceptual base of the new strategy and its effects on students. Demonstration is the "fulcrum of training design"; teachers require about 20 demonstrations of the strategy, about half of which should be videotapes of students. In addition, teachers need workshop opportunities to practice the new skill, especially the "opening moves." Even with these training elements in place, Joyce, Wolf, and Calhoun (1993) point out fewer than 10 percent of these desired instructional practices will be added to teachers' repertoires, unless workplace redesign is undertaken.

Coaching and action research are among those workplace redesigns that complement training by promoting transfer to the classroom. When the goal of training is transfer of skills from the workshop to consistent, correct use in the classroom, Joyce and Showers (1995) underscore the critical importance of participants understanding the theoretical base of the skill, viewing numerous demonstrations of the practice, practicing the skills with feedback, and receiving on-the-job coaching. "A large and dramatic increase in transfer of training . . .," they write, "occurs when in-class coaching is added to an initial training experience comprised of theory explanation, demonstrations, and practice with feedback" (1995, 112). This type of training enhances teachers' fluency with the new skill, improves their executive control over its use, and increases their confidence as they integrate the skill with ongoing instructional practices.

Provides generous amounts of time for collaborative work and various learning activities.

"We recommend that teachers be provided with the professional time and opportunities they need to do their jobs," the National Education Commission on Time and Learning concluded (1994a, 36). A fundamental lesson about school reform from the past decade is that far more time is required for staff learning and collaborative work than is currently available. Staff development days—typically for workshops—and brief meetings before, during, or after the school day when other responsibilities tug at the participants are grossly insufficient for the collegial learning and planning that are essential to successful school improvement efforts.

A follow-up publication from the National Education Commission on Time and Learning argues "The Commission's study of time and learning in schools clearly and consistently points to a need for more and better time for teacher learning" (1994b, 39). The Commission points out this time is needed for teachers to master their subjects, design learning experiences for students that result in the achievement of high academic standards, use improved assessment systems, and work with and learn from colleagues. "To lock teachers into the existing system, which defines a teacher's professional activity almost solely as the time spent in front of students in classrooms, is to guarantee failure," the latter report notes (39).

Hugh Price (1993), then vice president at the Rockefeller Foundation and currently president of the National Urban League, argues an important barrier to providing time for teacher development is our uncertainty about what to do with students while teachers are away from their classrooms. For that purpose, he proposes "academically productive ways" students could spend the equivalent of one day a week away from their regular teachers that "wouldn't cost the district a bundle." Price suggests as possible options school-based extracurricular activities, occasional large classes, course-related projects (higher-order assignments), and community service.

Purnell and Hill (1992) and Raywid (1993) suggest additional ways time can be found for staff development. Their recommendations include better use of existing time (for example, faculty and department meetings), schoolwide community service projects that would free most of the staff for collaborative work, extending the school day for a few minutes four days a week with an early release day on the fifth day, and adjustments in the master schedule to accommodate team meetings during the school day.

Conclusion

"The continuing issue for professional development is how to make more sustained, in-depth opportunities for teacher learning more widely and routinely available in schools across the country," Darling-Hammond concludes (1998c, 36). And as was previously described, this professional development must be considerably different from that typically available to teachers and administrators today.

There is good news, however, because, as Joyce, Wolf, and Calhoun observe, "Strong, well-supported initiatives are easier to make than are weak ones, and educators are perfectly capable of rapidly learning the skills and knowledge to sustain the most complex initiatives thus far put forward, provided that adequate support is given" (1993, 6).

Policy makers at all levels are responsible for creating the conditions for such initiatives. Given the barriers described in this chapter, this is no easy task, however. It requires vision, persistence, and recognition of the essential role professional learning communities must play in meaningful reform efforts. But those expectations are no less challenging than those we hold for teachers and principals—to educate all students to meet high standards of learning. When these challenges seem overwhelming, it is wise to remember the words of Margaret Mead, who is reported to have said: "Never doubt that a small group of thoughtful, committed citizens can change the world; indeed, it's the only thing that ever has."

Bibliography

Anderson, S., C. Rolheiser, and K. Gordon. 1998. "Preparing Teachers to Be Leaders." *Educational Leadership* Vol. 55, No. 5: 59-61.

Ball, D.L., and D. Cohen. 1996. "Reform by the Book: What Is—Or Might Be—the Role of Curriculum Materials in Teacher Learning and Instructional Reform." *Educational Researcher* Vol. 25, No. 9: 6-8.

Bradley, A. 1998. "Rethinking Teacher Pay." *Teacher Magazine* (April 1998): 16.

Caine, R.N., and G. Caine. 1997. *Education on the Edge of Possibility*. Alexandria, VA: Association for Supervision and Curriculum Development.

Caine, R.N., and G. Caine. 1998. *NASSP Bulletin* Vol. 82, No. 598: 1-8.

Calhoun, E. 1994. *How to Use Action Research in the Self-Renewing School*. Alexandria, VA: Association for Supervision and Curriculum Development.

Council of Chief State School Officers. 1997. *Fostering Excellence: How State Actions and Support Can Help Create Successful Schools*. Washington, DC: Author.

Darling-Hammond, L. 1996. "What Matters Most: A Competent Teacher for Every Child." *Phi Delta Kappan* Vol. 78, No. 3: 193-200.

Darling-Hammond, L. 1998a. "Teachers and Teaching: Testing Policy Hypothesis from a National Commission." *Educational Researcher* Vol. 27, No. 1: 5-15.

Darling-Hammond, L. 1998b. "Teacher Learning That Supports Student Learning." *Educational Leadership* Vol. 55, No. 5: 6-11.

Darling-Hammond, L. 1998c. *Doing What Matters Most: Investing in Teacher Quality*. New York: National Commission on Teaching and America's Future.

Elmore, R. 1996. "Getting to Scale With Good Educational Practice." *Harvard Educational Review* Vol. 66, No. 1: 1-26.

Fritz, R. 1996. *Corporate Tides: The Inescapable Laws of Organizational Structure*. San Francisco: Berrett-Koehler.

Fullan, M. 1991. *The New Meaning of Educational Change*. New York: Teachers College Press.

Guskey, T., and D. Sparks. 1991. "What to Consider When Evaluating Staff Development." *Educational Leadership* Vol. 49, No. 3: 73-76.

Jones, R. 1998. "What Works." *American School Board Journal* Vol. 185, No. 4: 28-33.

Joyce, B. (editor). 1990. *Changing School Culture through Staff Development*. Alexandria, VA: Association for Supervision and Curriculum Development.

Joyce, B., and B. Showers. 1995. *Student Achievement through Staff Development, 2nd edition*. White Plains, NY: Longman.

Joyce, B., J. Wolf, and E. Calhoun. 1993. *The Self-Renewing School*. Alexandria, VA: Association for Supervision and Curriculum Development.

Kerchner, C., J. Koppich, and J. Weeres. 1997. *United Mind Workers*. San Francisco: Jossey-Bass.

Lawton, M. 1998. "Evolution Debate Accents Deeper Science Disquiet." *Education Week* Vol. 17, No. 34: 1, 17.

Loucks-Horsley, S., P. Hewson, N. Love, and K. Stiles. 1998. *Designing Professional Development for Teachers of Science and Mathematics*. Thousand Oaks, CA: Corwin Press.

McLaughlin, M. 1994. "Strategic Sites for Professional Development." In *Teacher Development and the Struggle for Authenticity: Professional Growth and Restructuring in the Context of Change*, P. Grimmett and J. Neufeld, editors. New York: Teachers College Press.

Meier, D. 1998. "Can the Odds Be Changed?" *Phi Delta Kappan* Vol. 79, No. 5: 358-362.

Mohr, N. 1998. "Creating Effective Study Groups for Principals." *Educational Leadership* Vol. 55, No. 7: 41-44.

Murphy, C. 1997. "Finding Time for Faculties to Study Together." *Journal of Staff Development* Vol. 18, No. 3: 29-32.

National Board for Professional Teaching Standards. 1997. *State and Local Actions Supporting National Board Certification*. Southfield, MI: Author.

National Commission on Teaching and America's Future. 1996. *What Matters Most: Teaching for America's Future*. New York: Author.

National Education Commission on Time and Learning. 1994a. *Prisoners of Time*. Washington, DC: U.S. Government Printing Office.

National Education Commission on Time and Learning. 1994b. *Prisoners of Time Research: What We Know and What We Need to Know*. Washington, DC: U.S. Government Printing Office.

National Staff Development Council. 1994. *National Staff Development Council's Standards for Staff Development: Middle Level Edition*. Oxford, OH: Author.

National Staff Development Council. 1995a. *National Staff Development Council's Standards for Staff Development: Elementary Edition*. Oxford, OH: Author.

National Staff Development Council. 1995b. *National Staff Development Council's Standards for Staff Development: High School Edition*. Oxford, OH: Author.

Odden, A., and C. Kelley. 1997. *Paying Teachers for What They Know and Do: New and Smarter Compensation*

Strategies to Improve Schools. Thousand Oaks, CA: Corwin Press.

Pennel, J.R., and W.A. Firestone. 1998. "Teacher-to-Teacher Professional Development through State-Sponsored Networks." *Phi Delta Kappan* Vol. 79, No. 5: 354-357.

Perkins, S.J. 1998. "On Becoming a Peer Coach: Practices, Identities, and Beliefs of Inexperienced Coaches." *Journal of Curriculum and Supervision* Vol. 13, No. 3: 235-254.

Price, H. 1993. "Teacher Professional Development: It's About Time." *Education Week* (May 12, 1993): 24, 32.

Purnell, S., and P. Hill. 1992. *Time for Reform.* Santa Monica, CA: RAND Corporation.

Quinn, R.E. 1996. *Deep Change: Discovering the Leader Within.* San Francisco: Jossey-Bass.

Raywid, M. 1993. "Finding Time for Collaboration." *Educational Leadership* Vol. 51, No. 1: 30-34.

Renyi, J. 1998. "Building Learning into the Teaching Job." *Educational Leadership* Vol. 55, No. 5: 70-74.

Schlechty, P. 1997. *Inventing Better Schools: An Action Plan for Educational Reform.* San Francisco: Jossey-Bass.

Schmoker, M. 1996. *Results: The Key to Continuous School Improvement.* Alexandria, VA: Association for Supervision and Curriculum Development.

Schmuck, R, and P. Runkel. 1988. *The Handbook of Organization Development in Schools.* Prospect Heights, IL: Waveland Press.

Schwahn, C., and W. Spady. 1998. "Why Change Doesn't Happen and How to Make Sure It Does." *Educational Leadership* Vol. 55, No. 7: 45-47.

Senge, P. 1990. *The Fifth Discipline.* New York: Doubleday Currency.

Sparks, D. 1998. "The Educator, Examined: An Interview with Phil Schlechty." *Journal of Staff Development* Vol. 19, No. 4: 38-42.

Sparks, D. 2002. *Designing Powerful Professional Development for Teachers and Principals.* Oxford, OH: National Staff Development Council. Available online at http://www.nsdc.org/library/book/sparksbook.pdf

Sparks, D., and S. Loucks-Horsley. 1989. "Five Models of Staff Development for Teachers." *Journal of Staff Development* Vol. 10, No. 4: 40-57.

Sparks, D., and S. Hirsh. 1997. *A New Vision of Staff Development.* Alexandria, VA: Association for Supervision and Curriculum Development/National Staff Development Council.

Spillane, J.P. 1998. "State Policy and the Non-Monolithic Nature of the Local School District: Organizational and Professional Considerations." *American Educational Research Journal* Vol. 35, No. 1: 33-63.

Stigler, J., and J. Hiebert. 1997. "Understanding and Improving Classroom Mathematics Instruction." *Phi Delta Kappan* Vol. 79, No. 1: 14-21.

Walters, P.G. 1990. "Characteristics of Successful Organization Development: A Review of the Literature." In *The 1990 Annual Developing Human Resources,* J.W. Pfeiffer, editor (pp. 209-223). San Diego, CA: University Associates.

Wang, M., G. Haertel, and H. Walberg. 1998. "Models of Reform: A Comparative Guide." *Educational Leadership* Vol. 55, No. 7: 66-71.

ERS ORDER FORM FOR RELATED RESOURCES

Quantity	Item Number	Title	Base Price	ERS Individual Subscriber Discount Price	ERS Comprehensive Subscriber Discount Price	Total Price
				Price per Item		
	0538	*Handbook of Research on Improving Student Achievement, 3rd Edition*	$44	$33	$22	
	0529	*A Practical Guide to School Improvement: Meeting the Lessons of the NCLB*	$28	$21	$14	
	0530	*Supporting School Improvement: Lessons from Districts Successfully Meeting the Challenge*	$28	$21	$14	
	0496	*Understanding and Using Education Statistics: It's Easier (and More Important) Than You Think, 2nd Edition*	$28	$21	$14	

Postage and Handling** (Add the greater of $3.50 or 10% of purchase price.)

Express Delivery** (Add $20 for second-business-day service.)

**Please double for international orders.

TOTAL PRICE:

SATISFACTION GUARANTEED!
If you are not satisfied with an ERS resource, return it in its original condition within 30 days of receipt and we will give you a full refund.

Method of payment:

☐ Check enclosed
(payable to ERS)

☐ P.O. enclosed.
(Purchase order #_____)

☐ MasterCard ☐ VISA ☐ American Express

Visit us online at www.ers.org for a complete listing of resources!

Name on Card: _____ Credit Card #:_____

Expiration Date: _____ Signature: _____

Ship to: (please print or type) ☐ Dr. ☐ Mr. ☐ Mrs. ☐ Ms.

Name: _____ Position: _____

School District or Agency: _____ ERS Subscriber ID#: _____

Street Address: _____

City, State, Zip: _____

Telephone: _____ Fax: _____

Email: _____

Return completed order form to: **Educational Research Service**
2000 Clarendon Boulevard, Arlington, VA 22201-2908
Phone: (800) 791-9308 • Fax: (800) 791-9309 • Email: msic@ers.org • Web site: www.ers.org

ERS *Subscriptions at a Glance*

If you are looking for reliable K-12 research to . . .

- *tackle the challenges of NCLB;*
- *identify research-based teaching practices;*
- *make educationally sound and cost-effective decisions; and most importantly*
- *improve student achievement . . .*

then you need look no further than an ERS Subscription.

Simply pick the subscription option that best meets your needs:

✓ **Comprehensive School District Subscription**—a special research and information subscription that provides education leaders with timely research on priority issues in K-12 education. All new ERS publications and periodicals, access to customized information services through the ERS special library, 50 percent discounts on additional ERS resources, and more are included in this subscription for one annual fee.

✓ **Individual Subscription**—designed primarily for school administrators, staff, and school board members who want to receive a personal copy of new ERS studies, reports, and/or periodicals published and special discounts on other resources purchased.

✓ **Other Education Agency Subscription**—available for state associations, libraries, departments of education, service centers, and other organizations needing access to quality research and information resources and services.

✓ **Premium Services Subscription**—provides entire administrative staff "instant" online, searchable access to the wide variety of ERS resources. You'll gain access to the ERS electronic library of more than 1,000 educational research-based documents, as well as additional content being uploaded throughout the year.

✓ **Premium Plus Subscription**—All of the resources described in the Premium Services Subscription above, PLUS a print copy of all new ERS periodicals and publications.

Your ERS Subscription benefits begin as soon as your order is received and continue for 12 months. For more detailed subscription information and pricing, **contact ERS toll free at (800) 791-9308, by email at ers@ers.org, or visit us online at www.ers.org!**

Notes

Notes

Notes

Notes

Notes